HIS WORD LIVES

VIMA DASAN S.J.

HIS WORD LIVES

Homilies for Sundays,
Feast Days and Special Occasions,
for Cycles A, B and C

ST PAULS

ST PAULS
London SW1P 1EP, United Kingdom
Maynooth, Co Kildare, Ireland

ISBN 085439 526 1

Set by TuKan, High Wycombe
Produced in the EC
Printed by Biddles Book Manufacturers Limited, Guildford

ST PAULS is an activity of the priests and brothers of the
Society of St Paul who proclaim the Gospel through the media
of social communication

INTRODUCTION

The Word of God in the Scriptures is living water to the thirsty and light to those in the dark. It guides and counsels, comforts and supports, defends and heals. Philosophy and Religion may reform, but only the Word transforms, for it redirects our wills, cleanses our emotions, enlightens our minds and invigorates our total being. It teems with so many hidden meanings that what we understand is much less than what we leave behind, as we do after drinking from a fountain. It is so nimble, yet so full of subtle flame, because it is inspired by God. The Scriptures do not breathe out God, but God breathes out the Scriptures.

Therefore, as the faithful gather round the Eucharistic table on Sundays, Holy days and Feast days, Scriptures are read and homilies are preached. As a priest, I am always aware that our listeners do not so much have to have their heads stored with words, as to have their hearts touched by the Word. Hence I believe that a homily apart from the Word is a mistake in conception and a crime in execution.

When I wrote the homilies contained in this book for all Sundays and Solemnities of all three liturgical years, including those for special feasts and occasions, there were two purposes uppermost in my mind: to make the Word of God come alive in the world of today and to do it in the most effective way possible. To this end I followed a certain scheme and I would like to point out some elements of the scheme.

Need: There are two approaches open to the homilist who sits down to prepare. One is, to ask what does God say in the texts and apply it to some aspect of people's present need. The other is to ask himself first, what do people need to hear and then go to the texts and find the Good News that fulfils their need or at least suggests a response to the need. Mostly I have followed the second approach. This approach is more difficult than the first for it requires deep search into the texts, but that is part of the work a preacher has to put in. As St Jerome wrote: "Everything that we read in the Scriptures shines and glitters even in the outer shell, but the marrow is sweeter. He who desires to eat the kernel must break open the shell."

Subject: A homily may or may not be centred around a Scripture passage, but it must always have a subject. It must be about something significant bearing upon Christian life. Since at Sunday Masses and other holy feasts a homily is preached normally on Scriptural texts, I have followed certain proven homiletic methods to derive a subject from the texts: *Deduction* > deducing an application from a basic principle that a text provides; *Induction* > moving from a general statement of fact in the text, to particular truths; *Analogy* > comparing that which a text mentions as something already known to the listeners, with something that is not; *Suggestion* > taking a clue from the message, not directly stated but only suggested by the text.

Unity: The effectiveness of the homily depends much on the unity of its subject matter, for only with a unified subject one can focus listeners' attention on a particular message. Without such a focus, the preacher will tend to stray away wandering through the wilderness of his imagination shooting at every target that may cross his mind. A homily without unity within, will be like a rudderless ship on a wide sea of ideas driven here and there making for no haven.

Therefore, if a text presented several ideas, I have tried to find some bond of unity or some primary idea that will serve as a focus. If a text had several ideas, each independent of the other, I have tried to bring all the points into a general statement of one idea. Sunday Lectionary readings are three. Normally the first and the third reinforce each other, but the second usually stands alone apparently unconnected. However, I have made an effort to get a unified message from all three readings, so that the people feel that God has spoken to them through all three readings and the Church's intention of providing three readings for a single worship service, makes sense.

Theme: We speak of a 'Theme Song' which is a recurrent melody in a musical play. So too, we can speak of a 'Theme Homily', or, more correctly, the Theme of a Homily. At the start of each homily, I have given its theme. If the preacher can succeed in structuring his entire homily around a theme, the theme would reveal that the homily constitutes a unity and that it is not a series of thoughts strung together but thoughts that move towards a definite goal.

Application: A homily is not simply an exegesis, nor theologising, though they are needed in preparation for a proper Scriptural homily. Application is bridging the gap between the Word of God and people's life today. It is the application that bridges. An effective application needs to be personal to the listener. It has to be made in the present tense, for, after ten minutes of listening, people ask not "What shall we do?" but "What shall we do now?". The application has to be dynamic for its ultimate dynamic, for its ultimate purpose is to change people's lives in some way. The usual place for application is at the end of the homily, which I have done in most of them. But for the sake of variety, I have placed the application at the very outset in some; in some others, I have sprinkled the application throughout the homily.

Attention: As a preacher I can't assume that all I need is to catch the attention of the listeners in the first moments of my speaking. The essential nature of attention is unstable. It tends to come and go. Therefore, I have to do something throughout my homily that will keep bringing the attention of the listeners to what I am saying. To this effect, I have used in the homilies some *attention factors,* such as: variety, the startling, humour, surprise, the familiar, the vital, the novel, conflict, and story.

Story: I have made an extensive use of short stories real and imaginary. They are not for entertainment but to illustrate or prove or elucidate a point. A story charms the listeners to encounter the treasures hidden beneath. Even those who may oppose a truth, generally find it impossible to resist a story, for it worms its way into your heart, breaking down your defences against the divine.

Introductions and Conclusions: I have paid particular attention to the introduction and conclusion of each homily. A good introduction must be able to create interest in the hearers on the subject, prepare them for understanding the subject, establish rapport between the speaker and the listener, and get instant attention from the hearers. A good conclusion can be a restatement of the main text, or a reaffirmation of the central theme, or a memorable statement that condenses the sermon, or a concrete application, or a short story that illustrates the theme, or a challenge to action, or a prayer.

Brevity: While writing the homilies, I was conscious of the need to be brief. A famous preacher once told his congregation, "Every blade of grass is a sermon." A few days later, a parishioner saw him mowing his lawn. ""That's right, Father," the man said, "cut your sermons short." Some can easily talk for an hour on a subject, others can talk as long, without a subject. One reason why I have tried to keep to one subject in each homily is the need for brevity.

Myself being an Indian, conditioned by my own religious culture, my reflections on the Word of God are bound to have an Indian mould, as water takes the shape of the vessel it fills. Cultural differences can at times block communication. But there is no such danger here, for the Word of God became flesh precisely to bridge the gap between human cultures, and I am only proclaiming that Word in these homilies.

Nearly all the homilies found in this book, except some of those written for special feasts and occasions, have been already preached by me in the course of the last three years to the Congregation of Newmarket Parish, Suffolk, England. I am grateful to the Faithful of this Parish who encouraged me to make these homilies available also to those who are far and wide. A special word of thanks to Margaret Canning who tirelessly went on printing these homilies in the Parish Newsletter week after week, for the benefit of those who could not be present when the homilies were actually preached. A distinct word of gratitude to Michael Rogers. If faith can move mountains, his computer skills can do a similar feat! Whenever I messed up with my computer, while writing these homilies, I called on Michael to come and clear up the mess; he was always handy, sweet as candy.

Finally, I owe a large debt of gratitude to the Rt Revd Alan Clark, Bishop Emeritus of the Diocese of East Anglia, who invited me to work in his Diocese and to the Rt Revd Peter Smith, the present Bishop of the same Diocese, for his continued support given to me. But for their invitation and support, it would not have been possible for me to carry on this pastoral ministry of the Word of God.

Vima Dasan, s.j.

CONTENTS

YEAR A

ADVENT

CHRISTMAS SEASON

LENT

EASTER

ORDINARY TIME

YEAR B

ADVENT

CHRISTMAS SEASON

LENT

EASTER

ORDINARY TIME

YEAR C

ADVENT

CHRISTMAS SEASON

LENT

EASTER

ORDINARY TIME

HOMILES FOR FEASTS AND SPECIAL OCCASIONS

HOMILIES FOR FEASTS

HOMILIES FOR SPECIAL OCCASIONS

YEAR A

1ST SUNDAY OF ADVENT

BE THOU MY VISION

Readings: Is 2:1-5; Rom 13:11-14; Mt 24:37-44

Theme: We are called to meet Jesus as he comes daily into our lives, in order to prepare us for his final coming, when God's vision for mankind will become a reality.

Most people can see no further than their noses; but Isaiah read far into the mind of God and described God's vision for the world (Is 2:1-5). According to his description, a day will come, after the silence of ages and the waiting of years, after all thrones have been crumbled and crowns have fallen, when God will establish his Kingdom. In his Kingdom "all nations will stream towards the house of the Lord", for he will set all free to come out of isolation and form a family of nations. "All will take instructions from the Lord and walk in his path", for his instruction will be on justice, the great unchanging theme of his rule; and his path will be love, a love that can transform every human heart into bliss on earth. Above all, in his reign "one nation will not raise the sword against another", for there will be no need for the blast of war, the unmitigated evil, planned by ambition, executed by violence, and consummated by devastation. Peace will reign, the everlasting peace, never to be broken to pieces.

All people dream and those who dream at night wake up only to find that it was vanity. But the dream of God for our world was not to fade away into the light of common day, for it was not an Utopia, impractical or impossible of realisation. Christ again and again spoke about "the coming of the Son of Man" (Mt 24:37), and St Paul refers to it, saying "our salvation is closer and the day is drawing near" (Rom 13:11). Therefore we are certain beyond all doubt that one day the Lord will set up his rule, flooding the world with light and banishing the power of darkness, guiding all into the way of peace, drawing all to dwell in union of hearts and minds. But we do not know the exact day of his final coming. Any attempt to calculate the time of the end, a favourite preoccupation of many Christians, is doomed to failure; for it will be so sudden that "when two men are at work, one will be taken, the other will be left" (Mt 24:40); that means, we will be caught up to meet the Lord with scarce a moment's notice.

That will be his final coming. In the mean time, his reign has already begun. It began when Christ appeared, veiling his brightest glory, bearing our sins, dying on the cross and rising again. Christ himself had thus to inaugurate the reign of God, not only because it is he who will come at the end to reign as King, but also only he can make nations into a Brotherhood, not science, which can make them only into a Neighbourhood. It is in order that we may appropriate more and more the fruits of Christ's redemptive death and resurrection and begin to taste already now the peace, love, truth and justice of his Kingdom, that he keeps coming daily into our lives. He comes in the duties which we carry out, in the things that happen to us and in the people we meet. His coming will be a surprise. "The Son of Man is coming at the time you least expect" (Mt 24:44). This is true not only of his coming at the end of the ages and at the end of our lives, but also of his daily coming; hence the need for us to wait with minds and hearts always awake.

Visions are funny things; they never work unless you do. God's vision will soon become a reality, only if we make his vision our own, by practising today the vision of tomorrow and by living the life of the Kingdom here and now. This means, we have to "throw away our deeds of darkness", "to put on the armour" of faith, hope and charity (Rom 13:12), and work for peace and justice in the world. In international conflicts, tanks and missiles are deployed; in ethnic fights, guns and bombs are fired; in community disputes, knives and spears are wielded and in public life, cruel actions and unjust deeds slash and cut each other. We need therefore to build bridges between people, through strengthening our relationships with one another, by taking initiatives to forgive, by loving the alienated and by reaching out to the disadvantaged.

Our work for the Kingdom to come may be small and little, but it is needed. As from little fountains large streams flow, and as from little acorns tall oaks grow, so our little actions will mould the world to its glorious destiny, which is a promise from the Lord. It is this promise that makes every moment of our Christian life fly on wings of hope.

2ND SUNDAY OF ADVENT

A DAY WILL COME

Readings: Is 11:1-10; Rom 15:4-9; Mt 3:1-12

Theme: Since a day will definitely come when all people will be gathered together into one family as brothers and sisters, the Lord wants us to start living now in harmony with one another.

A day will come when justice will roll down like water and righteousness like a mighty stream; for the King "shall wear the band of justice around his waist" (Is 11:5). A day will come when the loathsome mask of inequality will fall and all people will stand equal and un-classed, so that "even the wolf shall be the guest of the lamb". A day will come when there will be no enemies to fear but only friends to love; and even "the baby shall play by the cobra's den", for "there shall be no harm or ruin on the holy mountain of the Lord" (Is 11:8-9). On that day all people, high and low, rich and poor, will sit together at the table of brotherhood and there will be neither East nor West, neither border nor breed, for the true nationality will be the human race. This is the picture of the Kingdom, a return to the primeval harmony of the Paradise, which Isaiah foresaw at the coming of Jesus Christ, "the root of Jesse".

Jesus Christ did come; but still, in our world, might is master and justice is servant, walking on wooden legs. Jesus Christ did come; but still, equality in many countries applies only to those in the grave: all people are born equal, yes, but eventually quite a few get over it. Christ did come, yes, but still there is nothing more common than the name 'friend' while there is nothing rarer than true friendship; some spend their lives making enemies, others exterminating them. Christ did come, but still many keep asking "Am I my brother's keeper?" – a perverse idea of freedom; many indeed love their fellow men, but only because they hope to profit thereby. As we draw nearer to the stars, we seem to withdraw ourselves farther from our neighbour. Hence, was Isaiah's vision just a fairy tale? No. Christ did indeed sow the seeds of the new Kingdom and this Kingdom is touching our lives right now, but it will fully come only in the future; meanwhile, we wait.

But our waiting has to be an active one. We have to prepare ourselves and the world to be ready to receive the new Kingdom when it arrives. Since it will be a Kingdom of justice, we must right now work for justice for all, until justice will form the basis of all governments, not pity. Since in the new Kingdom all will be equal, we must right now work for equality for all, and not remain satisfied with equality which begins only in the grave. Since harmony will be the soul of the heavenly music in the new Kingdom, we must right now strive "to live in perfect harmony with one another according to the spirit of Jesus" (Rom 15:5). Since it will be a Kingdom of friends, we must right now try to become to each other true friends in the Lord, not false friends who roll out the carpet for you one day and pull it out from under you the next. Since in the new Kingdom all will be brothers and sisters, we must right now come closer and closer to our neighbours. If all these demand a conversion of our lives, we must do it, as St John the Baptist urges us to "Reform your lives, for the Kingdom of God is at hand" (Mt 3:2).

Such a time of waiting may be the hardest time of all. But only those who wait in this manner "shall mount up with wings as eagles" (Is 40:31) towards the new Kingdom, which Isaiah saw in his vision. It was not a fairy story but the story of our salvation; and hence, it is our strong hope that such a Kingdom shall certainly come. To live without hope is the greatest human poverty that you can know. As a little child having a bad nightmare screams at night, so we too in the face of so much evil in the world may get disheartened and frightened. But we need not. As the mother hearing the child scream runs to the bedroom, turns on the light and hugs the child, saying 'It's all right; don't worry; I am here', so God comforts us saying,' I am with you; your days may be weary, but I love you. You are mine'. Hence let us get to work. Advent offers us a rare opportunity to prepare for the coming of the Lord and his Kingdom. Like the spoken word or the sped arrow, a neglected opportunity also cannot come back.

HAIL! FULL OF GRACE!

Readings: Gen 3:9-15; Eph 1:3-6,11-12; Lk 1:26-38

Theme: In Mary Immaculate we see the embodiment of great human values such as innocence and obedience to God's will, calling us to incorporate the same into our own daily lives.

He was born in 1792 into the Ferretti noble family, in a small village in Italy. His name was John. As he grew into manhood, he was intelligent and very handsome; but he had epilepsy. He prayed fervently to the Blessed Virgin Mary for a cure and miraculously the disease disappeared entirely. In thanksgiving to the Mother of God, he even officially took for himself the middle name of Mary. He was none other than Pope Pius IX, who, on 8 December 1854, proclaimed the Immaculate Conception of the Blessed Virgin Mary as a dogma of faith, which says that Mary was preserved free from original sin from the first moment of her conception. When God said to the serpent in Genesis "I will put enmity between you and the woman and between your offspring and hers" (Gen 3:15), he prophesied that Mary would be immaculately conceived. That prophecy was fulfilled when the angel said to Mary, "Hail, Full of Grace; Blessed are you among women" (Lk 1:28). These words of the angel to Mary express the positive meaning of the Immaculate Conception, for Mary was not only free from sin but she was free to receive the fullness of God's gifts. Hindenburg (1847-1934), a German soldier, Statesman, President of the German Republic 1925, was a Lutheran. Though a Lutheran, he kept a statue of Mary Immaculate in his study. People asked him, 'Why?' He said, "In Mary Immaculate I see the embodiment of great human values necessary in my life."

One great human value which Mary Immaculate embodies is innocence. Innocent people are beautiful people. Their beauty has nothing to do with the colour of their eyes, the tilt of their nose or the shape of their mouth: that is debasing the notion of beauty. Real beauty has to do with the person, not the body. In this sense, the most beautiful human being was Mary, for she was sinless from her conception. She was 'our tainted nature's solitary boast.' If we spend one-hundredth of the time and energy and expense in being beautiful instead of just looking beautiful, then this world would be a very beautiful place indeed. The innocent are pure in heart and their purity seems to glow in a special way, radiating a light that makes those around them glow too. With people of pure heart around, the market is sacred as well as the sanctuary. When we preserve the purity of our heart at any cost, by having no lust, no hatred, we can walk safely among the things of lust and hatred, as the sun which, though it passes through dirty places, remains as pure as before. Above all, the heart that is pure is God's paradise where he delights to dwell and makes it his lesser heaven. And yet, I am afraid that many of us seem to pray more for full purses than for pure hearts! May we always remember that God does not demand from us a beautiful vessel, but he does demand a clean one.

Another great human value which Mary Immaculate embodies is obedience to God's will. If Christ the Perfect Redeemer had to redeem the human race from all its sins, he could be born only to a woman who has herself been perfectly redeemed from all sins, especially from the sin of disobedience by which our first parents let loose all other sins upon the human race. Therefore, Mary was not only made sinless at her conception, but was given fullness of grace to obey God's will in everything, saying always, "Let it be done to me according to your word" (Lk 1:38) and thus remain sinless all her life. If we can say these same words daily and mean it, we have reached the highest point we can ever hope to attain. Our heart is right when we will what God wills. If God's will becomes our daily duty, then we can trust that the sovereign will of God will work in the ordinary circumstances of our lives for our good and for his glory. Surely, there will be suffering as it was for Mary in doing God's will. It is a myth that suffering is never part of God's will. However, by suffering God's will, we will learn to do God's will and at the end of the day, there will be no disappointments to those whose wills are buried in the will of God. On the contrary, to walk out of God's will is to walk into nowhere, for the power of God is identified with his will, and without his power we can do nothing.

Our joy at the celebration of Mary's freedom from sin and her freedom to obey God's will is found not only in what it meant to her, but in what it means to us today, because we also have been favoured by God. At our baptism, "God bestowed on us in Christ every spiritual blessing in the heavenly places, to be holy and blameless" (Eph 1:3-4). The blessing we received from God at baptism was similar to that of

Mary: freedom from sin and freedom to do God's will and thus to grow in holiness. But have we been growing in holiness since our baptism by preserving our innocence and by striving to do God's will in everything? We need to preserve our innocence not only to imitate the Immaculate Virgin but also to remain inwardly strong to face the trials of life. The strength of an innocent person is as the strength of ten, for such a person's heart is pure. No one is more dangerous than the person who is innocent, for innocence is unassailable. We need to strive to do God's will in everything not only in imitation of our blessed Mother, but also to defy the sin of the world. The sin of the world is not that it does not do the will of God but that it does not choose the will of God. Whether we like it or not, we are ruled by God's will and no one can escape it, for there is no other will but the Master's will, since all other wills are subservient to his. Hence it is always wiser not just to do God's will but to choose to do his will.

3RD SUNDAY OF ADVENT

HE KEEPS COMING

Readings: Is 35:1-6, 10; Jas 5:7-10; Mt 11:2-11

Theme: The Lord keeps coming to us in the midst of our daily toils and trials in order to lead us singing into everlasting joy.

Where God is, there is beauty. We experience the beaming of his beauty in the flowering spring and in flowing rivers, on the fruitful plain and on the mountain heights, when the morning shines and when the birds sing. Where God is, there is joy. We experience it in the joy of love and hope, in the joy of a peaceful conscience and of a grateful heart, in the joy of trustful soul and of glowing hope. We experience it even when "the plants and trees rejoice and bloom with joyful song" (Is 35:1,2). Where God is "sorrows and mournings flee" (Is 35:10), for he heals the broken bodies and bruised hearts with an overflow of the bright ocean of love. Just as torches burn most brightly when swung to and fro, so the healing presence of God brings out the rich qualities of a person under the cold, merciless wind of suffering. Where God is, the redemptive works of his Son Jesus continue. They were so profound and earth-shattering that they continue to vibrate even today throughout the world, freeing men and women from bondage and darkness.

However, the mighty presence of God in the world does not yet rule out the naughty presence of suffering. As long as we carry around our mortal bodies wounded by sin and until the Lord comes at the end of time, we have to accept suffering willingly and even joyfully. We must permit no distress to break our friendship with God. A boy and girl are playing on the beach building together sand castles, unaware of the approaching sea waves. Eventually the tide comes and sweeps away their castle. You know what they will do. They will have a hearty laugh and proceed holding hands to another spot on the beach to build together castles again. Likewise, we may build castles real and unreal but God may wipe them out; at times we may feel that the landscape of our lives is turned into a desert but even then we must hold on to God's hands and wait patiently for his coming, as "the farmer awaits the precious yield of his soil" (Jas 5:7), "without murmuring or grumbling against one another" (v.9). Patience is not a beggar's virtue but the passion of the great hearts.

The heart of a Christian must be great. If it is, the Christian will not only bear their own suffering willingly but also reach out to those who suffer, to lift their sorrows. Is it possible to list the ills of the present world that cry for help? Our dear world itself is sick for want of elementals: pure air, pure water and pure earth. For millions, life is like an onion which one peels crying. Besides, it is our presence with those who suffer which makes us authentic Christians. Christ himself pointed out his ministry to the blind, lame, deaf and poor for proof of his authenticity as Messiah (Mt 11:4). Hence a Christian heart has to go out, offering help to those who are in distress; after all, our helping hand is just at the end of our right arm. It does not matter if our charities are small or poor. Little things are great to little people, and great engines turn on small bearings. Every small act of kindness extended to the afflicted, every act of charity we do to get justice for the poor, bread for the hungry and healing to the distressed does bring God's liberating presence one step closer.

It is our unshakeable belief that the presence of God in all its splendour will break out at the final coming of Christ, when "all the ransomed will enter Zion singing, crowned with everlasting joy" (Is 35:10). But before that day, Christ wants to keep coming to us here and now. Why? To open our eyes, if we are blind, to see the glory of God's presence in his creation and to praise, and to see the misery of millions in our world and reach out; to open our ears, if we are deaf, to hear God's word and obey, and to hear the cry of the poor and help; to straighten our hands and knees, if they are feeble and weak, to meet our commitments to God and neighbour; to release our tongues, if we are dumb, to speak for justice and truth. Hence we must daily wait, especially during this Advent, for the Lord's visits. But all his visits will not be labelled; some of them come in disguise. Therefore let us always keep awake for the Lord's visit. The opportunity to meet him does not wake up people who are asleep.

4TH SUNDAY OF ADVENT

GOD IS WITH US

Readings: Is 7:10-14; Rom 1:1-7; Mt 1:18-24

Theme: We are preparing to celebrate the birth of Jesus, who is a God of puzzle and trouble, a God of presence and presents.

If there is one thing which even the best glue can't fix, it is a broken promise. A broken pledge produces ever-widening ripples of distrust: especially a promise made to a child, which if not fulfilled, ruins confidence for ever. God our Father always keeps his promises and therefore they are for us like life-jackets, keeping our souls from sinking into a sea of despair. God made a promise that "a virgin shall be with child and bear a son" (Is 7:14) who was to be the Saviour of the world; and God did keep his word, by becoming Man in the person of Jesus. But what sort of a God is our God who came in flesh?

He is a God of puzzles. Not only did he surprise us by becoming Man, but the *way* he became Man was still more puzzling. "Before Mary and Joseph lived together, she was found to be with child through the power of the Holy Spirit" (Mt 1:18), with the result that Jesus was in the line of David in the human sphere, but Son of God in the divine sphere; he is the God of the Jews as well as the God of the Universe. We experience God's surprises in our own lives. Some of them are gentle shocks of mild surprise, others are giant tremors of big surprise. We ask for health that we might do greater things, but we are given infirmity that we might do better things. We ask for riches that we might be happy, but we are given poverty that we might become wise. We ask for power that we may have the praise of men, but we are given weakness that we may feel the need of God. Hence we must never give up on God in times of disappointments, for God has his surprises.

He is a God of troubles. When he comes into our lives, trouble comes. Christ's birth was meant to bring joy to Mary and Joseph, but what an agony of mind Joseph had to wrestle with, when he found his wife pregnant, for which he was not responsible! This is true also in our lives. Our commitment to God, Church and neighbour brings with it slings and arrows of even outrageous troubles. If we are poor, we suffer from want of money; if we are rich, we suffer from troubles which money can't cure. Marriage vows are meant to bring joy, but often they bring sorrow. Sex is meant for faithful love, but at times it brings on intolerable pregnancies. But we know for sure, that when we have troubles, God comes. He came to Joseph to assure him saying, "Have no fear about taking Mary as your wife" (Mt 1:20), and he gave him reasons too. Likewise, when we are in trouble, let us trust that God is closest to us and will bring some good out of our troubles. As soft marrows abide in hard bones, blessings abide in troubles. Troubles are often tools by which God fashions us for better things. Anyway, what is the use of worrying? We'd better pack up our troubles in an old kit-bag and take them to the Lord.

He is a God of presence. When God became man, human nature was raised to a divine dignity. The Son of God united himself in some fashion with every human being; as a result, every thing material has received a spark of the spiritual, all creation has been illuminated by his divine light; God has pitched his abode here on earth. "Hence, they shall call him Emmanuel, a name which means 'God is with us' (Mt 1:23). If we know how to look around for God, we can see him smiling and hear him speaking, even in the smallest and most ordinary events in our lives. For example, I took up the phone and talked to a friend but he hung up suddenly and the line was cut. I was hurt, but then God smiled at me and said, "You talked a lot and listened very little; since you didn't listen, you learned nothing, helped nothing and communicated nothing. Stop this monologue and you will have friends". God is present in any Christian community. "Where two or three are gathered in my name, I am there" (Mt 18:20), said the Lord. We can see God's goodness in the kindness of others and experience his happiness in our own joy and peace. He is there in our illness comforting us. He is in our celebrations like Christmas, bringing families together in love.

He is a God of presents. His presence may be ordinary but his presents are extraordinary. He gives salvation from sins. He gives holiness, grace and peace. God is with us in moments of sorrow, giving solace; in situations of poverty, giving support and in times of worry, giving peace. He is with us to see through any struggle, to help us survive any setbacks and to strengthen us to endure any disappointments. Christmas is a time to reaffirm our faith that "God is with us" and "will be with us to the end of time".

CHRISTMAS DAY – DECEMBER 25

DAWN ON OUR DARKNESS

Readings: Is 52:7-10; Heb 1:1-6; Jn 1:1-18

Theme: Christ came into the world as the dawn on our darkness, so that those who believe in him and receive him into their life as their Saviour are in the light.

No one is light unto himself, not even the sun. Christ alone is the Light. Before his birth men were in darkness, confused about the very meaning of life, and like infants, were crying for light with no language but a cry. But God sent his light and brilliancy in Christ, before the jaws of death could devour men. Viktor Frankl was a prisoner of the Nazis in World War II. One early morning he and some other prisoners were digging in the cold hard ground. As he was struggling to find a reason for all his sufferings and slow dying, suddenly he became totally convinced that there was a reason, though he could not fully understand it. He writes in his book *Man's Search For Meaning*, "At that moment a light was lit in the distant farm house which stood on the horizon, as if it were painted there in the midst of the miserable grey". At that moment, he says that the words of the Gospel flashed into his mind: “The light shines in the darkness and the darkness has never put it out” (Jn 1:5). From that time, Victor was a different man, for it gave him hope and dispelled his despair.

There are times in our lives when we are thrown into darkness in which even shameful deeds do not bring disgrace. But if we open our hearts to Christ, he can dispel our darkness. When we do something wrong and try to hide it, our deeds are in the dark; but the light of Christ can reveal our deeds as they are, moving us to acknowledge our guilt and repent. When we don’t know what to do or what to say, our minds are in the dark; but his light can remove that ignorance, urging us to help those who are in pain or to speak on behalf of the poor unmindful of its consequences. When we don’t see any purpose in life, our life is in the dark; but his light can help us to find meaning in our life. When we can’t accept Jesus into our lives as our Saviour our religion is in the dark; but his life can offer us the gift of faith, if we truly open our hearts to him. When we fear death because we don’t hope for anything beyond the grave, our death is in the dark; but his light can reveal him as our resurrection. Hence, when our light is low and the quiet shadows are falling, when our blood creeps, the nerves prick and the heart is sick, we must seek the light of Christ.

So many centuries have gone by since the coming of Christ and yet, perhaps, we are still in the dark. How do we know that it is day and, for a Christian, the night is over? Is it that, at dawn, he can distinguish a mango tree from an apple tree, or an ox from an ass? Not really. When he looks at his neighbour and recognises in him or her his own brother or sister, then it is day for him; then he is in the light of Christ for love of neighbour is the heart of Christ’s message. As long as this is not the case, we are still in darkness which Christ alone can banish, for he is the brightest and the best of the sons of the morning, streaming light on our darkness. But he cannot remove our darkness all by himself, we have first to open our hearts to him. A famous artist drew a magnificent picture of Christ, thorn-crowned and carrying a lantern in his left hand, knocking at a closed door. He entitled the picture as “The Light of the World”. A friend of his who appreciated the painting much, said to him: “But, you have put no handle on the door”. The artist replied: “You forgot – the handle is on the inside”

Therefore Jesus is willing to fill us with his light, as sunlight is willing to flood a room that is open to its brightness; but we must open our hearts to the light, for we have the key. Oncc filled with his light, we can become light to others. As children of the light, we are called to become a beam of light in the midst of darkness and a ray of hope in the midst of despair. It is not enough to decorate our homes and trees with our Christmas lights. We ourselves must become lights and must light candles from our own light, instead of cursing the darkness. We are called to shed Christ's light on others by our example. Example is always more efficacious than precept, for precept begins, example accomplishes. Our example must be witness to our religious faith in the midst of a world that often ridicules religious faith as superstition; witness to human dignity in the midst of a world that often tramples on human rights. May we, then, become bearers of the light to get people out of darkness and the shadow of death and thus leave a trail of Christ's light behind us as we pass through this life.

HOLY FAMILY

A CHURCH IN MINIATURE

Readings: Sir 3:2-6, 12-14; Col 3:12-21; Mt 2:13-15, 19-23

Theme: A Christian family where the Gospel values flourish, with parents and children playing their respective roles in spite of the hardships involved, will not only be holy and happy but, increasingly, become socially conscious serving as an effective evangelising church in the world.

No other structure can replace the family. Family is the centre of our affection round which our hearts' best wishes entwine. We live today in a commercialised, go-it-alone, competitive and sometimes heartless society; but still the fact remains that no body grows alone, that people need people and it is in the family that the foundation of human relationship is laid, upon which faith and morality are built. Psychologists remind us that many of the personality problems of the grown-ups have their roots in family deficiencies during childhood. Family plays a central role in human formation and growth; it provides the suitable soil for Christian virtues to flourish. The Feast of the Holy Family presents to us an ideal family for Christians. It is not right to say that the Holy Family is too ideal for us to relate to. In many ways they were ordinary people. They were economically poor and, in spite of their privileged status with God, they too were constantly struggling to find God's will in their lives. And yet they succeeded in making their family holy and happy.

In a happy family, both parents and children contribute their share, each playing their respective roles. Parents need to realise that every word and deed of a parent is a fibre woven into the character of the child. Some parents of the modern generation talk as if they have nothing to do with it. But the truth is that what a father says to his children is not heard by the world; indeed, but it will be heard by posterity; and what a mother sings to the cradle goes all the way down to the coffin. Every Christian parent should leave no stone unturned in order to help their children to develop physical, mental, emotional and spiritual maturity.

But no one says that bringing up children is easy. There are hardships in parenting. Joseph and Mary endured such hardships when they had to flee to Egypt as instructed by God (Mt 2:14). In fact, they suffered all the anxieties and insecurities of poor parents. But their conviction that they were doing God's will and their faith in the divine providence sustained them in their travails. So too, Christian parents, if they centre their family life in God, can be sure that the grace of God will not be wanting to enable them to bear the hardships willingly, even joyfully.

Children on their part have to respect their parents' authority over them. Pity the home where every one is the head. Children have an obligation to care for their parents especially in their old age. "My son, support your father in his old age, do not grieve him in his life" (Sir 3:12). We never know the love of our parents for us, till we have become parents. The fourth Commandment cannot be discarded like the clothes and toys of childhood once we become independent adults.

A happy Christian family, has Christ as its centre and his teachings are the family guidelines. St Paul enumerates some of them, such as "mercy, kindness, patience and forgiveness" (Col 3:12). The Christian values which must mark out a Christian family are summarised in more concrete terms by Dr Paul Kelly, an orthopaedic surgeon and family counsellor, as 'The Seven Cs'. They are: first, Commitment: a lifelong caring for the other, no matter what happens. Second, Communication: a willingness to take time to listen, dialogue and share one's feelings. Third, Compatibility: an ability to get along, adjust and be flexible. Fourth, Compassion: a capacity to understand weakness and sympathise with failure. Fifth, Confession: the readiness to say, 'I am sorry', to be reconciled and forgiven. Sixth, Conviviability: a sense of humour, to laugh at oneself and make others to smile. Seventh, Children: one's own, adopted, grandchildren or those of close relatives, with whom life and love can be shared.

But a Christian family to be truly Christian cannot be just immediate blood relatives. It is all the children of God who have some relationship with the divine. In this broad sense, Christian family is communion of saints. This means that all people who are connected to God are mystically connected to one another. Concretely speaking, our every day's prayers and good actions cause a ripple effect in the world family of God's children, changing us as well as all others, both living and dead, who are in touch with the divine, and affecting the eternal destiny of all. A Christian family, thus grounded in Christian values and socially conscious, can serve as an effective evangelising church. A group of young people from many nations were discussing how the Christian Gospel might be spread. They talked of propaganda, of literature, of all the ways of disseminating the Gospel today. Then the girl from Africa spoke: "When we want to take Christianity to one of our villages", she said, "we don't send them books. We take a Christian family and send them to live in the village and they make the village Christian by living there". Yes. A Christian family is a church in miniature.

MOTHER OF GOD – JANUARY 1

MOTHER, DEAR!

Readings: Nm 6:22-27; Gal 4:4-7; Lk 2:16-21

Theme: We begin the New Year trusting in the protective love of our Mother Mary for, as she is the Mother of Jesus and so God's own Mother, she has been given to us as our Mother too.

Not long ago Mrs Indira Gandhi, a former Prime Minister of India, had invited the members of her staff and their spouses for a party at her residence. She welcomed everyone of them warmly and when she came to Mrs Accamma Alexander, the wife of Mr Alexander her principal secretary, the Prime Minister asked her a question which caused the guest no small surprise. "Well, Accamma, you are an Orthodox Christian, are you not? What is the attitude of your church to the Blessed Virgin? Does the Orthodox church hold her in great veneration as some other churches do?" "Certainly, St Mary is very dear to the Orthodox church and we all pray to her and are her devotees," replied Mrs Alexander. The party over, the Alexanders went home and thought no more about the Prime Minister's curiosity about a point of religion. Within a few days, a special messenger brought to them a packet containing a statue of the Madonna and the child. As a statue of the Madonna always shows, Mary can never be separated from Jesus, for he is the blessed fruit of her womb.

Mary is the mother of Jesus who is the Life of the world. Our ancient mother Eve was more of a stepmother than a true mother, passing on to her children the sentence of death before bringing them into the light of day. Her name indeed means 'mother of all the living', but she proved more truly to be the slayer of the living, since for her to give birth was to transmit death. But Mary is truly the Mother of the living for she is the mother of Jesus who is life itself. His power to give life had already been prophesied before his birth: "So shall they invoke my name upon the Israelites and I will bless them" (Nm 6:27). This prophecy was fulfilled at the naming of Mary's son: "The name Jesus was given to the child, the name the angel had given him before he was conceived" (Lk 2:21). Mary was not mother of Jesus just because she brought him forth into the world. To think that simply bearing children makes one a mother is as absurd as believing that a piano makes one a musician. Mary, as mother, not only brought forth her child but also did what all mothers do: watched over his growth into manhood, pleasing to God and to men.

Because Mary is the mother of Jesus, she is the mother of God, for Jesus is the Son of God. "When the designed time had come, God sent forth his Son born of a woman" (Gal 4:4). Napoleon once uttered these remarkable words: "If Socrates would enter the room, we should rise and do him honour. But if Jesus Christ came into the room, we should fall down on our knees and worship him". It has been our faith from the beginning that Christ is the eternal Son of God. He was born again in time, in a human nature, of Mary the Virgin. So we rightly call her mother of God. We don't mean that she is mother of the Godhead. No, she is the mother of thc humanity of God who became man. This is the marvel and mystery of our faith.

Mary is given to us as our mother too. Each of us lives by the life of Mary's child, so each of us is Mary's child. Since Jesus was truly made one of us in the womb of Mary, like us in all things except sin, when Mary gave birth to Jesus, she gave birth to a new human race as well. How fortunate we are to have Mary as our loving spiritual mother! "I kept looking at her as hard as I could," said Bernadette, "and she kept looking steadily at me!" The thousands who flocked to the grotto at Lourdes that February day of 1858 saw nothing but Bernadette. So eager were they to touch the invisible that they asked, "Tell us, does the Lady look at anybody but yourself?" "Yes, indeed, she does," replied Bernadette, "she looks all around the crowd, and she stops at some as if they were old friends". Yes. It has to be so, for we are all her beloved children. Any mother in a sense represents God and therefore it is said that because God could not be everywhere, he made mothers. It is so true of Mary, for in her not only God took his flesh but through her we too have become God's children.

The Feast of the Mother of God is also the beginning of a New Year. Yesterday I received two calendars, one is in my office and the other in the kitchen. The kitchen one wishes me: "A very happy and prosperous New Year." It was from the local bank. The other is from the church, displaying the picture of Mary. It is right and proper that we begin the New Year calling on the blessings of Mary our Mother. A child clings to its mother in good times and in bad times. Even blaming mother is just a negative way of clinging to her still. Like a child, let us cling to Mary our mother from the start of this New Year. No matter how old a mother is, she watches us, her middle-aged children for signs of improvement. Let us trust that Mary will watch over us all through our New Year's journey. Let us not hesitate to come to her, whoever we are. As every beetle is a gazelle in the eyes of its mother, so each of us, however low may be our standing in life are dear to her for we are all her children.

EPIPHANY

THE FEAST OF ALL NATIONS

Readings: Is 60:1-6; Eph 3:2-3, 5-6; Mt 2:1-12

Theme: Epiphany is the feast of all nations because on this day we celebrate the manifestation of Christ, the true light, to all nations, calling us to become more and more filled with this light, to clothe our own communities with the universality of this light, and to labour to bring it to those who are still in darkness.

Sadness flies on the wings of the morning light; but the greatest of all lights, the only true light from whom sprung the lights of the day and the sun, is Jesus Christ. In an age of electricity and artificial lights, it is difficult for us to appreciate the symbolism of light; but the truth is that Christ as light is the fullest expression of God's work in the world. Therefore, "Arise, shine, "cries out Isaiah, "for your light has come, and the glory of the Lord has risen upon you" (Is 60:1). Christ is not just a dim glow or a signal or a guide through the darkness or a light on a question or a ray of light in a dark world. He is the radiating, life-sustaining light who is power and glory. He is the light that guides us to travel safely over the tempestuous sea of the mortal life until we have made the harbour of peace and bliss. He is the light without which all things are deep darkness but by whom all things are made lightsome because it is the mind and wisdom of God. But Christ as light shines for all mankind. He is the light of the world.

The Epiphany is a festival of light, for on this day we celebrate the manifestation of Jesus Christ in the darkness of the world calling all humankind to come and bathe in his light. As Isaiah foretold: "The nations come to your light and kings to your dawning brightness" (Is 60:3). At the birth of Jesus, three wise men from the East, guided by a star, came to worship him (Mt 2:1). It is a custom to picture them as black, white and brown; thus, they represent all the people of the earth, particularly the gentiles. Hence, "The pagans now share the same inheritance, that they are parts of the same body, and that the same promise has been made to them, in Christ Jesus, through the Gospel" (Eph 3:6). Yes, Epiphany is the feast of all nations.

We are baptised so we have the light of Christ, but too often we think that is enough. The strange thing about Jesus is that not only you can never get away from him but also you can never get enough of him. Jesus Christ is God's every thing for man's total need. Therefore till all our deepest needs are satisfied culminating in our perfect union with God, our quest for more and more of Jesus must go on. Therefore meet Jesus daily. We need not look towards the stars to encounter him. He is being born every day in our lives. He comes anew to us in every suffering we face, in every hand stretched out to us for help. The Lord comes to us also in the Sacraments, especially the Eucharist and in the community of faith; not in any kind of community, but a community of believers which reflects the universality of Christ; hence it has to be a community that welcomes all peoples and races, that respects each one's perception of Christ – since Truth can take many shapes and various manifestations – and a community that provides equality for all, especially to the 'little ones', who are not just children but those individuals who are seen as the least important in society.

The more we Christians receive the light of Christ, the more we would want to give it to others who seek after it. While people may appear to us to be seeking after fame or fortune or just plain excitement, what in fact they ultimately seek is human fulfilment. Their search is basically for what is supremely good, true and beautiful. In a word, they are seeking after Christ. So we Christians have work to do. After Christmas, there are already signs in the streets that work has resumed, the sales have started, cards and decorations are looked upon as nuisances and schools are about to reopen. The 'back to work' motif is noticeable. Today's feast also is like a factory hooter calling us to work in order to bring Christ to all nations. As an anonymous poet has put it: "When the song of the angels is stilled, when the star in the sky is gone, when the kings and princes are home, when the shepherds are back with the flock, the work of Christmas begins: to find the lost, to heal the broken, to feed the hungry, to rebuild the nations and to make music in the heart".

1ST SUNDAY OF LENT

LENT IS IDEAL

Readings: Gen 2:7-9, 3:1-7; Rom 5:12-19; Mt 4:1-11

Theme: Lent offers us an ideal opportunity to renew our lives, by taking decisions based on the Word of God, and aided by the Grace of God operative in Christ.

Friendship will last if you put it first. But Adam and Eve did not. In their ill-woven ambition, hunting impossibilities on the wings of hope to reverse roles with their Creator and Friend, they ate the fruit forbidden by him (Gen 3:6) and lost his friendship. Their friendship with God was like sound health, the value of which they did not know until they lost it. Their rejection of God's word brought with it also the collapse of their harmonious relationship with their fellow human beings and Nature itself, introducing evil and suffering and ecological devastation into the world (Gen 3:7). But God's love has a hem to its garment that reaches the very dust touching the stains of the streets and lanes. In his love, God sent his Son Jesus Christ to restore man's friendship with him, which Jesus accomplished by his self-sacrifice. However, curses are like young chicken; they always come home to roost. So the curse suffered by our first parents began haunting the human nature, with the result that every one of us carry within our mortal frame a proclivity to reject God, in order that we might be God unto ourself: a fatal and perfidious ambition that first sprung from the blessed abode.

We commit only the oldest sin but in the newest kind of ways. Beneath the dignity of uniformity of international fashions in dress, human beings remain always the same, capable of outstanding courage and open to outrageous temptations. We are tempted to substitute one's own ways for God's ways; to use other people's and one's own gifts for totally selfish purposes; and to misuse one's position, talent and wealth for one's own vaulting ambition. The lure of catering to excessive bodily comforts without any self-denial, the readiness to substitute decent principles, which are for the ages, with expedients which are for the hour; to substitute the superficial for the real, the trivial for the tremendous – these are temptations to a false way of life and falsehood is the jockey of misfortune. Hence Jesus warned us about them. He also gave us an example on how to fight temptation. For example, in the desert he was tempted (Mt 4:1-11) to compromise his mission, substituting self-interest for God's, values of the world for the ways of God, the immediate and attractive realities for the will of God; but Jesus rejected them all and relied only on the word of God.

But we must be right about this. God never overpowers any one with temptations. He allows them often to test our faithfulness to him. Hence temptations are only suggestions for us either to accept or reject God's friendship. The pity is that some take evil suggestions as a cat laps milk; others start playing with them. How can you play with animal in you without the danger of becoming animal yourself? How can you keep your garden tidy while reserving a plot for weeds? We must resist evil at its mere suggestion. It is better to shun the bait than struggle in the snare. In every temptation we are called to make a personal decision either for God or against him, with a concern also for the social implications of our decisions. For when I sin, there is so much more evil in the world; but when I respond to grace, there is so much more good in the world. To help us to choose God in our decisions, the grace of God is always available in Christ, for "if by offence of one man all died, much more did the gracious gift of the one man Christ abound for all" (Rom 5:17).

Lent is the right time to take right decisions. During this Lenten desert journey towards Easter, the word of God will challenge us to choose God and his ways above all else, aided by the gracious activity of God in Christ. If we have to change our attitudes towards God, our neighbours and Nature around us, we must change. Change is only the interval between the decay of the old and formation of the new. We can't be like wood which might remain ten years in the water but never become a crocodile, because it can't change. In order to bring about the desired changes in our lives during this Lent, we are advised to go into 'desert', as often as we can, as Jesus did. Deserts are like stars but with a difference. Stars speak of man's insignificance right now. Our 'desert', can be any private moment in a private place, stripped of all distractions of the world. Jesus was also careful to use the right weapons to combat evil: they were prayer, penance and the word of God. So must we. Weapons must be as strong as the enemy; one can't shoot with butter but with guns.

2ND SUNDAY OF LENT

THE IMMORTAL DIAMOND

Readings: Gen 12:1-4; 2 Tim 1:8-10; Mt 17:1-9

Theme: If we take ourselves to prayer as often as we can, we too, like Christ, can have our own moments of transfigurations, when the touch of God could lift our darkness and melt away our fears.

It is a burden to some of us to be human beings; to some others it is a shame and disgrace to carry around a human body; still others ride through life as if internally mounted on some kind of beast within. But the transfiguration of Christ is the demonstration of what a human body is destined for, and what humanity is capable of. Our life may be a moment, less than a moment, but a moment will come when in a flash and at a trumpet call, we all will at once be transfigured into what Christ was on Mount Tabor, "dazzling as the sun and radiant as light" (Mt 17:2). Our humanity may be debased by slavery, corrupted by power or degraded into a mass of animated dust, but the light of God which it conceals, will finally break through. Yes. The fall of a leaf is a whisper to every living creature that humankind are earthenware vessels. The marvel is that each vessel carries within an immortal diamond.

The feast of the Transfiguration is a feast of encouragement. One day the devil decided to put a few of his well-worn tools up for sale. On display were some treacherous instruments including hatred, jealousy, lying and pride. Set apart from the rest, however, was a harmless looking device with a very high price tag. "What is that?", someone asked. "That is discouragement", Satan replied, "It is one of my most effective tools; with it, I pry open the hearts of God's greatest servants and bring on depression". Hence, when we are in trouble, we must take care not to fall into the devil's snare. Trouble has no necessary connection with discouragement. As arthritis is different from a stiff joint, so trouble is different from discouragement which has a germ of its own. If we are discouraged, we would soon slide into despair and there is no vulture like despair. On the contrary, we are encouraged by the Lord's transfiguration to be patient in the midst of troubles, for it radiates hope in the ultimate victory of the good. "Listen to my beloved Son", says the heavenly Father; and Jesus says, "Rise and have no fear".

The glory at which humanity will finally arrive, promised by Christ's transfiguration, is already possessed by us through baptism. This means that an enormous vitality and dignity lie concealed in ordinary humanity. Christians who believe that they possess an immortal diamond of glory will cease to be pessimists who always expect the worst and make the worst of it when it actually happens. Rather, they will soon learn on their Christian journey that in the midst of winter there is in them an invincible summer, always aware that "Christ has robbed death of its power and has brought life and immortality". (2 Tim 1:10). Such Christian optimists will smile through trials and tribulations for they know that what sunshine is to flowers, smiles are to humanity.

We may find our lives filled with trifles to be sure: but scattered along life's pathways, the good that even trifles can do is immeasurable. However, to grasp the significance of small things around us and sundry events in our lives, one has to be awake". They kept awake and saw his glory" (Lk 9:32). As long as our minds are asleep, we will lose much in life. Prior to our final glory, we will have our own imperfect transfigurations – in prayer for example, which could be a moment of grace to become more loving and alive to God. Even outside prayer, we will have our moments of happiness, for example when we go for a walk after a tiring day or when we re-establish friendship after a quarrel. But, once again, in order to experience God at such moments, one has to be awake. A woman at a bank asked the cashier to cash a cheque for her. Citing company policy, the cashier asked for her identification. The woman gasped! Finally she managed to say, "But, Jonathan, I'm your mother!" So, let us be awake.

3RD SUNDAY OF LENT

THE LIVING WATER

Readings: Ex 17:3-7; Rom 5:1-2, 5-8; Jn 4:5-42

Theme: A loving and obedient relationship with God, an enduring reliance on Him for one's own fulfilment and a progressive renewal of heart are basics to Christian life.

All over the world companies like Coca Cola and Pepsi spend millions on TV ads intended to stimulate our thirst and get us to buy their product. But most people today thirst for things of greater value. People thirst for justice, truth and love; they long for recognition, freedom and security, like the Samaritan woman of the Gospel; she too, oppressed by the prejudice and injustice of a foreign power and crushed by her own guilty conscience because she had had five husbands, was seeking after freedom and peace. But the tragedy is that many try to satisfy this inner craving of the human heart with material things. Material things can never fill our inner void for ours is a spiritual thirst; basically it is a thirst for God. St Augustine rightly said, "…for you have made us for yourself, and our heart is restless until it rests in you". Trying to satisfy our thirst for God with material things is like trying to distract a crying baby by giving it sweets and by making faces at it. Material pleasures are like a snowball in the river, a moment white, then melt for ever leaving us thirst for things of greater value.

But God has provided us a way to satisfy our inner thirst for himself. He has given us Living Water through his son Jesus Christ. Jesus said, "Whoever drinks the water I give him will never be thirsty" (Jn 4:14). The Living Water which Christ gives is God's life and since God is Love, we receive the very love of God when we drink Living Water; and hence St Paul would say that in our baptism "it was the very love of God that was poured into our hearts" (Rom 5;5) at our baptism. It is for this love of God flowing from his Holy Spirit that we actually thirst as people in parched lands thirst for water. It originated from the pierced side of Christ on the cross and continues to flow into the veins of his Church whose members we are. It gives divine life to our souls now and immortality to our bodies at resurrection. It frees us from clinging to material things, from clinging to unforgiving ancient hatreds and from clinging to sinful pleasures. Since the living water is the life of God who is love itself, we should immerse our hearts, with all the holes in them, into the ocean of God's love. Once immersed into the ocean, what does it matter whether our human heart has holes or not?

Where can we find this Living Water? It is in Christ who is the rock. As Moses struck the rock and water gushed forth (Ex 17:6), so when Christ was pierced with a lance, the living water flowed and still flows. As Christ was present to the Samaritan woman in her search for peace which even five husbands could not give, so he is present in our search for peace and in the midst of our pains. Christ is present in his

Words and Sacraments. By experiencing Christ personally in prayer, we can receive the water of peace; by following Christ's footsteps in our daily life we can drink the water of freedom and by serving his people, we can receive his water of joy. None of us need therefore ask like Israelites, "Is the Lord in our midst or not?" (Ex 17:7). But the pity is that some of us seem to be hardly aware of his presence, like people who go through a forest finding no firewood. A greater poverty than that caused by lack of money is the poverty of unawareness.

God's life that flows into us through Christ is given to be shared. That is why, in those who drink from it, it "becomes a fountain within them, leaping up to provide eternal life" (Jn 4:14). Are we prepared, like the Samaritan woman, to share this water of life with so many others who are in need of it, people such as those who live in blindness, in abject poverty, in wheelchairs, in sickness and in a thousand other hostile situations? Even the strong, rich and powerful will need it, for riches may fill your pockets but it usually leaves the hearts empty. Lenten prayers, fasting and good works offer us a precious opportunity to drink this life-giving water to the full and share it with others as well. Lenten liturgy brings us closer than ever to the fountain of living water. But let not the liturgy distract us from the life it brings, for the bucket is not the thing, but the water it contains.

4TH SUNDAY OF LENT

OUT OF DARKNESS

Readings: 1 Sam 16:1, 6-7, 10-13; Eph 5:8-14; Jn 9:1-41

Theme: In baptism we were delivered from darkness, so that we may walk in the light of the risen Lord.

The joy of seeing for the first time is unspeakable. During World War II, John Howard was blinded in an aeroplane explosion and could not see a thing for the next 12 years. But one day as he was walking down a street near his parents' home in Texas, he suddenly began to see 'red sand' in front of his eyes. Without warning, his sight returned again. According to an eye specialist, a blocking of blood to the optic nerve caused by the explosion had opened. Commenting on this experience, John said, "You don't know what it is like for a father to see his children for the first time". But according to the Gospel (Jn 9:7), something more spectacular happened to a man born blind, for Christ conferred on him, not only his physical sight but also his spiritual sight; he opened his inner eyes of faith and radiated his own light into the mind and heart of the blind man, so that the blind man believed in Jesus as one believes in the sun.

We too received the same gift of faith at our baptism, a faith without which there is neither hope nor love, for it alone grasps meaning, in the midst of the meaningless; a faith that sings like a bird while the dawn is still dark; for it can turn away any course, light any path, relieve any distress, bring joy out of sorrow and heaven out of hell. At baptism we too received the light of Christ, a light for which restless millions waited for ages, whose dawn makes all things new; a light that gives more than sight, for it enables us to emerge from the tombs of sin and death into the light of Christ's life. "There was a time when you were in darkness, but now you are light in the Lord" (Eph 5:8). That time was before our baptism. We were all blind and in the dark, until we came to see in faith who Jesus really is and the light he offers. Similar to the anointing of David (1 Sam 16:13) and the smearing of the blind man's eyes (Jn 9:6), we too were anointed in the Sacrament of Baptism, as a token of God's call to live and witness to the life of the children of the light.

We are the children of the light, if our hearts are pleasing to God, however low or lofty may be our stature. In the world, men are valued not for what they are but for what they seem to be. But God chose David as king, in spite of his shabby appearance, because he was a man according to his own heart (1 Sam 16:12). We are the children of the light, not because we are able to distinguish in daylight an ox from an ass but because we can recognise in our neighbours our own brothers and sisters. We are the children of the light if "we produce every kind of goodness, justice, and truth" (Eph 5:9) and commit ourselves to these values with courage, a courage that is grace under pressure. We are the children of the light if we live as true Christians in the world, unstained by its evil, like Christ's own light which can pass through pollution without being polluted. We are the children of the light if, enlightened by the beam of Christ's brightness, and bearing in our hands the light that shines for everyone, we bring light to those whose eyes cannot see because their hearts wish them to be blind.

Lent is the time for each of us to ask whether we are in the light or still in the dark. Do we overlook people in need and keep discussing only the abstract question of evil in the world like the disciples who asked whose fault it was that the man was blind? Are we blind and perhaps glory in being blind – the very limit of human blindness – to the sufferings of the poor and the sick, the oppressed and the abandoned? Are we afraid to support just causes, like the parents of the blind man who would not stand up for him, out of fear of authorities? Our fears always outnumber our dangers! Is our faith so weak that it cannot see any good beyond our sorrows? The heart of a Christian is like a creeping plant which withers for want of that faith which it needs in order to spread. Are we blind to our own faults, which are not in the stars but in ourselves? In order not to face them, do we always blame others? The greatest of faults is to be conscious of none. The time is drawing near, for the renewal of our baptismal promises in the Holy Saturday liturgy. May we, therefore, come out of darkness and begin walking in the light of the risen Lord.

5TH SUNDAY OF LENT

BEGIN HERE AND NOW

Readings: Ez 37:12-14; Rom 8:8-11; Jn 11:1-45

Theme: Anyone who is united to Christ through belief in him begins eternal life, here and now.

Even at our birth death does but stand aside a little. It eats up all things both the young lamb and old sheep. People die of cancer, old age, car accidents, war, starvation and disease. But for Christians, death is the supreme festival on the road to eternal life. We believe with the prophet Ezekiel that out of the graves new life will emerge (Ez 37:12); with St Paul we trust that God who raised Jesus from the dead will raise us also to new life (Rom 8:11), because the Lord said that those who believe in him, "though they should die, will come to life" (Jn 11:25). Eternal life is not something that will come only after our physical death, but it can begin here and now, in and through many other kinds of the living deaths that we face in life. The breakdown of marriages, being unemployed, becoming victims of crime and violence, bereavement, anxiety, self-doubt and guilt may well be experiences of death, that take us piecemeal, not at a gulp. But however devastating may be these deaths, those who make a leap of faith in the midst of such disillusionments, will find here and now eternal life; for the Lord said not "I will be", but "I am" the resurrection and the life (Jn 11:25).

But to experience eternal life here and now one must believe in Christ, precisely because faith unites us with him and he is that life. The raising of Lazarus was not meant just to console his sisters but to serve as the symbol of the presence of eternal life in the person who believes in Jesus Christ. This life of faith is not some vague affirmation about Christ. It is living with Jesus' spirit. "If any one does not have the spirit of Jesus, he does not belong to him" (Rom 8:9). It calls us to a behaviour which is inspired by Christ's own behaviour; it is unselfish life; it consists in dying to one self which is the same as living for God and for others; it is giving our time, our resources, our energy and ourselves in the service of our neighbour. As a little child who already possesses the power to grow into manhood or womanhood, we Christians, through baptism, already possess the power to live an unselfish life. Has this power grown in us, giving us deeper and deeper experience of the new life in Christ?

If not, we are called to begin a spiritual return, as the Israelites returned from exile to their homeland. If we still find ourselves in the tomb of selfishness, we are called to come out of the tomb, as Lazarus came out. Our selfishness makes us hard and stiff towards others. Hardness and stiffness are companions of death, not of life. Look at a man at his birth; he is tender and supple, but at death, he is hard and stiff. Therefore we need conversion, constant conversion, from the sinfulness of the flesh and the self to the new life of the Spirit and love. Of course, any change for the better would cause pain and suffering. Only from human emptiness can a person find the fullness of God; only from darkness, comes the dawn. In the sunlight of happy days, faith may be golden; but it is in the midst of sadness and suffering that we are called to take the leap of faith. It is in the moment of human darkness that we are called to believe in our immortal destiny, beyond death.

Lent is nearing its end. God calls us again to change. If we feel we are too settled to change, if we fear we have been too long in the grave of mediocrity, God can help us with his power. Lazarus came to life not by his own power but by the power of God. It is the power of God that enables us to break the fetters of fear-filled self-centredness. Therefore we must bring all our fears and frailties to God in prayer. Martha brought her sadness to the Lord and her sadness was transformed into a faith-experience, that her brother was not dead but alive with God. So instead of living in self-imposed Friday Darkness, let us bring our deepest fears and deadly darkness to God. God's power combined with our own Lenten sacrifices can transform the waters of chaos in our life into the wonders of creation.

PASSION SUNDAY

AGONY AND GLORY

Readings: Is 50:4-7; Phil 2:6-11; Mt 26:14-27,66

Theme: Those who suffer like Christ for the love of God and neighbour may hit the rock bottom of agony, but are sure to rise to the height of glory.

Our Lord Jesus died for love of God and humanity; and the fact that all through his passion he suffered alone brings out the depth of his love, for loneliness in suffering is the clearest indication of a person's capacity to love. The fact that he suffered, not because of weakness inherent in human nature, but as the result of human injustice and of his revolutionary message, proves his faithful love for God and humanity. In his suffering he acted upon his own word: "The greatest love a person can have for his friends is to give his life for them" (Jn 15:13). Our Lord did not suffer to wipe out suffering from our lives but to teach us how to suffer, to teach us that suffering will always accompany true love; and hence anyone who follows him must carry his daily cross (Mt 16:24). He taught us about the supremacy of love and of the qualities that exemplify it; namely, that love is stronger than violence, that humility is stronger than pride, that kindness is stronger than anger, that gentleness is stronger than rudeness and that peace is stronger than war.

The apparent futility of suffering runs through the whole of Christ's passion. His mission seems to end in failure. But he overcomes the apparent futility by abiding obedience to his Father's will. "He humbled himself, obediently accepting even death, death on the cross" (Phil 2:8) and he did so freely. "He gave his back to those who beat him" (Is 50:6), being fully in control of his destiny, whereas others during the passion acted as prisoners. Pilate was utterly imprisoned by his own weakness; the high priests were controlled not by truth but by their lust for the blood of Jesus; St Peter could not control even his tongue and denied his Master; Judas ended his life as the prisoner of his own helplessness. But Jesus was all the time free, so free that he would later say, "I am now ready for you". It is this freedom with which Christ chose to suffer for the love of us that crowned his passion. Of course, he needed help; help which he could not expect from his own disciples who slept when he suffered and woke up only to desert him. Hence Christ's constant prayer was, "The Lord God is my help" (Is 50:7).

Like Christ, those who love God and neighbour must be ready to face conflicts, sufferings and even death. In the past, many have laid down their lives for the sake of love. There are thousands who are at present imprisoned unjustly for their Christian convictions. To try to face each day as a true Christian, with courage, in a world which requires so many kinds of painkillers can be very hard. Struggle for social justice and human freedom will involve some forms of death: death to one's position, honour, wealth and power; sometimes even physical death. But if our love of God and neighbour is deep and strong, we will be able freely to accept these sufferings as a way of sharing in Christ's love. We would also be able to love, to reach out to others and diminish their sufferings. We would be able to see in those who suffer the face of the contemporary Christ, marred and scarred by the violence which human beings inflict upon each other and we would not remain silent; for such a silence would only inflict further violence, of neglect and carelessness, on those who suffer.

Victory comes through suffering. Passion was not the last word in the life of Christ. It was only the first word of the Holy Week that will reach its climax on Easter Sunday. So too, however many of our days seem to end in a depressing way, they are not the last word in our life. Rather, they are only the prelude to triumphs we have yet to experience in this life; and they point to the ultimate victory which will be ours in the next life. Hitting rock bottom in our personal life and falling into the depth of sin must not make us pessimistic. No matter how low we fall, there is always the possibility of rising from it to the heights. Palm Sunday should solidify our hope. Palms should be signs that we are willing to march with Jesus, not only in moments of triumph and glory, but also in times of fall and agony. For the passion and resurrection of Jesus, prove that life will prevail over death; that when death has done even its worst, life will still be victorious.

EASTER SUNDAY

THE EASTER RELEVANCE

Readings: Acts 10:34, 37-43; Col 3:1-4; Jn 20:1-9

Theme: Easter is relevant today for it confirms Christ's way of life as applicable to our times, offering to all believers the hope of new life here and now.

Easter lilies decorate our homes and churches during Easter. They symbolise Christ's resurrection. All through the winter these flowers lay buried in the cold frozen earth; but with the spring sunshine, showers and breezes, these lilies come alive, break through the ground and bloom. Likewise, Jesus, buried under the earth, rose again to new life; no ground could hold him. It is a historical fact that the risen Jesus radiated his new life in all its power and glory wherever he went and to whomsoever he appeared. The disciples to whom he appeared were suddenly transformed from a band of despairing men into a brigade of daring missionaries. Everywhere they preached the Good News of Christ's resurrection, the power of Easter began to work in people's lives: despair began to give way to hope; darkness began to give way to light; hatred began to give way to love and sorrow began to give way to joy.

But there is a question we must answer. If it is really true that Jesus rose from the dead, does it have any relevance for today after 2000 years, in an age of science and sophisticated technology? Yes, it does. The relevance is that by raising Jesus from the dead God has confirmed that the way of Jesus is the way of life for all in all times. What was the way of Jesus? Against the social trends of his times, he sided with the poor, cured the sick, helped the needy, praised and blessed those who were not regarded worthy in society. Instead of giving Jewish rituals top priority, he placed human beings in the centre of the stage. Identifying himself with the poor and the lowly, he provoked the powerful. When the wise men of the world put him to death, because they rejected his way, God raised Jesus to a new life, thus demonstrating that the way of Jesus is the true way of life. This is the Easter relevance for today.

Easter has relevance for today, not only because it offers the world a true way of life with an assurance of the resurrection of the body after we are dead, but also because it offers to all believers the hope of new life here and now. For example, every time we suffer a loss, fail in some enterprise or are disabled by an illness, we die a little bit; but if we believe in the presence of the risen Jesus in our midst, we will discover new dreams to pursue, new challenges to take on and new reasons to try again. Every time we are overwhelmed by problems, discouraged by disappointments or beset by worries, we are diminished in some way. But if we believe in the real presence of the risen Christ, we will find that the impossible becomes possible and the unreachable becomes reachable. If the risen Christ is not relevant for us today, to whom would we go to discover the radiance of the face of God? Why should we come together seeking his communion? If the risen Christ is not relevant for us today, where can we find forgiveness, the wellspring of a new beginning? Where would we draw the energy for following him right to the end of our existence?

It is because God wanted Easter to be relevant for today that he has arranged a way for us to meet the risen Jesus. The central way is through the Holy Sacrifice of the Mass. Jesus uses the Mass in union with the bloody sacrifice of Calvary to take away our sins. He uses the Eucharistic banquet to come to each of us. "He who eats my flesh and drinks my blood, lives in me and I in him", he said. Of Mahatma Gandhi, Pundit Nehru said, 'Where he sits is a temple and where he walks is hallowed ground'. It is much more true of Mary, the mother of Jesus and we too can say it of each of us because Christ has promised to make us his home and his temple. Hence, Christ is risen that we might rise in him today and after death; Christ has entered new life that we might live in him today and in heaven; Christ has come forth from the tomb that we might shake off the fetters of evil today and for ever.

2ND SUNDAY OF EASTER

OUR STAYING POWER

Readings: Acts 2:42-47; 1 Pet 1:3-9; Jn 20:19-31

Theme: The gifts of the risen Christ are given to us at baptism. They endure, with ever-growing strength, by our belonging to the community of believers.

An old gentleman walked into the fashionable florist's shop. "I want a beautiful corsage ", he said, "not a big one but just about the prettiest one you can make." He smiled broadly. "It's for my granddaughter and she is having her first date tomorrow." The florist was all sympathetic interest. "How old is the young lady?", he asked. "Two weeks," replied the grandfather. The florist turned in utter amazement. "Did you say… a date… a corsage… two weeks old?" "Precisely," said the old gentleman. "And I want a corsage that's exactly right. She we'll never have a more important date than that which she has tomorrow. My little granddaughter is getting baptised." Yes. When we are baptised, we have the most important date of our life, for it is on that date, "God and Father of our Lord Jesus Christ gives us new birth, a birth unto hope which draws its life from the resurrection of our Lord Jesus Christ." (1 Pet 1:3) We Christians need to believe in this, for it is this faith which is the master key of Christian life, which can unlock the divine store house and fetch Christ's new life into our souls.

We don't believe only in possibilities, which is not faith but philosophy; our faith is the assurance of things we hope for. We are assured that in our baptism, we receive the same gifts that Jesus granted to his community of disciples after his resurrection: (Jn 20:19, 23), namely, we are washed into the community of believers; we encounter Christ's wounds and are marked with the cross of Christ; we are baptised into Christ's death that we might share his resurrection; we are given peace, forgiveness and community with a commission for ministry. If this faith of ours as to what happens at baptism is weak, it is time to stir it up; unless our faith is raised up, it will lie prostrate and unless it is warmed, it will be frozen. One sure way to rouse up our faith is to put our faith into works. We all know that if we don't use a muscle, it begins to weaken. In fact, it can become so weak that it will begin to atrophy or die. Something like that can happen to our faith if we don't exercise it. As we cannot separate heat from fire so we cannot have faith without works.

Believers who are intent upon exercising their faith cannot but belong to the community of believers, for we were not reborn in baptism for self-sufficient aloneness. A wall will not be strong with loose bricks; the bricks must be cemented together. So the early Christians formed themselves into a well-knit family. "The brethren devoted themselves to the apostles' instructions and the communal life, to the breaking of bread and the prayers, sharing all things in common". (Acts 2:42) We too need to belong to the community of believers to derive support from one another and grow in our faith. Our faith is never perfect; we are partly unbelievers. We need others' faith to help our unbelief. Like life, our faith too has peak moments and zero moments. It too has mountain top and valley moments. When we are in a valley of doubts and our faith seems to flicker and threaten to go out, we need the community. We need to belong to it also in order that we might experience the presence of the risen Lord. St Thomas got his experience of Christ in the community of disciples. In the community he became a believer because there he met Jesus.

To belong to the community of believers is not always to see eye to eye but to walk arm in arm. It is fellowship which doubles our joy and divides our grief, a fellowship which flourishes at the fountain of forgiveness. To belong is to share, not our properties necessarily, but our time, energy, talents and if possible some of our material goods for common welfare. To belong is to serve and serving God with our little is the way to make it more. To belong is to come together to pray, to break the word of God and to break the living bread. A community of such believers is assured of the power of the Holy Spirit working in them. The Holy Spirit can work in at least two ways. It can explode, as it did at Pentecost, as if a lighted match was thrown into a can of petrol, bursting forth into "tongues of fire". But the power of the Spirit can also work through the Church, as the energy channelled through a car engine in a controlled burn with lasting effect and staying power. Through worship, fellowship and service, a Christian community is provided with staying powers.

3RD SUNDAY OF EASTER

JESUS IS A WALKER

Readings: Acts 2:14, 22-28; 1 Pet 1:17-21; Lk 24:13-35

Theme: The risen Jesus walks with us in our life's journey towards God, guiding us when we feel lost and supporting us when we feel down.

Jesus once walked on the earth and his walking was far more important than man walking on the moon. Today, we his disciples walk on the path he has set for us. With the Psalmist, each of us can say, "You have shown me the path of life; you will fill me with joy in your presence" (Ps 16:11; cf Acts 2:28). We are on a journey towards eternal life with God. God could not create us for merely mortal ends. We will one day reach our destiny. As long as we keep our sense of direction, taking time out to consult our faith; as long as we observe our speed limits, setting a pace that won't burn us out before we reach our destination; as long as we watch the road signs, such as the indications of spiritual danger and signs of progress; as long as we are concerned for other travellers, giving support to them; as long as we take care to refuel our spirits, making it a regular practice to pray, we are sure to reach our goal.

However, our Christian journey will not be exempt from the rocks and dust of simply being human. Gospel is good news, but Jesus never said it was easy news. We will encounter the harsh realities of our personal and social lives. At those moments we must persevere in our journey and our set path. Life always seems better on the other side of the hill; the grass always looks greener in another field. After the crucifixion of their Master, two of his disciples, disappointed because all their hopes had been dashed by his death, left Jerusalem and were on their way to Emmaus in search of the other side of Calvary (Lk 24:13). We cannot act like them. "In prayer, you call God a Father; so then, live out the time of your sojourn here in reverence for God" (1 Pet 1:17). This means that, when we are faced with difficulties in our Christian journey, we must not give up on God. We cannot always trace God's hands, but we can always trust God's heart, because God's goodness is equal to his greatness.

God never abandons his pilgrims. He always comes to help. Some years ago, a speedboat driver was at near top speeds when his boat veered slightly and hit a wave at a dangerous angle. He was thrown from his seat as his boat was sent spinning crazily into the air. He was propelled so deeply into the waters that he had no idea which direction the surface was. But he remained calm and waited for the buoyancy of his life-jacket to begin pulling him up. Once he discovered which way was up, he could swim for the surface. Sometimes in our journey we too find ourselves immersed in trials and troubles. But if we remain calm and wait on God, his gentle tug will pull us in the proper direction. Our "life jacket" may be other Christians or Scripture and the Eucharist as it was to Emmaus disciples. As their "hearts burned inside them" when Jesus explained to them the Scriptures, and as they "recognised the Lord" at the breaking of bread, we too can experience God as we listen to his Word and partake of his Bread. God knows that we need spiritual nourishments for our journey and he has provided them.

In our journey we are not alone. Jesus walks with us. He walks with us in our lack of understanding, our hurts and our bitterness, as he did with the two disciples. He asks us to surrender our difficulties into his hands and continue our journey. At times we can experience his presence with us; at other times we can't. He is like the sun in the sky, which at times is big and bright and clearly visible in the sky, but at other times, it disappears behind a layer of clouds and seems to have vanished from the sky. But we know from experience that the sun is always somewhere in the sky. So too, in our low points of our journey we should not be disturbed by the apparent absence of the Lord; we should rather use them as opportunities to show Christ our trust that he is still walking with us and he will appear to console and heal us. For a journey, maps and road signs are useful; but it is infinitely better to have the guide himself, someone who has been there before and knows the way. Jesus is that Someone who walks with us.

4TH SUNDAY OF EASTER

THIS DOOR IS SAFE

Readings: Acts 2:14,36-41; 1 Pet 2:20-25; Jn 10:1-10

Theme: Christ is our safe door to full life for, himself being the Shepherd, he directs us on the right path and offers us the security of his love and the freedom to be ourselves.

St Peter said to the crowd, "You crucified Jesus", and that awakened in them a sense of guilt and a movement towards conversion which urged them to ask, "What must we do?" (Acts 2:37) They were right, because true belief in Jesus as the Christ necessitates such a radical conversion that it finds expression in a new way of living. What about us? After being converted to Christ in baptism, is our heart still craving for power and money? These are good in themselves, but when they possess us, they lead us to trample the rights and dignity of other people. Is our heart still full of worldly ambition, which often leads one to ruthlessness, selfishness and jealousy, making it impossible to live the Gospel values of love and care? A learned professor went to the East to meet and learn from one of its many gurus. After welcoming the professor, the simple guru poured the man a cup of tea. He continued to pour until it began to spill on to the saucer. The learned professor exclaimed 'The cup is full, you cannot pour any more into it'. 'That is precisely the way it is with you', said the guru. 'You are too full of yourself to let God in'.

Letting God into our Christian life means that we live for values proclaimed by Jesus; it means that Jesus becomes our 'door'. "I am the door", said Jesus (Jn 10:7). In our society of electric and automatic doors we normally think about doors as territorial barriers against our fear of being robbed or about doors that stand between 'mine' and 'yours'. Whereas, when Jesus called himself the 'door', he meant that he stands between life and death and he is the gate to safe and full life. He said, "I have come so that they may have life and have it to the full" (Jn 10:10). Just imagine for a moment that you are a cosmonaut out in space, umbilically attached to the craft. The earth spins in beauty in front of you; you have completed your space mission and the air reserve for the 'walk' is nearly over. You reach for the hatch lever but you find none; you claw and scratch the bolted surface of the craft to find the door you came out of, but that is not there. Thus, the way in is gone and you are lost. Then, suddenly, from within, a new and unseen door is thrown open and you are pulled through it and you are saved. That is the gate of life in space. Jesus says he is a similar gate to life on earth and to eternal life in the next.

If we enter through Christ our door, we are safe because of the security of his love; if we enter through Christ, we will have the freedom to be our best self, because we can go freely in and out; if we go through him, we are sure to find pastures, the nourishment and the satisfaction that give purpose to life. Jesus is not only the gate to the sheepfold, he is the shepherd himself. As our Good Shepherd, he is our guide. A good career guide can save some wasted years, a wise marriage counsellor a marriage, a medical adviser can save a life, a caring priest a soul. But the Guide of guides is the Good Shepherd. How often we go to other councillors when we really need our Shepherd? Yes. In our sickness we need a saviour, in our wanderings a guide, in our blindness some one to show us the light. We can have all these helps in Jesus. We dead people need life, we sheep need a shepherd, we children need a teacher, the whole world needs Jesus the Good Shepherd.

Christ not only promises us that he is the gate that leads to life, but wants us to follow him because he is the Good Shepherd. He is our model especially in the acceptance of suffering for the values which he preached and for which he died on the cross. "Christ suffered for you and left an example for you to follow the way he took" (1 Pet 2: 21). One of the most excruciating forms of suffering in our modern rather unethical and unjust society is to stand up for truth, to endanger the security and comfort of one's own life for the sake of justice and peace – and then have no one pay attention; to challenge corruption in our system, to suffer the pain of confrontation in the process and to discover that the rest of the world is too busy to pay any attention – what a cross! But Jesus asks us to bear them as he did, for the sake of the fuller life these crosses would bring to ourselves and mankind. In fact, we have to learn to refer not only the painful but all other experiences of our life, good or bad, to Christ our Shepherd in order to find life through them all.

ARE YOU TROUBLED?

Readings: Acts 6:1-7; 1 Pet 2:4-9; Jn 14:1-12

Theme: A true Christian believes the good Lord is always here and hence he fears nothing but prays always.

There is no person – king or pope – in the world, without some manner of trouble. Trouble appears to crush one man now, but afterwards another. Some people invite trouble unaware that it will accept the invitation every time. A lot of trouble in the world is caused by people trying to reform other people first. We are not so much talking here about such troubles; we talk here about real troubles. Joseph is afraid of unemployment; Mark and his wife are fearful about their son who has had a nervous breakdown. Mary has recently received an eviction notice and she has no place to go; Peter is afraid that his affair with a woman would become public and he is not able to break off. Mrs Angela is very old and is dreadfully afraid of death. Apart from such personal troubles, we are all afflicted by national and international troubles such as the fear of nuclear war and of increasing violence and crime in our societies. To add to all these, there are our imaginary troubles. We fear loss and failure, criticism and rejection which may never happen.

Nearly all our troubles can be summed up in one word: fear. Fear is of two kinds. One is constructive fear. This is the fear that can lead to deeper understanding and more creative action. In fact, much of humankind's progress has been the result of fears of starvation, sickness and the like. Hence constructive fear can be an instructor of great sagacity and the herald of many revolutions. But there is another kind of fear which is destructive. This fear leads one to deterioration of the emotional state, to increased nervousness, unreasonable behaviour and impotence. As the saying goes, 'When an elephant is in trouble, even a frog will kick him'. This can be applied as well to an individual who has fallen into destructive fear. Counsellors advise us that when we are afraid of something, we must not allow ourselves to freeze into immobility, nor should we take to disorganised flight causing stampede in our life. We know how a herd of cattle can destroy itself in such flight. On the contrary, they tell us that the best reaction to trouble is that we take a calm and rational attitude to it, have a strong trust in our own inherent power to face it and move towards a constructive action in the belief that we are in God's hands.

It was to this belief in God that Jesus was referring to when he said, "Do not let your hearts be troubled. Have faith in God and faith in me" (Jn 14:1). We must believe that God is with us in our trouble. We may not see him, but he is there. We cannot see the wind but we can see it blowing the leaves in the trees. We cannot see electricity but we know it is there when we switch the lights on. We cannot see air but we could not live a minute without it. We cannot see love but we know it is there in those who care for us. Similarly we cannot see God, but we know he is there because of the wonderful world all around us. The promise of Jesus is that he is always with us and will save us in spite of our troubles. Just imagine. A man gets trapped down a sewage pipe. Only the top of his chest, his head and his arms are not submerged. If he had not kept his arms in the right position he would have fallen completely. The man cannot pull himself out. His freedom requires the Fire Brigade which does come to rescue him. So too the Lord is always around to rescue us from going under. But remember that the trapped man was rescued because he was calling for help.

Likewise, we must call upon God and pray to him in our troubles. Not just in times of troubles a Christian should pray; prayer should be the soul of Christian life. The Early Church realised the importance of prayer so well that when the Apostles found that they had no time "for prayer and the service of the Word" (Acts 6:2), they appointed seven Deacons to care for the material needs of the community so that they themselves could devote all their time to prayer and preaching of the Word. Therefore let us become prayerful people. To a prayerful Christian, every trouble is a spur and a valuable hint to go to the Lord. "Jesus Christ is the cornerstone. The man who rests on it will not be disappointed" (1 Pet 2:6), because the Lord will encourage us towards a calm appraisal of the problem that is causing fear and motivate us to use the available resources to overcome our difficulties. To be unable to bear an ill is itself a great ill, but the Lord will give us the ability to bear it. With the Lord's support, even if the worst happens, we will not be destroyed by it; even if everything seems to be collapsing, we will not be crushed. Yes. The Lord is good, there is no devil but fear.

6TH SUNDAY OF EASTER

TO BE CHAMPION HORSES

Readings: Acts 8:5-8, 14-17; 1 Pet 3:15-18; Jn 14:15-21

Theme: Converted to Christ by means of faith, we are ready to obey his commandments and receive his Holy Spirit, who will activate us into champion Christians.

Robert Cheesebrough believed in his product. He's the fellow who invented Vaseline, a petroleum jelly refined from rod wax, the ooze that forms on shafts of oil rigs. He so believed in the healing properties of his product that he became his own guinea pig. He burned himself with acid and flame; he cut and scratched himself so often and so deeply that he bore the scars of his tests for the rest of his life. But he proved his product worked. People had only to look at his wounds, now healed, to see the value of his work and the extent of his belief. We too say that we are believers in the teachings of Christ. But how true is our belief? If faith is the conviction that God does not tell lies, how deeply are we convinced that the teachings of Christ are true? Faith is more than assent but it is never less than assent; if so, how deeply have we assented to the Good News?

Nothing is more disastrous than to study faith, analyse faith, make noble declaration of faith but never actually accept it. "When the apostles in Jerusalem heard that Samaria had accepted the Word of God they sent Peter and John to them" (Acts 8:14). Their believing was their personal, interior acceptance of the truth of what Philip preached. Their baptism was their personal, public, sacramental expression of their believing. Many of us were baptised as infants; have we ever seriously and maturely considered the Christian message and accepted it and committed ourselves to it consciously and deliberately? If we have, our faith would have by now become obedience, because faith is always obedience. Faith and obedience are bound up in the same bundle. One who obeys God believes him; one who believes God obeys him.

Obedience to God for a Christian believer is, of course, obedience to the commandments of Christ. But in order to obey Christ, we first need the conversion of our hearts or a change from our previous life-style to "the new life in Christ", "venerating him in the heart" (1 Pet 3:15). This is so because the seat of faith is not in the brain but in the heart. Once our hearts are converted to Christ by means of our faith, we are ready to obey the commandments of Christ; and we will obey for love of him, not for any other reason. That is what he meant when he said, "If you love me, you will keep my commandments" (Jn 14:15). Once an angel was walking down the street, with a torch in one hand and a bucket of water in the other. "What are you going to do with the torch and that bucket of water?", someone asked. The angel said, "With the torch I'm going to burn down the mansions of heaven; and with the bucket of water, I'm going to put out the fires of hell. Then we're going to see who really loves God". Many people seem to obey Christ's commandments out of fear of hell or hope of reward in heaven and not for love of him.

If we obey Christ's commandments, then, and then only, he will send us his Holy Spirit. "If you obey the commandments I give you, I will ask the Father who will give you another Helper" (Jn 14:15-16). Don't we need the Holy Spirit? Surely we need him. What is it that makes some horses winning thoroughbreds? Why is it that some horses have more speed, strength and stamina than other horses? Essentially these traits come from within the horses themselves. Still they also need help from expert trainers and skilful jockeys to activate and develop their inner powers. Similarly, we have within us capacities such as to overcome obstacles and grow; to discover more beauty in the world and create; to be compassionate to the needy and be generous; to see things clearly from God's point of view and follow. Yet like the champion horses, we too need a special kind of helper, the Holy Spirit, to activate and develop our inner capacities to the full, so that we can reach a peak in personal growth, become Christ-like and enrich the lives of people around us.

ASCENSION

THE POWER WITHIN US

Readings: Acts 1:1-11; Eph 1:17-23; Mt 28:16-20

Theme: By ascending into heaven, Jesus has not left us orphans, because he is still with us through the indwelling of the Holy Spirit.

A priest, Walter Ciszek by name, was in Russia for 23 years, five of which were spent in the dreaded Lubyanka prison in Moscow and ten of which were spent in the harsh Siberian slave labour camp. He was finally released from Russia in 1963, in exchange for two Soviet spies held in USA. He died in 1984 at the age of 84. After release he wrote a book 'He leadeth me'. In this book he tries to answer the question: 'How did you manage to survive in Russia?' He says: "I was able to endure the inhuman conditions in which I found myself because I experienced somehow the presence of God. I never lost my faith that God was with me, even in the worst of circumstances". What was true of Fr Walter Ciszek is true of each of us. Jesus is with us; God is with us in the power of his Holy Spirit.

These days, we are especially conscious of the cost and importance of power: how to harness the solar power, wind power and wave power; the power of the trade unions, and the power of television. We talk of the uses and abuses of power by power-crazed people. But on this feast of Ascension, we are not thinking about any power other than the power by which Jesus ascended into heaven. It was by the power of the Father that he ascended. "The power which he used to raise him from the dead and to make him sit at his right hand in heaven" (Eph 1:20). And Jesus promised the same power to all his followers: "You will receive power when the Holy Spirit comes on you" (Acts 1:8). He fulfils this promise chiefly at our baptism and confirmation.

When do we experience the power of Jesus dwelling in us? When we read his words, when we deny ourselves for him, when we carry our cross after him or when we suffer persecution because of his name. But we need to pray for his Spirit to become active and alive in us. That is why his disciples, after his ascension, went directly to the upper room in order to pray for nine days before Pentecost. The power of God becomes active through prayer. Prayer means more than an occasional nod in the direction of heaven. It means sitting down or kneeling down on a regular basis and speaking to our heavenly father asking him for the gift of the Spirit. As we wait in prayer, we will begin slowly to experience God's power; we will begin to be able to forgive and to unite; with the power of the Spirit an individual's life will be transformed; suspicions will be replaced by trust; hostility can change into mutual trust; repulsion and violence can change into repentance. In a word, the whole person can be reborn.

When we take our seat on a train or climb the gangway onto a ship, the thought rarely crosses our minds as to whether there is sufficient power in the engines to move the train or ship. Most likely we take it for granted. Flying in a jet is quite different. Take off makes us very much aware of the tremendous power required to lift such a weight off the ground. We hold high expectations that it will succeed; after all, our life depends on it. What of the power of God within us on which peace and happiness in this life and eternal life in the next, depend? Do we simply take it for granted or are we truly aware of it? Probably most of us rarely think of it, which is a fatal mistake.

Thus our Lord's ascending to heaven is important to us, because it confirms his claim to be God's own Son; it completes the cycle of incarnation-redemption-glorification; it gives us hope that one day we too will be with them in heaven. But in the meantime he has not left us as orphans. Although he is not visibly with us, he dwells within us by the power of the Holy Spirit. That is what he meant when he said: "I am with you till the end of time" (Mt 28:20). Yes. Jesus is still with us.

7TH SUNDAY OF EASTER

PRAYER: A WASTE OF TIME?

Readings: Acts 1:12-14; 1 Pet 4:13-16; Jn 17:1-11

Theme: Our prayer, both personal and common, is born of our faith in God and models itself on the prayer of Jesus Christ.

If a person has no faith in God it is logical enough for him or her to call prayer a waste of time. But we have faith and yet one wonders how much and how often we pray. Prayer figures in all of today's readings. In the first reading we see the disciples praying together in the upper room; in the second reading the newly baptised are exhorted to praise God for his blessings. In the Gospel Jesus prays to his Father. Anyone who loves God, needs him and cares for him cannot afford not to make a habit of prayer. A woman was told by her husband that he was suing her for divorce. "Why? ", she asked. He replied, "You have always been indifferent to me. You never cared for what I did or thought". Suppose God the Father appears to you now and says, "We are close to breaking off". You say in shock, "Why?". He responds, "You are indifferent to me; you never pray; you never seek my company in prayer; you don't even ask for the earthly goods to which you are so much attached". We must therefore examine our habit of prayer. Self-examination is the high road to prayer.

The habit of prayer is good, but the spirit of prayer is better. We will have the spirit of prayer if our prayer is turning of our minds and hearts to God, a heart to heart conversation with him, an attitude of waiting and attending to him, a personal relationship with him which can be continuous even when we are engaged in other activities. A heart to heart prayer is different from saying prayers. While journeying on horseback one day St Benedict met a peasant walking. "You've got an easy job", said the peasant, "why don't I become a man of prayer? Then I too would be travelling on horseback". "You think praying is easy", said the Saint. "If you can say one 'Our Father' without any distraction, you can have this horse." "It's a bargain", said the surprised peasant. Closing his eyes and folding his hands he began to say the 'Our Father' aloud. When he came to 'Thy Kingdom come', he suddenly stopped, looked up and asked, "Shall I get the saddle and bridle too?" This is why, while praying, it is better to have a heart without words than words without a heart. Only that prayer that comes from a heart can also get into God's heart.

You can have a heart to heart conversation with God when you are alone, as Jesus does in today's Gospel. Speak to him in your own words. If you find this hard, do what a sick person did. He was in bed for several years but could not pray. A friend suggested that the sick person place an empty chair near the bed. He told him to imagine Jesus sitting in it. Then he asked him to converse with Jesus, just as the two of them were conversing now. The sick man tried it and had no more trouble after that. You and I can do the same. Along with private prayer we must also pray together with our fellow Christians as the Apostles did in the upper room. "Together they devoted themselves to constant prayer" (Acts 1:14). We must constantly pray as a Church. Prayer is the strong wall and fortress of the Church. If private prayer is the breath of faith, group prayers are the lungs of the church. Whether we pray alone or together, there must be both praise and petition in our prayers. "A Christian must glorify God in virtue of that name" (1 Pet 4:16). Do we glorify God enough in our prayer? One wonders whether complaint is the largest tribute Heaven receives! When we glorify God, we enjoy him; praising God energises and renews praying.

Among us, there may be experts in prayer, who knows! But remember, for Christians there is really only one prayer: the prayer of Jesus himself, in which all of us his faithful participate; that is why we always end our prayers saying: "Through Christ Our Lord". Hence we must model our prayers on his. How does he pray in today's Gospel? First he recognises the primacy of the Father's will in his life: "I have given you glory on earth by finishing the work you gave me to do" (Jn 17:4). In our prayer do we seek God's will or our own? The supernatural power of prayer consists not in binding God's will down to us but in lifting our will up to him; prayer is good but when used as a substitute for obedience, it is nothing but pharisaism. Secondly Jesus showed concern for his disciples when he prayed: "For these I pray, these you have given me" (Jn 17:9). How often do we pray for others? If we seek only our own advantage and blessing through God we are not seeking God at all! Hence let us pray and pray as Jesus has taught us. Prayer draws down the great God into our little hearts and it drives our hungry souls up into the fullness of God. He stands best who kneels most.

PENTECOST SUNDAY

WE HAVE A DREAM

Readings: Acts 2:1-11; 1 Cor 12:3-7, 12-13; Jn 20:19-23

Theme: The Feast of Pentecost, while renewing our dream that one day all people will form one community of nations assisted by the power of the Holy Spirit, calls all Christians to cooperation with the Spirit in the transformation of the world.

We all look forward to that day when there will be no more the tragedy of wars between nations, wars which are nothing but murders legitimised by the wearing of uniforms. We all look forward to that day when there will be no enemies in our midst, enemies who treat one another with hatred, a hatred which, like a poisonous mineral, can eat into the very heart of a religion. We all look forward to that day when the value of any culture will not be judged by its location on the globe but by its effect on character; that one day all the diversity of cultures will be joined together as one in the heart of the human race. We all look forward to that day when it will not be the races but individual people who will be seen as noble or ignoble, rejecting no one from the human race because of class or colour. We all look forward to that day when all people will speak in harmony and their minds apprehend alike. We all look forward to that day when peace will rule the day because Christ will rule the hearts. We all look forward to that day when all people will form one community of nations, with malice towards none, with charity for all; singing in one voice with the Psalmist: "Behold, how good and how pleasant it is for brethren to dwell together in unity". That is our dream.

Can this dream of ours, for a community of nations, become a reality? Yes, it can; provided we have the Holy Spirit assisting us. The Spirit of God achieved such a community on the day of Pentecost. When he came "like a strong driving wind, and tongues of fire rested on each of the apostles" (Acts 2:2), all barriers of nation and language were broken down by the fusing power of the Spirit; so that people who had gathered there from different lands "heard the apostles speaking each in his own language" (Acts 2:8). Language has the power to divide and the power to unite, depending upon the spirit of those who use it. Those who use their language, influenced by the Spirit of God, can create an understanding community; others will only divide it or destroy it. The Spirit brought together not only the dispersed nations but also the confused disciples, so that they were immediately transformed into the Body of Christ. The same Spirit can do the same today for the Church and the world.

But the Spirit of God needs us, his Church, to cooperate with him in the transformation of the world. It is not enough to have faith in the power of the Spirit; wherever there is genuine faith, it must blossom into works. We must first work to transform our own churches into united, loving, forgiving and sharing communities. Our parishes must become truly the Body of Christ, in which all our individual gifts are put at the service of the community, in the belief that "there are different gifts but the same Spirit, there are different ministries but the same Lord" (1 Cor 12:4). Having thus set our own house in order, we then reach out beyond the narrow confines of our particular churches. The words of Jesus, "As the Father has sent me, so I send you" (Jn 20:21) were directed towards us also. Therefore, as God's people, we are bound to function as divine agents in the world, to break down the walls of pride and prejudice and of hatred and war, that still plague our families, cities and nations.

Let us pray: "O Spirit of God! See your people gathered in prayer. Baptise us with your grace, like early morning dew. Soothe and quieten our minds with your message of peace. Mighty river! Flood our barren spaces, make fertile our deserts within, break us and heal us. Free us from party spirit. May we be less occupied with things that divide us and more with those that we hold in common. Help us to see ourselves as rays from the one sun and as streams flowing from one river. May we remain united to you and to one another. Warm-winged Spirit, rushing wind! Sweep the world out of the dusty corners of its apathy and breathe vitality into its struggle for justice and peace. Let your mighty fire freely burn, till earthly passions turn to dust and ashes, consuming in its heat all that divides the human race. Touch our hearts with the shock of your coming and fire us with longing, to spend and be spent in the ways of love and service to humanity, until our dream of a united world comes true."

INTIMACY IS FOR OTHERS

Readings: Ex 34:4-6, 8-9; 2 Cor 13:11-13; Jn 3:16-18

Theme: The spiritual riches we receive by developing an intimate relationship with each person of the Holy Trinity through prayer are meant to be shared with others.

Hyde Park in London is a favourite place for soapbox orators. Anyone can go there on a Sunday afternoon and talk on any subject under the sun, ranging from Politics to Religion. The famous English Catholic layman, Frank Sheed, went there often to talk about religion. When he was once preaching there on Holy Trinity, it began to rain. He used the rain to explain the unity in diversity of the Trinity. He said something like this: "The water that is falling is water, but it can exist in three different forms: gas, solid, and liquid – that is, in steam, in ice, and in falling rain". Of course, an analogy like this falls short of the reality. But it offers an insight into the Trinity. As there are not three different kinds of water but only water in three different forms, so there is only one God in three different persons. St Ignatius of Loyola, once in prayer, perceived the Trinity in the form of three musical notes which made up a single chord. However, with all such analogies, the Trinity is still a mystery to us; but we believe in this mystery and many of us also want to develop an intimate relationship with each person of the Trinity.

One way you can grow in close relationship with the Trinity is through prayer. Each night before falling asleep, set aside three minutes. During these three minutes, replay the day that has just ended. During the first minute, pick out the high point of your day, something good that happened to you – like escaping a car accident on the motorway. Speak to the Father about it and thank him for it. During the second minute, pick out the low point of the day – like chastising your child, not to correct but to vent your anger. Speak to Jesus about it and ask him to forgive you. During the third minute, look ahead to tomorrow, to some critical point – like having to confront someone who has been spreading false rumours about you. Speak to the Holy Spirit about it and ask for wisdom and courage to deal with it properly.

This daily exercise which combines prayer and self-examination, can lead you day by day into an intimate relationship with the Holy Trinity.

But remember; our intimate relationship with the Triune God must not serve only our own self-interest. We can't keep God to ourselves, can we? If we love our neighbour as God wants us to, then we have a duty to reveal the beauty and the uniqueness of our God to others. That is, our intimacy with the Trinity must be also for others. Moses did that. Moses was so intimate with God that God "used to speak to him... face to face" as "one speaks to a friend" (Ex 33:11). But he came forward to use this intimacy to win God's favour for his people when they sinned. "If indeed I do enjoy your favour, please, my God, come with us" he prayed (Ex 34:9). Even the intimate relationship that exists between Father, Son and the Spirit is not for themselves but for others. That is why the intimate love the Father has for his Son resulted in sending him to be our Saviour: "God so loved the world that he gave his only son" (Jn 3:16). The Father and the Son love each other so deeply that their love was poured out in the person of the Spirit on all those who believed. In the same manner, if we know and love God intimately, then we are urged to make sure that our intimacy is for others also.

Here are few examples to show how one's intimacy with the Trinity can benefit others too. Am I married? If so, I am called to share my love of God with my spouse, which then can overflow into my family life. Am I an employer? If so, I am called to express my understanding of a merciful God in mercy and justice for my employees. Am I an artist? If so, I am called to translate my appreciation of the beauty of God into works of art for others. Am I single? If so, I am called to reveal my knowledge of a compassionate God in my concern and support for others. Whatever may be our vocation in life, we Christians, who claim to have an intimate experience of our "God of love and peace", are urged to "agree with one another and live in peace and harmony" (2 Cor 13:11); so that the world would know, that our intimacy with God is for others. At Mass, we ask the Father to send his Spirit upon our gifts and then there is a sharing of bread and wine. Thus the Eucharist too, forces us to translate our intimacy with God into sharing, teaching us that intimacy is indeed for others.

CORPUS CHRISTI

EUCHARISTIC PEOPLE

Readings: Dt 8:2-3, 14-16; 1 Cor 10:16-17; Jn 6:51-58

Theme: Eucharistic people are believing, spirit-filled, contented, united, and caring community people.

Eucharistic people are people who believe in the real presence of Christ in the Eucharist. Years ago, on *Corpus Christi* priests carried the Blessed Sacrament through streets accompanied by worshipping throngs. In my parish, the priest used to stop at appointed houses where altars waited. One ten-year-old boy, who believed so deeply in the presence of Christ in the Eucharist, wanted to know why Jesus did not stop at their home. "Ask the priest," his mother replied. He did and got his wish. "Jesus came to my house," he said proudly, "I think I'll work for him." And he did. He became a priest. God allowed the Israelites to be hungry in the desert and then fed them with manna to show them that "not by bread alone does man live, but by every word that comes forth from the mouth of God" (Deut 8:3). And the supreme Word of God became flesh in Jesus, who is now present in the Eucharist.

Eucharistic people are spirit-filled people, because the reception of the Eucharist is a communion with the very life of Jesus for he said, "I myself am the living bread" (Jn 6: 51). In the Eucharist Jesus nourishes our spirits not only for this life but for eternal life also. It is with the Eucharist we become fully alive in our life of the spirit. Without the Eucharist, we become weak, incapable of loving others; without it, we become easy victims to temptations and depression; without it, we quickly lose interest in anything spiritual; without it, we lose our freedom in the Spirit and become enslaved by the materialism of the world.

Eucharistic people are contented people. According to an Indian fable, Lord Vishnu said once to his devotee: "I am weary of your never-ending petitions. I shall grant you three requests. Make sure you choose them carefully because having granted them, I shall grant you nothing more." The elated devotee did not hesitate. "Here is my first request," he said, "I want my wife to die so I can marry a better woman." His wish was immediately granted. But when friends and relatives gathered for the funeral and began to recall the virtues of his wife, the devotee saw he had been hasty. So he asked the Lord to bring her back to life. That left him with just one more petition. He consulted widely. Some advised him to ask for immortality. But what good was immortality, said others, if he did not have good health? And health, if he had no money? And money, if he had no friends? The devotee was so confused that he finally asked the Lord himself: "Tell me what to ask for." The Lord laughed and said, "Ask to be content, no matter what you get." Of course, we can never be contented by bread alone, nor by beer, nor by television, nor by cars, nor by balanced budgets, but by every Word that comes from God. Fortunately for us, we believe the Lord God who is the source of contentment is present in the Eucharist.

Eucharistic people are united people. Eucharist unites its recipients into one body of Christ. "We, many though we are, are one body for we all partake of the one loaf" (1 Cor 10:17). Like the kneading together of many grains into one visible loaf and like the juice that flows from many grapes together into an invisible liquid, the body of Christ we all share makes us of one mind and one heart. "If then," says St Augustine," you are the body of Christ and its members, it is your own mystery which is placed on the Lord's table; it is your own mystery which you receive. It is to what you are that you answer Amen and in so responding subscribe to it. Be member of the body of Christ so that your Amen will be true."

Eucharistic people are community people. The Eucharist creates unity and hence communion means community. Husbands and wives who receive the Eucharist pledge themselves anew not only to Christ but to each other. Single people who share in the Eucharist thereby commit themselves to share in the destiny of brothers and sisters. The talented who break bread with Christ thereby refuse to break away from sharing their talents with others. The prosperous who eat and drink with Christ must in turn share their table with the less fortunate family members of Christ. "Is not the cup of blessing we bless a sharing in the blood of Christ? And is not the bread we break a sharing in the body of Christ?" (1 Cor 10:16).

Eucharistic people are caring people. To receive communion is to receive others into our world of concern. There is something wrong in our relationship with the Lord in the Eucharist if our communion does not bring us into a caring relationship with our neighbours, especially the poor and the suffering. This is what Mother Theresa referred to when she said to a group of European visitors to her slum in Calcutta, "Your poverty is greater than ours; the spiritual poverty of the West is much greater than the physical poverty of the East. In the West, there are millions of people who suffer loneliness and emptiness, who feel unloved and unwanted. They are not hungry in the physical sense. What is missing is a relationship with God and with each other." If Jesus washed the feet of his apostles before instituting the Eucharist, it was to call all Eucharistic people to intensify our caring and sharing in the service of others.

BAPTISM OF THE LORD – 1ST SUNDAY OF THE YEAR

CALLED TO SOLIDARITY

Readings: Is 42:1-4, 6-7; Acts 10:34-38; Mt 3:13-17

Theme: As Jesus, sent by God to bring justice to all particularly to the poor and the oppressed, showed his solidarity with them by receiving baptism like them so, too, we were set aside at our baptism for that same apostolic life that Christ initiated.

Gift wrappings and presentation boxes make gifts so much more attractive. But at times they may distract us a little from the gift itself. The Gospel accounts of Christ's baptism are full of drama as our own baptism is full of attractive rituals. It would be a pity if these baptismal wrappings distract us from what they are meant to highlight. They highlight the fact that at his baptism Christ was commissioned to carry out his mission of bringing justice to all. So Isaiah foretold: "He brings justice; he will neither waver nor be crushed until true justice is established on earth" (Is 42:1-4). But what is justice? In the biblical sense, justice is meeting need wherever it exists and particularly where it exists most helplessly. And Christ was commissioned to bring this justice not to the selected few but to all because, "God does not have favourites" and "Jesus Christ is Lord of all men" (Acts 10:34-36). Likewise, when we are christened at our baptism the Christ-ing appoints us to our Christian vocation, setting us aside for that apostolic life which Christ initiated.

That is why the day when a person is baptised is more important than when a person is ordained priest or bishop, for if one is not anointed at baptism to carry out the mission of Christ, he can neither be a priest or a bishop. When the Roman youth reached manhood, he put on the Toga Virilis, the robe of manhood. When the Hindu youths of certain castes reached manhood, they put on the *yagnopavitam* or sacred cord. So at baptism, a believer puts on Christ, a new robe of righteousness to display to the world and a new cord of justice to establish in the world. Thus our baptism is dynamic; it points back to the work of God in us and forward to the life of faith. We are inclined to speak of our baptism in the past tense, "I was baptised" implying, perhaps, that our baptism is a static event now over and done with. It would be better to say, "I am baptised", meaning that baptism is an ongoing thing to be lived out daily. Therefore the question we must ask ourselves is whether as members of the new messianic people we are available to God as his instruments to bring justice to all.

Though Jesus' mission was for all, he was commissioned to bring justice particularly to sinners, to the poor and the little ones of society. This is the reason why he allowed himself to be baptised. The baptism of St John the Baptist was a baptism of repentance. It was a sign that the people repented their sins. But Jesus was sinless, always God's beloved Son. In spite of it, if he still chose to be baptised, it was to show his solidarity with us sinners, needing forgiveness; it was to identify himself with the poor, the distressed and oppressed, needing justice. Mahatma Gandhi did a similar thing. The film *Gandhi* is a three-hour epic, depicting the life of Mahatma Gandhi. In order to lead the oppressed people of India to freedom from British rule, Gandhi adopted means such as fasting from food, vigils of prayer, marches, protests and civil disobedience. One of the reasons why Gandhi put on a loin cloth and fasted from food almost to the point of death was to show solidarity with the Indian people, identifying with them in their physical sufferings, which finally brought independence to India.

If we are convinced that God has chosen us as his servants upon whom he has put his Spirit when we were baptised, the question we must ask is: To what extent are we ready to identify ourselves with the poor and the oppressed in order to relieve their burdens as much as we can? How deeply are we involved in the plight of people, in order to bring light where there is darkness and ignorance, sight where there is blindness and racism, freedom where there is oppression and ill-treatment? As adult Christians, are we prepared to take a public stand for the marginalised in society, a call we received at baptism as babies? In our present world, such public witness can be a daunting prospect as it could mean becoming unpopular and isolated, finding ourselves battling in a wilderness. At such moments of lonely suffering in the cause of truth and justice, we need to allow ourselves to hear that word from God: "You are my son/daughter, the beloved; my favour rests on you" (Mk 1:11). When we experience God's favour resting on us and his Spirit overshadowing us, we can go forth and do battle as Jesus did.

2ND SUNDAY OF THE YEAR

NICKNAMES OF JESUS

Readings: Is 49:3, 5-6; 1 Cor 1:1-3; Jn 1:29-34

Theme: Jesus the 'Servant of God' calls us to serve others as he did; Jesus the 'Lamb of God' calls us to be ready for sacrifices in being his disciple; Jesus the 'Lord' invites all Christians to unite under his one Lordship.

Nicknames are popular with people. Some of them are given to individuals just for convenience or humour. But often a nickname is a condensed description of one's outstanding qualities. For example, Ivan *The Terrible* is a nickname expressing the cruel character of the man; whereas *The Little Flower* is the nickname given to Thérèse of Child Jesus, capturing the gentle and humble character of the saint. Jesus too has some biblical nicknames.

The Servant: Jesus is the servant of God. "Israel, you are my servant", said the Lord (Is 49:3). This servant is a messianic figure referring to Jesus and what an all-out servant he was! When you are in some serious trouble, not many would come all out to serve you. There is a story of a man who had fallen into a well and was crying for help. A passer-by seeing the man in the well, said, 'Life is full of sorrow!' and went away. Another passer-by went a step further and said, 'if you are able to spring up to me, I can try to get you out'; but the poor man could not spring up to him. A third man came by the well, and on seeing him, actually climbed down into the well, took him out and brought him to safety. Jesus served us all in that manner.

He got himself personally involved in our redemption even accepting death on the Cross. But the "Servant of God" is more than a nickname because it challenges us to serve others as Jesus did. To be able to give a large part of oneself to others is the most satisfying thing in life. It is not always the talented ones who serve best, but the consecrated ones. We were consecrated to God and his people at our baptism, but do we live up to our consecration?

The Lamb: Jesus is the Lamb of God. "Look there! The lamb of God" (Jn 1:29), said St John the Baptist. Yes. The lamb went to his slaughter in silence but in strength, for the redemption of many, which he does even today. As you know, when a tiger dies, it leaves only its skin and when we die, many of us leave only our ashes; but when Jesus died, he left his name. Therefore, in the name of the Lamb of God, his followers even today continue to take away the sins of many and continue to sacrifice their very lives to liberate those who suffer as victims of poverty, injustice, oppression, racial bigotry and appalling human conditions. A wealthy young couple walked into a large orphanage one day to ask to adopt two children. The director, beaming with satisfaction, said, "Now we'll show you two of the nicest children in the orphanage". The wife turned quickly and then remarked kindly but firmly: "Oh, please, no! We don't want the nicest children; we want two that nobody else would take". That was a sacrifice, upon which even the gods would throw incense. The Lamb of God challenges us to make sacrifices similar to his for love of our neighbour. If the heart is denying sacrifice, it means love is dying.

The Lord: Jesus is the Lord. "Grace and peace to all those who, wherever they may be, call on the name of our Lord Jesus Christ" (1 Cor 1:2-3). Yes. Christ is not valued at all unless he be valued above all. As the Lord, he is the goal of human history and the centre of the human race. Yet so many in the world are still away from him, on an endless road, in a hopeless maze. But how can the Lord bring them also into his fold, if his own household still remains divided? A great musical conductor called Toscanini was rehearsing a Beethoven symphony with one of the great orchestras of the world. After a long day, the orchestra was not still producing the sort of music he had expected. Distressed by this performance, Toscanini turned to the orchestra and said, "Gentlemen, you are nothing, I am nothing – Beethoven is everything". If only we Christians could consider the differences which exist between our churches as nothing, and believe that the Lord is everything, Christian unity under the same Lord would soon become a reality.

COME AFTER ME

Readings: Is 8:23-9:3; 1 Cor 1:10-13, 17; Mt 4:12-17

Theme: Christ, the light of the world who illumines our hearts and shines for all, urges us to repent if we have caused divisions in his Church and unite with our fellow Christians in bringing his light to the rest of mankind.

A young man who later became a Cardinal was returning by sea from Italy to his native England. While the boat was detained in Sicily, young Newman fell ill and nearly died. During his convalescence, he wrote these words: "Lead kindly light, amid the encircling gloom", because he believed that the prophecy of Isaiah had come true: "People who walked in darkness have seen a great light" (Is 8:23). We too have our hours of darkness. The death of a lifelong spouse, an unexpected rejection by a loved one, a smashed dream of business success or the loss of good health can throw us into a temporary darkness. But at such tragic moments, true believers have in the past seen the light of Christ, a light that illumines the shadows of our hearts with the radiance of his splendour, guiding us to travel safely over the tempestuous sea of this mortal life, steering the vessel of life through rough storms of trials and troubles, until we have made the harbour of peace and bliss.

It is true that the light of Christ first shone in Galilee but it was meant to bring light to every one who comes into the world. Hence Jesus chose some to be his apostles telling them: "Come after me, I will make you fishers of men" (Mt 4:19). 'Fishers' is not just a metaphor but a mission, a mission to bring the light of Christ to cover the earth, as water covers the channels of the deep, to carry faith to the doubting, hope to the fearful, strength to the weak and comfort to the mourners. It is a mission entrusted not just to the apostles, bishops and priests but also to the laity who serve in the Church as altar servers, readers and eucharistic ministers, as well as to those who serve outside it, such as the parish pastoral councils, the teachers, the catechists and parents. In fact, all the baptised and confirmed are called to be fishers for Christ. If Jesus, the dawn on our darkness, has made us into the brightest sons of the morning, it is in order that we, like fishermen, may leave behind our narrow cells and launch out into a larger sea of life as apostles of the light.

Our apostolate will be a mighty force if it comes from one united Church. Together we can win, divided we fall. We Christians are gathered together by the same Word, joined together by the same Baptism, framed together by the same Spirit and built together by the same Christ. Why can't we then worship together as one Church? Disunity has been endemic in the Church right from its beginning. Already then, St Paul had to appeal: "Let there be no factions, rather be united in mind and judgement" (1 Cor 1:10). Although the week of prayer for Christian unity soon ends, we must continue to pray for unity first among ourselves as Catholics, that we may speak in harmony and our minds apprehend alike, that common be our prayer, common be our resolutions and common be our deliberations; and we must continue to pray that the members of different churches may soon be bound together in the visible unity of one faith.

If we Catholics have caused any bitterness between Christians because of our self-interest and self-concern, it is time to repent and repair the offences. If we have neglected the Lord, the bond of unity, because we have trusted in our own wisdom and strength, it is time to repent and reform. If we have failed in our commission to be the apostles of Christ's light, the greatest of all lights, the only true light, the light from whom springs the lights of the day and that of the sun, it is time to repent. We need not wait for Lent to repent. "Repent! The Kingdom of God is at hand" (Mt 4:17), asks the Lord today. It is consoling to know that it is easier to repent of the sins we have committed than to repent of those we intend to commit! If only we could truly repent and reform our lives, the Lord will send forth his Spirit speedily into the dark places of our guilt and woe, and arm us with the piercing power of his light.

BE-HAPPY RULES

Readings: Zeph 2:3, 3:12-13; 1 Cor 1:26-31; Mt 5:1-12

Theme: The eight beatitudes of Jesus which offer a spiritual vision of true happiness to both the rich and the poor hinge on two main pillars: humility and mercy.

Vision is the art of seeing things invisible. Any youth setting out to make a success of life must have a vision. One without a vision does not really care. In the Beatitudes Jesus offers a spiritual vision of true happiness. The wisdom of the Beatitudes is of perennial and universal validity. They are not easy and clear answers. They are not like advertisements neatly packaged like a television commercial. In them Christ offers a new set of attitudes, be-happy rules, but in a style and stance of paradox. The Beatitudes go beyond common sense to God's sense of things. Therefore, as long as we govern ourselves by our own common sense, we can neither understand nor practise the Beatitudes. Men and women of all generations found peace and consolation in the Sermon on the Mount. Mahatma Gandhi drew inspiration from the Beatitudes for his concept of nonviolence. Dr Martin Luther King was convinced that his struggle on behalf of the poor and the oppressed would succeed only if it were based on justice, love and forgiveness, proclaimed in the Beatitudes. Although the beatitudes given by Jesus are eight, they rest on two main pillars: humility and mercy.

Humility is poverty of the spirit. Humble people acknowledge their need of God and believe God is the ultimate guarantee for happiness. Therefore, "they seek the Lord, obey his commands" with the result that "they graze and rest with no one to disturb them" (Zeph 3:13) This is what Jesus meant when he said, "Happy are the poor in spirit, for theirs is the kingdom of heaven" (Mt 5:3). The humble are meek and gentle even towards those who are rough and tough, because their love for God sets them free to love others, unlike the proud who are so busy measuring the worth of others with their false tape measures. As meek and gentle, the humble will one day have "the earth for their inheritance" (v.5). The humble are pure of heart because they are single-minded in their seeking and pleasing God which allows them to "see God" (v.8). The humble readily accept sorrows in their lives. They do not complain about sorrow, poverty, hunger or any other pains in life; for they recognise them as signs of that future life where "they will be comforted by God" (v.4).

Mercy is to give compassionate attention to others. It means to forgive our persecutors. It means a willingness to suffer in support of those who struggle to return to the path of peace. It means to hunger and thirst to correct the injustices in our society that perpetuate inhuman conditions. After graduating from medical school Dooley enlisted in the Navy as a doctor. The big day of his life came one hot July afternoon off the coast of Vietnam. That's when his ship rescued 1000 refugees who were drifting helplessly in an open boat. Many of the refugees were diseased and sick. Since Dooley was the only doctor on the ship, he had to tackle single-handedly the job of giving medical aid to those people. It was back breaking, but he discovered what a little medicine could do for sick people like this. He said, "Hours later, I stopped a moment to straighten my shoulders and made another discovery – the biggest of my life. I was happy treating these people, happier than I had been ever before". Dooley's experience that hot July afternoon was the fulfilment of the Lord's blessing on the merciful.

Beatitudes are golden rules for happiness. The blessed may be poor in riches but they don't mind it because they trust in a caring God and so they are happy. The blessed may happen to be materially rich, but because they are poor in spirit the result is that God becomes so dear to them that wealth means nothing to them and therefore they are happy. They may sorrow, but realise that they are sharing in Christ's own sorrow and hence they are happy. In their hunger and thirst for God they do not mind the deprivation of worldly pleasures because they are enriched by the friendship of God and hence they are happy. They are so merciful that they may look like soft-hearted fools to the proud but they are sure of receiving God's mercy assuring them eternal life and hence they are happy. Ten Commandments alone are not the recipe for happiness. They are only foundations for it. They mostly tell us what not to do and what not to be. The Beatitudes on the other hand tell us what to do and what is to become. They counsel attitudes and actions which are the flowering of every virtue leading us to a blessed state.

SALT AND LIGHT

Readings: Is 58:7-10; 1 Cor 2:1-5; Mt 5:13-16

Theme: To be the 'salt of the earth' and the 'light of the world', particularly in working for social justice in today's world, may arouse opposition but we can overcome *them* in the power of the Spirit.

Before the days of widespread health problems relating to high blood pressure, salt was regarded as an unequivocal good. It was salt that preserved food and kept it from spoiling. Salt was traded by caravans just as people traded gems and gold. Jesus says that we his disciples are the "salt of the earth" (Mt 5:13), because we are essential to the world since we carry in us his life which he won by his death and resurrection for all humankind. He also says, we are "light of the world" (Mt 5:14). A mother and her small child once drove past the restored home of Abraham Lincoln in Springfield. It was night and the national shrine of the United States was brightly lit. "Look, mama," the child said excitedly, "Mr Lincoln left his lights on". The mother smiled. "Yes", she replied; "he left them on for the whole world to see". Although Lincoln has been dead since 1865, he is still a tremendous inspiration to all people. But in much more true sense Christ, "God from God, Light from Light" remains and will remain to the end the shining beacon for all people of all times. No world leader or founder of religion has left a more lasting impact than Jesus Christ. Christ has shared his light with us his disciples and asks us to be what we are: the light of the world.

We are asked to be salt to our world preserving it from spoiling because of greed, injustice and lust, preserving it from decaying because of dishonesty, disloyalty and disrespect. We are called to be salt in the world transforming it through Christian values such as sharing, human rights and decency. We are urged to be the light of the world, illuminating our homes and communities with truth, justice and peace and guiding the world along the way shown by Christ. We are not to parade our light but we are expected to be a light. Mother Theresa of Calcutta left a comfortable life in an European cloister to work among the very poor in India. She did not do this to be a good example to other people. She did it out of love and her love became a light for the world. Commenting on this, former media personality Malcom Muggridge said in effect: “I can’t tell you how much I owe to Mother Theresa. She showed me Christianity in action. She showed me love in action. She showed me how the love of one person can start a tidal wave that can spread across the world”.

Our being the salt and the light of the world must be in answer to the particular needs of our time and the present world cries for works of justice more than for anything else. We need to be like the salt in preserving the world from getting more and more corrupt because of injustices done one to another. We need to be the light in dispelling the darkness of greed and selfishness of certain sections which drive millions to go hungry, naked and homeless. The Lord’s appeal, “Share your bread with the hungry and shelter the homeless and clothe the naked” (Is 58:7) still resounds today and it resounds louder than ever. Nakedness can obviously be taken literally in terms of those without adequate clothing. But it has also a wider meaning. The naked are those whose human dignity is denied, who stand before the rest of humanity without protection, power or hope. The nakedness of such individuals is due to the greed of the rest of humanity. It is the obligation of the Christian to clothe the naked by working to establish a world order in which exploitation is replaced by an equitable sharing in the blessings of creation, a sharing which is based on a recognition of the dignity of each person, regardless of race, colour or religion.

While we serve the world as its salt and witness to the light of Christ, we will be called to make sacrifices and even meet opposition from those who prefer to live in darkness and refuse to approach the light. This may sting like salt on an open wound, but we need not lose courage, for we are doing only God’s work and we rely chiefly on the power of the Spirit. St Paul found success only through the power of the Spirit.” I did this”, he wrote,” so that your faith should not depend on human philosophy, but on the power of God.” (1 Cor 2:5). Yes; what can philosophy do? It can provide us a refuge for definitions. It is true we can’t do without philosophy since everything has its hidden meaning which we must know. But philosophy can hardly lead us to full truth. Philosophy begins in wonder; but at the end, when philosophic thought has run its course, usually the wonder remains. Philosophy and science are good servants of Christ, but they are poor guides when they rule out the power of the Spirit. Without the Spirit of God, we can do nothing; we are like ships without wind, branches without sap and coals without fire. Even prayer without the Spirit is like a bird without wings.°

6TH SUNDAY OF THE YEAR

PERFECTION IS NO TRIFLE

Readings: Sir 15:15-20; 1 Cor 2:6-10; Mt 5:17-37

Theme: God's love for us made practical by his commandments challenges us to seek a deeper and inner kind of holiness in and through their observance and to become increasingly holy as God is holy, which is possible aided by the power of the risen working in us.

Some look upon the Ten Commandments as ghostly whispers of a dead age; some dislikc them, others hate them. Yet it is for the benefit of man that God made the Laws. We come to worship God not because he is the greatest celebrity of all, but because he is thc greatest good. How can this God make laws which are bad for us? God's love for us is made practical by his laws. Hence his laws last longer than those who break them. Those who go on breaking them will pay for it. They may not pay weekly, but they will pay for it at the end. In a sense, no one can break the laws of God; we can only break ourselves against them. Thus, "Before man are life and death; whichever he chooses will be given him" (Sir 15:17). Those who obey the law, live; otherwise they die. Because God's laws are an expression of his friendship and of his concern for his people, Jesus proclaimed (Mt 5:17) that he had come not to abolish the laws but to fulfil them.

Jesus fulfilled all of God's laws when he sacrificed his very life on the cross for love of God and the human race, a love that sums up all laws and perfects them. In so doing, he called us his followers also to seek as he did a deeper and inner kind of holiness, rather than the mere external observance of the laws. This means that not only crimes of violence like murder are forbidden but also harbouring of any anger, which is the root cause of murder; not only the act of adultery must be shunned, but even lustful thoughts which are the seeds from which plants of adultery grow. Likewise, not only false oaths must be avoided but also any dishonest motive behind our words (Mt 5:21-37). By this new teaching, Jesus is challenging us to become as holy as God our Father is holy. Our church is charged with the grandeur of a holy God; that is why we light candles and incense the altar. We who come to worship this holy God are not all holy because we use holy water, but by seeking on the other six days of the week the inner holiness of our hearts and minds. In each action, therefore, we must look beyond the action to find whether we are holy within as God is.

Is it possible to become as holy and as perfect as God is? Many would probably place such perfection in the realm of fantasy. Yet, it is better to strive for this ideal and fall short than never to have tried at all. Besides, we are not left to struggle towards perfection all by ourselves. Through Christ we have received "God's wisdom, a mysterious, hidden wisdom, which eye has not seen, ear has not heard, but planned by God before all ages for our glory" (1 Cor 2:7). What is this wisdom? It is the spiritual eye that can see the effects of God's love and saving power working in us through Christ's redemption. We are called to use it. A blind man slowly turned around the corner of a street feeling his way with his white cane. A young man coming from the opposite direction dashed round and collided with him. "Why don't you look where you're going?" barked the hurried young man. The blind man gently replied, "Why don't you go where you are looking?" Many times we fail to use the 'wisdom eye' given to us by God.

God did not make us perfect, nor can we suddenly become perfect as God is. We are pilgrims after perfection moving little by little towards it. Therefore you are becoming perfect when you show a little more patience towards those with whom you have to live, even though their company may not be congenial to you; a little more firmness to continue the work which duty demands but is repellent to you; a little more humility to remain at the post to which God has led you, though not fitting with your talents; a little more common sense to take people as they are; a little more strength to endure an event which disturbs your peace; a little more cheerfulness so as not to show you are hurt; a little more unselfishness to understand the thoughts and feelings of others; and a little more prayerfulness to draw God to your heart. These may be trifles, but trifles make perfection though perfection is no trifle.

7TH SUNDAY OF THE YEAR

THE NOBLEST REVENGE

Readings: Lv 19:1-2, 17-18; 1 Cor 3:16-23; Mt 5:38-48

Theme: Jesus taught us by word and example not to hate our enemies nor take revenge on them, not only because love and nonviolence have to be the 'soul power' of Christian disciples but because in hating others we hurt ourselves more.

Dr Martin Luther King, following the footsteps of Gandhi's nonviolent methods, laid down his own life to win civil rights for the American blacks. He enforced upon his followers his own ten commandments of love. According to his commandments, love and nonviolence had to be the 'soul power' of the Civil Rights Movement. According to another Master, Jesus Christ, love and nonviolence have to be the 'soul power' of Christian disciples. Jesus, therefore, asks us not to hate our enemies and not to take revenge on them. In our Lord's time, if a Roman officer tapped a Jewish citizen on the shoulder with his sword, the citizen had to do whatever the officer commanded him. If he ordered him to carry some object for a distance of one mile, he had to obey. Referring to this humiliation the Jews suffered under the Roman forces, Jesus says, "Should anyone press you into service for one mile, go with him two miles" (Mt 5:41). Why did Jesus give this strange advice?

The question is answered by Dr Smiley Blanton who is a famous psychiatrist. One day a new patient walked into his office. The patient noticed a copy of the Bible on Dr Blanton's desk. "Don't tell me that the great Dr Blanton reads the Bible", said the patient. Dr Blanton replied: "I not only read the Bible but meditate on it. It is the greatest text book on human behaviour ever written. If people followed its teaching, a lot of psychiatrists would close their offices and go fishing". What did he mean by that? It is simple. He meant to repeat Leviticus: "You shall not bear hatred for your brother. Take no revenge and cherish no grudge" (Lev 19:18). He meant to repeat Jesus: "Offer no resistance to injury but love your enemy" (Mt 5:39). A teaching such as this certainly goes against our worldly way and what is that way? "Sir, the enemy are before us, as thick as peas", said the servant to his master. "All right, shell them", came the order. That is the 'way', a "wisdom of the world" which of course "is absurdity with God" (1 Cor 3:19). Yes. This is an absurdity because those who hate their enemies end up hurting themselves far more than they hurt their enemies.

We hurt ourselves by hating others. Hating people is like burning down your own house to get rid of a rat. The fire of hate compressed within our heart would soon burn fiercer and burst into flames consuming not only our own selves but also engulfing the world. Some say that the world will end in fire, others say in ice, but after knowing what hate has done so far between races, nations and communities, we can also say that the world could end by hate. We hurt ourselves by contemplating on revenge because, by doing so, we keep our wounds green which otherwise could heal. In any case, can blood be washed with blood and can injury repair injury? Of course, it is human to strive to get even with an enemy, but it is Christian to forgive, for we are all children of God who loves both the good and the bad without any discrimination.

Jesus always practised what he taught us and this is true also of his call that we love our enemies. Once a sparrow fell in love with a white rose, but the rose said to the bird, "Unless I am turned into red, I will not be able to love you". The sparrow, now lost in deep thought, wondered and searched hard for means to turn the white rose into red. At dawn the next day, the sparrow was struck with the bright idea of pricking itself with a thorn and letting its blood flow on the rose. Having accomplished its loving task, when the rose had turned red, the sparrow breathed its last, nestling close to the rose. This is how Jesus loved us, shedding his blood for his enemies. Hence, love even your enemy, not because it will drive the enemy nuts, but because those who deserve love least, need it most. Hate not your enemy, life is too short for hate; and think of no revenge, and if you want to take any revenge at all, remember that the noblest revenge is to forgive.

8TH SUNDAY OF THE YEAR

ARE YOU ANXIOUS?

Readings: Is 49:14-15; 1 Cor 4:1-5; Mt 6:24-34

Theme: Though moderate anxiety is desirable and healthy, we need to avoid succumbing to neurotic anxiety by trusting in the motherly concern of God and by seeking his Kingdom first.

John was my classmate in high school, but a week before the finals he dropped out. He could not handle anxiety. During class tests he would break out in cold sweat and his mind would go blank. He was in school for the first two years but latter he stopped going to lectures; they were too scary for him, because he was afraid he would not be able to remember the important points that would come for the test. By the end of the second year, he felt uncomfortable even to enter the school library. Soon he stopped going to the students coffee bar, for he was afraid he would meet there some of his teachers or cleverer students. And then the amazing thing happened: he became almost too anxious to leave his own room. Anxiety has been called 'the official emotion of our age'. If some are worried about the end of the world, others are worried about the end of the month. Blessed is the person who is too busy to worry in the daytime and too sleepy to worry at night.

Anxiety is an intense feeling of apprehension, concern and worry. Anxiety can arise in response to some specific identifiable danger or in reaction to an imaginary or unknown threat. Normal anxiety comes to all of us at times, usually when there is some real danger. Neurotic anxiety is an exaggerated feeling of dread even when the threat is mild or nonexistent. Moderate anxiety can be desirable and healthy, because it helps us to avoid dangerous situations and leads to necessary action; but intense anxiety is more stressful; it can produce physical harm such as ulcers, headaches, blood pressure and a variety of other stress-related diseases. It can also produce psychological and mental reactions. For example, it can hinder our normal ability to think and remember, causing the mind to go blank at times. It can also cause trouble in getting along with others, blocking effective human relationship and affecting efficiency in work. When Jesus asks us not to worry, he was referring to the exaggerated, abnormal anxiety.

Those who do not believe in God and in a God who cares for us are liable to be bogged down with worries more than others. We Christians who worship God as our Father should not needlessly worry. God is like a mother to us. "Does a woman forget her baby? Yet, even if these forget, I will never forget you" (Is 49:15) was God's own assurance. The basic cause of most of our worries is a failure to live our life on a day today basis. The crosses we make for ourselves by a restless anxiety as to the future are not crosses from God. Of course, it is wise to be prudent and wise to plan for the future and take responsible actions to solve our problems. Providence of God does not assist the idle. But Jesus taught us that we should not be too anxious about the future because we have a heavenly Father who knows what we need and will provide: "I am telling you not to worry about your life and what you are to eat nor about your body and what you are to wear. Your heavenly Father knows you need them all" (Mt 6:25,32). A person who believes what Jesus has said will agree with the hymn writer who wrote: "I know not what the future holds, but I know who holds the future". In any case, it does not make sense to worry about the future, because why open an umbrella before it starts to rain?

Therefore, instead of getting worried about our material needs, Jesus asks us to seek God's kingdom first. "Set your hearts on God's kingdom first and God's saving justice and all these other things will be given you as well" (Mt 6:33). Every one wants the kingdom of God but few want it first. But the divine promise is that if we give God our first priority in our lives, we can rest assured that our needs will be supplied and there will be no need to worry. What does it mean to seek God's kingdom first? It means hungering and thirsting for God's favour, lest we be in perpetual hunger and thirst. It means endeavouring to live by faith; when we feel low and empty, it is not because the hand of God is tightfisted, but because the hand of faith is weak. It means waging a ceaseless warfare against sin within us, for we know that Christianity is a battle, not a dream. It means taking a radical break to turn from earth's rubbish to heaven's treasure. It means labouring to have my bank in heaven than to have my heaven in a bank. It means holding loosely all that is not eternal.

9TH SUNDAY OF THE YEAR

HEARERS AND DOERS

Readings: Deut 11:18, 26-28; Rom 3:21-25, 28; Mt 7:21-27

Theme: If we both believe in and live by the Word of God, keeping the balance between hearing and doing, we are laying an unshakeable foundation for our lives.

Just imagine. You are on a journey to explore a new territory through a mountain forest. You leave your car at the entrance to the forest. It is overcast but dry. You make rapid progress up the hill through well maintained trails. Unexpectedly, mist and rain whirls around and you are forced to turn back in haste. You come to a fork in the path but can't be sure which is the way back to the car. A signpost would be a blessing but there is none. Your instinct tells you to take the left hand one. But your instinct turns out to be wrong. Your mistake sends you miles off route and you are cold, tired, hungry and miserable when eventually you reach the car late in the day. All these travails could be avoided if there were signposts along the way. Our life, though it is like a mountain trail, has signposts along the way. The Word of God which is expressed in the Ten Commandments and the teachings of Christ is one sure signpost, and God says, "Let the words of mine remain in your heart and in your soul; they are a blessing if you obey them" (Deut 11:18). God actually told the people to bind his words to their wrists and foreheads, thus stressing their importance.

However, it is not enough to hear God's words. We must do something about them. Knowing is not enough, we must apply; willing is not enough, we must do. Some years ago, a young man applied to teach religion in a Catholic high school in India. When the principal asked him if he were a practising Catholic, he replied: "No. I am a Hindu, but I know Catholic teaching thoroughly. I went to Catholic schools all my life. I'd gladly take a test to prove my competence". The principal explained to the young man that the heart of Catholicism lay not in knowing Catholic teaching but in living a faith-filled Catholic life. Yes. Un-practical religion is un-scriptural religion. Those who mouth the word of God without living it will not enter the Kingdom. We can't talk our way to heaven. Those admitted into heaven are not those who shout, "Lord, Lord", but "those who do the will of my Father" (Mt 7:21). Our faith in God's Word has to take on flesh in practice. Faith without works is a body without clothes, no warmth. Faith and practice are as inseparable as fire and heat.

Therefore there is a need to keep the balance between faith and action, between hearing the Word and doing it. Jesus once touched upon this balance when he said, "If you love me, keep my commandments". If we keep to this balance, we will not fall into legalism. What is legalism? It is not simply the keeping of the laws. It is the keeping of the laws based on the false belief that salvation comes through the keeping of the laws. As St Paul asserts, salvation comes not from the mere observance of the laws but, "through the free gift of God's grace by being redeemed in Christ Jesus" (Rom 3:24). Therefore I can't say, "I don't eat meat on Friday; I don't miss Sunday mass; I keep all the laws of the Church. God therefore must be pleased with me and must save me". This is equivalent to saying that one saves oneself and no saviour is needed. But at the same time one must avoid the danger of concluding that faith in the Saviour alone is enough and law does not matter and that it is all right to do one's own thing. No. We must observe the divine law as well.

If we both believe in and live by the Word of God, we are laying an unshakeable foundation for our lives. Jesus said, "Any one who hears my words and puts them into practice is like the wise person who built a house on a rock" (Mt 7:24). What does this 'rock' signify? It is the intimate union with God that results from both hearing and doing Jesus' words. It is a relationship with God that is so deep that most events in life become meaningful. It is contemplation in action that allows a person to face crises directly, without being torn apart at the slightest confrontation. Those who build their lives on the solid rock will not buy into the values promoted by the world, values that excite the nerves with sensual kicks but leave our hearts empty. On the contrary, their lives will be set so firmly on the values of Christ that no adversity will be able to destroy the fulfilment they find in Christ. It is true that none of us can be spared from some kind of setback and sufferings in this life, but on the solid bedrock of active faith in Christ we will survive the worst.

10TH SUNDAY OF THE YEAR

THE UNLIKELY CANDIDATES

Readings: Hos 6:3-6; Rom 4:18-25; Mt 9:9-13

Theme: Jesus calls each of us, even the apparently unlikely candidates among us, to new vision and to new mission, and if we accept his call, our rewards will be much greater than the sacrifices we make to follow him.

Douglas Hyde was the editor of The Communist Daily Worker; yet Jesus called him and he became a great apostle of Christianity. Piri Thomas was a drug pusher, thief and an attempted killer; yet Jesus called him and he became a great apostle of Christianity. John Newton was a slave trader; yet Jesus called him and he became a minister and went on to write great hymns such as 'Amazing Grace'. Paul of Tarsus persecuted Christians; yet Jesus called him and he became one of the greatest apostles of Christianity. St Matthew was a hated tax-collector. Honest men in his profession were so rare in his time that the citizens erected a monument to him when they found one. St Matthew was hated as a sinner and outcast, because he was a Jew who sold his services to the Roman conquerors, to collect taxes for them from his own countrymen. Thus, St Matthew had already made a mess of his life. Jesus, who was well aware of this, was still willing to give him a second chance by inviting him to follow him, which he did and he became one of the closest associates of Jesus. Each of these men were unlikely candidates to get a second chance from Jesus, but they got it and rose to become new men for a new world.

These men tell us, that each of us, without exception, is a candidate to be called by Jesus, to receive a second chance, to live a fuller life in him and to work in better ways for the spread of his Kingdom. Perhaps we have made mistakes or wasted opportunities in the past; perhaps we drank ourselves out of a good job or messed up our marriage; Perhaps, through no fault of ours, we are in an awkward situation now; for example, an accident may have disabled us, or economic misfortunes may have impoverished us; or we have been thrown into a situation, which is oppressing our spirits and suppressing our potentials. Therefore, we may conclude that we will never receive a second chance from Jesus. But in truth what Jesus normally does is the opposite. He often chooses the most unlikely candidates imaginable. This is because Jesus looks beyond what we are, to what we can become; he is not interested so much in our liabilities as he is in our possibilities.

Jesus calls each of us, the apparently unlikely candidates in particular, to new visions and to new missions. He calls us to a new vision of love, and to rise above rituals and sacrifice, to embrace the deeper meaning of life as a loving community, because it is love that God desires, not sacrifice (Hos 6:6). He calls us to a new vision of faith and to concretise our faith in Jesus, just as Abraham did, who "did not doubt or disbelieve but drew strength from faith" (Rom 4:20). He calls us to a new vision of our own life and to take new directions and explore new paths towards further growth. He calls us to a new mission: a mission that takes its inspiration from Jesus himself who shared bread with outcasts and sinners (Mt 9:11); to a new mission that promotes mutuality in relationship, equality before God and commitment to the wellbeing of the marginalised in society; to a new mission that translates faith and love in terms of mercy, social consciousness and justice. He calls us to discover in ourselves, a previously unused charism or undeveloped talent and to place it at the disposal of this mission.

If we accept Jesus' call and follow him, obviously we have to be ready to make some sacrifices; but we are also sure that what we will receive in return from God will be lot more than what we give up. St Matthew gave up a comfortable life but he got in return a life filled with adventure; he gave up a good income, but he got in return the satisfaction of doing something that would be lasting and significant; he gave up a life that would end in twenty years or so, but he got in return a life that would never end; he gave up his tax-collector's job and got in return the job of recording for all ages and all nations the greatest news the world has ever heard; St Matthew was not a skilful writer, but what he wrote down remains, even today, as unfathomable treasure for all to ponder and pray over; similarly, if we answer the Lord's call, we will have to give up certain things but we will also receive gifts from God, gifts that might, at times, put our best dream to shame. He may not return possession for possession but he will surely give us riches. That is why, perhaps, whenever my purse is emptied for God, my heart is filled.

THE HONEYCOMB JUST FLOWS

Readings: Ex 19:2-6; Rom 5:6-11; Mt 9:36, 10:8

Theme: More labourers are needed in the Lord's vineyard to share with others the love and reconciliation we have received from God, taking inspiration from the Eucharist which is a symbol of how to give freely and generously.

A bell is a bell only when you ring it; a song is a song only when you sing it; so, too, the love in your heart will stay as love only when you give it away. The gifts that God has given to each of us are meant to be shared with others. "There is one thing that I know," said Albert Einstein, "that man is here for the sake of other men. Many times a day I realise how much of my life is built on the labours of my fellow men; and I must earnestly exert myself in order to give in return as much as I have received". Of all the gifts we have received from God the greatest is his love. "You yourselves have seen how I carried you on eagle's wings and brought you to myself" said God to Moses (Ex 19:4). What God said of his love for the Egyptians applies to us a thousand times more, because we have been reconciled to him through his own Son Jesus Christ: "What proves that God loves us is that Christ died for us while we were still sinners" (Rom 5:8). Of course, together with such gifts of love and reconciliation that we have received from God through Christ comes our duty to share them with others.

As Jesus gave a share in his authority and power to his disciples so that they would go to the lost ones and proclaim that the Kingdom of God is close at hand (Mt 10:7), so he has given us gifts and talents that we may bring God's love, mercy and reconciliation to others in need. But are there enough labourers among us who have responded to the call of Christ? Is not what Jesus said then still true today: "The harvest is rich but the labourers are few" (Mt 9:37)? St Francis Xavier, labouring in India 400 years ago, wrote this to St Ignatius in Europe: "Many out here fail to become Christians only because there is nobody prepared to undertake the task of teaching them… I have often felt moved to go to the universities of Europe, especially the Sorbonne in Paris, shouting like a madman, saying to those who have more learning than goodwill to employ it advantageously. If only, while they studied their humanities, they would also study the accounting that God will ask for the talent he has given them! Many might be moved to say, 'Lord, here I am; What would you have me do?'"

The Lord needs labourers who will constantly pray to the owner of the harvest that he will send out more labourers to gather in his harvest. The Lord needs labourers who will raise their families as seedbeds for vocations to the priesthood and the religious life. When we witness to our love for God by bringing peace and compassion to our neighbours, when we witness to the reconciling mercy of God in word and action, when we as a Christian community reflect the Gospel qualities as alternatives to the values of the world, and when we address the spiritual and human needs in our parishes, civil communities and nations, we are labourers in the Lord's vineyard gathering in his harvest. We may not have money to give away to worthwhile causes, but all of us can give words of encouragement to someone in need; we may not have miraculous powers to heal, but all of us have the capacity to comfort and affirm people who are hurting in some way. Whatever gifts we have – the gifts of listening and reassuring, the gifts of serving and volunteering – have been given to us by the Lord to be given away.

The Eucharist we celebrate is a symbol of how to give freely and generously whatever we have received. Under the signs of bread and wine, Jesus shares the gift of himself with us and inspires us to give ourselves to others generously. Generous giving is the mark of a true Christian. A witty writer once wrote: "There are three kinds of givers: the flint, the sponge and the honeycomb". If you want to get anything out of the flint, you just hammer it to get only chips and sparks; some people are so stingy and hard, that they give nothing away if they can help it. If you want to get anything out of the sponge, you must squeeze it and the more you squeeze it the more you will get; some people are good natured and they can easily yield to pressures. But the honeycomb, just flows with abundance and sweetness. Giving that flows from love flows like honey from the comb.

12TH SUNDAY OF THE YEAR

"DO NOT BE AFRAID"

Readings: Jer 20:10-13; Rom 5:12-15; Mt 10:26-33

Theme: Though the presence of sin in the world and its resistance to God's work will make it difficult for us to help God in spreading his Kingdom on earth, God will not allow sin to overpower us.

A father was feverishly pushing the lawn mower around his yard, wondering if he'd finish before dinner. Mikey, his six-year-old walked up and, without even asking, stepped in front of his father and placed his hands on the mower handle. Knowing that the son wanted to help him, the father stopped pushing but the mower quickly slowed to a stop. "Get out of here, kid, you're in my way", he wanted to shout but didn't; instead, he said, "Here, son. I'll help you". As he resumed pushing, the grass cutting continued, but more slowly and less efficiently than before, because Mikey was "helping" him. This is the way our heavenly Father not only allows us but calls us to "help" him in spreading his kingdom. The call Jesus gave to his disciples saying, "What I say to you in the dark, tell in the daylight; What you hear in whispers, proclaim from the housetops" (Mt 10:27), was addressed not just to them but to us all, clergy and laity; we are all called to help our heavenly Father to proclaim the Gospel of Christ by word and deed, so that our ministry brings love where there is hatred, pardon where there is injury, faith where there is doubt, hope where there is despair and joy where there is sadness.

But in our Christian ministry we must be ready to face sufferings, hardships, sacrifices, rejection, even persecutions. Jeremiah is perhaps the greatest example of a minister who had to face such trials. "All those who used to be my friends watched for my downfall" he cried out (Jer 20:10). Christ himself had to face sufferings in his ministry and he did not avoid them. He did not attempt to evade the hands of those who scourged him, the blows of those who struck him, or the spittle of those who spat on him. What of the sufferings of the martyrs? They found themselves hard-pressed, beset by dangers from violent storms of hatred, dangers not so much to their bodies but rather to their faith. So it will be for us when we minister. When we try to reflect in our lives the values of the Kingdom, choosing life over death, faith over disbelief and integrity over sin, we will have to face crosses, because there is sacrifice involved in rejecting the world's sleazy ways and its lies. When we denounce by word and deed falsehood, injustice and selfishness, we may be led, like Jeremiah, to lonely isolation deserted even by our close associates.

Why should those who minister for the Gospel of Christ suffer? The answer is simple: there is sin in the world. "Sin entered through one man and through sin death" (Rom 5:12). As long as there is sin in the world, our attempt to free the world from sin will face resistance. Sin will resist truth, for the tragedy of sin is that it first affects man's mind, the highest faculty given to him to perceive thc truth. Sin will resist justice, for the essence of original sin was to usurp God's right to be the Lord of all. Sin will resist love, the greatest of God's commands, for sin is basically my right to my claim to myself. Sin will resist light, for it has been always a thief at night who will not only rob my soul of its life but also God of his glory. Sin will resist obedience, for all wars, disease, death, even natural disasters can be traced back to that one act of disobedience in Eden. Sin will resist holiness, for sin is not a splash of mud on my exterior but a wound in my soul inside me. Sin will resist grace, for it always begins and ends with a departure from God who is the source of all grace.

Because of such resistance from sin, we the ministers of Christ have to suffer. But we need not be afraid, because we have a heavenly Father who will not allow us to suffer alone without his support, or to suffer beyond our strength, or to suffer in vain. "Do not be afraid," said Jesus, "every hair of your head has been counted and you are worth more than hundreds of sparrows" (Mt 10: 31-32). Do we value ourselves as God does? Years ago, Stanley Coppersmith of the University of California wanted to know why some people succeed while others with equal talents and opportunities fail. To find this out, he studied 1700 students for six years, following them through the key growth years. He discovered that the most important factor contributing to success or failure is a person's self-image. In other words, if we perceive ourselves as valuable and as loveable as we are to God, we will be able to succeed in our ministries, riding over even great difficulties.

13TH SUNDAY OF THE YEAR

LOSS AND GAIN

Readings: 2 Kgs 4:8-11, 14-16; Rom 6:3-4, 8-11; Mt 10:37-42

Theme: To lose one's life, the most precious human possession, is to die to evil that we may rise to full life, is to carry one's daily crosses that we may share in the power of the risen Christ and to make sacrifices for others so that they too may share in the new life of Christ.

Of all the possessions we have, the most valuable is life. Human beings may still kill each other in wars; barbarism and disregard for human life may still belong to our age; human life may appear cheap when we see bloodshed so much. Yet it is only other people's lives that men treat cheaply. It is always true that one's own life remains for ever the most precious. Yet, our Lord tells us in today's Gospel: "Lose your life for my sake" (Mt 10:39). This saying of Jesus must have left his listeners staggered and bewildered by its sheer incredibility. We too will never understand Jesus until we understand that he came down from heaven in order to turn our worldly ideas about life upside down and to replace our worldly dream of the good life with a vision of a cross for eternal life. Note well his words: "He who loses his life for my sake will find it" (Mt 10:39). What does it mean?

It means to die to evil so that we may live for eternal life. Today there is far too much public discussion about evil, drunkenness, infidelity and sex. Discussion, plenty, yes; but confessions, how many? To talk of sin is easy, but to give up sin? When Charles Foucauld, a hero of France but still an evil man, entered a church one day, he knocked at the confessional of Fr Huvelin and said: "Come out, I want to talk to you about a problem". Fr Huvelin answered: "No, come in, I want to talk to you about your sins". Foucauld, struck by divine grace, obeyed. Later he became a solitary in the desert and one of the saintly men of our times. A distinguished man called on Fr Vianney, the Curé of Ars, and said, "I have not come to go to confession, but to talk things over". The Curé said, "I am not good at discussion, but I am good at consolation". Once inside the confessional box, the penitent encountered divine grace, found new energy and love to displace the old ego and his personality was reborn.

To lose life for Christ's sake also means to be ready to suffer for the sake of our faith in him. It means to carry our daily crosses, our sicknesses, loneliness, and struggles which are part of our earthly existence. These may not lead us to the Calvary of martyrdom but they normally lead us over very rough roads which, however, bring us in the end the reward won by Christ on his Calvary. To lose one's life for Christ means to bear sufferings not only of our own but also those that come in our service for others, especially the needy, the strangers and outcasts in society. In fact, the people whom the world remembers after they are gone are those who served others. Once a schoolboy was asked what parts of speech 'my' and 'mine' are. He answered that they were aggressive pronouns. He was right. Pride and greed are devouring so many human beings in our world that the idea of service as a life-giving value is getting almost lost. So many people are in business only for what they can get out of it. They may well become rich, but one thing is certain: they will not be loved and love is the true wealth of life.

Although losing one's life is the only way to gain life in Christ, our losses and pains that we accept for Christ's sake will not go unrewarded. An elderly married couple in the first reading took into their home the prophet Elisha and his servant Gehazi and as a result were rewarded with the promise of the birth of their first son (2 Kgs 4:16). Even if we are not suitably rewarded in this life for losing something for the sake of Christ, there is a promise of Eternal Life which should be the greatest reward a person could ever have. So St Paul says, "If we have died with Christ, we believe that we are also to live with him" (Rom 6:8). The unfortunate thing is that many people are not willing to make even the smallest exchange with Jesus Christ. They are like the rich young man in the Gospel who went away sad because he had many possessions. A cowardly patient can refuse to have the operation needed to cure the illness because of the pain that is the price of health. It should not be so with us. We must see the supreme wisdom that is in our Lord's saying, "He who loses his life for my sake will find it" and try to live by it.

14TH SUNDAY OF THE YEAR

COME TO HIM

Readings: Zec 9:9-10; Rom 8:9, 11-13; Mt 11:25-30

Theme: As the least among us have greater reason to thank God, for he chooses the little ones to be the recipients of his special blessings, so the most weary among us have greater necessity to come to Christ for comfort, since God has entrusted everything to his Son.

Bees suck honey from flowers and hum their thanks when they leave. Are we thankful enough to God for all his blessings? Or, perhaps, by our lack of appreciation for his manifold gifts, do some of us make God feel that he is casting pearl before swine? Jesus teaches us how to be thankful to God. At a time when he was facing mounting opposition and the inability to secure the confidence of the elite and powerful, he thought he had reason enough to praise God saying, "Father, Lord of heaven and earth, I thank you" (Mt 11:25), just because God had given him twelve ordinary men as disciples. As bread once eaten is forgotten, so we tend to forget the gifts of God and we don't remember them even when we come to him for new ones. It is a pity that human nature is such that we are slower to recognise blessings than evils. How humiliating it is for us personally when we have worked very hard on something expecting some appreciation but fail to receive it! Ingratitude especially to God is a great folly because it is so unkind. "Blow, blow thou winter wind", writes Shakespeare in *As You Like It*, "thou art not so unkind as man's ingratitude".

We need to thank God not only for big blessings but also, and especially, for small ones because our God has chosen to love and reveal himself especially to the small, the poor and the ordinary ones. "I bless you Father for hiding these things from the learned and clever and revealing them to mere children" (Mt 11:25) prayed Jesus. Our God is not like the ancient pagan Gods who revealed themselves in the mighty and powerful personalities of kings and rulers. Only the Pharaoh, for example, had the right to have the pyramid that would ensure him immortality and he was presented as the beloved of Gods. Our God the Lord of heaven and earth is different. "See how your king comes to you, humble and riding on a donkey", prophesied Zechariah

(Zec 9:9). Jesus did exactly that when he entered Jerusalem as king. This is to proclaim that the humble and the poor are God's special friends. Because such people are not proud, greedy or self-righteous, God has easy entrance into them. They are also free from material ties so that "their interests are not in the unspiritual, but in the spiritual" and therefore, "not doomed to die" (Rom 8:9,13).

Because the poor and lowly on earth are God's blessed ones, we must not conclude that they are not free from the weariness and burdens of human life. In fact, they often suffer more than the rich and the powerful. But all of us rich or poor, strong or weak, have our share of weariness and burdens. For example, all of us feel fatigue from hard work. All of us feel boredom which comes from a vague dissatisfaction with life. All of us have moments of severe depression. Lady Macbeth was so depressed that she uttered in despair, "What, will these hands ne'er be clean? Here's the smell of blood still. What's done cannot be undone" and eventually she committed suicide. Often weariness comes from life's burdens. Some have the burden of responsibility to lead, to direct, to be a parent or teacher; some have the burden of being sick, widowed or divorced. There are burdens some carry in looking after others. And yet, no matter what kind of weariness we feel or what kind of burden we bear, Jesus says, "Come to me all you who labour and are overburdened and I will give you rest" (Mt 11:28).

Jesus has every right to call us to him for comfort and consolation, for renewal and rebirth, because he is well aware of the unique relationship that exists between him and God, since he is Son to God the Father. This knowledge provides the basis for the most sublime claim of Jesus: "Everything has been entrusted to me by my Father" (Mt 11:27). So come to Jesus; he is our Master who came to console his fallen servants; he is humble though we be proud; he is our judge who is gentle, though we be arrogant. Come to Jesus; as our God, he is the potter who speaks in lowered voice, though we the clay may discourse in tones of a king. Come to Jesus; he is our Creator and how can the Creator not love his own work? How can the sculptor not care for what he has made? If he thought of his dignity, who of us will survive through the trials of life? Come to Jesus; he will not fail to treat even our incurable sickness with fitting remedies. He knows that if he did not console us, we will die. If he does nothing but threaten us, we all would perish. So come to him; he will compassionately bend down very low to raise us up.

15TH SUNDAY OF THE YEAR

THE MIRACLE OF GROWTH

Readings: Is 55:10-11; Rom 8:18-23; Mt 13:1-9

Theme: God's Word spoken through signs and wonders since the dawn of creation, culminating in the unique Word made flesh in Christ, is still alive and active in the world and those who hear and keep it will bear much fruit.

Our world seems to be trapped in a cycle of hopelessness, a hopelessness that is more virulent than the AIDS virus, threatening to destroy our capacity to imagine and wonder. For example, very few people ever spend time imagining what it would be like when the world lives at peace. On the contrary, so many of us spend a long time imagining what nuclear war might do to the world. We seem to have lost our capacity to delight in 'possibility', probably because we don't really believe in the power of God's Word. "Be fruitful, multiply; be masters", said God to our first parents and later he added through the prophet, "The word that goes from my mouth does not return empty" (Is 55:11). Jesus himself being the Word of God sowed his words as seeds of life on earth, enabling the fallen man to return to God together with all creation; and he too promised that his words falling on rich soil "will bring forth sixty- and hundred-folds" (Mt 13:8). This means that the word of God's blessings spoken at the dawn of creation and later personified in the person of his son, Jesus, is still alive and active in the world, so that creation can still retain the hope of being freed, like us, from its slavery to decadence.

If the word of God, which is the sign of his presence, is still alive, when do we hear it? The delightful truth is that God, like the sower in the parable, has scattered the signs of his presence generously throughout his creation. Have you ever worked in a fertile field of earth and planted a garden and saw it come into bloom? Then, you have heard God calling you to prepare for your resurrection. Have you ever listened to the birds carolling in the early morning and at dust? Then, you have heard him calling you to trust in his divine providence. Have you ever sat before a woodfire with old friends? Then you have met the Lord who wants to be your best friend. Have you ever walked the paths of quietness along the forest floor? Then you have met the Lord of peace. Have you ever dwelt in the valley of remembrance and on the hills of home? Then, you have met God who is love. Have you ever seen the miracle of Spring, the fruits of Summer and the beauty of Autumn, followed by the repose of Winter? Then, surely you have met the Lord of life.

Thus, we can hear God's life-giving word in any of our life's experiences. But human life is a complex book with pleasant and unpleasant aspects. Sometimes, God's word can be heard more clearly than the "churchy" word by people who are sensitive to "creation groaning in a great act of giving birth" (Rom 8:22). That is, God can speak to us very powerfully through pains and problems, our imperfections and weaknesses and through the agonising ambiguities of human life, especially in death, the darkest of all. However, it is not enough just to listen to his word with our minds nor to treasure it in our hearts. For God's words to become seeds of life, we must put them into practice. A businessman once said to Mark Twain: "I want to make a pilgrimage to the Holy Land before my death; I want to climb to the top of Mount Sinai and read the Ten Commandments aloud". "You could do something even better" replied Twain, "You could stay in your Boston home and keep them".

Those who not only hear but keep God's word will see how immense is the power of his word to reproduce and bear fruit in their lives and through them in the lives of others. Just think for a moment of the tremendous good done by the parents of Mother Teresa. Certainly, much of the good has been accomplished by their child, but it would never have happened had not those parents raised their daughter in a faith-filled family. Our effort in putting God's word into practice may be small. That does not matter; after all, a seed is indeed small. But we must realise that there is no proportion between what we contribute to God's kingdom and what he accomplishes through us. A single act of kindness, for example, will be multiplied in God's hands; The harvest of a lifetime of dedicated service to some noble cause will be increased a hundredfold by him. This is the way it ought to be because, even in the midst of hopelessness, the blessing of God given to man that his word will never return to him without watering the earth still stands. All around us we see the Miracle of Growth.

LIGHT A CANDLE

Readings: Wis 12:13, 16-19; Rom 8:26-27; Mt 13:24-30

Theme: Although there will be evil in the world as long as human nature remains tainted by sin, we are not to be indifferent to it but with patience and prayer keep resisting it the hope that one day the Lord will wipe it out altogether.

God is still in his Heaven, but all is not right with the world. Several years ago a man got so disgusted with the large-scale evils in the world that he put up a popular car sticker which read: "Stop the world; I want to get off". Yes; evil enters like a needle but spreads like an oak. Only evil, I think, has enough oil for every wheel. But we shouldn't be surprised at the presence of evil in the world. As long as our human nature is what it is, tainted by sin, do not search for a perfect society or a perfect family or perfect anything. There is small choice in rotten apples. Do not look for a perfect Church either; that would be hunting after an illusion and would only land us in an unhealthy spiritual elitism. The Church is not only a training ground for saints and apostles; it is also a haven for sinners, for the disturbed and the inadequate. This will remain so because evil has become a necessary part of the universe. A perfect humanity never existed and will never exist; good and bad, like "wheat and weed" (cf Mt 13:25) will always coexist. If so, what should we do in the face of evil?

First, we must be patient. In his parable of the sower, when the servants ask their master whether they should go and weed out the tares, the Lord says, "No, because when you weed out the tares, you might pull up the wheat with it" (Mt 13:29). This is a call to be patient with evil. The Chinese proverb says, "One moment of patience may ward off great disaster, one moment of impatience may ruin a whole life". If I am not mistaken, there is an inscription scratched on the Tower of London which reads: "It is not adversity that kills but the impatience with which we bear adversity". Secondly, we must pray that the evil forces of darkness may not overpower humanity. If we find it difficult to pray, let us call the Holy Spirit to help. "The Spirit comes to help us in our weakness" (Rom 8:26). Thirdly, let us hope that a day will soon come when the Lord of the harvest would wipe out all evil from the face of the earth. Our hope is founded on the belief that, "there is no God other than him who cares for everything and he has only to will, and his power is there" (Wis 12:13,18).

But our patience with evil or our hope in the Lord should not make us remain passive or indifferent to evil. Apparently, some people want to have peace of mind by not having any opinion about good or bad. That is tragic. Our attitude towards evil cannot be indifference. "The worst sin towards our fellow creatures is not to hate them", said Bernard Shaw, "but to be indifferent to them". If we passively accept evil or remain indifferent to it, we are as much involved in it as those who help to perpetrate it. However, the worst thing one could do in the face of evil is to run away from it. *Rascals In Paradise* is a book written by James Michener. In its introduction, the author tells how in the late 1930s, a learned Australian saw World War II coming. He got out a world atlas and looked for the safest place to be when the war came. He decided on a little-known island in the South Pacific. One week before Hitler invaded Poland, the Australian moved to his safe haven. The island was Guadalcanal. As fate would have it, it was destined to become the site of one of the bloodiest battles of World War II.

Therefore, instead of running away from evil or remaining indifferent to it, the Lord is calling us to do our bit to remove evil wherever we can and if we can't, at least protest against it. Instead of cursing the darkness, he is calling us to light a candle. A little boy, not familiar with an echo, thought he had heard in the woods the voice of another boy not far off. He shouted: "Hello, there!" and the voice shouted back, "Hello, there!" He cried again: "Who are you?" and the voice replied, "Who are you?". He cried once more: "You are a mean boy," and the cry came back: "You are a mean boy". Then this little boy went home and told his mother that there was a bad boy in the woods. His mother understood how it was and said to him, "Well, speak kindly to him and see if he does not speak kindly to you". The boy went to the woods again and shouted, "You are a good boy". Of course, the echoing reply came, "You are a good boy". "I love you", he said loudly. "I love you", replied the faithful echo. The story of the echo is the story of good and bad in life.

TREASURE HUNTERS

Readings: 1 Kgs 3:5,7-12; Rom 8:28-30; Mt 13:44-52

Theme: Since true happiness is found not in any earthly treasure but in Christ, a Christian is called, not by choice but by the baptismal obligation, to become a lifelong adventurer searching after the riches hidden in Christ.

Happiness is within the reach of everyone, however dull, mean or wise they may be. Life is meaningless if it is not happy; where happiness fails, life is only a mad lamentable experiment. So, all people search for happiness, though the search itself often becomes the chief source of unhappiness. As St Augustine said, "Indeed man wishes to be happy, even when he so lives as to make happiness impossible". But just think for a moment the tremendous joy the two men of the parable in the Gospel must have felt, when one discovered a hidden treasure and the other a priceless pearl (Mt 13:44-46)! One discovered the treasure by chance, while the other discovered the pearl by deliberate search. But the joy both experienced was overwhelming; it was so overpowering that it seized their feelings, thoughts, penetrating their inmost beings; to secure and to possess this joy, they were ready to make any sacrifice and give up everything that now seemed valueless, compared to the joy and happiness the treasure and pearl brought to them.

Yet, the happiness which a treasure or a pearl can offer can never be that true and lasting joy for which every human heart yearns. Sometimes, human as we are, we allow ourselves to be haunted not by reality but by images of that reality, not by the substance of joy but by its shadow and to be obsessed by a fairy tale, spending our lives searching for a magic door that opens only to a lost kingdom of joy. True joy is the treasure of a human soul which lies in the fulfilment of the spirit. Such a joy can be found only in God's kingdom, which is present in Jesus Christ. Therefore we must seek Christ in order to find our true treasure. The field of our search can well be the Bible, for Christ is the pearl of great price found in the Bible. If we can discover Christ, we have found the Way, the Truth and the Life; if we have found him, then we have access to the hidden treasures of God's wisdom, given to Solomon, a wisdom which is "a discerning judgement to distinguish between good and evil" (1 Kgs 3:9). The joy we find in Jesus is not to be confused with pleasure which may dry at the very moment it charms us most; nor should it be confused with the religious levity that has no deep roots. The joy of Christ is so unique that there is nothing in our afflictions that can disturb it and to any one who has discovered it, no sacrifice would be too heroic to possess it.

Those who claim to have discovered Christ and experienced the joy of his Kingdom, God bless them. But may God save them if they think that they have unearthed God's Kingdom once for all, as if it is an investment that can be banked safely and then cashed in times of need! To discover Christ has to be a lifelong treasure hunt, an ongoing adventure, for the treasures hidden in Christ are unfathomable. "Life itself is either a daring adventure or nothing," said Helen Keller. Without adventure, our civilisation would have decayed long ago. This is true also of our spiritual journey, because our discipleship of Christ is meant to be an adventure. If we have enough faith to see the mystery in Christ and the excitement that is there, we will be adventurous disciples and our life will not be dull or tedious; if we have enough confidence in the power of God's word to generate joy, we will be adventurous and not sad or long-faced Christians; if we have enough courage to take risks for Christ, we will not be so reluctant at times to make sacrifices while searching for him.

To search for Christ and discover the riches hidden in him is not a choice for us Christians; it is an obligation by virtue of our baptism in Christ. We have been chosen by God, not only to be coheirs to the riches in Christ but also to share them with others. We are children of God with a special call and a mission; we are "the ones God chose specially long ago, and intended to become true images of his Son" (Rom 8:28); we are "those he called and justified and with whom he shared his glory" (Rom 8:29). Are we conscious of this call? On one occasion, St Francis of Assisi was going through the fields. A peasant ran to him and asked him if he was the Brother Francis. When the man of God humbly replied that he was the man he was asking about, the peasant said: "Try to be as good as you are said to be by all men, for many put their trust in you; therefore, I request you, never to be other than you are expected to be". Yes; as chosen people of God, Christians are expected to search and find their joy in Christ and share it with others.

18TH SUNDAY OF THE YEAR

"I'M ONLY A SPARK, MAKE ME A FIRE"

Readings: Is 55:1-3; Rom 8:35, 37-39; Mt 14:13-21

Theme: The Eucharist reveals God's enduring love for the human race, it nourishes our spirits as the Bread of Life, it stands as a sign of Christ's compassion for all the needy today and it calls all Christians to works of charity even with whatever little they may have.

The Curé of Ars once saw in his church a farmer silently kneeling before the tabernacle. This man used to spend most of his time in the church. Once the Curé asked him, "What are you saying to the Lord all the time?" "Actually nothing", he replied, and pointing to the tabernacle, said: "I look at Him, and he looks at me". One wonders how many of us have such deep faith in the presence of the Lord in the Eucharist! Do we realise the immense love of God revealed through the presence of his Son in the Eucharist? If so, we too would be able to say with St Paul, "Who will separate us from the love of Christ?" (Rom 8:35). He is there as our bread of life and living water, calling, "All you who are thirsty come to the water; come to me that you may have life" (Is 55:1). On the day when the Lord multiplied some loaves and fed five thousand (Mt 14:19-20), the crowd were so determined to meet him that they were not discouraged by the physical effort involved in following him through the desert. Their desire to meet Jesus, whom they believed could make a difference in their lives, prevailed over the physical difficulties they encountered. How determined are we to meet the Lord in the Eucharist?

Jesus is in the Eucharist as our bread of life, feeding us with his own body, yes; but he hopes that we in our turn will go out to feed the hungry. He is there as our water of life satisfying our eternal thirst with his own blood, yes; but he hopes that we in our turn will go out and quench the thirst of others. He is uniting us with God and with one another feeding us with the same bread, yes; but he hopes that we in turn will go out and show our unity with the rest of the human race by caring for the poor, the needy, the weak and helpless. When he multiplied loaves and fed so many, the miracle was not meant just to reveal his power. The miracle was also to feed the hungry because "his heart was moved to pity" (Mt 14:14). Therefore, as the multiplication of the loaves was a sign of the forthcoming institution of the Eucharist, so the Eucharist stands today as the sign of Christ's compassion for all the needy in the world. Unless our breaking of bread at the table leads us to breaking of ourselves for the benefit of others, the Eucharist cannot be for us a bond of love with God.

Speaking on charity to the poor, Pope Paul VI once urged all men of good will to examine their consciences to see whether they are really compassionate for the poor in the world. He touched upon various ways by which one can care for the poor. "Conscience, a new conscience for our times is calling each of us to self-examination. Am I really doing all I can to help the poor and hungry? Am I prepared to pay more taxes in order that the government can do more for development? Am I prepared to pay more in the shops for goods imported from abroad so that the people who produce those goods are paid a decent wage? Am I prepared to leave my country to help the younger nations?... It is still true to say that charity begins at home. But home, today, is all the world".

Perhaps some of us easily excuse ourselves from works of charity saying, "I am limited in my resources; let those who have plenty give". But in today's Gospel Jesus encourages us to look beyond what is possible and share even the little we may have. The five loaves and two fishes were the only food available in the desert and, according to St John's Gospel, that belonged to a boy in the crowd. Jesus used that small quantity from a small boy and fed five thousand people. This means that one concerned person, like one grain of wheat, is important. However little may be our talents and gifts, if we offer them to Jesus, he can perform miracles with them. Let us pray in the words of Amado Nervo, a Mexican poet: "I'm only a spark, make me a fire; I'm only a string, make me a lyre; I'm only an ant-hill, make me a mountain; I'm only a drop, make me a fountain; I'm only a feather, make me a wing".

19TH SUNDAY OF THE YEAR

"LORD, I'M DROWNING!"

Readings: 1 Kgs 19:9, 11-13; Rom 9:1-5; Mt 14:22-33

Theme: It is in times of adversity that we must cling ever more, not to ourselves, not even to the Church but to Christ, the Lord of the Church, with the unshakeable faith in his still powerful presence with us.

With respect to all sea-loving people, one tends to agree with the observation of Carl Sandburg: "The sea speaks a language polite people never repeat. It is a colossal scavenger slang and has no respect". Who can count the number of human lives that the oceans have destroyed and swallowed! But for the timely help of Jesus St Peter himself would have drowned. The raging waves of the sea are often compared to the storms of human life. But what do we do when being ravaged by the turbulent waves of adversity? Do we have that faith of St Peter to stretch out our hands to cling to Jesus? (Mt 14:31). What do we do when we are lashed by stormy marriage, straying children, an impossibly demanding vocation, and a walking into the future with some dread disease? What do we do when we are gripped by an overwhelming history, a history of drugs or drink or the iron shackles of worldly desires that claim us again and again? It may be that our love of the world has gone beyond a limit and therefore we have lost the power to walk upon the waters and the world is about to engulf us, for it always devours its lovers. But even then, when we feel our foot slipping beneath us, are we able to cry out to him, "Lord, I'm drowning"?

When human frailty made him falter, St Peter turned once more to the Lord, who immediately stretched forth his hand to help him. It is when we are in trouble that we must seek out Christ more. To trust a doctor to cure you when you believe you are getting better is very easy. But to trust your physician when you feel as if the sentence of death were in your body – that is faith. It is unfortunate that some of us run away from God, like Elijah, when he is most needed. Elijah the prophet unable to face violent opposition gave himself up to despair and hid in a cave; but God called him out to meet him (1 Kgs 19:9). It is a reminder that we cannot afford to take our eyes off Jesus at any time. In the early days of sailing, a boy went to sea to learn to be a sailor. One day when the sea was stormy, he was told to climb to the top of the mast. The first half of the climb was easy. The boy kept his eyes fixed on the sky. But half way to the top, he made a mistake. He looked down at the stormy waters. He grew dizzy and was in danger of falling. An old sailor called him out: "Look back to the sky, boy! Look back to the sky". The boy did and finished the climb safely.

To cling to Christ is not exactly clinging to his Church. If the sea is our life, the boat is the symbol of the Church especially with St Peter, the first Pope in it. For the Church itself is a frail craft manned by all too human mariners. Therefore the boat alone won't save us from going under. We do not put our faith in any ultimate sense in the Church. Of itself it cannot provide final security. Don't we know how the Church itself is at present being rocked by innumerable problems and unanswerable questions? Are we not aware that the Church itself is going through rough and troubled waters in many parts of the world? Yes. Jesus alone can carry us and sustain us. Not ourselves, not even the boat – the Church – but the Lord of the Church alone. It is true that it is in the boat we come to know Christ and recognise him; however it is not in the boat but in Christ we must believe; it is not to the Church but to Christ we must cling.

To cling to Christ, especially in times of turmoil, we need strong faith in his mighty power and in his presence even today in our midst. Faith is more an encounter with Christ than it is a belief about him. It is more an experience of his divine presence itself than an acceptance of dogmatic pronouncement about him. Sometimes people ask about the need of faith. Faith is like a purse. A purse will not make you rich; yet without some place for your money, how would you acquire wealth? Likewise, faith of itself could not contribute a penny to salvation but it is the purse which holds the precious Christ. Of course, such a faith in Christ will not remove all our difficulties, but it will give us the strength to cope with them. It won't eliminate all the darkness that sometimes surrounds us; but it will let enough light filter through to allow us to recognise Christ's presence in that darkness.

ASSUMPTION – AUGUST 15

"DRAW US, MARY!"

Readings: Rev 11:19, 12:1-6,10; 1 Cor 15:20-26; Lk 1:39-56

Theme: The Assumption of Mary is not only a demonstration of God's deep love for her, but his fitting response to her faithfulness to his will and it reminds us of our own future glory which will be ours if we too strive, aided by grace, to live a life of faith and obedience to God's will.

Shah Jahan, a Mogul emperor in India, loved Princess Arjemand, his favourite wife, so deeply that in her memory he built the Taj Mahal which means 'The Pearl of the Palace' and has been described as a 'love song in marble'. A great Persian architect who was engaged by the emperor to build it as 'the one perfect thing in the world' took seventeen years to construct this enchanting edifice and completed it in 1645. It is an enduring monument to love that still inspires tourists from the over the world. Like Shah Jahan, God too, but in a more powerful and enduring manner, loved Mary the mother of Jesus so deeply that he could not bear her death and demonstrated his undying love for her by raising her from the dead and taking her into heaven, body and soul. Referring to this extraordinary glorification of Mary, Scripture describes her as a woman "adorned with the sun, standing on the moon, and with twelve stars on her head for a crown" (Rev 12:1). Mary herself had an intuition into what God would do to her at her death which she expressed in her Magnificat: "My soul proclaims the greatness of the Lord and my spirit exults in God my Saviour... from this day forward all generations will call me blessed, for the Almighty has done great things for me" (Lk 1:46-49).

It was fitting that Mary should share in this manner her Son's complete triumph over sin and death, because it is not possible to tell the story of Jesus without acknowledging her presence. If we tell of his birth, for instance, we can hardly forget about Mary. If we speak of the cross, she stands beside it. Nor can we talk about the story of our own salvation without her. We think of her at Calvary and call her, 'the Mother of Sorrows'. We remember her words at Cana and ask her to intercede for us. Her presence in the midst of the disciples at

Pentecost brings to mind her title, 'the Mother of the Church'; and especially at Christmas time, we think of her oldest title, 'the Mother of God'. Therefore it is fitting that the Lord whom she received when he entered the village of this world should on this day receive her into the holy city. Yes; on earth, there was a no more worthy place for Mary to receive the Son of God than the temple of her virginal womb; nor in heaven is there a more worthy place for her than the royal throne to which her Son has today exalted her.

Mary assumed into heaven reminds us of our own destiny. Christ our Lord is like a good salesman or an artist. Good sales people carry with them the best sample of their products. Artists showing their works hang their finest paintings. So, too, Jesus attracts all of us to the destiny that awaits us by setting before us Mary as the most sublime expression of his redemptive work, because of which all of us believers will rise one day body and soul glorified like Mary. "Just as in Adam all die, so in Christ all will come to life again" (1 Cor 15:22). This means that we are like a tulip plant. In spring this flower has a beautiful body but by the time fall comes, the tulip's body loses all its beauty and at winter only a bare bulb remains. So, too, at the fall of our lives, our body would lose all its beauty and strength because sin would have taken its toll in our human nature. However, when the time of our resurrection comes, we will emerge with a beautiful new body.

Mary not only reminds us of our destiny but, while on earth, she also showed us how to reach our destiny. The way she showed was one of faith and saying always 'yes' to God's will, accepting his plan that he has marked for each of us. By always doing the will of the Father, she allowed him to overshadow her ordinariness and do great things in her. If we follow the same way, God will do mighty works in and through us also. Once a priest said in his homily: "Death is not something that happens to us, but something we do". What he meant was that we are faced daily with opportunities to let go and let God be God. Again and again we are offered the challenge to surrender in trust to God's way, to God's timings, to God's mystery and love. When God asks for the ultimate surrender of the core of our being, then our practised 'yes' can flow more easily from our trained lips and hearts.

But we need to take note of this: Mary was able to live a life of faith and absolute surrender because she was also aided by the grace of God. It is so with us and the grace is available to us through Mary. We need therefore constantly to pray to her, which must not be difficult. By her Assumption she has not disappeared from us. She has only assumed a new and more powerful way of being present with us. As the Dutch catechism says, "Mary is more in the world now than any other woman. Cleopatra is remembered. Mary is addressed. She is the most closely present of all women". Because Mary is with us, we honour her with shrines. Hence we pray to her: "Draw us Mary after you and we shall run towards the fragrance of your perfumes".

20TH SUNDAY OF THE YEAR

"WOMAN, YOU HAVE GREAT FAITH!"

Readings: Is 56:1, 6-7; Rom 11:13-15, 29-32; Mt 15:21-28

Theme: Heaven is open to all those whose faith in Christ is personal, persistent, cheerful and practised daily, especially in the service of others.

One day, it seems, a certain curious person in heaven asked St Peter "How many Hindus are in heaven?" St Peter replied: "No Hindus". Then he asked: "How many Muslims?" "Not even one", replied St Peter. The man was surprised. He said: "Oh, then, there are only Christians in heaven?" "No, there are no Christians in heaven either", replied St Peter. "How many Catholics?" "No Catholics either". Then St Peter said, "Heaven is not meant for any particular group of people. Here, there is no distinction between Hindus, Muslims or Christians for all are welcome in heaven". What else could St Peter have said? Did not God tell his chosen people, referring to the Temple in Jerusalem which was a symbol of heaven for them, "My house shall be called a house of prayer for all peoples" (Is 56:7). Therefore Jesus, in response to the "great faith" of a Canaanite woman, healed her daughter (Mt 15:28) and she became one of his disciples. Following his Master, St Paul became "an apostle to the Gentiles and took pride in that service", even "arousing envy" in his own people (Rom 11:13-14). In fact, we ourselves feel envious of the faith which the gentile Canaanite woman put in Christ and are compelled to ask ourselves whether our Christian faith is as good as hers.

Hers was a personal faith: when the woman cried out, all the disciples went to Christ and said, "Send her away" (Mt 15:23). To that Jesus said, "I was sent only to the lost sheep of Israel" (v.24). But when the woman herself, still crying out, came to him and said: "That is true, sir, and yet the dogs eat what falls from their master's table" (v.27); then he granted her request, saying, "Let it be as you desire" (v.28). Yes; When the disciples entreated him, the Lord put them off, but when the woman herself personally cried out begging for this favour, he granted it. Is our faith personal?

Hers was a persistent faith: it seems that nothing could discourage her. She first met a wall of silence, but kept asking; then she met a rebuff, but she threw herself at the feet of Jesus and she was rewarded. How persevering is our faith? Shortly after World War II, workmen were clearing out the debris from a bombed-out house in Cologne, Germany. On one of the cellar walls of the house they found a moving inscription. It had apparently been written there by a fugitive Jew who had used the basement to hide from Nazis. The inscription read: "I believe in the sun even when it is not shining. I believe in love even when I feel it not. I believe in God even when he is silent".

Hers was a cheerful faith. Cheerfulness, as you know, is not the same as merriment; while we make merry, our teeth are smiling, but while we are cheerful, our hearts are smiling. The Canaanite woman had an irrepressible cheerfulness. We are not aware of all other difficulties she might have had in the course of her life. But her ready response to Jesus' apparent insult when he called her a 'dog' (Mt 15:26), suggests that she won't let the rough side of life get her down. She turned the insult round with a flash of humour and got what she prayed for. Are we always looking on the gloomy side of life? If our faith is strong, we would always be cheerful within. The moment I am unbelieving, I am unhappy. God loves a cheerful giver; a ready wit not only enables me to bear the burdens of life but it also gladdens the heart of God.

What can we do to strengthen our faith? Faith is like a muscle; the more we exercise our muscle, the stronger it grows. Our faith too responds to exercise. Therefore we can study the Gospels and talk about them. We can be more attentive during the Eucharist. We can take up the habit of daily prayer. But there is one way to exercise our faith that seems to be especially powerful and that is the way of service. Albert Schweitzer, the great missionary doctor, says something along the following lines in his book, *Reverence for Life*, "Do you really want to believe in Jesus? Then you must do something for him. In this age of doubt there is no other way. If for his sake you give someone something – which Jesus promised to bless as though it were done to him – then you will see that you really did it for him. Jesus will reveal himself to you as one who is alive".

21ST SUNDAY OF THE YEAR

"WHO DO PEOPLE SAY THAT THE SON OF MAN IS?"

READINGS: Is 22:15, 19-23; Rom 11:33-36; Mt 16:13-20

Theme: To believe in Christ as the Son of God is a gift of faith which is given to those who deserve it, enabling them to make a personal and decisive commitment to Christ and to become partners in building his Kingdom.

When Jesus asked his disciples who do men said he was, the disciples mistakenly thought that he wanted to know his popularity rating. As all of us know, being popular is important; otherwise people might not like us. But Jesus was not interested in knowing how popular or famous he was, because he was only too aware what fame brings to a person: to have it is a purgatory and to want it is a hell. Besides, even those who have not achieved anything can project themselves as famous and provoke an uproar through the services of professional image-makers on TV, radio and the press. Therefore, Jesus was not so much concerned about his fame among the public: what he really wanted to know was whether each of his disciples fully understood who he was. Fortunately, St Peter on behalf of the rest gave him a very convincing and courageous answer (Mt 16:16): "You are the Son of the living God".

Jesus addresses the same question to each of us. "Who do you say that I am?" This is a personal question that demands a personal response. It is a critical question that calls us to commit ourselves one way or other. It is a decisive question whose answer will determine our entire destiny. Whether we are in Newmarket or in New York or in New Delhi, we can't dodge the issue or avoid this question. If Jesus is truly God's son, then, either we confess that and act accordingly or else we deny it and do our own thing.

How does one come to the knowledge that Jesus is truly the Son of God? By studies and research? Not necessarily. Great thinkers and scientists, in spite of their marvellous contribution to the quality of our lives, have often been failures in ordinary human situations. The fact that men or women can plan a mission to the moon does not mean that all of them can change a baby's nappy. G. K. Chesterton was one of the great thinkers and writers of this century; but it is said, on one occasion, he wrote a brief note to his wife saying, "I am in Liverpool. Where should I be?" Thus, in practical matters he was disorganised. In spite of it, if Chesterton, an Anglican, came to embrace the Catholic Church, what was or who was behind him? It was the gift of conversion which he received from God at the end of his long years of study. This is why, Jesus said to St Peter, "You are a happier man, because it was not flesh and blood that revealed this to you, but my Father in heaven" (Mt 16:17). Thus, at the end of the day, it is this gift of faith from God that draws one completely to Jesus Christ: the faith which sees the invisible, hears the inaudible and touches the intangible.

But to receive this gift of faith one must deserve it. We will deserve it if we do our human part to experience the living Christ in daily life. If Jesus is the Son of the living God, he must be living amidst us. We must therefore use all the means available to experience him. One sure way of experiencing Christ is the daily meditation on the Bible. An African Chief wanted to know the secret of Britain's greatness. Queen Victoria, holding a Bible in her hand, said "Tell the Chief that this Book is the secret of our greatness". Let us read from it something daily. Another sure way of experiencing Christ is the sharing of our faith experiences in small groups with our fellow Christians. Those who regularly share like this will find that sharing turns the prose of life into poetry. Still another sure means of meeting the living Christ is prayer. As Tagore said, "God respects me when I work, but he loves me when I sing his praises". Hence, in the rush and noise of life, we must find intervals to kneel before God in prayer, with all our frailty and humility. Remember that the bird that soars on highest wings has to build her lowly nest close to the ground.

Unless we personally experience and come to believe in Christ as the Son of the living God, not only we can't commit ourselves to him, but also we can't be partners in building God's Kingdom. Building God's Kingdom was not only entrusted to St Peter when he gave the keys of the Kingdom, as God gave the key of the household of David to Eliakim (Is 22:21); nor did Jesus entrust to popes alone the responsibility to build his Kingdom. The laity also have a role to play in this building. The Pope cannot run the Church on his own or on three Hail Marys. He needs you and me. What can the Pope alone do? He is of course the first Christian and the first model of holiness. But the Pope is as mortal as we are. The corpse of the Pope takes no more room than his sacristan's. Therefore the laity's role is essential in building God's Kingdom. Let us thank God in the words of St Paul: "How deep are the riches and the wisdom of God" (Rom 11:33), to have entrusted to us the work of building up his Kingdom. But let us first make ourselves fit instruments of his Kingdom, by daily deepening our faith in Jesus Christ as the Son of the living God.

22ND SUNDAY OF THE YEAR

CROSS IS NOT LOSS

Readings: Jer 20:7-9; Rom 12:1-2; Mt 16:21-27

Theme: As long as we live in an imperfect world we have to carry our daily crosses, but to a Christian who often stands in the shadow of the cross of Calvary his/her own cross soon becomes bearable as well as enriching to his/her life.

We are all living in an age of illusions. Some select the illusion that appeals to them most and embrace it with passion in order to be happy. One such illusion is the notion that all pain and discomfort should be instantly eliminated, that only what is pleasant and easy is worth seeking, that every fancy must be satisfied without any cost, that human development should be achieved without self-denial and that we can and should live in a perfect world. This notion is not just an illusion, but a lie. It is a lie, repeated by many, as if repetition could transform a lie into truth; for the truth is that we do not live in such a world, nor is it God's plan that we should. It is a lie with which our world may be obsessed as with a fairy tale, but St Paul warns us that we "must not model ourselves on the behaviour of the world around us" (Rom 12:2). Above all, this illusion is a lie which is an abomination to the Lord, for he said, "Take up your daily cross and follow me" (Mt 16:24). The Lord asks us not to run away from crosses but to see them as opportunities to grow, by taking up our daily cross, by sacrificing ourselves for others and by making room in our lives for God's ways.

The cross is a necessary part of life. After seeing many dying I have come to the conclusion that there is no pain in dying, the pain is in living. We do not know whether to call it a dying life or a living death. Most of our comforts grow up between our crosses. If human life has its own necessary crosses, Christian life adds its own crosses. Leave out the cross, and you have killed the religion of Jesus. It is a cross to follow Christ, for in following him, we are expected to suffer rather than sin; it is a cross to reject the world's sleazy way of life and live by God's way. It is a cross to be faithful to the duties of one's vocation, such as marriage, parenting, priesthood or religious life. Jeremiah went through torments to be faithful to his call to preach the word of God to the people. He found the cross of preaching so heavy that he once shouted at God saying: "O God, you have seduced me; you have made me a daily laughing stock, the butt of every joke" (Jer 20:7). Hence, the cross is not an arm of Christian truth; it is the heart of it.

But the arresting Gospel promise is that the cross enriches life. As Christ says, "Anyone who wants to save his life will lose it; but anyone who loses his life for my sake will find it" (Mt 16:25). Is not love sometimes enriched through shared suffering? Is it not a fact that sometimes success and comfort do endanger love more easily than pain and sacrifice? Yes, they do. We sometimes have to lose certain things in order to find better things. If, for example, we worry too much about our health, we lose it by becoming hypochondriacs. People gain years of added life by giving up smoking or drinking alcohol. Great hearts are made by great troubles. Those who are never tried usually possess a poor, tottering faith. What shakes us first, strengthens us afterwards. One has to bear his own cross in order to feel for those whose life is a cross; none of us can come to the highest maturity without enduring the summer heat of trials. It is not a loss even to die, says Jesus, for it is only a lasting gain. Therefore fear not the cross; along with other aspects it brings healing. It is when God seems most cruel to us that he is most kind. God's wagon rumbles most heavily when it is bringing us the richest freight of his graces.

However, a cross is still a cross; it will be always a burden to human nature. And yet, there is a way for a Christian still to love his cross instead of trying to get rid of it. Once a man wanted to get rid of his shadow, jumped into the water, ran in several directions but all in vain. His shadow continued to follow him. Then a wise man advised him: "It is very easy to get rid of your shadow. All you need to do is to go and stand in the shadow of a tree". Likewise, if we want to get rid of our dislike for the cross, let us go as often as we can and stand in the shadow of the cross on which Christ was crucified for love of us. From the moment Christ died on the cross, the power of evil received its mortal wound; evil dies hard, yes; but from that moment it was doomed. Therefore a Christian soul will feel resurrected under the cross of Calvary, the very spot where misery reigned; it will find tremendous consolation on the very spot where agony reached its climax. In the shadow of the cross of Christ, a Christian will learn that every trial has a triumph in it; within every suffering, there is hope and hence his cross is not a loss.

23RD SUNDAY OF THE YEAR

LOVE IS CONCERN

Readings: Ez 33:7-9; Rom 13:8-10; Mt 18:15-20

Theme: The key to fulfilment in life is love, which is concern for the welfare of others shown in many ways – including in praying for each other and correcting one another in fraternal charity.

We must all have something to love. Captives have been known to love even spiders on their prison wall. Love is a must for the survival of our society. People will not care what you know until they know that you care. Love is the key to life in fullness. A wanderer once found a key in the valley close to a huge mountain. It was a magic key that could open the doors of every treasure house in the world. With the help of this key he collected as much gold and jewels as he wished at various places. On his way back he heard a voice from the foot of the mountain: "Before you go out, forget not the most important thing!" Suddenly the door of the opening was closed; but it was closed for ever, because he had forgotten to take along with him the most important thing: the key. We all long for the key to fulfilment, but we often forget that the key is love. St Paul tells us: "Avoid getting into debt, except the debt of mutual love" (Rom 13:8). He is perfectly right, because the Kingdom of God is ruled by love and a Christian community that does not glow with love is unsatisfactory. But what is love? Love is concern.

Love as concern shows itself in the interest we take for the welfare of others and in the help we offer to be better Christians. Such a loving concern will sometimes also take the form of warning someone who is doing evil. Suppose a mother caught her five-year old daughter with a stolen chocolate bar just after they returned from the supermarket. One natural reaction of the mother would be to do nothing or to pretend the problem is not there. An alternative reaction may be to shun and reject the daughter out of hand, even to hate her. But both reactions would not be Christian. A loving Christian reaction would be that the mother warns the child about the evils of stealing and have the child return the candy to the supermarket manager and apologise. "If you do not warn the wicked to renounce his ways, then he shall die for his sin, but I will hold you responsible for his death" (Ez 33:8), said the Lord to the prophet. This is a harsh warning to those who neglect their Christian responsibility to help another to move away from evil ways.

Love as concern is not having nice feelings for one another. It will mean at times the obligation of correcting one who has fallen into a serious misconduct. Suppose a ticket seller for an airport limousine service said to a father, "Sir, your son looks young for his age. Take a half-fare ticket. If the limousine driver questions you, just say, the boy is under twelve. Save yourself a few pounds". If the father had the sense of Christian responsibility, not only to do what is right but also help others to do what is right, he would have the courage to speak the truth and say, "I appreciate your concern for us, but I want my son to be truthful even when it works to his disadvantage". "If your brother does something wrong, have it out with him alone between your two selves" (Mt 18:15), said the Lord to his disciples. One of the most difficult things in life is to confront a person directly who has done something wrong. A few wrongdoers will immediately admit their guilt. However, a confrontation to reconsider what he or she has done, will sufficiently influence the person towards better conduct.

Love as concern has another beauty. It will draw people together to pray. If personal prayer is the breath of faith, community prayer is the lungs of the Church. God is love and where love is, there God is.

Therefore, when we gather together for prayer, we are sure to have God in our midst. Our Lord, after ending the matter of correcting one another, makes immediately a promise: "Whenever two of you agree about anything you pray for, it will be done for you" (Mt 18:19). This means that if the offender and the offended join together in a community prayer and pray for peace, there is a great possibility of ending the quarrel. Ordinarily, significant changes take place when two or three people get together to achieve some goal. If it is so in ordinary human affairs, magnificent things can happen in the spiritual order, when people join together to pray for something. Thus, love as concern, not only draws us together to pray but also brings peace and harmony among us. When prayers are strongest, mercies are nearest.

24TH SUNDAY OF THE YEAR

WON'T YOU FORGIVE?

Readings: Sir 27:30-28:7; Rom 14:7-9; Mt 18:21-35

Theme: The heart of Christianity is love but the power of love is in forgiving others, which is not easy but possible, if we consider how self-destructive is unforgiveness, how generous is God in forgiving our sins and if we learn to look at others' offences from God's viewpoint.

Two neighbours had a lifelong quarrel. One of them became gravely ill. His wife called the priest and explained to him, "Father, Pat has been fighting with Mike for years. Pat is going to die. Can't you patch up their quarrel?" After much persuasion the priest induced the dying Pat to call in Mike for a reconciliation. In a few minutes, Mike was at the bed side. He suggested, "Let's us make up, Pat. Let bygones be bygones". Pat agreed rather reluctantly. Mike prepared to leave. As he approached the door, Pat raised himself on one elbow in bed and shaking his other fist at Mike, he shouted, "Remember, Mike, this counts only in case I die". None of us finds forgiveness easy and cheap. When people treat us unjustly, everything inside us screams for revenge. A father whose son had been murdered, confessed his anger and his desire to throttle the perpetrator when he said "I can never forgive them". Many people regard it as their right to return evil for evil; if they cannot they feel they have lost their freedom. Hatred is settled anger and the desire to hold hatred against someone who has injured us lies deep in the human heart.

Yet forgiveness is the cornerstone of all the major religions in the world, because love and kindness are nothing if not a big dose of forgiveness. That is why Jesus asked his disciples to love even enemies. The true sign of Christianity is love, not standing up and singing twenty hymns by heart or giving a list of religious organisations we belong to, or summarising the last ten sermons we have heard (if they are summarisable at all!). The heart of Christianity is love, but the power of love is in forgiveness. The Lord asked us to forgive seventy times seven (Mt 18:22), that is, to be always ready to forgive. Forgiveness for a Christian cannot be an occasional act but a permanent attitude. Though forgiveness is a difficult thing to do, it warms the heart and cools the sting. To be forgiven is such a sweetness that honey is tasteless in comparison with it. But there is one thing sweeter still, and that is to forgive. As it is more blessed to give than to receive, so forgiving others is a more enriching experience than being forgiven. In other words, to be forgiven is the root and to forgive is the flower.

Unforgiveness is self-destructive, because it breaks the bridge over which we must all pass ourselves, for every one is in need of forgiveness. A mean and revengeful disposition shuts out God's forgiveness and the wrath of God is kindled against the hard and relentless. "He who exacts vengeance will experience the vengeance of the Lord who keeps strict account of sin" (Sir 28:1). Unforgiveness is self-destructive because if you refuse to let go your anger, that anger can get you imprisoned for a lifetime, making you feel sick and so uninterested in life that you won't see anything beautiful any more. Thus, it is impossible to hate someone without suffering yourself for that hatred. It is like trying to get even with someone by throwing cactus at that person with your bare hands; your opponent may get hurt, to be sure, but so do you. On the contrary, if you forgive a bad person, you implicitly assure them that they are still valuable as a human being, with an ability to overcome their errors. In other words the less blame we give to others, the less blame they give themselves.

There are Christian ways of exercising mercy and forgiveness. First, give yourself time so that anger can cool and you can view the circumstances in a more rational manner. One mother, whose son had been brutally killed said that she had written a letter of forgiveness to the man in prison, who had done this terrible deed, but she said, "I am not yet ready to meet him face to face". Secondly, view these hurts and offences from God's point of view. God uses hurts to improve our character. Offences and injuries suffered by us become in God's hands the best teachers for developing our character and spiritual effectiveness. See the offenders not as your enemies but as humans who are hurting just as you are. Thirdly, do what the official in the parable (Mt 18:32) failed to do: sit down in God's presence and recall how much and how often God has forgiven you, in spite of the magnitude of the wounds and hurts we have inflicted on others. He forgives all our sins in half the tick of the clock, so that we pass from death to life more swiftly than I can utter the words.

25TH SUNDAY OF THE YEAR

AMAZING GRACE

Readings: Is 55:6-9; Phil 1:20-24,27; Mt 20:1-16

Theme: Those who trust in God's generosity in dealing with men will commit themselves totally to his will and they will experience in return his abundant and amazing grace.

An arrow which falls short of the mark and a candle which smokes but yields no light is a waste. So, too, the life of a Christian whose commitment to the Lord is not total is a waste. The test of a true commitment is not how much we give to the Lord but how much we don't give him. St Paul was a totally committed apostle, so that he could assure his Christians beyond any doubt that, "Christ will be glorified in my body, whether by my life or by my death" (Phil 1:20). This kind of total commitment and abandonment to God's will is reflected in the labourers who came late to work in the vineyard. They made no agreement with the Master about their pay but were content to place themselves in his hands and trust him to do what was right (Mt 20:7). God has entrusted each of us with a mission and calls us to give ourselves unreservedly to it. Cardinal Newman once wrote: "God has committed some work to me which he has not committed to any other. I have my mission. I will trust him. He does nothing in vain. He may prolong my life; he may shorten it; he knows what is he about. O my God, I will put myself without reserve in thy hands".

Those who dedicate themselves totally to the Lord, will experience his surprising and surpassing generosity. For example, in a spirit of total dedication to the Lord, if we not only forgive those who offend us but forget their offences, we will see how "rich he is in forgiving our own sins" (Is 55:7). We will see how he takes the ruined sinners and builds them to be temples of his indwelling and how he takes even the castaways of the devil and uses them for himself. In our total dedication to the Lord, if we serve him not just fulfilling our duties but offering to do more, not just by doing what is expected of us but also by doing the unexpected, we will see how surpassing is his own generosity towards us. God has a way of giving by the cartload even to those who give away by shovelfuls. He does not count or measure. He makes too much wine at the Cana wedding, more than 100 gallons of it; he multiplies too much bread for the crowd, with 12 baskets of bread left over; he pays a day's wage even to those labourers who came to work at the eleventh hour (Mt 20:9). Yes; when God does things, he does them in a big way.

Stories abound about people who turned themselves completely to the Lord and experienced God's amazing grace. The man who wrote the hymn Amazing Grace had been a slave trader and had taken part in the most inhuman and cruel treatment of people. He called himself a wretch who deserved nothing but contempt and punishment but instead found himself pardoned and raised to a position of trust and responsibility. How could he otherwise describe it but as Amazing Grace? Many people seem to feel poor always because they never give themselves to the cause of God, whereas, people like John Calvin felt that his life was always rich because his one purpose in life was to serve the Lord. Therefore when the physician told him that he must cease from working so much or he would die because he had a complication of a painful disease, he replied, "Would you have my Master come and find me loitering?" No servant of God can get tired of serving the Lord. He may be tired in the service, but never tired of it.

And yet, it is amazing how reluctant some of us are to turn to the Lord in an act of total conversion. Perhaps we don't still trust that God will be generous in forgiving us. We forget that if it comes to a pitched battle between sin and grace, we shall not be so bad as God shall be good. It is also amazing how half-hearted many of us are in our service to the Lord. We don't seem to realise what C. S. Lewis had realised. He wrote: "The Lord cannot bless us until he has us. When we try to keep within us an area that is our own, we try to keep an area of death. Therefore in love, he claims all. There is no bargaining with him." Why is it that some of us serve the Lord sometimes and serve ourselves at other times. Perhaps it is because our minds operate on market forces: in a market, people are paid what they are worth, so we think that God too will act in the same way towards us. But the Lord insists that it is not so with him, saying, "My thoughts are not your thoughts, my ways are not your ways" (Is 55:8). God has his own form of justice and it is heavily weighted in favour of the poor who entrust all their cares to him and give their entire selves to him.

26TH SUNDAY OF THE YEAR

A HEALTHY MORAL LIFE

Readings: Ez 18:25-28; Phil 2:1-5; Mt 21:28-32

Theme: A vital principle of perfect health is a healthy moral life based on Christian morality which is founded on three pillars: assurance of grace, personal responsibility and self-forgetfulness.

Health is the first wealth, hence we must seek our bodily and mental health; but that is not enough. A vital principle of perfect health is a healthy moral life. Diseases are at times the price of immorality. Sickness always empties the purse but it also shows, at times, how a person has debased his moral currency. Periodical fits of morality are not enough. A good moral sense must regulate all our conduct. A breakdown in moral order leads to breakdown in civil order. As Bertrand Russell would say, "Without civic morality communities perish; without personal morality their survival has no value." The question, "What is moral and immoral?" may be still debated by many. But to a Christian the answer is clear: a healthy moral life must be based on Christ's teachings. After the dawn of Christianity, we believe that it is no more possible to invent a new morality than to place a new sun in the sky. It is our belief that if Christian morality expires, no human spark will be left and no glimpse of the divine will be seen. But Christian morality is founded on three pillars.

The first pillar is the assurance of grace. Christian moral life is lived under the gracious forgiving eye of God. "He who has chosen to renounce all his sins shall certainly live" (Ez 18:27) is God's assurance. The call of grace is so insistent and compelling that by its force many can and do change. Fr De Grandis, the well-known healing priest, writes: "I recall an incident involving a West Indian woman who had experienced back pain for quite some time. I prayed with this woman and finally, through the Spirit's guidance, decided that it was a case of unforgiveness. The woman admitted the need to forgive one of the members of her family and through confession, as I said the words of absolution, the pain went away. Just in the absolving of the sin of unforgiveness, the pain left immediately". Such happenings show that God's plan is a plan for life. Even when life seems to be hanging on by a mere thread, the Lord of Life holds our hope. But this utter grace of God available for us all the time has to be balanced by the need for a whole-hearted response on our part.

Therefore, the second pillar of Christian morality is the awesome gift of personal responsibility. Since a human being is free, to be a person is precisely to be responsible. To be responsible is to do one's duty. The sovereignty of God never excuses us from our duty. It is our Christian duty, for example, to check our initial reaction to the call of God, as did the first son in today's parable. He first said 'no' to his father's call, but "afterwards thought better of it and went" (Mt 21:29). Human as we are, we often develop our opinions in the dark room of prejudice. We often mistake our prejudices for our convictions. Hence it is a Christian responsibility to develop a reflective attitude to life. To think is an effort; but to rethink is a greater effort. In order to think God's thoughts, we often have to rethink our thoughts. Our sense of responsibility can meet with many obstacles. One is the temptation to substitute fine words for action, like the second son in the parable, who first said, "yes" to his father, but "did not go" (Mt 21:30). We must strive to translate our noble promises into noble performances. An acre of performances is worth a whole world of promises.

The third pillar of Christian moral life is self-forgetfulness. Self-forgetfulness is not adopting mock-humility. It is rather, "always considering the other person to be better than yourself, so that nobody thinks of their own interests first, but everybody thinks of other people's interest first" (Phil 2:3-4). Thinking of other people's interest first, may entail larger considerations. It may entail, for example, a concern for the general good of our society, because no one can be perfectly moral till all are moral and no one can be perfectly happy till all are happy. It may entail a genuine effort to work against racial injustice, to open one's ears to the cries of those whose human rights are violated and abused because of their skin colour and to eradicate prejudice and discrimination from society. It may also entail a concern for environment, because the earth we abuse and the living things we kill will in the end take their revenge on the human race, with the result that in exploiting them at present, we are only diminishing our future.

27TH SUNDAY OF THE YEAR

NO REPENTANCE IN THE GRAVE

Readings: Is 5:1-7; Phil 4:6-9; Mt 21:33-43

Theme: God calls us to make every effort and pray for conversion of our hearts, so that in loving response to God's own compassion towards us we can be compassionate to those who have hurt us and forgive them.

Divine love can admit no rival. The love of God is anchored in his character which is Love. God's hands may at times turn against his people, but never his heart. Like the master of the vineyard in today's parable. God gave the people of Israel his love and friendship and a beautiful vineyard to tend (Mt 21:33), but like the tenants of the parable, they rejected God's friendship and betrayed his love. It hurt God so deeply that he complained: "What more could I do for my people than I have done?" (Is 5:4) But God's love is long and enduring, hence he sent his own Son hoping that they would respect and honour him. Nonetheless, they abused him and killed him. But God's love was still unflagging. He chose to use the tragic death of his Son to give new life to his people. He chose to outdo the hatred of his people by a generous outpouring of his Holy Spirit on them. This means no matter how far we wander away from God, he gently seeks us out and brings us back to himself. This compassionate love of God towards us is to be an example of what we should do to one another.

We have many opportunities to show compassion to others. When we are hurt by someone, that can either cause bitterness and hatred or become an occasion for generous forgiving. We can be compassionate to an alcoholic in our family, to a spouse whose affection has become cold or to a teenager who rejects our family values. When we are let down by somebody whom we have helped, we feel like complaining, "After all that I did for them"! But such personal wounds can offer us a great chance to show God's own compassion to the ungrateful. Why is compassion so difficult? Why are our immediate responses so often selfish, tough and hostile? Perhaps the world weighs too heavily upon us, a world where violence is the rhetoric of the period, where the hands of liberty and democracy are dyed red with innocent blood and where those who bear the brand of Cain rule many countries. Perhaps we are afraid that compassion is dangerous, for it can change our lives, forcing us to see things through God's eyes, compelling us towards an interior conversion of our hearts.

But why should we fear the conversion of our heart? Is not the fruit of the Kingdom essentially conversion? Do not the Bible and the teachings of Christ again and again remind us that religion must be first in the heart, that it is the interior dimension of the Law which makes its observance worthwhile and that without the interior disposition our worship is mere formalism, a trap of hypocrisy? Yes. If the heart is the source of action, the 'purity of source' must be the motto of Christian life. Of course, the Christian religion is not merely or solely interior; Jesus did not condemn exterior practices, but only those without right interior disposition. St Paul gives a new twist to this need for interior conversion when he says, "Finally, brothers, fill your minds with everything that is noble, everything that is good and pure, everything that we love and honour and everything that can be thought virtuous or worthy of praise" (Phil 4:8). St Paul is right because, as it is physically impossible for a swine to deliver a lecture on astronomy, so it is just as much impossible for an unmended heart to enjoy the fruits of God's Kingdom.

God is patiently waiting for our conversion, from hearts of stone to hearts of flesh. The vineyard owner made three efforts to get the tenant farmers to change their ways. So too God fondly waits for us to turn to him. God is patient because he never cuts what he can untie. He knows that patience achieves more than force. Besides, God is wise and patience is the companion of wisdom. But a day will come when God's patience will run out. When the vineyard owner saw that more patience was futile, he passed judgement on the tenants, holding them accountable for their actions (Mt 21:41) It is the same with God. God, who has promised pardon if we convert, has not promised to preserve our lives till we convert. We must repent and return to God now. Now is the time to repent and there is no repentance in the grave. But let us not forget: we cannot be converted all by our own free will. We need God's help and so we must pray. "Present your needs to God in prayer and he will stand guard over your hearts and minds" (Phil 4:6) The touchstone of true conversion is prayer.

28TH SUNDAY OF THE YEAR

TOWARDS A BANQUET OF NATIONS

Readings: Is 25:6-10; Phil 4:12-14,19-20; Mt 22:1-10

Theme: God who has planned to transform our world into a fellowship of nations calls us to cooperate actively with his plan whatever may be our life-situation, trusting that he is with us and will be our strength.

In spite of all appearances to the contrary, God has a plan for this bankrupt world. He is not running an antique shop. He knows what he is doing to make of this world. His plan is to take us all to that Kingdom of God which will be a fellowship of all nations in peace, unity and joy with God. The Mount Sion seen by Isaiah in a vision is a symbol of this Kingdom to come. It symbolises God's lavish generosity with the prospect of total absence of hunger, mourning, death and shame, when "God himself will wipe away the tears of his people as the mother wipes away the tears of her child" (Is 25:8). When Jesus compared the Kingdom of God to a wedding banquet (Mt 22:2), he too revealed that God is at work in the world in order to take us all to the final Kingdom in which no one will feel left out, no one will go away hungry, and where there will be plenty of buzz, excitement and every one will get a lift. Who could not be excited by the arrival of such a Kingdom in which the lonely will be alone no longer and where all our deepest needs will be met?

But God's plan for our humanity requires that we work with God to realise it. Great plans need landing gears as well as wings. It is not enough that we know about God's plan, we must apply it; it is not enough that we are willing to become part of the Kingdom, we must do it. Hence God invites us to get caught up with his desire for our humanity and work with him to wipe away tears from cheeks and to take away people's shame. The venerable servant of God, Canon Cotolengo, when but a boy of five years, was measuring with a cord one room after another. His mother, rather confused, asked him what he was trying to do. "Dear mother", was the reply, "I want to see how many beds can be placed in this house: when I am grown up I should like to fill the whole house with sick people". A tear of emotion glistened in his mother's eyes. In 1832 he founded at Turin the 'Little Asylum of Divine Providence', and today it is world famous. It shelters 5000 men and embraces within its precincts a Church, a number of houses, terraces and courtyards.

Like Canon Cotolengo, there are some who respond to God's call with passion and reach out to others to realise God's vision for the human race. But there are many who like the invited guests in the parable (Mt 22:5) are complacent in their response to the Lord's invitation. He calls his people, for example, to come to the weekly Eucharistic banquet on Sundays, but many ignore it because they have more important things to do, like shopping or sleeping a little longer. He calls people to become more prayerful, but many can't find time; he calls people to be more helpful to others, but many can't look beyond their own needs; Such people call themselves Christians but do not follow the way of Christ. All Christians accept the call of the Lord to build his Kingdom, when they are baptised and confirmed. But accepting God's call is like graduating from college. Graduation is not the end of one's learning, but the launching pad for further learning. So too our baptism and confirmation must be the inauguration of our commitment which must become an ongoing process requiring constant updating.

The vision of God for the world as a fellowship of nations is to some extent unrealisable in our lifetime and will always remain a matter of hope. Most of the time, life for us, as for St Paul, is a matter of full stomach and empty stomach, poverty and plenty, joy and sadness. As we work towards the realisation of God's abundance, we have to learn to live with its absence. St Paul knew both hunger and plenty. But he had learned to cope with either one and he knew that neither of them could separate him from his goal because, as he asserts, "there is nothing I cannot master with the help of the one who gives me strength" (Phil 4:13). Like St Paul, we too must trust that the Lord is with us always and he will be our strength, whatever be our life situation: whether we are in poverty or in abundance, in the valley of darkness or in pastures fresh and green. We must have this trust, because there is no situation so chaotic that God cannot turn it around into something surprisingly good; in fact, it is when we have nothing left that we become aware that the Lord is enough.

29TH SUNDAY OF THE YEAR

DOUBLE CITIZENSHIP

Readings: Is 45:1, 4-6; 1 Thes 1:1-5; Mt 22:15-21

Theme: As citizens of heaven we have duties towards God, so as citizens of this world we have duties to our fellow human beings, which we must carry out in spite of difficulties, believing in God's transforming energies that are still afloat in the world.

Whatever makes people good Christians makes them good citizens. This is so because as Christians we are citizens of two worlds: the world we see of body and matter and the unseen world of the spirit. As such we have duties in both worlds, to God and society. Seeing the image of Caesar on a coin, Jesus said, "Give to Caesar what is Caesar's, and give to God what is God's" (Mt 22:21). It is hoped that our double citizenship and the obligations we have to each will never clash. If they ever do, the Christian must resolve the conflict as St Thomas More, the martyr did. King Henry VIII of England was validly married but appealed to Rome to annul the marriage. Since there was no honest basis for annulment, Rome refused. Henry took matters in his own hands and remarried. He then ordered his friends and officials to sign a document declaring that they agree he acted rightly. Many signed but More refused with the result that he was executed.

More had two obligations: one to God and one to his country. When they conflicted, More resolved it by remaining faithful to God.

God has the first claim over us before we give our allegiance to anything earthly. As the coin that bears the image of Caesar belongs to him and must be given back to him, so the human person created in the image of God belongs to God whole and entire. God who has made us the object of his love is the Creator God, "apart from whom all is nothing" (Is 45:6). God is the source of every good. For those who have everything as well as for those who have nothing, there is only one single good-God himself. God is all powerful so that he can lay prostrate the whole world whenever it may please him. He rules the life of each one of us so completely that nothing that happens to me is accidental or incidental and nothing that is attempted in opposition to God can ever be successful. After admiring the photograph of Mahatma Gandhi and an image of Jesus Christ, an admirer of Gandhi said, "Well, I bow down before Gandhi, but I kneel down only before Christ". Yes. Worship is due only to God and that is why we come every week to the Sunday Eucharist.

But our belonging to God is inseparable from our belonging to this world. Our faith in God has to be dynamic, leading us to actions for others, as St Paul saw in the lives of Thessalonians for which he admired them saying, "We thank God, for you have shown your faith in action and worked for love" (1 Thes 1:3). Hence we are called to be true citizens of this world. As citizens of a country, we have to obey and respect its civil regulations and contribute our share to the welfare of the state as a whole. As citizens we have also duties to our fellow human beings, duties such as what husbands and wives, parents and children owe to each other. We must add here also what the rich owe to the poor, the strong to the weak and the educated to the ignorant. It is a question of justice to the whole community. Justice is traditionally represented by the figure of the scales, signifying equality among all. Normal life would be impossible in a society without justice and without it there would be no true fellowship in a Christian community.

As citizens of this world, when we go about our duties to our fellow human beings, there will be times when we feel frustrated. When we encounter the vast anonymous systems of governments, we are liable to lose confidence in the power of democracy. When we face a society with a growing division between those who have and those who have not, when we see large cities struggling with the problem of overcrowding and so much loneliness and isolation, when we see so much violence and serial killings, when we see communities crumbling with families breaking away, we feel powerless and even lose the sense of responsibility for the common good. Still we cannot give up hope because the Lord who empowered the king Cyrus saying, "I called you by your name… though you do not know me" (Is 45:4) and asked him to preside over the restoration of his people in exile – that same Lord is still with us. His transforming energies are still afloat in the world, empowering us Christians to be bearers of his "grace and peace" (1 Thes 1:2) for the restoration of this world.

30TH SUNDAY OF THE YEAR

MADE FOR LOVE

Readings: Ex 22:20-26; 1 Thes 1:5-10; Mt 22:34-40

Theme: Our love of God is proved by our love of our neighbour, by bringing the salvation we have received from God to our fellow human beings, especially to the most helpless in society, in a way that satisfies their present needs.

Love is the definition of Christian living. One day there came parading in a street in London a lovely little girl with a great purple heart flaming on her blouse. Across the purple heart were inscribed the words, 'Made For Love'. Looking at her, any one would believe it. But God tells us in today's readings that not just pretty little girls are made for love, but all of us, created in the image of God who is Love, are made for love, to love God "with all our heart, all our mind and all our soul" (Mt 22:37). It is but right that all our heart should be in love with God when the heart of God is so much in love with us. However, love for God is not love for him at all unless it expresses itself in our love for others. So the Lord adds, "Love your neighbour as yourself" (Mt 22:39). Therefore a close connection exists between what we do to our neighbour whom we see and what we do to God whom we cannot see. On these two commandments hang the law and the prophets. The Ten Commandments are not replaced by the law of love; they are fulfilled in it.

The commandment to love our neighbour as proof of our love for God was already implicit in the Old Testament. "You must not be harsh with the widow or with the orphan; if you are, they should surely cry out to me and surely I shall hear their cry", said the Lord to Israel (Ex 22:22-23) But Jesus made the link between the two commandments more explicit, adding that both are of equal importance. Therefore, the law of love which is the basis of Christian morality requires of us that we love God by helping those who are in need: the poor, the orphan, the marginalised who are liable to exploitation, injustice, oppression and prejudice. Saints like Fr Damien of Molokai saw the inseparable link between love for God and serving others so clearly that they spent themselves in loving service to the most abandoned in society. Fr Damien who came from Belgium to the Hawaiian island Molokai in 1873 served the lepers there until he too contracted leprosy and died in 1889.

Serving the helpless and the disadvantaged for the love of God may mean bringing solace and comfort to the lonely, to the disheartened and to those who are sad in our own immediate surroundings. But our service to the needy has a wider implication in our times; it means working for social justice. There can be no genuine love without justice. It is true that Churches speak out against injustices. But that is not enough. We individual Christians must get involved in removing injustices which the poor and powerless suffer in our societies. "Love implies," wrote Pope Paul VI "an absolute demand for justice which recognises the rights and dignity of one's neighbours. Unless the Christian message of love and justice shows its effectiveness through action in the cause of justice in the world, it cannot gain credibility with the people of our times". Our works to bring justice to the people cannot be merely humanitarian. Humanism celebrates the importance of a human being, yes, but it is like whistling in the dark, for it has no relationship with love for God. On the contrary, a Christian's love for the needy emanates from his or her love for God just as perfume rises from the flower.

As God has been compassionate to us by giving us salvation, so we must be compassionate to others and bring God's salvation to them. But the salvation we bring to others must take place here and now. It must involve healing the wounded and reconciling the injured and the outcasts of our society. It is unfortunate that many of us live for ourselves and are dead to others. We shed tears mostly for ourselves at the least hurts, and our tears of self-pity so blind our eyes that we cannot see the tears in the eyes of those who are truly hurting. Therefore, if we want to serve the needy, we need conversion. We need to turn away from idols such as selfishness and materialism. Selfishness is the greatest curse of the human race. Materialism is the organised emptiness of the spirit, for it is the logical result of thinking that above and beyond this world there is nothing else. Are we really converted to Christ's teaching on love? When the Thessalonians were converted, they became true servants of God and "great examples to all believers" (1 Thes 1:7). What about our conversion?

31ST SUNDAY OF THE YEAR

THE SERVANT LEADER

Readings: Mal 1:14-2:2,8-10; 1 Thes 2:7-9,13; Mt 23:1-12

Theme: All Christians are called to show leadership through service, as Jesus and great Christian leaders in the past have done, but are warned against pharisaism in leadership.

The highest honour in the Church is not leadership but service. Leaders in the Church are those who have responsibility of priesthood or apostolic activity. Jesus demands from his Church, leadership through service. "The greatest among you must be the servant of all" (Mt 23:11). Church leaders are servants of God doing only God's work, not their own because, unless the Lord builds the house, they labour in vain. As in other institutions, leaders in the Church also have authority, but authority in the Church is service. Only authority that serves is seldom resisted and only a servant-leader can inspire God's people. Our chief want in the Church today is leaders who know the way, show the way and go the way. A servant-leader shares in the authority of Christ who alone is his Master and there is nothing holier or better or safer for a Christian leader than to content himself with the authority of Christ. If leadership in the Church is not through service, then our Churches where souls are to be lifted will soon become empty, while beauty parlours where faces are lifted will be packed.

Service was one of the most striking signs of Christ's own life. He wants the same from leaders in his Church. A leader who does not serve, but toys with his leadership and counts it to be like a trade, was never called to lead. Service has been the keynote of great Christian leaders in history. Martin Luther King said: "If any of you are around when I have to meet my day and if you get somebody to deliver the eulogy, tell him not to talk too long. Tell them not to mention that I have a Nobel Peace Prize; that is not important. Tell them not to mention that I have three or four hundred other rewards; that is not important. I'd like somebody to mention that day that,' Martin Luther King tried to give his life serving others'. St Paul reminds the Thessalonians that "like a mother feeding and looking after her own children", (1 Thes 2:7) he felt so devoted and protective towards them, and that he never accepted any payment for his apostolic work so as not to be a burden to any one. Such whole-hearted services can be hard, so hard that pressed into service could mean pressed out of shape. However, a candle loses nothing by lighting another candle.

Christian leaders are always to be warned against 'pharisaic' behaviour. They are to be warned against preaching something and not practising it themselves. Hence Jesus said of the Pharisees, "Listen to them but do not imitate their actions" (Mt 23:3). A leader who is not a practising Christian is like a crooked stick which will have only a crooked shadow. More depends on the leader's walk than talk. Christian leaders are warned also against "causing many to stumble by their teaching" (Mal 2:8). When a leader teaches the Good News, he has to bear in mind that a leader's teaching will affect eternity and no one can ever tell where his influence will stop. Jesus also warns against seeking self-praise instead of God's glory. Praise seems to be the best diet for many; human nature so deeply craves praise that even the deafest can hear praise. But Jesus condemned the thirst for self-praise in Pharisees. In fact, Pharisaism of any kind in a Christian leader is hypocrisy. Hypocrisy is the homage which vice pays to virtue. But remember that a hypocrite is living more lives than one and hence destined to die more deaths than one.

The call to leadership through service is not addressed only to the clergy and to those who hold apostolic office in the Church. All Christians are called to show leadership through service. People who do not seek to serve God and their fellow human beings, cannot be Christians. The very motto of a Christian should be 'I serve'. We each have a responsibility to show the authenticity of the Christian message through our love and service. Poor responsibility! It is so burdensome to some self-serving Christians! In the days of astrology, it was customary to unload one's responsibility upon a star. But today, it is easily shifted to the shoulders of God or Fate or Fortune or Luck and often to one's neighbours. However, there are still among us Christians who inspire us by their dedicated service. When Marion Hill Preminger, an internationally known actress and hostess, was asked why she suddenly gave up all to work with Albert Schweitzer in the steaming equatorial jungles, she replied: 'Dr Schweitzer says that there are two classes of people – the helpers and non-helpers. I want to be a helper'. Let us each find out where we can render a service and render it with all our heart.

ALL SAINTS – NOVEMBER 1

THEY JUST SHINE

Readings: Rev 7:2-4, 9-14; 1 Jn 3:1-3; Mt 5:1-12

Theme: The feast of All Saints, when we honour the canonised and un-canonised saints, as well as those who are still on earth living saintly lives, reminds us that all of us are called to become saints, aided by the grace of God.

It is a great deal better to live a saintly life than to talk about it. Lighthouses do not ring bells and fire cannon to call attention to their shining – they just shine. However, today being the Feast of All Saints, we can't help talking about saints and their holiness. Some saints in heaven are canonised by the Church. She does so in admiration of their heroism in being holy and to serve us as ideals in practising some particular Christian virtues. For instance, St Perpetua was a young mother in prison as punishment for her faith in Christ and she gave birth only a few days before her martyrdom. The soldier who witnessed her crying out in the pains of labour said to her, "What will you do while you are suffering in the arena?" And she answered, "Then another One will suffer in me." The One she referred to was Christ within her. Such was her heroic faith in Christ that she was canonised as saint in order to inspire our own faith in Christ.

Many of the canonised saints whom we venerate today are remembered for their extraordinary mystic speculations, miracle-working or uncommon austerities. Among them can be counted also those saints who went into the deserts to live alone in prayer and penance. They went there not because they hated human society, nor because they believed that living in a hole would make one holier but because they sought after loving union with God with all their heart undisturbed by human society around them.

We venerate today also the uncanonised saints who are now in heaven. They were ordinary men and women like us, who lived and loved, worked and played, struggled, succeeded and failed in their daily works; but they are in heaven now because they made every effort while on earth to be holy by following the teachings of Christ to which they had made baptismal commitment. Among them, let us not forget, could be members of our own families. In this respect, today, we venerate also those who are still living on earth but making every effort to live out their Christian faith to become holy.

If these are the saints whom we venerate today, because they were holy or becoming holy, one is tempted to ask. "What is the essence of holiness common to all of them?" The essence is their life according to the Beatitudes as taught by Christ. They did not and do not receive their holiness suddenly in a meeting, but in actively responding to the call of the Beatitudes: "To be poor in spirit, to be pure of heart, to be humble, to thirst after justice, to show mercy, to make peace, to accept sufferings and sorrows for the name of Christ" (Mt 5:1-12). In other words, their holiness consists in thinking as God thinks, willing as God wills; it has love for its essence, humility for its clothing, the good of others as its employment, and honour of God as its end. It goes without saying that such a life of holiness has to pass through trials and tribulations, even daily martyrdom. But those who persevered in living out the Beatitudes are in heaven now as saints. They are those, as the Book of Revelation graphically puts it, "who survived the great period of trials and washed their robes and made them white in the blood of the Lamb" (Rev 7:1). Yes. They were true "children of God" on earth and now have "come to his light" and "like him" (1 Jn 3:1-3).

We all have a calling to become saints. We can't be content with placing a statue of a saint in the middle of a bird-bath and let the whole business of saints go at that. While celebrating the Feast of All Saints, we remind ourselves about our own call to become saints. The destiny of a Christian is not happiness, nor health, but holiness. God is not an eternal blessing-machine for us; he did not come to save us out of pity; he came to save us because he created us to be holy. Perhaps some of us recoil from the thought of becoming saints, because we are so conscious of our sinfulness; but many of the insights of the saints stemmed from their experience as sinners. We say that God creates us out of nothing and we call it a wonder. But there is something still more wonderful that God does: he makes saints out of sinners. Each of us can achieve holiness by practising the virtues described by the Beatitudes and achieve it where we are in our own lives, not pining for the life situation of a particular saint. The childlike confidence of St Thérèse of Lisieux, for example, does not need a Carmelite convent for its practice.

But being a saint is not pleasure but pain, to be honest. To live out our baptismal commitment day after day could be a living martyrdom; to practise in every detail the Beatitudes could be a daily cross. But there is no detour to holiness; Jesus came to resurrection through the cross, not around it. However, in our consistent endeavour to become saints, we have the saints in heaven to help us. They are right by God's side interceding for us. The help they give us and their nearness to us should be very reassuring. In all our difficulties we are never alone: a host of God's saints are ever with us. The ritual of incensing at Mass is carried out on the altar where rest the relics of the saints. This incensing is a symbol of our trust that the saints will take our prayers before the throne of God.

Therefore as we resolutely set ourselves on the way towards saintliness, let us keep praying for this saintliness and keep our hearts always open to receive God's grace. For just as the sun pours down its rays from above abundantly upon all, only those who have eyes can see them, and then only if their eyes are open, so too, when God sends down from above his abundant help to all, only those whose hearts are open can benefit from his grace and power to practise virtue.

32ND SUNDAY OF THE YEAR

WE BUILD OUR DESTINY

Readings: Wis 6:12-16; 1 Thes 4:13-14; Mt 25:1-13

Theme: Our Christian destiny is eternal life with the Lord, but the way to our destiny is the wisdom from above, which calls us to use foresight, to be reflective and prayerful while we deal with those facts of daily life as they relate to everlasting life.

It is the fate of the coconut husk to float and for the stone to sink. Every thing on earth has its destiny. So, each one of us has our destiny. Our destiny is that we all will rise again after death. Jesus rose from the dead, thus promising us also life after death. "We believe that Jesus died and rose again. And it will be the same for those who have died in Jesus. God will bring them with him" (1 Thes 4:14). At our resurrection a mysterious transformation will make our mortal bodies immortal and incomparable, so that we will be capable of enjoying heavenly bliss. Someone said to a Christian, "What is your age?" and he replied, "I am on the right side of 70". They found out he was 75 and they said," You told us you are on the right side of 70?" "So I am," he answered. "That is the right side, for it is the side nearest to heaven, my blessed home". Heaven is our blessed home, for it is being with Christ. We can never think of heaven without Christ. Heaven without Christ is day without the sun, feasting without food and seeing without light.

But to reach our heavenly home, we must live our lives now wisely. Wisdom is not knowledge; it is similar to knowledge but superior to it, for knowledge can produce vile results as well as honourable ones. A genius could, for example, turn his talent to the stealing of cars and the forging of cheques. Wisdom, however, will never lead us into evil. While common sense will suit itself to the ways of the world, wisdom will try to conform to the ways of heaven. Since wisdom is not the growth of human genius, it must be sought from above and it is available: "By those who love her, she is readily seen and found by those who look for her" (Wis 6:12). Hence, if you lack knowledge, you go to school; if you lack wisdom, get on your knees. By observing people's behaviour, you can tell whether they are wise. For example, wise people will seek here on earth only those things which they can have for ever and grasp only those riches which death cannot tear from their hands. Wisdom is an affair of values and hence wise people will deal with facts of life as they relate to life eternal. This means wise people use foresight.

Foresight looks ahead and if we do not look ahead, we will find ourselves behind. A Christian who uses foresight avoids evil by anticipating it, and makes his roof before it rains. We need this foresight in order always to be ready to meet the Lord when he comes. While his final call in death seems crucial, we must also be ready for his daily calls. A Christian who uses foresight will be reflective. Being reflective is being prayerful, without allowing oneself to be burnt out by the frantic pursuit of earthly things. A reflective Christian always keeps asking, 'Do I have the extra oil of good works to nourish my lamp of faith?' The five wise virgins in today's parable thought and reflected before they left and took their extra flask of oil. That few minutes of reflection paid off, for the bridegroom arrived late and they had enough oil (Mt 25:4). Foresight never does desperate things at the last moment. Nine-tenths of wisdom is being wise in time. Hence a foresighted Christian, while waiting for the Lord keeps always awake, so that he or she may sleep in his peace and awake in his glory.

One who is awake to meet the Lord whenever he chooses to come is a prayerful Christian. Yes; but such a prayer will not be detached from active life. A truly prayerful Christian will be like a man ploughing a field who keeps his eyes fixed on the furrow but sometimes looks up to set his eyes on a distant mark to keep the furrow straight, while at other times he pauses to greet a neighbour. A prayerful Christian will move from prayer to work and from work to prayer. It is not enough just to have faith without good works, as it is not enough to have only a lamp without oil in it. To be doing good works till the Lord comes is the same as living our Christian life well, doing what God wants us to do. At the Last Supper Jesus said to his Father, "I have glorified you on earth. I have finished the work you gave me to do" (Jn 17:4). We Christians must be able to say the same of ourselves, just for the sound of it, and so live that one day we can say it with joy. Always remember that as we are so we do and as we do, so it is done to us, because we are the builders of our own destiny.

33RD SUNDAY OF THE YEAR

USE IT OR LOSE IT

Readings: Prov 31:10-13, 19-20, 30-31; 1 Thes 5:1-6; Mt 25:14-30

Theme: We are called to develop our talents, big or small, and to put them to maximum use for God and humanity, without comparing our gifts with others enviously and to be ever ready to give an account of them to God who is the owner of all gifts.

We all have so many fine qualities of mind, soul and body, given freely to us by God: they are like the talents handed by the master to his servants in the parable (Mt 25:15) before he left on his trip. God expects us to develop our talents and gifts. He expects us to put them to maximum use for God and for humanity, like the woman in Proverbs. She is praised, because with her gifts she brought her husband happiness day by day, made clothes for her children and reached out her hand to the poor (Prov 31:10-31). Are we all putting our gifts to their maximum use? Not really. Experts say that an average person uses only 10% of the mind's potential. Would we ever tolerate our car operating at only 10% of its capacity? God expects us to put to maximum use even our small ordinary talents. Many ordinary people are slow to realise that their contribution can really affect the quality of life around them. Even a single personal gift is important. None of us should be like the one-talented man of the parable who could not see that his talent was of value to God and humanity. What matters is not how big or how many are our gifts, but how faithful and wholehearted are we in the use of them.

We should not compare our gifts with others enviously, thus limiting ourselves to meagre tasks. Of course, our gifts vary, but why? A Jew went to his rabbi and demanded to know why God distributes his gifts unequally. The rabbi whispered: "Not so loud. God might hear you and say, 'If you are anxious to know, come up here and find out'". That is wise advice. Each of us receive God's gifts in different measures and he has a purpose. Each is born into a different family, in circumstances that are different. The influences on individuals vary and the opportunities they receive differ, even though God gives sufficient to all. Yet, how easily we envy those who live more glamorous lives than we do, those who acquire notoriety and very easily gain great wealth! The media, especially TV, glorifies the actor, singer or footballer, even though their personal lives may be very empty and poor. The majority live unglamorous, undistinguished lives, but are they any less happy for it?

Just think of the variety of gifts God has given to every human being. All have the gift of love, but a love which by its very nature demands sharing of life with others. We Christians have the gift of light (1 Thes 5:5), but and as children of the light we are called to enlightened conduct doing good and not evil, reflecting God's own goodness in the world. We have the gift of God's word which is so precious and powerful that we have no right to hide it. We must preach it and teach it. All people have the gift of a basic sense of justice which calls us to combat injustice in the world and to plant seeds of justice in the soil of human hearts. Many have artistic gifts. Artists, sculptors and musicians are called to use their gifts to beautify creation and to glorify God. All have the gift of time and are called to use it not only on themselves but in the service of their community. All have gifts of money, more or less. People who make maximum use of their money will not hold it back and hoard it for themselves. Rather, keeping their own personal needs simple, they will be generous in sharing it with others.

But we are all bondservants entrusted with talents that are not ours. The Lord who is the source of all gifts will return to ask for an account. The man who goes on a journey abroad and returns after a long time is an image of Christ who has journeyed to the Father and is expected to return again (Mt 25:14). The test required to ensure a favourable judgement is whether we made full use of our gifts for the growth of his Kingdom on earth. Are we secure with our accounts? Once the Wall Street Journal reported that more business people fail because of poor record keeping than for any other reason. They think that things are going along fine, but when an unexpected bill comes they go bankrupt. Likewise, some people think that they are in good spiritual shape, when in fact they may have nothing in their heavenly bank account. Our present life is a fertile field ready to be filled. The seeds of truth, justice, love which we plant today will surely germinate soon and flourish to the glory of the Kingdom of God and when the Master returns unexpectedly, like a thief in the night, we will be lauded for breaking new ground. On the contrary, if we neglect our opportunities to plant and nurture the Christian seeds, we will loose not only the opportunities but also our talents.

34TH SUNDAY OF THE YEAR – CHRIST THE KING

OUR SHEPHERD KING

Readings: Ez 34:11-12, 15-17; 1 Cor 15:20-26,28; Mt 25:31-46

Theme: Since Christ's Kingship rests in love and service and will judge us on the last day by the criteria of our own love and service, we the citizens of his Kingdom are expected to prove our loyalty to him by serving others, especially the most helpless in society.

We have no kings in the world today. A crown today is no more than a hat that lets in the rain. Kings have lost their privileges as the stars which complete their time lose their splendour. How then are we still proclaiming Christ as our King? It is because the Kingship of Christ belongs to the majesty and power of a different world. Christ is not the king of clubs ruling with ruthless force and might but a King of love and service. He is not the king of diamonds desirous of wealth and glory and glitter but a shepherd King. Of him, God foretold: "As a shepherd I am going to look after my flock myself" (Ez 34:11-12). Jesus said of himself: "I am the Good Shepherd who lays down his life for his sheep" (Jn 10:11). Yes. The shepherd King's love for us was so great that he came among us to experience for himself what it was to be truly human, including our death. He looks after us even today with tender care leading us to the waters of baptism, anointing us with the oil of confirmation and feeding us with the bread of eternal life. He continues to take upon himself the pain and the anguish of humanity, dying anew each day and each day rising ever more triumphantly as King.

If, then, we would look for Christ's reign in this world, we need only hear his word: "I was hungry and you gave me food; I was thirsty, a stranger, ill and you gave me water, clothing, comfort and friendship" (Mt 25:35-36). It is there in the sufferings of every human family that we will see him reigning. We shall not discover him clothed in the garments of unbridled power which demands our attention and respect; We shall discover him in the pains of human flesh, in the rhythms of conflict and peace, in our struggles for justice and in our desire to be witnesses to his life and his love for us. We will see him as our King reigning over the frailties of humankind, "until he has put all his enemies under his feet and the last of the enemies to be destroyed is death" (1 Cor 15:25-26). Therefore all those who want to enter Christ's Kingdom and all those who want to promote his Kingdom on earth are called to imitate his own active service to the needy. To us, such a service may seem hard at first but this is the only way we can succeed in seeing the full reign of Christ.

Our shepherd King calls us to help him to build up towards its fullness his Kingdom of justice, love and peace. He calls us to alleviate the distress of the suffering millions of the world, brought into our living rooms by way of satellite television. Can we say that our heart reaches out not just to the needy at our doorsteps but to those also who are in greater need in the Third World? In a parish bulletin one time there was the following indictment:" I was hungry and you formed a humanitarian club and discussed my hunger. I was imprisoned and you crept off quietly to your chapel and prayed for my release. I was naked and in your mind you debated the morality of my appearance. I was sick and you knelt and thanked God for your health. I was homeless and you preached to me of the spiritual shelter of the love of God. I was lonely and you left me alone to go and pray for me. You seem so holy, so close to God. But I'm still very hungry and lonely and cold". So if we want to honour Christ our King, we must do something to the least of his brothers and sisters.

If Christ is the royal ruler of the universe and if doing something for the needy is the same as doing it for Christ, then even the least among us is royalty and even the little we do to them is royal service. It is by the criteria of active love that on the day of judgement, every one, Christian and non-Christian, will be judged. All our rituals, our ceremonies, our protestations and our piety will be considered useless and trivial if they were not based on true love for one another demonstrated in daily life. Some of the famous textbooks of many children are those maths books which have the answers in the back. They can keep working until they get the right answers. That is the kind of help our shepherd King is giving us. He provides us the right answers to the questions on our final exam, so we can get it right. Christ has no wish to spring a trap on us. He tells us exactly what he wants. Note that sin is not mentioned in this particular depiction of the Final Judgement, nor worship, nor the word 'love'. Only deeds are mentioned, deeds of love. In the evening of life, we will be examined on those deeds.

YEAR B

FIRST SUNDAY OF ADVENT

WAITING FOR THE LORD

Readings: Is 63:16-17,19; 64:2-7; I Cor 1:3-9; Mk 13:33-37

Theme: If only we have those eyes that see and those ears that hear Christmas can be a pointer to the constant coming of Christ in our lives.

Once I went to see my parents after a long absence. My mother lovingly scolded me saying, "Do you know how long we have been waiting for you?" I said, "I understand, mother, but do you know how long I was waiting to be born?". All of us wait to be born, to be nourished and to be loved. Travellers wait for buses and planes; students wait for the results of their exams. Waiting is part of life. Life is not like instant coffee, there is always more to life than we can fully grasp at any one time. If it is so with the life of a human being, what of the life of God, whose glory shines not in one sun but in numberless suns and whose greatness flashes not in one world but in ten hundred thousands of infinite globes? When we see the stars and hear the mighty thunder, his power throughout the universe displayed, can we ever imagine that we can at any one time grasp the Immensity of God? Can we ever fathom the depth of God's love, "who so loved us that he gave his only begotten Son" (Jn 3:16)? We say "God is love", but can we at any given moment possess all his love, which is the same in days of calm or in days of storm and which is deeper than our sorrows, deeper than our death and deeper than our sins? Even to write of God's love would drain the ocean dry. Hence all that we can do is to wait for God to let himself be known and be possessed as he pleases.

Advent calls us to wait for the Lord. The First Sunday of Advent liturgy underlines this waiting. Isaiah expresses our intense desire as we wait for the Lord: "Oh, that you would rend the heavens and come down" (Is 64:1). St Paul assures the Corinthians that they "lack no spiritual gifts as they wait for the revelation of our Lord Jesus" (1 Cor 1:7). Jesus in the Gospel asks us "to be awake and vigilant" (Mk 13: 33). Surely we must wait for the Lord who will come at the moment of our death. Death is no respecter of men, but lays his icy hands even on kings, as their sceptre and crown crumble down. You cannot take a newspaper without finding that death has a corner in it. Hence advent calls us always to be ready to meet the Lord at our death. But as Christians, we should be ready not just for the final coming of Christ but for his constant coming every day of our lives.

If we are alert, we can find the Lord popping up in the ordinary activities and possibilities of life. If I am watchful, he may be tapping me on my shoulder when I meet my neighbour. If only we have "those eyes that see, those ears that hear" (Is 64:4), we can meet him in his supreme visit which he makes in a thousand ways. If we look wide-eyed at all creation, which reflects God, when the flowers of the earth are springing, the birds of the sky singing and a world of blended beauties smiling, we can sense through the sacred feelings they arouse in us the rustling of his garments and the coming of his feet. Even when the wintry winds are howling and the heavens darkly scowling, we can feel the awesome majesty of his giant steps. Yes, to meet the Lord, we must be prepared for life, not just for death.

Advent is the countdown time for the celebration of Christmas. But Christmas is only a pointer to the constant coming of Christ in our lives. When we do Christmas shopping and buy gifts suited to each friend, Jesus comes in the respect we show to the uniqueness of each individual; when we send Christmas cards with the messages of love, Jesus comes through the warmth and affection we express to others; when we decorate our homes and lanes for Christmas, Jesus comes through our desire to bring beauty into other people's lives; when we prepare our Christmas family meal, Jesus comes through our readiness to make peace with all and form one human family. The Lord who is willing to come as light is willing to flood a room but we have to wait for him with our minds and hearts open and vigilant. God's love is pressing round us on all sides like air.

2ND SUNDAY OF ADVENT

HE IS HERE

Readings: Is 40:1-5, 9-11; 2 Pet 3: 8-14; Mk 1:1-8

Theme: During Advent we need to get into a symbolic desert experience in order to experience God who is already here.

Life is like heady wine. Everyone reads the label on the bottle, but hardly any one tastes the wine. That is why there is such a craving in each of us for better life. The search for a better life goes on, but often, in the wrong places. Here is an Indian story: A neighbour found Nasuruddin on hands and knees. "What are you searching for, Mullah?" "My key." Both men got on their knees to search. After a while the neighbour says, "Where did you lose it?" "At home." "Good Lord! Then why are you searching here?" "Because it's brighter here!" We must search for the better life where we lost it and we lost it where God is; and where God is, there is "new heaven and new earth", (2 Pet 3:13).

When shall we enter into this new heaven and new earth? Is it only after death? No. God is present here and now. When the Lord was made flesh, God in the person of Jesus literally entered into this material world, into a human body experiencing all the sufferings and death we experience, but dramatically rising again from the dead. Therefore, this God is with us in the midst of our sins and sufferings, giving us an experience of his presence and raising us to better life, as he raised his Son Jesus. Hence Isaiah proclaims, "Here is your God; he comes with power; he comes like a shepherd feeding his flock" (Is 40:10-11). It happened in the ocean: a little fish said to an older fish, "Excuse me, you are older than I, so can you tell me where to find the thing they call the ocean?" "The ocean is the 'thing' you are in now", replied the older one. "Oh, this? But this is water. What I am seeking is the ocean", said the disappointed fish, as he swam away to search elsewhere. How many of us are looking elsewhere for a better life, when we are actually living in the ocean of God's presence, which is bliss itself!

In order to experience God who is with us, we need to go for a "Desert Experience" like St John the Baptist, who was a voice in the desert heralding the Lord's coming (Mk 1:3). I do not mean that we must go into a physical desert, but to any place where we can be alone with God and pray: a corner in the back-yard, a nook in the basement or a park bench. But to pray one requires certain aids. First is simplicity. In city life, we are easily enchanted by what is pretty, plastic and superficial. In order to pray, we have to get rid of this excessive baggage, because it blocks our way to Christ and to seeing things as they are. The second aid is silence. We need to be still, to be healed of our disturbed spirits. We need a place of quiet in order to calm our tingling nerves and hear God speak. The third aid is solitude. We cannot allow ourselves to be driven all the time by an instinct to perform, to produce and to do many things. Sometimes we have to stand alone in solitude to discover who we are and who our God is.

Going for a desert experience in order to experience God like St John the Baptist also means that, like him, we take a Camel Hair Route. St John was clothed in camel hair, wore a leather belt and ate grasshoppers, thus appearing strange to his contemporaries. He was not trying to attract their attention; rather he was departing from the ordinary norms of society in order to jolt himself from the dullness of conformity. He was deliberately choosing a different experience to see if such an experience gives the intoxicating experience of God. It did. Likewise, we too, sometimes must experience what it is like to be outside the ordinary pattern of human behaviour. For example, what would it feel like not "to keep up with the Joneses" in the suburbs? What would it feel like to eat a few meagre meals some week in order to understand world hunger? What would it feel like to give one tenth of all that one owns, to charity? What would it feel like to ration the use of one's car, in order to comprehend the energy crisis?

During this Advent, therefore, we need to get into a symbolic desert experience, in order to experience God, who is already here amongst us. "Here I am with you", says God, "and you keep thinking of me, talking of me, with your tongue and searching for me in your books! When will you shut up and see?" St Thomas Aquinas, one of the world's ablest theologians, suddenly stopped writing. When his secretary complained about his unfinished work, St Thomas replied: "Brother Reginald some time ago, I experienced something of the Absolute, so all I have written of God seems to me now to be like straw". How could it be otherwise?

THE IMMACULATE CONCEPTION

FALL AND RISE

Readings: Gen 3:9-15, 20; Eph 1:3-6, 11-12; Lk 1:26-38

Theme: The Immaculate Conception of Mary calls us to have a look not just at the fall of the human race, but at its later rise to grace, a look not just at the sinlessness of Mary, but at her God-filled life, and a look at our own life, not merely as sinful, but as life shot through with hope.

Sin is so devastating that as one leak will sink a ship, so one sin will destroy the sinner. What is sin? To put it simply: it is an attempt to be the author of one's own happiness rather than to receive this happiness from God. And the greatest of modern sins is to be conscious of none. In our present age, even the grown-ups laugh at sin and at the idea of the fall of the human race from grace. Adults laugh at the virtues of chastity and purity calling for free rein to be given to passions. Adolescents laugh if you warn them of the depraving and debasing influences of sin. Married couples laugh at the sanctity and stability of marriage as God intended. Abortionists laugh at the notion of sacredness of human life. And yet, sin is real and not artificial as many would think. Sin brought death and death will disappear only with the disappearance of sin.

However, today's feast of the Immaculate Conception of Mary calls us not just to concentrate on the evils of sin but to contemplate the goodness of God. Indeed, the human race fell from its original grace by sin, but the truth is that it rose again from his fallen state. It is true that in the beginning there was a tree (Gen 3:8), but in the work of redemption there came another tree, the wood of the cross. It is true that in the beginning, there was an angel whose word spoken in darkness brought death, but at the annunciation there was another angel, the angel of light whose word brought salvation. It is true that in the beginning there was a man and a woman through whose disobedience sin and death entered the world, but in the plan of redemption there came a virgin Mary through whom Jesus the Saviour was born. It was fitting that the mother of the divine Saviour should herself be sinless.

Once again, we will not do full honour to the Immaculate Virgin

Mary if we only meditate on her sinlessness. Rather, we are called to contemplate the "fullness of grace" (Lk 1:28) in her, for which she was made sinless. To many of us, Mary's fullness of grace is a mystery. Perhaps, an example will help. When a potter throws a lump of clay on the wheel, there comes a moment when that clay becomes centred, spins smoothly and gently beneath the potter's fingers, and there is a deep harmony between potter and clay. All the tiny sand particles that make up this clay lump, now move together and are focused in the one direction. They are totally centred and it is only now that it becomes possible for the potter to mould this lump into most beautiful shape. Likewise, Mary's fullness of grace means that she was totally centred on God, one in whom every fibre of her being was turned Godward, one who was completely flawless clay in the hand of her potter. It is this God-centredness of Mary that we celebrate today. Thus, today's feast calls us to take a positive look at the 'landscape' before us: a look not just at the fall of the human race from its original grace, but its later rise; a look not just at the sinlessness of Mary, but at her God-filled life.

But there is a third positive look that today's feast calls us to take. This look is at ourselves. When we look over our mistakes and foolishness, we feel guilty, embarrassed and ashamed. But we need not stop there. Mary's sinlessness from her conception onwards is God's proof that no matter how bad we are or have been, life is still shot through with a 'rising' hope. The misery and suffering consequent upon original sin are still with us in the forms of war, killings, natural disasters, ethnic strifes and heartless inhumanity of person to person. Yet, life is vibrant with this 'rising' hope. Our hope is strengthened by the fact that we too have had a sharing at our baptism in Mary's fullness of grace. As St Paul says, God has "bestowed on us in Christ every spiritual blessing in heaven" (Eph 1:3) and Mary's sinless conception demonstrates what is possible when human life is touched by the grace of God.

Hence, may the feast of the Immaculate Conception of Our Lady give us another opportunity to have a positive look at the fall of the human race from original grace, at the sinlessness of Mary and at our own faults and mistakes. Positive outlook is a source of great inspiration; it enables us to hold our head high and to claim the future for ourselves. For negative thinkers, one cloud is enough to eclipse the sun. Positive thinkers believe that the angel's words to Mary, "Do not be afraid" (Lk 1:30) was addressed to them also and hence, when engulfed by darkness around, they move forward asking, 'Is there enough darkness in all the world to put out the light of even one small candle?' They are right. For these are people who concentrate not on the fall but on the rise.

3RD SUNDAY OF ADVENT

THERE IS ONE AMONG YOU

Readings: Is 61:1-2, 10-11; 1 Thess 5:16-24; Jn 1:6-8, 19-28

Theme: We are called to straighten up the rough and rugged spots in our lives so that Jesus who stands always in our midst can have easy entrance into our hearts with his joy and peace.

We hear people saying to us, "we must put God in our lives" but God is already here! Our business is to recognise him. The gold necklace we wish to acquire is around our neck. "There is one among you, whom you do not recognise" (Jn 1:26), said St John the Baptist, pointing to the then physical presence of Christ. The same Lord is now present in our minds in a mysterious way. It is his continued presence, though invisible, that gladdens our hearts, even amidst our shady sadness. The sweet mark of a Christian is not faith, not even love, but joy, because we are all strings in the concert of his joy. Did not the angel announce at the birth of Jesus, "I bring you glad tidings of great joy."? Hence St Paul asks us to "Rejoice always" (1 Thess 5:16) and Isaiah shouts out, "I rejoice heartily in the Lord, the joy of my soul" (Is 61:10). Joy is never within our power in the same way that pleasure is. Only Christ can fill us with joy. Joy is the flag which is flown from the castle of the heart when the King is resident there.

Jesus, ever-present, enters into our hearts in the silence of prayer, provided we do not resist him by hiding behind layers of distractions, drowning his voice with noise from television sets and stereos. He comes to us through his words in the scriptures. If we listen to his words in Sunday readings, not like listening to a cassette rerun, his words will come alive, questioning and enlightening our minds, challenging and testing our wills, moving and inspiring our hearts. He comes through the sacraments, which are those intense moments of grace and 'peak' experience of God. There are many other ways in which the Lord comes into our lives. His ways are always behind the scenes, but he moves all the scenes he is behind.

But we need to "make straight the way of the Lord" (Jn 1:23), not that we must strew roses, roses all the way, but at least we must not throw thorns and thistles and so block his way. One sure block that obstructs his way is pride. Pride is a "psychological inflation", more disastrous than, what the economic experts call "runaway inflation"; the latter deprives us, only of adequate purchasing power, but the former deprives Jesus of any space in a human heart, that is swollen from an exaggerated idea of self-importance. Although Jesus himself said that, "John the Baptiser was greater than any man born of a woman" (Lk 7:28), St John was so humble that he felt unworthy "even to untie his sandal strap" (Jn 1:27). Pride and grace never dwelt in one place.

Clinging to one set life-style, against the constant warning of Christian conscience, could also hinder the coming of Christ into our hearts. A crow once flew in the sky with a piece of meat in its beak. Twenty other crows set out in hot pursuit and began to attack it viciously. When the crow finally dropped the meat the pursuers left it alone and flew off shrieking after the morsel. Said the crow, "I have lost the meat but gained this peaceful sky". Likewise, when we drop from our lives 'that something' which is un-Christian, the peace of Christ flows into our hearts. Of course, the most common stumbling block that impedes the coming of Christ is selfishness. It is only when my selfish house is burnt down that I get an unobstructed view of the moon at night. Advent calls us to straighten up those rough and rugged spots in our lives so that Jesus can have easy entrance; to work quietly on the chunks of darkness hidden within us, in order to make our way towards the light of Christ; and to get in tune with all the mysterious ways of Christ so that when he comes, we can recognise him. We obtain salvation not through action, nor through meditation but through recognition.

HIGHLY FAVOURED DAUGHTER

Readings: 2 Sam 7:1-5, 8-11, 16; Rom 16:25-27; Lk 1:26-38

Theme: Like Mary, if we believe and obey God's word, we too can conceive Christ spiritually and make him present in the world.

Man's greatest wisdom is to know that God sent his Son into this world to break the chains of sin. Humanity's greatest joy is to possess the peace of Christ, which makes 'the heart to swell with rapture. Humanity's greatest blessing is to hope that beyond the grave the followers of Jesus shall reign above the sun. God bestowed on Mary all the greatest favours in the order of grace. Whether the sun was shining or the sky was black, Mary was always led by his grace. A little fish in the Thames became suddenly apprehensive lest drinking so many pints of water in the river each day, it might drink the Thames dry. But Father Thames said to it: "Drink away, little fish, my stream is sufficient for thee". Likewise, Father in heaven kept constantly assuring Mary; "My grace is sufficient for thee". Why the extraordinary favour done to Mary alone? Because, as St Paul tells the Romans, "when the mystery of Jesus Christ, hidden for many ages, was finally revealed, God expected human beings to believe and obey" (Rom 16:25-26), and Mary was the first disciple of Christ to believe and obey.

Mary believed. Her faith was humble and hence she first believed and only then reasoned upon it. "What a piece of work is man! How noble is his reason." Yes, God wanted Mary to submit even that noble reason to faith. A man was dangerously hanging on to a single branch on the top of a tree from where he could not climb down. He cried out to God, "Oh, God, save me; you know I believe in you. All that I ask of you is to save me and I shall proclaim your name to the ends of the earth". "Very well", said the voice of God, "I shall save you. Let go of that branch". The distraught man yelled out, "Let go of this branch? Do you think I am crazy?" Some people cling to their reason so adamantly that they are never able to see the light of faith. Mary's faith was ever active and hence she not only accepted the divine truth but dwelt upon it, used it and developed it. Her faith was ever active and hence "the handmaid of the Lord" did not exclude even death from her faith. Whatever is alive must die. Look at the flowers; only plastic flowers never die.

Mary obeyed. Her obedience was risk-taking when she said, "Let it be done according to thy word" (Lk 1:38), She did not realise the full implication of the 'word'. Words are inadequate reflections of reality. How can you claim to know what Niagara Falls are like, just because you have seen Niagara water in a bucket? Her obedience was loving. She loved God and hence trusted in him and obeyed. After all, the important religious distinction is not between those who worship and those who do not worship, but between those who love and those who don't. Mary's obedience was persevering. God the supreme Artist, who painted a picture of stunning beauty on her, not only brought her joy, meaning and hope through splashes of colour but also smeared on her lily-white soul black and ugly stains of pain and hardship. And yet, Mary kept on saying "yes" to him till the end of her earthly story.

The Messiah as foretold by prophet Nathan to King David in the book of Samuel had already come in the person of Jesus, fulfilling the messianic hopes of all nations. Now, he wants to come into each one of us individually at Christmas. However sinful we may be he still invites us to his Birthday Party, for "nothing is impossible for God" (Lk 1:37). But at the party, he will challenge us, as he challenged Mary, to accept the role God has designed for each of us in life. Like Mary, if we believe and obey his word, we can also make Christ present within us and through us his light can illumine the world.

CHRISTMAS DAY

STANDING BEFORE THE CRIB

Readings: Is 52:7-10; Heb 1:1-6; Jn 1:1-18

Theme: Standing before the crib we see Jesus, we observe and hear what Mary and Joseph are doing and saying; so we receive the divine light they shed on our lives as we bow in humble worship of their Son.

I see the child Jesus. In him I see God who has lavished his generosity upon me; but when I look at myself, I am ashamed to see a 'kindergarten' heart in an adult body. In him, I see a God who humbled himself to my human level. But I have been like a virtually empty vessel which rattles noisily the small coins it actually has. I see Mary. She is beautiful, on account of the goodness of her heart. Beauty without goodness is worse than wine and will intoxicate the holder and the beholder. I see St Joseph. He is silent even when Mary is near. This silence is not the absence of sound but of self. Each has surrendered themselves to God in the manger. Our world regards silence as a deficiency. Therefore some radios, even on Christmas Eve, keep us awake until dawn playing 'Silent Night'.

I survey the crib. I see what we regard as essential for modern civilisation. There is not even a door or a window (which we moderns keep shut even during the daytime). There is no watchdog that welcomes guests entering a modern house by barking at them, if not in fact biting them. Mary is not wearing slacks, which is not slack enough these days. St Joseph is not smoking a cigarette, while some of us consume three packets a day, as if they contained all the vitamins necessary. And yet, though civilised things are absent from the crib, we have, here the first civilised persons in the world: Jesus, Mary, Joseph. After all, what use are civilised things without civilised individuals? Twenty-five civilisations before ours have been destroyed, not by enemies from outside, but by people inside (at least in part).

I hear Mary telling Joseph, "I hear people's gossip about us, having a baby without living together as husband and wife". Joseph says "Don't worry, Mary. Worry never accomplishes anything, except wrinkles which gives another thing to worry about. Leave gossip alone; those who gossip are caught in their own mouth-trap". Mary says, "God could have given us at least a cradle for the baby". Joseph says, "My dear, at least we have this crib. Some people are so poor that even cockroaches shun them. One advantage of being poor is that it does not cost much. And though those who sleep on the floor never fall out of bed, riches are not always blessings". Mary says, "Joseph, don't speak loudly; the baby is sleeping". Joseph says, "Yes, we mustn't disturb him. He sleeps so soundly even in poor swaddling clothes". Of course, man's conscience and not his mattress has most to do with his sleep.

I touch the floor of the crib. It is very cold. We people have become so cold towards one another that God has become a human being to warm us up. Often, we are neither cold nor hot, but lukewarm and a lukewarm Christian makes a good bench warmer although a poor heart warmer. I kiss the feet of the child Jesus. All the legislation in the world cannot abolish kissing. The word 'kiss' was invented by poets to rhyme with bliss. So when I kiss Jesus I kiss the eternal bliss, but I must take care that I do not kiss as Judas did.

HOLY FAMILY

A FAMILY REVOLUTION

Readings: Sir 3:2-6, 12-14; Col 3:12-21; Lk 2:22-40

Theme: The survival and happiness of our natural families depend on our caring and working for the welfare of our world-family.

There is a Mexican proverb which says that none but a mule denies his family. Our family home is the place where we grumble the most but are treated the best. It is a kingdom of its own in the midst of the world! It is the haven of refuge amidst the turmoils of our age! The bonding together in family groups is both instinctive and necessary to human welfare. As Pope John Paul II has said: "We must treasure our families, for the future of humanity passes by way of the family."

However, our blood family is not the only family we must be concerned about. It is true that we have cause to love our relations better than others, but that is no reason to think that they are our whole world. The world is much larger than our kith and kin. There is a world-family on whose welfare the happiness of our natural family depends. There was once a man who was busy building a home for himself. He wanted it to be the nicest, cosiest home in the world. Someone came to him to ask for help because the world was on fire. But it was his home he was interested in, not the world. When he finally finished his home, he found he did not have a planet to put it on! Yes. It is impossible to have security for our blood family without working for the welfare of the world-family. That is why God has put into every human being a deep instinct, not just for the natural family as we know it but also for other family groups like parishes, civic organisations and work communities; it is an instinct that is urging us to endeavour to come out of the privacy of our blood families in order to work for world-family.

The Holy Family of Jesus, Mary and Joseph, started a family revolution by putting the welfare of the world-family before their own. At the presentation in the Temple Simeon prophesied that Jesus would be the Saviour not just of Mary and Joseph but of the world and his role would bring great suffering upon the family of Mary and Joseph (Lk 2:34-35), for the sake of the world. Then Anna, the prophetess, speaking emphatically about the deliverance of Jerusalem (Lk 2:38), made it clear that Mary should see her son in a context wider than her own family, that she would have to learn to be more than just his mother and that normal family life would have to be sacrificed for the sake of her son's mission in the world. Jesus himself was to teach later to his own family and through them to all of us that his real family is not made up of blood relations but of those who belong to the house of God where "those who do the will of the Father are real brothers and sisters." (Mt 12:50). Thus the Holy Family was much larger than Mary, Joseph and Jesus in Nazareth; it was inextricably linked to the rest of the world and to God's plan to restore peace and hope to the world.

In imitation of the Holy Family, all Christian families are invited to reach out to the whole world and use their own natural families as the base for building a family of all nations. A Christian family could begin linking itself with the world-family in many ways. One sure way is hospitality. Hospitality is love of the stranger, the exact opposite of the fear of stranger. The great campaign for Civil Rights in America began when a black woman, Rose Parkes, refused to be banned from sitting at the back of the bus simply on the grounds of her colour. Such discrimination is a warning sign of the endemic disease which is at its most horrific in the wholesale slaughter that we have seen in Europe, and which is described emphatically as 'ethnic cleansing'. It is a disease that erupts daily in many homes when the family shuts their door on any stranger who does not belong to their blood; at times, we also see people from ethnic minority groups being subject to harassment, to intimidation and even to death threats in the streets. The only way to overcome fear of the stranger is, in Gospel terms, to practice love of the stranger, the love which recognises in the stranger one's own brother or sister.

Every revolution was first a thought in one individual's mind and when the same thought occurs to another individual, it is the key to that era. Similarly, the family that first thought of making their family into a movement for a world-family was the Holy Family. If the same thought occurs to each of the Christian families today, that could be the key to a new world order in which natural families are not destroyed but transformed into instruments for forming one family of all people on earth.

THE MOTHER OF GOD

CONTEMPLATIVE MARY

Readings: Num 6:22-27; Gal 4:4-7; Lk 2:16-21

Theme: The most suitable gift that we can offer Mary, the Mother of God and our own Mother, is our commitment to practice a life of contemplative prayer.

Scattered around the earth, like stars across a summer sky, you will find churches named in honour of the blessed virgin Mary. In the tiniest towns and the largest cities, in urban and suburban areas, you will find churches named in honour of her. Something there is in the Catholic heart that loves to name a church after Mary. Pope John Paul II hardly writes anything without emphasising her importance for the Church. Millions of the faithful visit her Shrines in Fatima, Lourdes and Walsingham, (to this list we might add Medjugorje, though, as we know, it does not have the official sanction of the Church hierarchy). We know why such veneration is offered to Mary. She is the Mother of God! "The Blessed Virgin," wrote St Thomas Aquinas, "by becoming the Mother of God, received a kind of infinite dignity because God is infinite; this dignity therefore is a reality that a better is not possible, just as nothing can be better than God."

The veneration offered to Mary is not only because she is the Mother of God, but also because she is our Mother. She is the spiritual mother of all the human race. For when Mary gave birth to Jesus, she gave birth also to a new human race. As St Paul says, "when the designed time had come, God sent forth his Son born of a woman, born under the law, to derive from the law those who were subject to it, so that we might receive our status as adopted sons" (Gal 4:4-5). Because Mary is our mother, she is a powerful advocate for us in heaven. Therefore, in all our needs, we must not hesitate to pray to Mary. If you are in danger, she will hasten to free you; if you are troubled, she will console you; if you are sick, she will bring you relief; if you are in any kind of need she will help you. She does not look to see what kind of person you are. In fact, the poorer and the more ordinary you are, the more readily she will come to your help.

Her special concern for the more poor and ordinary among us, is due to the fact that she herself was poor and ordinary when she lived on earth. She experienced uncertainty and insecurity when she said, "Yes" to the angel. She knew what oppression was, when she could not find a room in which to give birth to Jesus. She lived as a refugee in a strange land, with a strange language and strange customs. She knew the pain of having a child who caused controversy wherever he went. She knew the loneliness of the widow and the agony of seeing her only son executed. Therefore Mary who is the mother of us all is a special mother of all the poor, the oppressed and lonely and she is closely related to all those who are rejected, despised and pushed about. In fact, it was she who introduced into the Gospel God's option for the poor when she sang in her Magnificat "He has raised the high, the lowly, and filled the starving with good things" (Lk 1:52-53).

On this feast of Mary, the Mother of God and our own Mother, we would want to offer her a gift, a gift that would please her heart greatly and which would also be fitting on this New Year's day. That gift could be our resolution to develop a habit during this coming year of praying like her. Mary's way of praying was contemplative and meditative or reflective. Luke gives us an insight into this way of praying when he tells us at the end of the birth narrative: "Mary treasured all these things and pondered deeply about them" (Lk 2:19). Let not the word 'contemplative' startle you. To treasure and ponder is to be contemplative. It is to sharpen, refine, something in the heart and meditate upon the Word of God in silence.

Silence is the element in which great things fashion themselves. Contemplative silence in particular is that in which we look when there is apparently nothing to see and we listen when all is seemingly quiet. Contemplative silence is eloquent silence which is often better than eloquent speech because speech is of time but silence is of eternity. Such a silence is full of potential wisdom because in it truths bind themselves together and take root. God is with us, as you know, but often we are not with him because we are driven most of the time by an instinct to perform and produce. Hence we need contemplative silence in order to be healed of our disturbed spirits and perceive God. We need to be quiet in the depth of our being in order to calm our tingling nerves and to be able to have an intense and intoxicating experience of God. Above all, to derive the maximum benefit from the words of the Scripture we need contemplative silence. To listen to the words of the Scripture is like seeing the cool crystal water sparkling in the cup. But to contemplate on them is like drinking of them. It takes calm, thoughtful, prayerful meditation on the Word, as Mary did, to extract its deepest nourishment because, in the word of God, more is meant than meets the ear.

Therefore let us offer the resolution to Mary that we will be contemplative in prayer as she was. If we can offer this resolution, not only the Mother of God will be highly pleased but also the "blessings of the Lord" promised by God (Num 6:23-27) will follow us through the coming New Year. Offer Mary this gift and "the Lord will bless you and keep you; the Lord will let his face shine upon you". Offer her this gift. "The Lord will look upon you and give you peace."

EPIPHANY

JOURNEY

Readings: Is 60:1-6; Eph 3:2-3, 5-6; Mt 2:1-12

Theme: Those who persevere in their difficult spiritual journey, guided by the star of faith all the way, will invariably meet Christ who will heal them and transform them into new persons to take a new direction in life.

Marco Polo journeyed to India and China; Christopher Columbus journeyed to America; Admiral Byrd journeyed to the South Pole; Armstrong journeyed to the moon. They all undertook daring adventures. Likewise, the Magi, as narrated in the Gospel, journeyed to find the newborn babe Jesus. Leaving the security of their homeland, they ventured forth into a strange country in order to find the Saviour. Like all men, these astrologers too were in constant search after human fulfilment, but they believed that only in the Saviour Jesus they could finally find what they had been searching for all their lives. We too are making our individual journeys, searching after something which alone will give meaning to our existence; we are searching for something permanent and eternal. Happily for us, by the gift of faith in Christ which we already possess, we are in no doubt that we can find our perfect fulfilment only in Jesus.

But we need a guide for our spiritual journey as the Magi needed a star to guide them to Jesus. Our guiding star is obviously the divine teachings of Christ. The more truly we follow our Lord's teachings in daily life, the more surely we will encounter him and the more easily he will be able to reveal himself to us. How does the Lord reveal himself to us? His ways are many. It could be through an inward illumination that draws us closer to God; it could be through a sense of wonder which is fundamentally religious; it could be through a clearer vision of what human life is all about; It could be through an intimate experience of love for God and for neighbours; or it could be through a spiritual insight which is called enlightenment. Whatever the way in which Jesus reveals himself to us, the end result of his revelation will be the bursting of his divine light into the whole of our being, filling us with his peace and joy.

However, our journey towards a closer encounter with Christ will not all the time be smooth and easy; neither was it so for the Magi. The Gospel says that when they set out on their journey, they saw the star "as it rose" (Mt 2:2). The next time the star is mentioned is on the road to Bethlehem as they neared the end of their journey. "There in front of them was the star they had seen rising" (Mt 2:9). The implication seems to be that in between they had travelled in darkness. It was for them like a night-time journey between two ports. It will be the same for us. As we start our journey on some road following our individual 'vocation' in life, trying to follow the teachings of Jesus as our guiding star, we may initially be attracted by a bright ideal or vision or hope. But when we are on our way, we must be ready to meet clouds that would blot out the light of faith and make us stumble and the darkness of faith may even discourage us from continuing our journey towards Christ. But we must not be discouraged or give up. We must keep going on. If we are daring enough to keep going forward, we will see that the darkness will pass and once again we would have the glimpse of the initial star that we saw when we set out on our journey.

When we encounter Jesus at any point in our Journey, two things will happen. The first is that we will be moved to offer him a gift.

Have you ever sat at the presentation of Gian Carlo Menotti's one-act Opera, Amahl and the Night Visitors? The story is about three Magi who stop on their way to Bethlehem at the hovel of a poor crippled boy named Amahl. When Amahl hears of their mysterious search for a child, he secretly follows behind. He watches in awe as the Magi present their gifts to the child. He is disturbed that has no suitable gift for the child, until it occurs to him to offer the only thing he possesses, his crutches. As he presents his crutches, he is healed. We too, when we offer to Christ as our gift that something which is still holding us back from coming closer to God, we will be healed. And the second thing also will happen: Healed as we are, we will travel through life by a different route (Mt 2:12), as the Magi did after adoring Jesus. That is, we will put away the worldly attitudes, values and goals which we might have thus far held dear and we will take on those of Christ, proclaiming by word and deed that Jesus is the Saviour of the world.

1ST SUNDY OF LENT

LENT IS LOVEABLE

Readings: Gen 9:8-15; 1 Pet 3:18-22; Mk 1:12-15

Theme: Lent is meant to be enjoyed, not to be endured, for it invites us to begin again, to grow into maturity and to emerge spiritually stronger through self-discipline.

One could love Lent. Like all loveable things, Lent is meant to be enjoyed rather than to be endured. No matter what kind of a mess we have made of things up to this point, Lent once again offers us an opportunity to leave our past behind and start again. We may have broken our last Lenten resolutions; but lovers' quarrel is the renewal of love. So, Lent invites us to begin again and renew. This is the wonderful thing about Christian life. It is a series of new beginnings. We can always start again. Like the gardeners who plant new seeds every year to see blooms in May, we are invited to sow deep within our hearts seeds of God's words during Lent, to reap Easter fruits in abundance.

Lent is a growing period. We grow by giving a mature response to

God's covenanted love which rings aloud in his promise, dressed in symbolic language, "I set my bow in the clouds to serve as the sign of the eternal covenant between me and the earth. Never again shall a flood destroy all mortal beings" (Gen 9:14-15). God fulfilled his promise when Jesus died on the cross and rose again. "This is why Christ died for sins once and for all so that he could lead you to God" (1 Pet 3:18). This means that whatever our experience or the power of evil, that is not to be 'our final story'. God intends life for us, not death. We grow during Lent by accepting this "Good News". No matter how much the power of sin and its effects have flooded every area of our lives, salvation is possible for those who enter the ark and separate themselves from evil.

Lent is a training period. It trains us to combat evil through desert experience, as Jesus himself did for forty days (Mk 1:12-13). There are desert areas in our lives where decisions are needed and resolutions must be made. Often the very thing which would release God's power in us is the very thing we avoid. Christ asks us to look into the wilderness of our innermost selves, where there are no kindly friends to colour our faults with soothing words. Christ asks us to see ourselves as we really are, and to rid ourselves of anything ungodly and unchristian, saying, "This is the time of fulfilment. Reform your lives" (Mt 4:17). Therefore Lent offers a period of self-discipline. Self-discipline never means giving up anything. In self-discipline, we are not giving up the things of the earth, we are only exchanging them for better things. Discipline hurts. Yes. There will always be some initial pain in reforming our lives. Even children, learning to play the guitar, feel initial pain by pressing their fingers against the strings! Thus, trained by Lent, we would emerge spiritually strong, as Jesus emerged from the desert, as a wiry athlete ready for the ultimate test of his strength in the struggle against evil. Our Lord's struggle against evil still goes on, but now the battleground has shifted from the desert into our own spirits.

Let us begin Lent with confidence, because whether we gaze with longing into the garden or with fear into the desert, God walked there first. Let us begin Lent with hope, because the symbols of ashes and purple and sombreness of Lent will soon be eclipsed by the light and flowers and alleluias of the Easter season, as the drab and darkness of winter will be transformed into the colour and promise of spring. Let us begin Lent with enthusiasm because, although what we do for Lent – our fasting, abstinence, prayer and works of charity – may indeed be small, they are important victories for the Kingdom of God and they are defeats for the evil present in our lives. Hence, we must make love, not war, with Lent; and in love, there is always one who kisses and one who offers the cheek. Lent offers its cheek, but are we prepared to kiss?

2ND SUNDAY OF LENT

HE TOUCHED ME

Readings: Gen 22:1-2, 9-18; Rom 8:31-34; Mk 9:2-10

Theme: If we take ourselves to prayer as often as we can, we too, like Christ can have our own moments of transfiguration, when the touch of God could lift our darkness and melt away our fears.

Science commits suicide if it denies God. It cannot deny, for the supernatural is not its field of enquiry. However, many moderns, influenced by science, dismiss the reality of the Spirit as primitive myth. But Jesus by his Transfiguration revealed that God is indeed real. Because what happened at the Transfiguration of Christ was only the explosion of the Spirit already present in him, breaking through with brilliance, giving him a rare glimpse of God's face, transporting him for a while to the realm of God and touching the chords of ineffable joy within him.

Such a transfiguration, but in an imperfect manner, could happen to any human being, because God is an unutterable sigh planted in the depth of every human heart. It could happen to any Christian because God indwells by his Spirit in every soul redeemed by Christ. It actually happens to saints. Touched by God, St Paul challenged, "If God is for us, who can be against us?" (Rom 8.3). Touched by God, St Augustine exclaimed, "Our hearts are made for you, Oh God, and they shall not rest until they rest in you". Touched by God, St Francis of Assisi sang, "Make me a channel of your peace". So God can touch any heart that opens its doors to His love. Even an alcoholic, when moved by the concern of a beloved wife, or a lonely and bereaved widow when comforted by the concern of a caring relative, or a confused and depressed young man when received by a kindly elder could experience their moments of limited transfiguration, for it is the same transforming power of God which is transmitted when someone tells another "I love you".

At such moments of our own imperfect transfiguration, wonderful things can happen to us. For example, our attitude to suffering could change, for then we will realise that here on earth we can't walk in a straight line to victory and that the destiny of every Christian is written between two mountains, Calvary and Mount Tabor. Even Jane Torvill would testify that Olympic medals for ice dancing are not won simply by eating wheaties. We will also realise that even calamities can bring us blessings in the end – as to a bird, sheltering each day in the withered branches of a tree which is suddenly uprooted by a whirlwind, forcing the bird to fly a hundred miles till it finally comes to a forest of fruit-laden trees. The touch of God could lift our darkness and melt away our fears, for all fear is bondage. We fear even love and that is why we fear sacrifices, which was not the case for Abraham to whom even sacrificing his only son was meaningful because he loved God (Gen 22:9-12). Without meaning, sacrifices can destroy us, but with meaning they can transform us.

But one thing is certain. If we want to have our transfigurations, we must have our Tabors, namely we must take ourselves to prayer. It was when Jesus climbed the Mount to pray that he was transfigured and heard, "This is my beloved son, in whom I am well pleased" (Mk 9:7). At prayer, the Lord will speak and we must "listen to him" (Mk 9:7) The Lord will speak to us in any manner, either by putting an idea in our mind or giving us a new perspective of life; either by stirring up new desires in our heart or by calming our turbulent emotions or by actually whispering words to the listening ears of our souls. But in whatever manner he speaks, if only we listen, we will be transfigured, reborn and healed. Such a healing that comes from the touch of God can never be promised by the most reputable therapist of clinical psychotherapy. The healing touch of God will kindle in our hearts such a spark of hope and love that we can go forward into our dark future, carrying an invisible lamp burning in our heart, proclaiming to the rest of the world, "He touched me".

3RD SUNDAY OF LENT

BACK TO BASICS

Readings: Ex 20:1-17; 1 Cor 1:22-25; Jn 2:13-35

Theme: A loving and obedient relationship with God, an enduring reliance on him for one's own fulfilment and a progressive renewal of heart are basics of Christian life.

Roots are basic to trees. Foundations are basic to buildings. Principles are basic to religion! It is easier to fight for basics than to live up to them. But that does not mean that we can give them up. A religion takes its eternal motivation from its basic principles. Hence "Back to Basics" can serve us as a relevant Lenten campaign. This Sunday's scriptural readings call us back to three important basic principles of Christian life.

First is Relationship. Christianity is not just a religion, it is a relationship. The essence of the ethics of Jesus is not law but a relationship of person to God. God gave us Ten Commandments (Ex 20:1-17), and we are told that, since the beginning of civilisation, millions and millions of laws have not improved on them a bit. However, we would be fooling ourselves if we hope that the evils of this world can be cured by commandments or legislations. Only goodness within human beings can achieve that. But for us to be good, we must be in relationship with God for "God alone is good". Commandments were given to us, not to enslave us but to free us for a relationship of love with God. A Catholic who comes to Mass simply out of obligation is still a slave of the law. A Catholic who never comes to Mass claiming to have been freed by the Spirit from all external laws, needs to ask: what do I really want, God's will or my own? A Catholic who loves God would come to Mass anyway, law or no law. Let us strike a loving relationship with God, who dwells in the deep well within us. It is sad that, in some cases, sins like stones and grit, block that well so much that God is buried beneath and he has to be dug out.

Second is Reliance. Reliance on God is more basic to our fulfilment than dependence on material things. No doubt, money is the sixth sense which enables us to enjoy the other five. But the picture of the merchants being driven out by Jesus from the Temple (Jn 2:15-16) warns us of preoccupation with money. Cattle, sheep, hay and corn can be bought in the "Market Place"; but only in the "Father's House" can we find deep peace. Reliance on one's own way of looking at things could also endanger man's salvation, as was the case with Greeks and Jews about whom St Paul writes. The Greeks expected Jesus to be another Plato, offering a new package of ideas in answer to the problems of evil and death. But Jesus did not. The Jews thought that God becoming a human being and being crucified on the cross, was sadness. And yet, in the end "God's folly was wiser than men and his weakness more powerful than men" (1 Cor 1:23). How can we forget that we, who were deceived by the wisdom of the serpent, were 'freed by the foolishness of God'?

Third is Renewal. Religion is in the heart, not in the knees. Hence progress in the faith-journey supposes a progressive change of heart, which alone is true renewal. A person who can't change his own heart cannot change anything. If I cannot protect my own feet with slippers, how can I carpet the whole earth? A change of heart brings about purification of motives. We should all, at times, be ashamed of our finest actions, if the world understood our motives. Thank goodness it cannot. But the Lord can: "Jesus was well aware of what was in man's heart (Jn 2:25). Jesus drove out the people who were doing business in the temple, not because it was business; for even as business it was a valuable service at a feast; but because their motive was diluted by their manipulative intention to make a "fast buck". Hence during Lent, let us aim at the renewal of our hearts; with God's help, all of us can. For the almighty God who drew out a fountain of water in the desert for His people can draw from our hearts, however hard, tears of compunction.

4TH SUNDAY OF LENT

THE CHAOS OF THE CROSS

Readings: 2 Chron 36:14-17, 19-23; Eph 2:4-10; Jn 3:14-21

Theme: At the chaotic moments of our life, if we pray and reflect under the shadow of the cross of Christ, our dark days will become great days, for the providence of God presides over human affairs.

There is a divinity that shapes our destiny. Men may cast their lots, gamble with their deeds, create chaos and confusion in the world and move the wheels of history with blood-stained hands. But the providence of God that presides over human lives finally brings order out of chaos. The history of Israel was largely a history of chaos. The Jews suffered a collapse at the hands of a foreign power, were deported to exile and "By the streams of Babylon they sat and wept" (Ps 137). However, just when it seemed, as if all were over for them, King Cyrus of Persia, inspired by God, not only released them from exile but helped them rebuild their Temple (2 Chron 36:20-23). Thus, God's mercy overcame his own wrath, drawing his people, through their chaotic history closer to himself.

The chaotic history of Israel repeated itself in the life of Jesus. Every time history repeats itself, the price goes up. The chaos of the cross became the ultimate chaos in human history, because on it, goodness itself was crucified as a common criminal. But once again, God drew life out of that bleeding cross, so that, it was by the cross we were all saved, "when we were dead in sin" (Eph 2:5); and what a glorious and universal salvation that was! "The Son of Man was lifted up on the cross, so that everyone who believes may have eternal life in him" (Jn 3:14-15). It is the same cross which, until today, stands tall and high in the hearts of millions who continue to sing, "Nearer my God to Thee, nearer to Thee! Even though it be a cross that raiseth me".

This means that the history of the chaos of the cross is not contained in thick books but lives in our very blood. We have our own chaotic moments in life but through them all, God intends to bring us to life and to make us truly "his handiwork, created to lead the life of good deeds" (Eph 2:10). We have heard it said, "Where there is life there is hope". But we Christians who believe in the power of the cross dare say, "Where there is death there is life". It is because we believe that the crucified Christ lives with us we hope that, in times of crisis, God will help us to find a way to survive; that when we face difficulties, he will help us to devise ways to overcome them; that, when tragedies like fire or flood devastate our homes, he will help to rebuild what we have lost; that when some of our precious dreams are destroyed by a mistake, he will inspire us to start over again; that there is always hope even for a family where all love between the members seems to have died and that there is always the hope for a better future for people who suffer under severe economic and social conditions. Yes, order will always emerge from chaos; new life will always spring from the Cross. This is our faith.

But this faith is a gift from God, not given to us on a plate, but planted within us like a seed which must grow. It will grow not when we grow more successful and wealthier in life but when we stand at the foot of the Cross and prayerfully reflect upon the chaos of our life. For it is during such prayer and reflection that our faith will deepen, to the extent that even death will appear not as a going down but as a going up; not a crumbling into dust but a skyward sweep. As a result, our weeping may endure for a night but joy will come in the morning (cf Ps 30:5); life will no more be like "a tale told by an idiot full of sound and fury, signifying nothing", as it did to Macbeth. We may be in the midst of winter but at prayer we will learn that there is in us an invincible summer. As long as we pray and reflect upon the confusion and convulsions of our life, under the shadow of the Cross, our dark days will become great days. Of this let us be certain: the well of providence is deep and hence the buckets we bring to it must not be small.

5TH SUNDAY OF LENT

BE NOT AFRAID

Readings: Jer 31:31-34; Heb 5:7-9; Jn 12:20-33

Theme: Fearless dying to one's self-will and self-seeking, in obedience to God's will, preserves one's life for eternity; for life is fruitful in the same measure as it is laid out.

Once a school boy was asked what parts of speech 'My' and 'Mine' were. He answered that they were aggressive pronouns. How true he was! As a heavily laden cart lumbers along creaking, so our "self" mounted by its "ego" often goes groaning. Unfortunately, all of us are serving a life sentence in the dungeon of self. Jesus came to show the way out of this dungeon. But the way he showed is puzzling. He said, "The man who loves his life loses it, while the man who hates his life in this world preserves it to life eternal" (Jn 12:25). It is a paradox and a bitter one. Because of such bitter sayings, Jesus lost many of his followers. In that he was poor in public relations but then he came not to please but to lead. Only politicians stand for what they think the voters will fall for; but Jesus was not a politician and hence he spoke only the truth.

Jesus taught us to yield up the love of life for the sake of the life of love. What he taught, he also practised. He suffered the shame and pain of the cross to die for the life of his foes. Because he died, his life lives on in the untold souls. In a way, we are in debt to Adam, the first benefactor of our race, for bringing death into the world. Because Jesus died, his seed prevails, filling the earth as the stars fill the sky; his pain is our peace and his death is our life.

The paradox of life through death would not puzzle us so much if we were to look at the nature and human growth. A seed lies smothered and submerged in the dark earth before it blooms and blossoms. The whole future of that seed remains unfulfilled if it is not put to earth to die (Jn 12:24). Look also at any sphere of human life. By putting to death the traditional forms of expression in art, music and literature, some artists gave birth to new forms; by putting an end to transportation by horse and buggy, travel by the car came in; by putting to rest the Old Testament ritual of circumcision, Jews became

Christians; by burying the Latin liturgy, mass in the vernacular was born; by their death Mahatma Gandhi in India and Martin Luther King in America became powerful influences in the liberation of their people; by dying to some of our old attitudes and forms of behaviour we discover a new way of life.

Therefore, as Jesus told us, life is fruitful in proportion to which it is laid out. Our highest life does not consist in self-expression but in self-sacrifice. It is not what we take up but what we give up that makes us and others rich. Hence do we want eternal spring in our heart? Then we must welcome winter on our head. Do we want to enjoy the glory of sunshine? Then we must live through the night and death. If we are afraid of death, probably we are afraid of life as well.

Dying to self would often mean, sacrificing one self-will, for the sake of God's will, which is his law, "placed within us and written upon our hearts" (Jer 31:33). God wills only our good, hence the greatest of his laws is our greatest good. Nine tenths of our difficulties are overcome when our heart obeys God's will. The mother and guardian of all virtues is obedience. That is why, summing up Jesus' thirty years of hidden life, the gospel says, "He was subject to them" and that to the end "Son though he was, he learned obedience from what he suffered" (Heb 5:8). We give God very little when we give him our possessions; but when we give him our own will, we give him ourselves and in any giving, only when we give of ourselves, we truly live. Besides, if we deliberately sacrifice our own will for that of God, he, with all his mighty power will ordain the remotest star and the last grain of sand to assist us.

Of course, dying to self very often means sacrificing ourselves for the sake of others. Only by dying to our self-seeking and vain ambitions, can we bring life to others, spreading joy and inspiring hope. Like Jesus, many heroic men and women found love for God and fellow men as values worth dying for. If one has found nothing worth dying for, then probably found nothing worth living for. Let us not be afraid of such dying before we actually die. For death is only a parting of the cloud which hides the sun.

PASSION SUNDAY

AT THE FOOT OF THE CROSS

Readings: Is 50:4-7; Phil 2:6-11; Mk 14:1-15, 47

Theme: Standing at the foot of the cross, we marvel at the incomparable Christ, we thank him for his indefatigable love, we feel sorry for paining him with our sins, and we pray for selfless love.

Lord, I MARVEL at you. You are incomparable. In infancy you startled a king; in boyhood you puzzled the learned doctors; in manhood you walked upon the waves and hushed the sea to sleep; and finally you hung upon the cross and removed the sting of death. Great men have come and gone but you live on. Herod could not kill you, Satan could not seduce you, death could not destroy you and the grave could not hold you. You are incredible. You never wrote a book but more books have been written on you than on anyone else. You never wrote a song but you provided a theme for the best musicians in the world. You never practised medicine but you have healed more broken hearts than any other physician. All this by your death on the cross. Like the flower that blooms and in blooming it dies, like the pelican in the mediaeval legends that feeds its young ones with its blood and in feeding it dies, you died giving life.

Lord, I THANK YOU. I thank you for the poverty, the pains and the passion you, suffered for me. You slept in a manger that was not your own, you cruised on the lake in a boat that was not your own and were buried in a tomb that was not your own. You are the maker of the universe and yet you were made a curse on the cross. Your holy fingers made the meadows, yet they grew the thorns that crowned your head. You made the forests, yet they gave the tree upon which you hung. You made the sky, but it darkened over your head when you died. It was for love of me that you suffered all these. I can see upon the cross inscribed in shining letters: "God is Love". Yes, your love is so great, so vast and so mighty that I may count the leaves of the forest trees or the sparkling drops of dew at sunrise, but never can I tell the depth of your love. That is why it has lasted longest and stood the hardest test. I was born in my mother's pain and I will not perish in my own, because you love me.

Lord, I am SORRY. Evil men put you to death but that dark evil sleeps in me as well. Like the crowd that was jubilant singing "Hosanna", but soon turned into an angry mob shouting "Crucify him", I too have praised you with songs and pained you with sins. I have often twisted you with the fickleness of my human nature that cannot be consistent for two days in a row. It was the Judas in me that betrayed my commitments to you. Like Pilate who blew hot and cold in the same breath declaring you innocent but condemning you to death, I too have been a bundle of contradictions, believing one thing and practising another. Like St Peter, I have been week and cowardly. As he wept I want to weep: indeed, there are many tears in my heart but they never reach my eyes. Like the soldiers who crucified you on the excuse that they were simply carrying out orders. I too have been good at blaming others for my faults and, in doing so, I have only made them the worse. Lord, give me true repentance. I cannot repent too soon because I do not know how soon it would be too late. I know I am a sinner, but do not know how great; you alone know, for you died for my sins.

Lord, I PRAY. You have often pierced my mind with the arrows of your words; now pierce my heart with the arrows of your love. Let my love for you be selflessness: whenever I loved you right I was virtuous but whenever I loved you wrong, I sinned. Mend me, a bruised reed, so that this poor reed is tuned for you. Enter into my life more deeply; my life will be filled with meaning only when you enter into it. Hold me fast as I journey in faith. As I can't let go of the rope while I climb a mountain, so I can't let go of your hand as I climb the everlasting hills. You did not come to explain away suffering or remove it but you came to fill it with your presence, so that the streams of my life become snow-white, when they clash against the rocks. Be with me, therefore, when I suffer. I have heard you whispering in my pleasures but even when you shout in my pains. I have failed to hear you. Sharpen the ears of my heart so that I may hear you saying, "I am with you", and open the eyes of my soul, that I may see the Easter morning that lies just beyond Calvary.

HE IS RISEN

Readings: Acts 10:34, 37-43; Col 3:1-4; Jn 20:1-9

Theme: The resurrection of Christ has created hope for our present and future existence, inspiring us to work fearlessly and courageously to remove all that is bad, sad and mad, from the face of the earth.

Easter is a celebration not of the emptiness of the tomb but of the content of that tomb; its main content is "we too will rise again as Jesus rose". Over the magnificent mausoleum that holds the mortal remains of Queen Victoria and those of her royal husband are inscribed the words:" Here at last I will rest with thee, and with thee in Christ I shall rise again". The root of all good works is the hope of our resurrection. The resurrection of Jesus Christ was not simply for God's glory. It was for the human race in need of it. The Lord is risen for you and me. An older cathedral stood on the site of the present St Paul's in London. It perished in the Great Fire of 1666. After the fire, the brilliant young architect Christopher Wren designed a new cathedral which took 35 years to build. The first stone that Wren picked up from the ruins of the old building bore the inscription "I will rise again". Our Lord has written the promise of our resurrection, not in stones and book alone but in every leaf in springtime. Through baptism we already share in the risen life of Jesus promised by the message of Easter; we die with him and we rise with him.

Resurrection has created hope for our present and future existence. God is present now in all our material creation, which will one day be completely transformed and brought to its fulfilment. Faith in the resurrection has changed the way we live our ordinary life. What will be destroyed is of only passing value and what will be transformed is of surpassing value. This is the result of the resurrection. Every healing hereafter is a partial resurrection and every change is towards greater life: the child leaving the womb, the adolescent entering adult life, the adult moving through the middle age crises and the person leaving this world in death, all move towards fuller life. All negative elements in our life can be dealt with creatively; death has been conquered by life in his resurrection and so we can continue to work with hope against poverty, hunger, sickness, violence and war.

In Christ there is no fear; there is only peace and joy. The world and its fears hold no power over Christ, but even his closest followers failed to enjoy this glorious freedom he offered. Judas feared that he may be in the wrong ball-game, so he betrayed him, only to experience the deeper fear of despair. The disciples feared the loss of status and of lasting commitment to Jesus, so all abandoned him and one denied him. Pilate feared losing power and prestige. The establishment was afraid of being usurped by the newcomer called Jesus. The crowds and the soldiers were afraid of going against public opinion and hence all tried to destroy him. But Jesus feared not even death, since he was concerned with eternal life. His first words after his resurrection were "Fear not".

Belief in the resurrection is not an appendage to the Christian faith; it is the Christian faith. St John Chrysostom said: "We were once living in the shame of sin, but now we live in confidence and justice. We are now not only free but saints, not only saints but just men and women, not only just men and women but sons and daughters, not only sons and daughters but heirs, not only heirs but brothers and sisters of Christ, as co-heirs and members, not only his members but temples, not only temples but instruments of the Holy Spirit". Yes. Easter, like all deeper things begins in mystery but like all hidden things ends in great courage. Let us keep our risen God always alive in our hearts and live a courageous life for him.

2ND SUNDAY OF EASTER

BELIEVING IS NOT SEEING

Readings: Acts 4:32-35; 1 Jn 5:1-6; Jn 20:19-31

Theme: Faith in the risen Lord without seeing him is possible and is powerful; it conquers the world for Christ through communities that love and share.

If God were to tell me, 'I want to deprive you of all your faculties except one; which do you want to keep?' I will tell him, 'Leave me with my eyes'. Our sight is the most perfect and most delightful of all our senses. Therefore the hunger of the eye is not to be despised. It is no wonder that St Thomas was insisting that he must see the risen Christ with his eyes in order to believe. But strangely enough, Jesus chided him for his insistence and declared, "Blessed are they who have not seen and have believed" (Jn 20:29). To think of it, many of us are not different from St Thomas. We may not be insisting that we should see God with our eyes; but we often put similar conditions for belief.

Frankly, is it possible to believe in the risen Jesus without seeing him? Why not? Suppose I am blindfolded and a water bucket is placed in front of me. Keeping my eyes closed, I can still know whether the bucket is empty or full. One way is through experiencing: to reach out into the bucket and feel or experience if there is water in it. A second way is through reasoning: to drop an object like a coin into it. If the object hits the bottom of the bucket with a loud sound, you know the bucket is empty. A third way is through trusting others: to ask someone you trust and if he says there is water, you believe it. Likewise, we can believe that Jesus is alive either by spiritually experiencing him in our hearts or we can believe in Jesus through reasoning. One way of reasoning is as follows: after the death of Jesus his disciples were completely distraught. But on Easter Sunday something changed them in an amazing way. Suddenly they exploded with joy and happiness: unless they had seen the risen Christ, such a transformation was not possible. Or we can believe in the risen Lord by trusting the testimony of the Scripture: therefore believing without seeing is possible.

Such a faith in the risen Lord has mighty power, precisely because it comes without seeing him. It has power even to conquer the world in the spiritual sense. Throughout history there have been men who have wanted to conquer the world. Alexander the great was consumed with lust for power. Napoleon thought his goal could be achieved by military might. For the same reason, Hitler was responsible for more bloodshed than anyone on earth. But these men did not know what true conquest is. True conquest is to conquer one's own ego because every human being is one's own enemy, as it were one's own executioner and when nature decides to destroy us in the struggle for life, it first cultivates the ego in us. What use it for our world to have narrowed down to a neighbourhood, before it has broadened to brotherhood? Therefore when we curb our own selfishness and begin to love our fellow human beings as the extension of ourselves, then only are we conquering the world. This conquest is made possible by faith in Christ, because it is through faith we all become children of God and are able to love one another as brothers and sisters. "Everyone begotten of God conquers the world and the power that has conquered the world is this faith of ours" (1 Jn 5:4). Hence, to us believers, our faith is like the hair of Samson in virtue of which we can have great strength, and it is our 'Elijah's chariot' by means of which we can mount above the earth to conquer it.

But in order to conquer the world for Christ, it is not enough for us believers to proclaim our faith in the risen Lord through words alone. All words are just pegs to hang ideas on. For one thing, no one can live by words alone, though at times, some have to eat their own words! We need to put our words into action. If it is true that by our faith we have become God's children, then our Christian communities have to be dedicated to the common good of all God's children, as the early Christian communities were. "The whole group of believers was united, heart and soul. Everything they owned was held in common." (Acts 4:32) It was not communism, for it was voluntary sharing; It did not involve all private property but only as much as was needed and it was not a membership requirement in order to be part of the Church. Because of the unity brought about by the Holy Spirit, the believers were able to give and share freely and so eliminate the poverty that was among them. A similar loving concern for those who are needy in our communities will speak to the world volumes about the presence of the risen Christ in the world. The world would then believe him without seeing him.

3RD SUNDAY OF EASTER

STEP BY STEP

Readings: Acts 3:13-15, 17-19; 1 Jn 2:1-5; Lk 24:35-48

Theme: If we can face truth about ourselves and confront it, we will be converted. If we are converted, we are consoled by Christ. If we are consoled, we commit ourselves to Christ.

Confrontation with truth is wiser than concealing it. Pushing any truth out very far, you are only met by a counter truth. Hence St Peter confronted his audience with the truth about the choice they had made in the past: "They dismissed the Holy One and preferred the release of a murderer" (Acts 3:14). Can we face the truth about the bad choices we have made in the past? Perhaps we chose excessive drinking instead of moderation, or took unfair advantage of others instead of sharing with them the excess wealth we have, or perhaps we chose to find our human fulfilment in accumulating physical comforts instead of seeking the peace that comes from experiencing Jesus personally. St John confronts his readers about their knowledge of Jesus, insisting that "the way we can be sure of our knowledge of Jesus is to keep his commandments" (1 Jn 2:3). Can we face the truth about our own knowledge of Christ? Is our knowledge recognisable in our action? We are going to Mass once a week, yes; but do we care about his commandments the rest of the week? We may not be killing our neighbours, but perhaps our motives do not reflect honesty and integrity while dealing with others. Therefore we are called to conversion.

Conversion is the natural result of confronting the truth about ourselves. Conversion of heart can indeed be difficult because there is nothing harder to see than the naked truth; but remember, there is nothing safer than following the truth. The three readings today call for conversion. St Peter pleads: "Reform your lives, turn to God" (Acts 3:19). Jesus commands that "in his name penance for the remission of sins is to be preached" (Lk 24:47). St John, while urging us to convert from sins, encourages us to know that "we have Jesus Christ who is an offering for our sins" (1 Jn 2:2). Conversion is of absolute importance. It is the hinge of the Gospel. All of us need to change for we are all wounded within: bitter from weariness and sick within.

Hence if we are not what we ought to be, if we are not what we want to be and if we are not what we shall be, let us convert, so that we become something very different, at least from what we used to be.

Consolation is the reward of conversion. A converted person is like the finger that touches the strings of a harp which can be compared to our Saviour, bringing forth the melody of peace. Conversion places us in Christ who is the Prince of Peace. We are like the Pilgrim in John Bunyan's *Pilgrim's Progress*: they laid the Pilgrim in a large upper chamber, facing the rising sun. The name of the chamber was Peace. "Peace be with you" (Lk 24:36) was the greeting of the risen Lord to the apostles, whose level of anguish had reached its high-water mark. If only we could make a definite break from earth's trash to heaven's treasures, we too could experience the peace of Christ shooting through the guilt, resentment, anger, anxieties, isolation and fears that reside deep in our hearts, crying out for Christ's risen peace. As a pearl is found beneath the flowing tide, so we can experience his peace even under the strain and stress of life. When our hearts are filled with the peace of Christ, a peace which is joy and power, we can't help sharing it also with others. We will invariably become committed messengers of the risen peace.

Commitment to share the peace of Christ is a mission entrusted to us by the Lord. The most powerful force in the world is the Christian. We touch others with the peace of Christ by the way we live, by what we say, by how we conduct our business, by how we work, by how we relate to others and by how we stand for justice and love. This is Christian witness in the true sense and its influence on others is enormous. *Reader's Digest* once quoted Albert Schweitzer, commenting on how he gave up a career as a concert pianist in Europe and became a medical doctor to the poor. He said: "As I look back upon my youth I realise how important to me were the help, understanding and courage... so many people gave me. These men and women entered into my life and became powers within me. But they never knew it. Nor did I perceive their help at the time". Yes. The most powerful influence in the name of Christ often takes place without people involved being aware of it.

THE GOOD SHEPHERD

Readings: Acts 4:8-12; 1 Jn 3:1-2; Jn 10:11-18

Theme: Jesus, our Good Shepherd who died for us, continues to care and die for us even today and calls us to become in our turn caring shepherds to one another.

In his book on the Holy Land, M. Thompson relates this tragic story. One day a young shepherd was tending his flock in the vicinity of Mt Tabor. Suddenly three Bedouin rustlers appeared. The young man knew what he was up against, but he did not flee. He stood his ground and fought to keep his flock from falling into the hands of the outlaws. The fight ended with the young shepherd laying down his life for his sheep. "I am the Good Shepherd", declares Jesus, "who lays down his life for the sheep" (Jn 10:11). We are the sheep. To take away our sins, he died on the cross. He did so out of sheer love for us. There was no selfish motive in his death. He was not like a hired shepherd who tends the sheep for money. Jesus was not merely doing his job. He was committed to love us. False teachers and false prophets do not have this commitment. Our Good Shepherd laid down his life for us, of his own free will. When Christ came down from the cross, they borrowed a bed on which to lay his head. They borrowed an ass in the mountain pass for him to ride to town. But the crown he wore and the cross he bore were his own.

Our Good Shepherd continues to care for us even after he has gone away from our physical sight. He gives himself in the sacraments, especially in the Eucharist. As Pope St Gregory said: The Lord laid down his life for his sheep that he might convert his Body and Blood in our sacraments and satisfy the sheep whom he had redeemed with the nourishment of his own flesh. Our Good Shepherd still heals the sick, a ministry which he had already begun with his apostles. It was in the Lord's name that St Peter cured a crippled man. "In the power of the name of Jesus, that cripple stood perfectly sound" (Acts 4:10). The Lord Jesus literally lays down his life for his sheep even today through those servants of God such as Archbishop Oscar Romero. The Archbishop was shot dead in San Salvador on March 24,1980 with a single shot to the heart after saying Mass, because he spoke out against tyranny and for freedom, because he demanded human rights for his people under oppression. Yes. The love of our Good Shepherd for us is the same yesterday, today and tomorrow.

Is our own love for our fellow human beings as determined as Christ's love for us? Can we say that we are truly followers of our Shepherd in our care, concern and selfless service to others? I am afraid that not all can say a resounding 'Yes'. A layman said to a priest after Sunday service, "You preachers talk a lot about giving but when you get right down to it, it all comes to basin theology". The clergyman asked, "Basin theology? What is that?" The layman replied: "Remember what Pilate did when he had the chance to acquit Jesus? He called for a basin and washed his hands of the whole thing. But Jesus, the night before his death, called for a basin and proceeded to wash the feet of his disciples. It all comes down to basin theology. Which one will you use?" Our Good Shepherd expects all of us both clergy and laity to be good shepherds to one another according to each one's vocation in life. Husbands and wives by doing more than enough for each other, parents by making extra sacrifices for the good of their children, teachers by spending extra hours to instruct weak students, doctors and nurses taking up extra work to show they care for their patients, and parishioners by generously supporting their parish community. In a word, all of us are called to be deeply concerned about each other and committed to each other's welfare.

Perhaps, we need some strong motives for selfless service to others. Indeed, a good motive clothes itself with sudden power so that even a pebble will bud, shoot out winged feet and serve us for a horse. The first strong motive is the example of our Good Shepherd himself. He did not ask, "How much?" – he gave himself, his all. He did not ask, "How far to go?" – he went all the way. If you need another very strong motive, here is one: "See what love the Father has bestowed on us in letting us to be called children of God" (1 Jn 3:1). If there is one subject more than any other on which we would like to write, it is the love of God, but if there is one which quite baffles me and makes me feel ashamed of my feeble words, it is this subject. The love of God is the most amazing thing under heaven if not in heaven, because in his love God has not only created us in his very image but regenerated us as his children. The result is that even if all people on earth were to hate you, this honey of God's love would turn their gall into sweetness. How come, then, can't we love God as our Father and all men and women as our brothers and sisters!

WE ARE THE TERMINALS

Readings: Acts 9:26-31; 1 Jn 3:18-24; Jn 15:1-8

Theme: Those who are united to Christ both in good times and bad, especially by being a part of a loving and caring Christian community, find true joy and bear much fruit.

A poor German schoolmaster who lived in a humble house in a small village, carved over his doorway this proud inscription: "Dante, Moliere, and Goethe live here!" That schoolmaster had learned that the secret of a rich life lies in one's spiritual companionship. Jesus wants his followers to be united with him like the branches to a tree and to enjoy continually his spiritual company. "I am the vine, you are the branches" (Jn 15:5), he says. In so far as we abide in him and he in us, we will bear much fruit, because he is the source of life and in so far as we do not, we will be absolutely ineffective, because without him we can do nothing. We are called to be united to Christ to the extent that each of us must be able to say with St Paul, "I live; yet not I, but Christ lives in me". Unfortunately, we seem to have frozen these words of the Apostle into some kind of theology or to have stiffened them into a dogma until the life has gone out of them. If a schoolmaster can say that Dante and Moliere and Goethe live with him, why can't Christians say that Christ lives in us and we in Christ?

The conditions to live united to Christ are clear. We live in him, by keeping God's word continually in our mind and making it the guide of our actions; by maintaining a prayer life; by receiving the sacraments that draw out his grace; by avoiding all sins and yielding to the direction of the Holy Spirit. Above all, we abide in Christ by being united with one another as a community of love. There can be no such thing as a lonely Christian in a loving community. Our love for one another has to be real. In a real community the good of one will be the good of all and the pain of one will be the pain of all. "Little children, let us love in deed and in truth and not merely talk about it" (1 Jn 3:18). Love that is only talk has no value. We are to be grapes not simply to hang around the vine but fruits from which people can eat and drink. We are called to be the fruit and drink especially of the lonely, the ill, the poor and the dispossessed in our neighbourhood and communities. We are meant to be sources of nourishment that revive the spirits, feed the hopes and enliven the bodies of others.

What is required of us is not just seeking Christ, but abiding in him. In moments of great financial need we may cry out to Jesus to deliver us; in times of great illness we may beg him for a cure. When one of our children is about to fail in an important endeavour we plead with him to save him; that is all right. But we have to be with Christ also at other times. If we get angry with God when a trusted friend betrays a confidence, if we are incensed with him when a dishonest person succeeds where we have failed, if we are bitter with God when a loved one dies, that means we are not abiding in Christ. The pains of life are not signs of being cut away from Christ; on the contrary they are indications of the opposite. Because we are united to Christ like branches, God will prune us to promote growth of the branches. He will discipline us to strengthen our character and faith. Hence pains of life need not frighten us away from Christ.

If we remain in Christ both in good times and bad, we will enjoy much peace and consolation, as the members of the early Church did: "The Church was at peace and enjoyed the increased consolation of the Holy Spirit" (Acts 9:31). If we remain in Christ, we will find joy in him, not the superficial joy of prosperity suggested by slick television commercials, but a joy that comes from the fulfilment of one's potential, a joy that will produce much fruits such as curbing violence and bringing back peace in our streets and removing injustices and establishing equality and a joy that is a power with which we can do all things good for God and the world.

Probably, most of us have at one time or other walked into a bank or an airline office to be told by the staff: 'Sorry, you will have to wait, the computer system is down'. We can see that the computer terminals are there, some switched on. The screens are lit up; they may even perform some limited functions. However, we know they are quite helpless, because they are not connected to the 'mainframe'. Like the computer terminals, we have to be plugged in to Jesus, the mainframe, if we want to be of any use.

THE LOVE STORY

Readings: Acts 10:25-26, 34-35, 4-48; 1 Jn 4:7-10; Jn 15:9-17

Theme: God has loved us in Jesus by giving himself unto death and we are called to fan the Spirit of love poured into us, so that we love others as God has loved us.

Boy meets girl. They fall in love and marry. That was the *Love Story*, a film I saw in 1975; a moving tale of a millionaire's son who gives up his fortune to marry a poor, ostracised girl. We all enjoy a love story, for in each of us there is a spark of love. But sadly enough, love is often only a dream; some dream in technicolor, others add sound effects. Jesus said, "No one can have greater love than to lay down his life for his friends" (Jn 15:13). We celebrate an example of such heroic love in England on D-Day, since on this day we actually honour heroic love. It was on 6 June 1944, a group of paratroopers called 'The Screaming Eagles", out of love for humanity and in defence of freedom, spearheaded the invasion of Normandy, knowing full well that many of them would die, and in fact one company jumped with 208 enlisted men and 11 officers but only 69 enlisted men and four officers came back. Yes: love is real, not just a fantasy and to love even heroically is possible and loving is the soul of life. Without love in life, what would happen to our world?" Hence Jesus commands: "Love one another" (Jn 15:12). His commandment is a prescription, the type of prescription we find in a cooking book which says, "You cannot cook Chicken Birani without rice". Rice is a prescription and a condition. Likewise, Jesus says that without love, the live ingredient, human life is hell.

We are called by Jesus to love others as God loves us. God's love which is true love is different from sexual love, for sex is occasional union but true love is constant. It is different from free love, for true love is neither free nor carefree but binding and demanding. It is different from love at first sight, which usually ends with divorce at first slight. It is different from family love, for a relative tends to help primarily or only a blood relative. It is different from love between friends, for you can be kissed by a fool and fooled by a kiss. God's love is different because it is giving, and giving unto death. Can such a love be real or is it like a ghost which everyone talks about but nobody has seen? Is it like a teddy bear that has no skin on its face? No. God's love is real and was made flesh and blood in Jesus. "God's love was revealed in our midst when he sent his only Son to the world that we might have life through Him" (1 Jn 4:9).

We are urged to show to one another the kind of God's love Jesus revealed, as we live as members of a Christian community. We are all necessarily born into a community through baptism, as the first gentiles were admitted to the community of the faithful by St Peter (Acts 10:47). Since love is the fairest flower that blooms in the garden of God, it is obvious that love must be the soul of every Christian community. But what is obvious is often overlooked. A parish priest wrote to all his parishioners explaining that the annual cost of heating the church had risen to five thousand pounds. To overcome the problem of costs, the building was to be weather proofed and he suggested that people dress more warmly. "But", he continued, "the best way the parishioners can help is to bring a friend to church with them; for body heat is still one freely available natural energy resource". The priest's suggestion was an obvious one for, on average, the heat from three people is equivalent to a 1 kilowatt electric fire. It is often easy, however, to overlook the obvious. Are were overlooking the obvious characteristic of our parish community which is 'love'?

To love one another is not a platitude but a prescription, not a counsel but a command. Jesus uses the word 'love' eight times in sixteen lines of his speech. Laying down of one's life will often mean a lot of little laying downs of our selfishness for the good of others. But it is also possible to lay down even one's life for others. Has not Christ's command inspired martyrs and soldiers and missionaries in every century since the time of Christ? When we are selfish and refuse to love, we build a wall around ourselves and condemn ourselves to a winter of loneliness and bitterness. But when we love and care, the wall falls down and we experience a springtime of joy and peace. Let us allow the Holy Spirit which has been "poured" into us (Acts 10:45) to fan the flame of love into a furnace.

ASCENSION

A COSMIC TRICK?

Readings: Acts 1:1-11; Eph 1:17-23; Mk 16:15-20

Theme: The feast of the Ascension springs hope of our immortal destiny, while urging us to continue the work of Christ on earth, so that this earthly life may give all a foretaste of our destiny.

Ascension is a feast and hence a celebration. But we can have trouble celebrating it if we get tangled up in the mechanics of the event. If Jesus was "lifted up", how? Was it a matter of disappearing feet into a cloud? If a "cloud" took him from their sight, how? Where exactly was he taken to and from whence the cloud come? These mechanical 'how's have a way of blinding us to God's truth. Nicodemus who came at night to meet Jesus is a case in point. His was a severe case of the 'how's. How can a human being enter the womb again? How can a senior citizen be born again? Such were his questions. If we are busy asking similar questions about the ascension, it is going to be only a fantastic feat or a cosmic trick and not a feast and a celebration. If we are only concerned with the mechanics of the ascension, we will turn it into a biblical sideshow complete with wires and mirrors. We won't be able to figure it out. In fact we are not supposed to figure it out. Instead we are called today to grasp at the significance of the ascension.

Ascension is about our destiny. It says that we are destined to a life beyond the one which we now enjoy. We are destined to be with God in a union which cannot be destroyed by death. Death in this life is frightful. Over the past hundred years, the average life expectancy has been pushed forward from the late thirties to the seventies and eighties. An occasional science fiction novel will treat of some elixir of immortality, but this is not true life. Real immortality is the journey's end of a pilgrimage with Christ, through a death and a resurrection to an ascended life, like his. Thus Jesus' ascension contains a message of hope for the human race, and St Paul prays: "May God enlighten the eyes of your mind so that you can see the great hope to which he has called you" (Eph 1:18). Therefore we are meant to be optimistic people, full of hope. We are not to place our hope in an impossible dream, like a little child hoping that Christmas day will never end. Rather our hope is like the expectation of a person awake at night, looking forward to the dawn. It is the kind of hope that springs eternal in the human breast. But this does not mean that we Christians have no interest in life here and now. On the contrary, our hope impels us to make our earthly life as a kind of foretaste of the immortal life.

Ascension is about our present world. It calls us Christians to continue the mission of Christ on earth. Christ's mission was not just to give us hope for the future, but to change the quality of life here and now, so that we can begin to experience already now the riches of the eternal life to come. Jesus entrusted this mission to his disciples when he said, "Go into the whole world and proclaim the Good News to all creation" (Mk 16:15). It is this mission that the angels urged the disciples to undertake, instead of "standing there looking up at the skies" (Acts 1:10). One of the tallest buildings in Ireland is Cork Country Hall. To emphasise its height, there are statues of two men gazing up at the building. The apostles must have been like these statues staring up into the sky. Perhaps to many of us our religion is just staring into the sky! If it is so, we have failed to see a real connection between it and our everyday lives. Christianity is very much about the here and now. It is not about standing around waiting for something to happen; it is about making that something happen. We make it happen by witnessing to the Good News of Jesus Christ through word and deed.

Ascension is about endings and beginnings. On the day of his ascension, Christ's personal ministry on earth ended, but the operation of the Holy Spirit in his followers to continue his ministry began. The time for preparing his apostles for their mission to build his Church was over, but the time for their participation in the expansion of that Church began. It has to be so for us also. Once the liturgical celebration of the feast of the ascension is over, our work of witnessing to whatever we believe in Christ has to begin. We come to church to praise God, to hear his word and to eat his bread. But we don't stand here all day looking up to heaven. We leave this place to witness to Christ in the world. Christ has no one else except us, to continue his mission. As Teresa of Avila would put it: "Christ has no body now on earth but yours, no hands but yours, no feet but yours; yours are the eyes through which he is to look out to the world with compassion; yours are the feet with which he is to go about doing good, and yours are the hands with which he is to bless us now".

7TH SUNDAY OF EASTER

ALWAYS, ONE MORE!

Readings: Acts 1:15-17, 20-26; 1 Jn 4:11-16; Jn 17:11-19

Theme: There is no better way to love the world as God has loved us than to give persistent witness to the resurrection of Christ through our word and deed.

A cross-country bus made a scheduled stop at a depot that was located near four different restaurants. The driver announced, "Folks, we'll be here for thirty minutes. The bus line has a strict policy never to recommend an eating place by name, so I am not permitted to tell you which restaurant of the four here is the best. However, I can say this: while we are here, if any of you should need me for any reason, I'll be at Tony's Diner directly across the street"! Our actions, more than anything else, tell people what our true beliefs are. Therefore, the most efficacious kind of witness to our Christian beliefs is our actions according to those beliefs. If, for example, we want others to appreciate prayer, there is no better way than to become more prayerful ourselves. If we want to lead others to greater involvement in the Mass, we can do no better than to become more involved ourselves. Likewise, if we want others to believe in the resurrection of Jesus, we can do no better than to witness to his resurrection ourselves. The early Church chose Matthias to replace Judas, because he was a "witness to the resurrection" (Acts 1:21). But what is that makes you and me witnesses to Jesus' resurrection?

The resurrection of Jesus represents victory over death, not only for himself but also for us. Hence, we witness to his resurrection, if we are truly joyful people, secure in the hope that we too will rise with Jesus. The resurrection is God's vindication of Jesus, the assurance that whatever Jesus preached and stood for was God's will for the human race. Hence, we witness to his resurrection if we make Christ's teachings and life as our norm of behaviour. The resurrection is the confirmation of the value of human life, because in our resurrection that which is human now will be glorified. Hence, we witness to his resurrection, if we respect and honour other human beings, indeed all creation. The resurrection represents a new kind of existence, a new life with God, a spiritual dimension to our human life. Hence, we witness to his resurrection if we have a spiritual attitude to our life on earth, without succumbing to materialism.

Such a Christian witness is of paramount importance in our world today. Like the infant Church as portrayed in the first reading, the Church has been always needing one more such witness. Christ's prayer at the Last Supper was an earnest plea made to his disciples to bear witness to him. "Father, consecrate them by means of truth. As you have sent me, so I have sent them into the world" (Jn 17:17-18) was his prayer. Yes. We were consecrated, set apart and commissioned at our baptism and confirmation to bear witness to him and to his word. It is for this reason that we are instructed every Sunday by God's word and strengthened by the Eucharist. The world into which we are sent to bear witness may indeed frighten us with all its problems: poverty and oppression, injustice and violence, abortions and addictions. Yet, we are not to run away, but confront the problems and eliminate them. Our task is to influence the world and renew it by means of the Good News. We are not believers in Christ's resurrection just for our own sanctification; we are believers for the transformation of the world as well, because of the love we have for the world.

We love the world because God loves us. And how does God love us? A holy man was engaged in his morning meditation under a tree whose roots stretched out over the river bank. During his meditation he noticed that the river was rising and a scorpion caught in the roots was about to drown. He crawled out on the roots and reached down to free the scorpion but every time he did so, the scorpion struck back at him. An observer came along and said to the holy man, 'Don't you know that's a scorpion and it is the nature of the scorpion to want to sting?' To which the holy man replied: 'That may well be, but it is my nature to save; must I change my nature?' This holy man represents God. It is God's nature to love and save. How often we have hurt him with our unfaithfulness and how far we have run away from his embrace! But still he has been pursuing us with his love. "If God has loved us so, we must have the same love for one another" (1 Jn 4:11) The world may turn a deaf ear to our Good News; it may resist our every attempt to transform it; it may even strike back at us like a scorpion when we try to redeem it. But that is no reason why we should give up on the world if we love the world as God has loved us.

PENTECOST SUNDAY

REJOICE!

Readings: Acts 2:1-11; 1 Cor 12:3-7, 12-13; Jn 20:19-23

Theme: The Holy Spirit which in-dwells in every Christian is a healing and explosive, consuming and unifying, cleansing and life-giving, consoling and comforting power.

An elderly gentleman passed his granddaughter's room one night and overheard her repeating the alphabet in an oddly reverent way. "What on earth are you up to?" he asked. "I am saying my prayers", explained the little girl. "But I can't think of exactly the right words tonight, so I'm just saying all the letters. God will put them together for me, because he knows what I am thinking". Christians who have similar childlike faith rejoice that though their lives may be in shambles, God will put them together. The God in whom they believe is not up in the sky but dwells within them as the Holy Spirit. They know that, as the Holy Spirit came on the nascent Church at Pentecost, so he came on them also, though in a less spectacular way, at their baptism and confirmation "to lead them to complete truth" (Jn 14:26). True believers are deeply aware of their utter dependence on the Spirit for "no one can say 'Jesus is Lord' except in the Holy Spirit" (1 Cor 12:3), nor can they even pray without him.

We rejoice today, because the feast of Pentecost reminds us of the gentle and explosive power of the Holy Spirit when it blows like wind. At times it blows gently. When fear rises in us while sick and old because we are not sure whether anybody will care for us in time to come, when hopelessness grows in many of us who are young because we are afraid whether we will find any job, when anger is deep in many of the depraved and poor among us because we see the rich growing richer, when apathy leads some of us to dependence on alcohol and drugs as the easiest way to cope, the Spirit can bring calm and quiet to our troubled hearts. But the Spirit of God does not blow always gently. In fact, at Pentecost, he "came from heaven like the rush of a mighty wind" (Acts 2:2) Since then, the same mighty Spirit has been known to blow down great but corrupt institutions or to burn to ashes gigantic but unjust social systems.

We rejoice today because Pentecost reminds us of the consuming and unifying power of the Spirit when he burns as fire. At Pentecost, he came "as tongues of fire" (Acts 2:3) and he consumed the hearts of the disciples so powerfully that he drove them out of Jerusalem, scattering them like seeds all over the earth, filling them with words which changed many lives, but which eventually got almost everyone of them killed. The Spirit of God is a unifying fire as well. At Pentecost, those who received the Spirit spoke foreign languages and were understood by all, thus signalling the arrival of the Spirit to unite all people of God, which he continues to do even today through our baptism. As St Paul says, "It was by one Spirit that all of us, whether Jew or Greek, slave or free, were baptised into one body" (1 Cor 12:13). We also rejoice for this world. Because of the presence of the Spirit in the world, the separated members of the human race will one day be restored to unity, like the limbs of a single body, by being joined to Christ, their common head.

We rejoice today because the feast of Pentecost reminds us of the cleansing and life-giving power of the Holy Spirit when he flows like water. Referring to the Spirit, Jesus said," If anyone is thirsty, let him come to me and drink. Whoever believes in me, rivers of living water shall flow from his heart" (Jn 7:37-38). We are washed clean and brought back to life by the water of baptism. It is not the water itself that does them, but the Holy Spirit who is in and with the water, and faith. Water by itself is an ambiguous symbol, bringing to mind both rain and flood, drinking and drowning. It is the Spirit holding the baby in the water that transforms it for him or her, into cleansing and life-giving water. Without the holding, the water would drown us. So, even though our hearts may have become arid, we can still find a river of living water in it, because of the presence of the Spirit in it.

We rejoice today because Pentecost reminds us of the consoling and comforting power of the Spirit whom Jesus called, "the Comforter" (Jn 14:16). As a mother holds the wounded and frightened child, and with her breath inspires trust, rekindles confidence and gives life back again, so the Holy Spirit is with us in times when we are blown down, too weak even to pray. He will hold us and breathe us back to life. Should we wither and fade, he will gather us up in his arms. He is ready to use our limbs, our heart beat, and our breath as rhythms of God's own Spirit to bring comfort. Finally, when the tents which we are in now become burnt to ashes, he will hold us in peace for ever.

Let us not hesitate to seek the aid of the Spirit, whatever may be our standing in life. He is not a tame force carefully bottled in ecclesiastical institutions, available to be served out in rational doses according to the decisions of the hierarchy or the ministry of specially illuminated saints. He is the Lord of the Church, not subject to human control and, like the wind, he blows wherever he chooses. Let us therefore constantly pray to the Spirit, especially today, to come and fill our empty hearts. It is hard for an empty bag to stand upright.

TRINITY SUNDAY

THERE IS A KEY

Readings: Deut 4:32-34, 30-40; Rom 8:14-17; Mt 28:16-20

Theme: The feast of the Holy Trinity is not a celebration of the mystery of the Trinity, nor of the doctrine about the mystery, but a celebration of God's dynamic and intimate friendship with us.

Trying to explain the Trinity is like crossing the ocean on a raft, or like flying to the stars with wings of narrow span. Once St Augustine was walking on the sand thinking about the mystery of the Trinity. There he observed a child carrying water in a pot and pouring it in a nearby pool." What are you doing?" asked the saint. "I want to pour out the whole water of the ocean into my pool", announced the child. Laughing, the saint exclaimed: "You will never succeed in that". Then the child stood up and said, "I do exactly as you do: Do you think, with your small understanding, you will be able to discover the mystery of the Trinity?" No, we can't. We may have grasped the mystery of the atom, but not the mystery of the Trinity.

Therefore, on this Trinity Sunday, we are not so much concerned about the mystery of God being one but three persons, nor about the doctrine of this mystery. Some Christians wrongly assume that Trinity Sunday is the only feast-day which celebrates a doctrine rather than an event. They assume that other festivals celebrate such events as our Lord's birth, the crucifixion, the resurrection, the ascension or the coming of the Holy Spirit, but on this Sunday we celebrate a doctrine.

This assumption is not only untrue but unnecessary; because, why should we celebrate a mere doctrine? After all, many a doctrine is nothing but the skin of truth, set up and stuffed; and it is often an attempt not to tell the truth but to satisfy the questioner. What we are actually celebrating is God's dynamic and intimate friendship with us, through the three persons of the Trinity.

One friend in a life time is much; two friends are many; three are hardly possible. But what is impossible for us is possible for God. In God we have three intimate friends. Intimate friends are faithful to each other. Moses pictures God as an ever faithful friend, listing all the mighty works which he did for his people, asking them finally, "Did anything so great ever happen before? Was it ever heard of?" (Deut 4:32) It is this love and faithfulness of a friend in God the Father that we celebrate today. Friends share things, ideas; they discuss and decide together. Jesus, the second person of the Trinity not only called us his friends but as a true friend has himself shared his very life and teachings with us. These he shared to serve as our model for our lives. He conveyed his earnest wish to share his life, through us, with the rest of the humanity as well, when he asked "Go and make disciples of all nations" (Mt 28:19). It is this sharing and caring of a friend in Jesus, that we celebrate today. Friends may be physically apart, but even in separation they are united with each other in spirit. This is what the Holy Spirit, the third person of the Trinity does in us. Now that the Lord is physically absent from us, we are still united with him through the indwelling Spirit in us. "The Spirit that we have received is a Spirit through which we cry out to God, 'Father'. The Spirit himself gives witness with our spirits that we are the children of God" (Rom 8:15). It is this guidance and support of a friend in the Spirit that we celebrate today.

Therefore, on this Trinity Sunday, we are not so much concerned with the mystery of the Trinity, though mysteries are part of our religion. Rather we are focusing on the qualities of God as our friend: his love and faithfulness, his caring and sharing. If indeed we are created in the image of such a God and baptised into his family, then we must reflect in our lives the same qualities of friendship in our relationship with each other. In fact, we do reflect, in some way, these qualities in the liturgy. Our liturgy may be full of ceremonies but for any friendship to grow, it needs to be surrounded also with ceremonies and not crushed into corners. Think about what happens in liturgy. A group of clergy and laity come moving into the assembly. The people sing and then the choir sings and then the president sings; the president prays, and then all the clergy join in and then all the people join. A lay person reads and then we sing and another lay person reads and then the cantor sings and then the preacher preaches and we listen and respond. Thus, we all are relating and responding back and forth as friends of the same family in the very image of the life of the Trinity. Indeed, our liturgy is a ritual of friendship.

But what we reflect in the liturgy as the very image of the life of the Trinity ought to be seen in our relationship with one another in our daily life. In our families, in marriage, in parenting, in our work and play, the very nature of God as a loving, caring and sharing friend must come through. Our love and care have also to reach out even beyond our families and close groups. When we see human society trying to build peace by preparing for war, when we see our fellow human beings living on the streets and eating out of rubbish bins, when we see pain, illness and sufferings, we need to get into the life of the Trinity, that life of friendship of which we have a foretaste as we gather here for the liturgy. That is the way we can be the manifestation and active agents of the Holy Trinity here and now. Trinity may be a riddle wrapped in a mystery, but there is a key and that is friendship, which cannot only unravel the mystery a little, but also help to create a friendly world.

CORPUS CHRISTI

HUNGER FOR BREAD

Readings: Ex 24:3-8; Heb 9:11-15; Mk 14:12-16, 22-26

Theme: Hungering for the bread of life and feeding the hungry are necessary prerequisites for participation in the Eucharist.

The basic need of the human heart never changes and the answer to that need never changes either. The need is God and the answer is Jesus Christ, God made flesh. We are all human machines, so to speak, designed by God to run on himself and hence it is Christ and nothing else who can fuel our spirits. That is why Christ has given his body and blood in the Eucharist as our food, a gift which God has freely bestowed on a hungry people who look longingly for someone to feed their hearts. But an individual must be conscious of his hunger for God in order to appreciate the Eucharist. Oftentimes our hearts become immune to this basic hunger, for we give up our hearts rather too fully to the pleasures found in material things. There is so much in the world that ruffles our spirits, so much that saddens and depresses us and so much that seeks to profane our spirits. We need to resist this onslaught of the world on us and seek the Lord our God in prayer and in the Eucharist. We are at our greatest when, upon our knees, we come to commune with God in prayer, and we are at our highest when, upon our feet, we come to receive the Eucharist.

However, the Eucharist is not just food for our hungry spirit; it is also a sign of the millions of people in the world who are hungry for material food and hence is a constant reminder that those who come to the Eucharist to be fed spiritually by God are bound to do their utmost to feed the hungry stomachs of the poor in the world. Professor Michael Todaro, who writes one of the widely read texts in Economic Development, estimates that at least 1,375 billion people live in absolute poverty, lacking even the minimum food, clothing and shelter required for survival. More than 750 millions of these desperately poor folks are malnourished. According to the 1988 World Bank Report, the number of people with inadequate diets in developing countries, excluding China, increased from 650 million to 730 million between 1970 and 1980. Since then, tragically, matters have gone from bad to worse.

When so many are in need of food for survival, how is it possible, one wonders, for many Christians in the developed countries, to eat more than they can lift. So many restaurants in the West are so crowded that nobody goes there anymore. Many seem to live to eat rather than to eat to live. Many countries go on piling up armaments; if asked why, they might say that they want to fight for the freedom of the oppressed in the world. But does not every gun that is made, every warship launched, every rocket fired a theft from those who hunger and are not fed (though, of course, we recognise the terrible contribution made to these problems by corrupt governments in the developing world)? Some satisfy themselves just by preaching on charity to the poor. But the fact is that a good meal makes a person feel more charitable towards the world than any sermon. A hungry stomach has no ears. How can you talk religion to an individual with bodily hunger in their eyes? A hungry person is more interested in three sandwiches than three persons of the Holy Trinity.

That is why, Jesus himself, before preaching about eating his body and blood, fed the people. The scene of taking bread, giving thanks, breaking and giving at thc Last Supper (Mk 14:22), already had occurred at the multiplication of loaves (Mk 8:6). There, they all ate satisfactorily with twelve baskets of bread left over. In other words, both the Eucharist and the multiplication were meant to be special signs by which the Lord wanted us, in our turn, to share and feed the hungry. The body of Christ which is broken and shared among us, the blood of Christ poured out for all, is what we are called to be for one another.

We are called to feed the hungry not just out of pity. If all alms were only from pity, said Nietzsche, all beggars would have starved long ago. We Christians are expected to feed the hungry in response to the covenant we have entered into with God and our neighbours through baptism. According to the covenant God made with his chosen people through Moses, sealing it with blood (Ex 24:6), God was faithful to his promise and so, as the Scripture says, he fed his people with the finest wheat and honey; their hunger was satisfied. Christ too, as the high priest, offered the perfect sacrifice by shedding his own blood on behalf of all people (Heb 9:12), thus fulfilling the promise of God's previous relationship with Israel. It is this fidelity and love of the Lord that must urge all those who are baptised to be faithful and loving in their turn to God and to the needy among them. If we believe that by receiving the body and blood of Christ, we are renewing our covenant with God and with one another, then we must be actively concerned about the hungry in the world who are our brothers and sisters in Christ.

There are many mothers who after the pains of childbirth give their children to strangers to nurse. But Christ could not endure that his children should be fed by others. So he nourishes us himself with his own body and blood. If you really believe this, then, when you place a Eucharistic spark in your soul, you have implanted therein a divine seed of love. Surely such a stroke of love should be enough to waken anyone from the slumber of indifference towards those of God's children who have no food even to survive.

IN THE CAUSE OF JUSTICE

Readings: Is 42:1-4, 6-7; Acts 10:34-38; Mk 1:7-11

Theme: As Jesus at his baptism inaugurated his mission of bringing justice to all, for each has a human dignity as the child of God, so we, at our baptism committed ourselves to the same mission in the world.

Some years ago a Brahmin believer in the Lord Jesus Christ was baptised in the Meeting-room, Broadway, Madras. He came to the ceremony wearing as all Brahmins do the 'Yagnopavita', or sacred thread, dangling round his neck. Immediately after his baptism, as he came out of the water, he snapped the thread and threw it into the water in which he had been immersed, thereby signifying that the old life as a Brahmin had come to an end and that he would henceforth live in the newness of Christ's life. We too were baptised, but perhaps much of its significance has escaped us.

Yet this is the day we too began a new life in Christ and the nature of that new life was exemplified by what happened to Christ at his baptism. At his baptism Jesus was called God's beloved son; so too we at our baptism became children of God so that we can relate to each other as brothers and sisters. On the day of our baptism the spirit of God rested on us, as it did on Christ. There was something else that happened at Christ's baptism. That was his identification with sinners. Jesus, though sinless, allowed himself to be baptised by St John (Mk 1:9) like all other sinners, to show that all persons including the poorest of the poor and the most sinful have their basic human dignity as the children of God. Thus, at his baptism, Jesus inaugurated his mission entrusted to him by his Father, to bring back the human dignity to all the little ones who suffer, deprived of their dignity in various ways. His mission was therefore "to open the eyes of the blind, to free those in prison, and to bring out all those who languish in darkness and depression" (Is 42:7). When "the Holy Spirit rested on him in the form of a dove" (Mk 1:10) God stamped his approval for Christ to begin his saving mission, particularly, to "bring forth justice to the nations" (Is 42:1). Like Christ did that day in the Jordan, on the day of our own baptism (or on the day that we finally accepted the baptism we received as infants) we committed ourselves to carry on the mission of Christ to serve the cause of justice.

Therefore, after the example of Christ and by virtue of our own baptism, we have been called to serve the cause of justice. The cause of justice that calls us to serve leaves us in no doubt as to where and how it needs to be served today. The cause of justice calls us to free ourselves from the false values of our society so that we can see those of other cultures and races as people like us and as God's children. The cause of justice calls us to mourn the sins that enslave us, the sin of unemployment and hunger in the midst of plenty and the sin of exploitation of the weak by the strong. The cause of justice calls us to offer our compassion for those who are depressed and lonely, for those who live under stress and fear of harassment because they belong to a particular ethnic group. The cause of justice calls us to work for healing between those who are burning with hatred, to build the Kingdom of love where none shall despise another, where none shall discriminate against another, where all shall be caring, loving children of a compassionate and all-embracing God.

Obviously, to work for the cause of justice will demand from us certain personal sacrifices because everyone's freedom necessarily costs everybody. But we will not feel our sacrifices to be burdensome, if we recognise the truth, as St Peter did, about the dignity of every human being: "The truth that I have come to realise", wrote St Peter, "is that God does not have favourites, but that anybody of any nationality who fears God and does what is right is acceptable to him" (Acts 10:34-35). Being acceptable to God is one's most basic human dignity. It is this basic dignity of every individual that Pope John Paul II has been stressing in whatever he writes. Whether he writes on human rights or the rights of workers, on the distribution of goods or work in the world, on evangelisation or mission, on inter-faith dialogue or ecumenism, on the Gospel of life or civilisation of love. It goes without saying that when we accept each other as what he or she is before God, we will respect and love one another, work for each other's human right and be willing to sacrifice anything for the cause of justice.

2ND SUNDAY OF THE YEAR

OUR COMFORTABLE PATTERNS

Readings: 1 Sam 3:3-10, 19; 1 Cor 6:13-15, 17-20; Jn 1:35-42

Theme: We are called to change from our comfortable patters of conduct, thinking or religious practice which we have set for ourselves, so that our work for a better world may succeed.

There was a missionary in Africa who was intrigued by the behaviour of a Bedouin. He often used to lie flat on the land in the desert. One day the missionary asked him why he did that. The Bedouin stood up and said: "Friend, I listen to the voice of the desert which cries: 'I like to become a garden'". As in the desert so in every human heart, there is a burning desire to be changed into something better. God works on this basic desire of the human heart and calls each of us to change from the comfortable pattern we have set for ourselves and become a part of the new world order. Samuel was living a sedate life serving the Lord's sanctuary at Shiloh, and God's word came to him calling him to become a prophet (1 Sam 3:4). St Paul warns the Corinthians to stop abusing their body and respect it, because it is for the Lord (1 Cor 6:13). St Andrew and his companion had probably become comfortable in their relationship with St John. Now that the One whom St John had been announcing was actually on the scene, their comfortable patterns had to change and they were urged by St John to go and join Jesus and begin again (Jn 1:35). We all work for a better world, for better relationships, for a more just society; but to achieve these, we too have to change ourselves from our comfortable old 'grooves'.

Our comfortable pattern which needs change may centre around our body. If our body and sexual powers are used solely for selfish gratification, enslaving it to a set of non-Christian values, our pattern must change. "Your body is the temple of the Holy Spirit. That is why, you should use it for the glory of God" (1 Cor 6:19). Perhaps some of us are possessed by possessions and accumulate luxuries, when millions in the world are starving. Most of the luxuries are not only not indispensable but positive hindrances to the elevation of spirit. It is when there is plenty of wine that sorrow and worry take wings.

Our comfortable pattern may revolve around our mind. Many of us

Christians are not free because we have passively submitted our minds to the opinions of the crowd so that, for self protection, we hide in the crowd, even if it is a lynch mob. Some people have got a negative mind-set which looks for the worst in almost every situation. They are perpetually critical and always negative. Such persons have to free themselves from this negative trap and move into positive thinking. If we are upset, our conditioned mind nearly always is the cause, except in the case of physical pain. That is why something that upsets you may not upset another person. A diamond looks precious to us but is regarded as valueless by some African tribes. We recoil at dirt, while children enjoy playing with it. It all depends on our mind-set.

Our comfortable pattern which needs a break may even concern our religious practice. Samuel was no wicked adult. He was a minister in the holy place attending the lamp of God. "He was lying in the sanctuary of the Lord where the ark of God was" (1 Sam. 3:3) when God called him to be instrumental in realising his plans which were bigger than the temple and rituals. Some of us feel so comfortable with our routine religious practices, that we fail to achieve a change of heart through them. A saint said to a group of disciples whose hearts were set on a pilgrimage, "Take a bitter gourd along. Make sure you dip it into all the holy rivers and bring it into all the holy shrines". When the disciples returned, the bitter gourd was cooked and served as sacramental food. "Strange", said the saint slyly, after he had tasted it, "the holy water and the shrines have failed to sweeten it". Yes. What will sweeten our life even in the midst of our unavoidable pains is the kind of religious heart that we carry, not the rituals we perform.

Are we ready to change? What destroys life in us is not accidents or tragedies, but unwillingness to change. It is true that all change is not growth, as all movement is not forward. But if it is the voice of God calling us to change, it must be for the better. Let us seek to change ourselves, not others. It is easier to protect your feet with slippers than to carpet the whole of the earth. To change, we need support. Jesus is here to support us. He tells each of us, "Come and see" (Jn 1:39). Let us come to him with our ill-woven comfortable patterns. Jesus is the divine physician and his prescriptions are never out of balance. The highest sin and the deepest despair together cannot baffle the power of Jesus. Come to him and change.

3RD SUNDAY OF THE YEAR

THE SIAMESE TWINS

Readings: Jon 3:1-5, 10; 1 Cor 7:29-31; Mk 1:14-20

Theme: If we have become engrossed in the material world and have stopped collaborating with God to realise his Kingdom initiated by Christ, we are invited to repent and change.

A Russian youth who had become a conscientious objector to war, through reading of Tolstoy and the New Testament, was brought before a magistrate. With the strength of conviction he told the judge that he believed in a life which loves its enemies, which does good to those who despitefully use it, which overcomes evil and which refuses war. "Yes", said the judge," I understand. But you must be realistic. These laws you are talking about are the laws of the Kingdom of God and it has not come yet". The young man straightened and said, "Sir, I recognise it has not come for you, nor yet for Russia or the world. But the Kingdom of God has come for me! I can't go on hating and killing as though it had not come". In a way, the Russian youth summed up what we believe about the Kingdom of God. In creating the world, God's loving purpose was to establish his Kingdom by sharing the gift of his life with his creation. When Jesus said," the Kingdom of God is close at hand" (Mk 1:15) he meant that God had already initiated his Kingdom by sharing his life with us through Jesus and this Kingdom longs for its completion.

As part of the evolving purpose of God leading the human race towards his Kingdom, our world as we know it has its positive value. We admire this world and love it. It lies before us like a land of dreams, so various, so beautiful, so new! This world, after all our science and sciences, is still a miracle, wonderful, inscrutable and magical. It is a fine place and worth the fighting for. However, this world, a bride of such surpassing beauty, is a maiden never bound to anyone. Those who have to deal with the world," should not become engrossed in it, because it is passing away" (1 Cor 7:31). We should live this life to the full but never forget its ultimate goal which is the Kingdom. This means that as we carry out our daily responsibilities such as paying mortgages, feeding and educating children, attending to civic duties and business, we must also respond to God's voice coming through the mouths of the poor, lonely, forgotten and homeless. This also means that we can acquire money and riches, but never fail to reckon the real value of money in terms of love and service. In our search for riches, we must not lose the things which money can't buy.

How soon will the plan of God for his Kingdom be realised? It depends much on how earnest we are to be on God's side and cooperate with his plan. A friend of Abraham Lincoln one day tried to console the President in his many problems by saying: "I hope that the Lord is on our side". Lincoln replied kindly but firmly that this was not his hope. Everyone was amazed! Then he went on to say: "I am not at all concerned about that, for we know that the Lord is always on the side of the right. But it is my constant anxiety and prayer that I and this nation should be on the Lord's side". If we are on the Lord's side and for his Kingdom, we will use the countless gifts he has given to each of us to advance his Kingdom. Unfortunately, some of us are like Jonah. His flight westward, when the call of God was to go eastward (Jon 1:3), is a powerful symbol of the many attempts people make to hide from their destiny, failing to use the gifts God has given them. However, despite our failures to be constantly on the Lord's side to bring about his Kingdom, the Lord always wins, for he can bring out good even out of evil and he can accomplish his goal by the repentance of his people.

Therefore, if we feel that we have not been cooperative enough with God to realise his Kingdom, we are called to repent. "Repent, believe in the Gospel" (Mk 1:15). To believe in the Gospel is to take God at his word and believe in our destiny. To repent is to change. It is coming to one's senses with a corresponding change in conduct. It is changing our perspective to God's perspective. It is reviewing our gifts, obligations, opportunities and activities in the light of God's Kingdom. It is turning more and more away, for example, from selfishness and laziness or prejudice and stubbornness or from greed and possessiveness. Thus, repentance and change are like Siamese twins. If one is sick the other cannot be well. But take care not to postpone repentance. Deathbed repentances are possible but not desirable, for those which seemed to be deathbed repentances have seldom turned out to be worth anything, when the patient has recovered. Hence repent now, for the time is now. Change now, for the Kingdom is here.

SUPER POWERS

Readings: Dt 18:15-20; 1 Cor 7:32-35; Mk 1:21-28

Theme: Christ who wages war against evil in the world calls all his followers, whatever be their status in life, to join him in the fight.

The evil spirit, sometimes called the angel of death, is around the world so pervasively that you can almost hear the beating of his wings anywhere. He enters into individuals as he did into the man of today's gospel. A gentle man told me that his mother was a witch, so he left her. He further said, when he entered his mother's house, he felt the same evil sensation which he felt when he entered a pornography shop. The evil spirit can enter a nation sowing the seeds of division and feeding on the blood of the innocent victims as he has in Bosnia. The evil one can enter even some of the most astounding modern discoveries such as the Press and TV, so that Pope John Paul II once urged people to "simply shut off" television, if it glorifies sex and violence and threatens family life. Satan has attacked us all so that all people are in a sense evil and will declare so when occasion is offered. I myself, when I am good, I am very good, but when I am bad I am better.

But history is littered with wars which everybody knew would never happen. Salvation history is no exception. Ever since Satan launched its attack on the human race, God set up his own Kingdom on earth, through his Son Jesus Christ to wage war against evil, which Satan never expected. Jesus possessed the power of the Spirit and had the authority of God. Power without authority always looks dangerous. Authority without power always looks comical. Jesus had both to confront evil. To show that the Kingdom of God is mightier than that of Satan, Jesus in the Gospel rebukes the evil spirit "to be quiet and come away" (Mk 1:25) and he does. Moses, in today's first reading, promised that a new prophet will arise and God will put his words in his mouth. And that was fulfilled in Jesus and hence when Jesus spoke people were spellbound. It is said that Beethoven and Mozart, the greatest of all music composers, by their music lifted up mortals to heaven and brought angels down from heaven. But Jesus by his eloquent preaching did the same: he brought heaven down to earth and lifted earth to heaven.

However, the authority of Jesus appears to be weak today. The evil power seems to be winning, so much so that when choosing between two evils, some people always like to try the one they have never tried before. Jesus asked people to turn the other cheek and to pray for those who harm us. Who does it? Only wars and feuds and permanent grudges remain deep rooted. Jesus spoke of the lilies of the field. Today you can nearly use that passage in a comedy routine. People are proud of their sleepless nights, blood pressures and desperate need for tranquillisers for they consider these as the battle scars and war wounds of a successful businessman. Jesus spoke a lot about forgiveness, but that is a dirty word in the world. Thus his gospel does not seem to be the popular bandwagon, nor his new way of thinking the latest fad. But then, this is only the situation for the moment. There will be a day when he will completely overthrow the kingdom of darkness, for he said, "I have not spoken on my own authority. My Father commanded me what I should say" (Jn 8:28). Hence, applause or no applause, Jesus will continue to fight against the power of evil till it is finally wiped out.

But a King cannot fight his war alone. He needs an army and we are his army. We need first to put on the armour of Christ before we join him in the battle against evil because, on becoming the soldiers of Christ, we do not cease to be the citizens of his Kingdom. If we do, we may wish to be heroes but remain practically zeros. One sure way to put on the armour of Christ is to heed the Lord when he speaks God's words to us during the Eucharist in the readings of Scripture. If we heed his words we can become truthful, for He says, "This is why I was born – to bear witness to the truth" (Jn 18:37). If we heed his words, he will lead us to freedom, for he said, "If you abide in me, you will know the truth and the truth shall make you free" (Jn 8:32). If we heed his words, we will find fulfilment, for he said, "he who drinks of the water I will give, shall never thirst" (Jn 4:13). If we heed his words, we will share in the very power of the Spirit, for he said, "he who believes in me will do the work I do, and far greater than these he will do" (Jn 14:12). And then and then only, each of us in the army of the eternal King will be able to light the candle of goodness, instead of cursing the darkness of evil.

To light a candle of goodness and dispel the darkness of evil is a call Jesus gives to each of us whether single or married. Single and married people both receive their vocation from God. Either state is capable of leading to God. Each state carries with it the obligation to bear witness to the love of God. But St Paul also appreciates those who choose to remain single, detached from a partner in order to be attached to God, giving a sign in their lives that this world as we know it is passing away and thus pointing to a higher form of life to which God calls us in Christ. Marriage, argues St Paul, restricts availability to the Lord whereas the single state increases it. Freedom from family responsibilities increases one's availability for the service of God and of the neighbour. "The unmarried man is busy with the Lord's affairs, concerned with pleasing the Lord, but the married man is busy with this world's demands" (1 Cor 7:32). Appreciation of the dignity of being single which facilitates self-sacrificing generosity is sometimes lacking. But to be Christ's messenger of truth and goodness, of justice and love is a vocation of every follower of Christ, whether single or married. Christ no longer has a tongue to tell the story of his love, no hands to feed the multitudes with bread and wine, no feet to go where his lost sheep pine in the desert. He wants to use our tongues, our hands and our feet as his own, to overthrow the kingdom of evil. "How beautiful upon the mountains, are the feet of him that brings good tidings, that publishes peace" (Is 52:7).

5TH SUNDAY OF THE YEAR

CAN LIFE BE BEAUTIFUL?

Readings: Job 7:1-4, 6-7; 1 Cor 9:16-19, 22-23; Mk 1:29-39

Theme: Life can be beautiful, even in the midst of all the ills in the world, if we learn to live through the mystery of suffering for the sake of the Gospel and its promises.

Some years ago a TV station showed the soap opera *Life Can Be Beautiful*. Yes, it can be but not in the soap opera sense. We would have to be hermits to avoid seeing the pain and the misery in the world. When I hear somebody sigh, "Life is hard", I am always tempted to ask, "Compared to what?" We see marriages heading for rocks, neighbours having nervous breakdowns, teenagers at odds with their parents, crime, violence and destruction in the cities. Each of us personally experiences suffering, illness and death. It is a funny old world; you are lucky if you get out of it alive. Hence we sympathise with Job when he cries out, "Is not man's life on earth a drudgery?" (Job 7:1) Because of so much evil in the world, many deny the very existence of God. At the end of the Second World War, Rabbi Rubenstein, confronted with the realisation that 6,000,000 of his fellow Jews – God's chosen people – had been exterminated as useless parasites by Hitler, came to the conclusion that there is no God.

But to blame God for all the ills in the world is not the answer. The first place to look is within every human being: one's inhumanity to another. Wars are started by human beings, food shortages are deliberately caused to keep the world prices up, and millions are abused, exploited and manipulated by their own fellow human beings. But the question remains: Why God permits evil? We would be lucky if we knew the answer. Why Jesus himself had to endure a horrifying death is a mystery. God is no Shylock demanding his last pound of flesh. Perhaps God allows suffering as a purifying fire, to remind us that a human being is a noble animal, splendid in ashes and pompous in the grave, and that under all skies, all weather, our happiness lies elsewhere and not here. But whatever the reason, human life is a meaningless absurdity without God and hence suffering is not a problem to be solved but a mystery to be lived.

We must live through the mystery of suffering not like Job who became so profoundly pessimistic that life seemed to him as an hereditary disease, divided into the horrible and the miserable. For such pessimists, things are always going to get a lot worse before they get worse. But we must live through the mystery of suffering like St Paul who voluntarily made himself a slave for a deeper hope and a higher motive, namely, "for the sake of the Gospel in the hope of having a share in its blessings" (1 Cor 9:23). Yes, God does not offer us a bed of roses, but he will lead us through pains to full life in Christ. Hence, adversity is like a toad, ugly and venomous, but it wears a precious jewel in its head. God will move in a mysterious way to perform his wonders. The clouds that we dread so much are big with mercies and will break in blessings on our heads.

That is our hope. If we do not hope, we will not find what is beyond our hopes. Hence putting on the armour of hope, let us each get actively involved in alleviating some of the sufferings of others, as

Jesus did. Instead of battling with the question, "Why suffering?" Jesus moved to heal the afflicted. "After sunset, as evening drew on, they brought him all who were ill, whom he cured" (Mk 1:32-33). All that is necessary for the victory of evil is that good men do nothing when others suffer. Hence let us reach out and touch the worried, the weak, the suffering; and let us witness to the truth that God still loves all men in their weakness and fragility. We Christians, blessed with this hope, are not storerooms but channels; we are not cisterns but springs.

6TH SUNDAY OF THE YEAR

"BE HEALED"

Readings: Lev 13:1-2, 44-46; 1 Cor 10:31-11:1; Mk 1:40-45

Theme: Although the first human beings, who were created to be fully alive and healthy, sinned against God, God sent his Son to restore him to full life and health by reconciling us with God, his neighbour and himself.

Through all the works of God runs the golden thread of bloom, not the iron thread of doom, and it was so evident when he created the human race. He made them fully alive and fully healthy, "to be fruitful, multiply and fill the earth" (Gen 1:28). But they sinned and since then, sin has become so pervasive that if we were to confess our sins to one another, we would all laugh at each other for lack of originality. Wages of sin are always liberal and on the dot, and hence human nature became diseased, so diseased that even minor pleasures are accompanied by minor pains. However, God is a compassionate God. Even when he has to strike us, he does so only with his finger, not with all his arm. Therefore, the merciful God sent his son, Jesus Christ, to restore men to their original health. That is why, to anyone who prays, like the leper in the gospel, Jesus is always ready to answer, "I do will. Be healed" (Mk 1:41).

But God, who is perfect, never acts in half measures. If he writes, he writes with a pen which never blots; if he speaks, he speaks with a tongue which never slips; if he acts, he acts with a hand that never fails. Therefore when the Son of God went about healing people, he aimed at healing not just their bodies but their souls as well. It meant that his mission was not just to heal us but to save us. That is why, while sending his apostles he said, "Preach the good news of salvation and heal the sick". Whenever he healed, he would often say, "your faith has healed you" or "your sins are forgiven thee". If he devoted one third of his healing ministry to drive out evil spirits, it was to signal victory over the reign of the Evil One, who is the greatest enemy of man's salvation. Thus, Jesus wants to heal us in order to save us and he wants to save us in order to heal us.

Jesus saves us by reconciling us with God, with our neighbours and with our own selves. When we are reconciled with God, "whatever we do, we will do for the glory of God" (1 Cor 10:31), with a cheerful spirit and a cheerful spirit helps a great deal to recover from illness. As the saying goes, "The best doctors are Dr Diet, Dr Quiet and Dr Merryman". When we are reconciled with our neighbours, "we try to please all in any way we can" (1 Cor 10:33); we not only forgive others but also find a special cemetery plot to bury all their faults, and thus be freed of anger and hatred which, if prolonged, causes ulcers and heart diseases. When we are reconciled with ourselves, we will readily forgive ourselves also, and will not brood over our own wrong-doings because rolling in the muck is not the best way of getting clean. As a result, even our emotions, which are strings in the human heart which become sick because, at times, we vibrate them violently, are freed from stress, anxieties and fears. Thus human health comes to a great extent as an indirect but precious consequence of reconciliation, namely salvation.

This salvation, which brings with it human health, is God's gift in Christ and not a merchandise in market that gold could buy. If it could, only the rich would be healthy and be saved and the poor alone would be sick and damned. No. It is a gift offered to all. And it is offered free of charge. The doctor gave my father six months to live, but when he could not pay the bill, he gave him six months more. Let us all therefore turn to Jesus, the all-sufficient physician of humanity, yearning for his free gift of salvation which is health in the ultimate sense.

7TH SUNDAY OF THE YEAR

TRY FORGIVENESS

Readings: Is 43:18-19, 21-22, 24-25; 2 Cor 1:18-22; Mk 2:1-12

Theme: The enduring mercy of God towards sinners is a spur for all forgiven sinners to show mercy to their offenders, for their own sake and for the sake of others.

Sin's misery and God's mercy are beyond measure. God's goodness surrounds us at every moment and we walk through it almost with difficulty as through thick grass and flowers. But when it comes to God's forgiving our sins, his mercy matches only his infinite love. From the Middle Ages comes this legend about a nun who claimed that she had a vision of Christ. The bishop asked, "Sister, did you talk to him?" And she said "Yes, I did." He continued, "If you have another vision, ask Christ this question: 'What was the bishop's greatest sin before he became bishop'?" About three months later, the nun came to see the bishop. "Did you see the Lord again?" asked the bishop. "Yes," she replied. "Did you ask him the question about my sin?" "Yes, I did." "And what did he say?" She smiled and answered, "The Lord said, 'I don't remember anymore.'" When we recall the number of times God has forgiven our sins, big and small, we can only thank him in the words of Addision: "When all thy mercies, O my God, my rising soul surveys, transported with the view, I am lost in wonder, love and praise!

It is not surprising, then, that God who alone can forgive sins came forward to forgive the sins of Israel saying, "You burdened me with your sins; It is I who wipe out your offences; your sins, I remember no more" (Is 43:24-25). Jesus too revealed that as the Son of God he had divine power and mercy to forgive sinners, when he told the paralytic, "My, son, your sins are forgiven; Get up and walk" (Mk 2:5). Sinners never had to drag mercy out of Christ as money from a miser. Christ was so compassionate and generous with sinners. Christ also shared his power to forgive sins with his Church. He made it part of the Church's visible ministry in order to give human beings that comfort and support which we weak human beings need in our pilgrimage on earth. The Sacrament of Reconciliation, the divine means through which we receive forgiveness from our sins when we admit and confess our sins, gives us an experience of the loving mercy of God; we are swept up in a feeling of relief, a sense that if God is with me who can be against me! The overwhelming presence of Christ gives us strength for our future life, a support for the drudgery of everyday living that we can never find in our private thoughts.

As forgiven sinners, we too are called in our turn to forgive others. By forgiving our offenders, we help them to improve their lives. When we forgive, we accept the offender as he is with all his weakness and he knows that we still respect him as a human person in spite of the offence. And that gives him a sense of self-worth on which he can build a better life. The Duke of Wellington was about to pronounce the death sentence on a confirmed deserter. Deeply moved, the great General said, "I am extremely sorry to pass this severe sentence, but we have tried everything and all the discipline and penalties have failed to improve this man who is otherwise a brave and a good soldier." Then he gave the man's comrades an opportunity to speak for him. "Please, your Excellency," said one of the men, "there is one thing you have never tried. You have not tried forgiving him." The General forgave him and it worked: the soldier never again deserted and ever after showed not only gratitude to the Iron Duke, but also he became his friend. As the saying goes, 'Friendship flourishes at the fountain of forgiveness'.

When we forgive others, we not only help others, but also we help ourselves. To be brooding over hurts drains us of energy and creativity. It is never wise to nurse an injury. We must learn to extract what wisdom we can from our hurt and then bury it. If we forgive most, we will be most forgiven. That is, we heal our own wounds in binding up those of others. St Augustine said, "There are many kinds of alms, the giving of which helps us to obtain pardon for our sins, but none is greater than that by which we forgive from our heart a sin that someone has committed against us". Besides, the more we forgive, the stronger we become; the weak cannot forgive; forgiveness is the attribute of the strong. Above all, nowhere we imitate Christ more than in showing mercy to our offenders.

JOY IN CHRIST

Readings: Hos 2: 16-17, 21-22; 2 Cor 3:1-6; Mk 2:18-22

Theme: As we wait for perfect joy in heaven, we can have a foretaste of it here on earth in Christ Jesus, whom we can meet in prayer, in acts of love and mercy and through a life of confidence in God.

There is a story about a monastery where the monks were unable to die, but simply grew older and older. Tired of their endless existence, the monks began to pray for their own deaths. One night, the abbot had a dream in which it was revealed to him that the gate used by the angels to come to and from heaven was right above their monastery. In effect, the monastery had become a part of heaven. He realised that this was why the monks never died. The abbot related his dream to the monks. They decided to demolish the monastery and rebuild it several miles away. As soon as they had done so, the ancient monks began to die and they were very happy, for they were now really in heaven released from their mortal bodies. The message of the story is that we can have perfect joy not on this earth but only in heaven, for Christ who is the perfect image of God is there and he is not the child of eternity but the Father of it.

However, we can have a taste of the perfect joy of heaven here on earth, on condition that Christ is with us. When the Pharisees asked Jesus why his disciples were not fasting, he replied, “How can the guests at a wedding fast as long as the groom is still with them?” (Mk 2:19) Christ represents himself as the bridegroom and calls the community of believers as his bride. Therefore, as long as the bridegroom is with them they have only to rejoice and celebrate. Yes. As long as Christ is in us and we in him, we will be happy. The greater our closeness to Christ, the greater will be our joy. This is not surprising, for Jesus Christ is God’s everything for man’s total need. He is the risen Saviour and hence he is made up of all delights; he himself is all that is desirable. This is why saints who had tasted, when alive here on earth, the heavenly delight of Christ by their intimate union with him, could never get away from him. Yes. Joy in Christ is the happiest of all joys.

How do we experience the presence of Christ in our daily life so that we can delight in his joy? We can experience him in prayerful solitude. God "led his people into the desert and spoke to them" (Hos 2:16). We need not literally go into any desert in order to commune with God in prayer but we need to give ourselves some time daily to be alone with God in silence. As you know, great joys as great griefs are silent. Remember, solitude is the audience chamber of God. To experience Christ, we must also try to live a life of love for God and mercy towards others. God said to his people, "I will espouse you for ever in love and mercy" (Hos 2:21). Don't we know how faithful God has been in his loving mercy towards us? If we want to experience his Son Jesus, we too must daily respond to God's faithfulness by our own acts of love and mercy. Above all, we can experience the joy in Christ if we live a life of trust and confidence in God. St Paul once boasted that, "it is not I who live, but Christ lives in me." How did he manage to get so close to Christ? He says, "It is through great confidence in God, through Christ" (2 Cor 3:4). To those who place all their trust in God, all shall be well, and all shall be well and all manner of things will be well.

Therefore, we who know that perfect joy is to be found only in heaven, but on this earth, we can still have that pure joy in various degrees of intensity, should also know where to find it and how to get it. One day a big dog saw a little dog chasing his tail round and round. "What are you trying to do?" he asked. "I'm looking for happiness", answered the little dog. "Someone told me that happiness is in my tail, and when I catch it I will have it. So I'm chasing my tail till I get it." "I'm looking for happiness too", said the big dog. "I've been told the same thing. But I've discovered that every time I chase my tail it runs away from me. So I go about doing what I should do, and I find that happiness comes after." There are people in the world who are frantically chasing after joy and happiness, but can't find it. Pure joy is to be found only in Christ. As sorrow for sin is the keenest sorrow, so joy in the Lord is the loftiest joy.

CELEBRATE TO LIBERATE

Readings: Deut 5:12-15; 2 Cor 4:6-11; Mk 2:23-3:6

Theme: On every Sunday, the Lord's Day, which is our Sabbath, we celebrate our liberation from death to life with Christ so that we may spiritually equip ourselves to liberate others as well.

That day was the day of rest. Therefore on that day, no work was permissible, not even medical care could be given. A wound or fracture, for instance, could not be attended to. It was a big debate among the Jewish religious leaders whether on that day a knot could be tied or untied. An egg laid by a hen on that day could not be eaten, because the hen in her effort to lay the egg, violated the law of that day. Not even self-defence was permissible on that day. Violation of the law of that day was liable to punishment with death. And that day was the Sabbath day. It is true that God had instructed the people of Israel to rest from work on the seventh day of every week. But the Jewish learned leaders had turned the law of God into a spider's web to ensnare the unlearned, into a stone mill-wheels in order to grind the poor down into an abject state and so instil fear into the simple.

Sabbath, in Hebrew, means rest. But the Jewish leaders had put so much emphasis on observing the rest, that they forgot the purpose of the rest, God had said, "No work may be done," on that day so that they could rest thanking God for "liberating them out of Egypt" (Deut 5:15). God had commanded that "all slaves, males and females" (Deut 5:14) must also be given rest on that day, so that they too could have Exodus experience of freedom and celebrate their human dignity. In other words, in God's mind, Sabbath was meant to give freedom not only from all works, but also freedom for certain special kinds of work, for instance, to promote human values, to protect human dignity and to provide for human needs. However, Israel's memory about the purpose of Sabbath faded into mere laws and rules. Therefore Jesus had to set the people's priorities right. He allowed his disciples to "pull off heads of grain" (Mk 2:23) and eat them on the Sabbath, in order to remind the Jews that Sabbath was also meant to provide freedom for human needs. He himself cured "the withered hand of a man" (Mk 3:5) on the Sabbath, in order to remind the Jews that the question to be asked on the Sabbath is: how much good I can do for people, and not how much good I can refrain from.

What was Sabbath day for Israel is Lord's Day for us now, which is Sunday, when Jesus our Lord passed from death to resurrection taking us along with him to new life. Hence for us too Sunday, our Sabbath, is a day of celebration, when we gather together in the church to celebrate our liberation from sin and death. For us too, Sunday is a day of rest, rest from work. Work is the inevitable condition of human life, yes; but we often tend to intoxicate ourselves with work, so we don't see during the week how we really are. Our soul gets restless, even furious during working days and wants to tear itself apart and cure itself of being human, at least on the Lord's Day. So we give time to ourselves on Sundays to rest and reflect. In our reflection, earthly things will assume their true size. In our prayerful reflection we will be able to see that in the wilderness of perplexity and affliction of this life, it is God who is guiding us to new life, and that will give us strength, as it did to St Paul, to "carry about in our bodies the dying of Jesus, so that in our bodies, the life of Jesus may also be revealed" (2 Cor 4:10), until we reach our immortal home. And yet, is it not a pity that millions who long for immortality do not know what to do with themselves on a rainy Sunday afternoon?

Thus on every Sunday, we not only celebrate our liberation from sin and death, but also we celebrate in order to liberate. By devoting extra time to spiritual things, we liberate ourselves, for instance, from the modern society's materialist penchant for production and consumption through widespread trading even on Sundays. By celebrating the Lord's Day, we also spiritually equip ourselves to liberate others. If we have truly celebrated the Lord's Day at Sunday worship, then we will respond to the needs of people in the world which we express in the prayers of the faithful at Mass. We will continue the music we sang in the church and sing the goodness we find in our neighbours, and we will carry the Gospel message we heard at the worship and promote justice and peace for all. Indeed, if all of us celebrate the Lord's Day in this manner, as days to liberate ourselves and others, then God by giving us the Sabbath each week would have given us fifty-two springs in every year.

10TH SUNDAY OF THE YEAR

FREE FOR OTHERS

Readings: Gen 3:9-15; 2 Cor 4:13-5:1; Mk 3:20, 35

Theme: To be free just for oneself is perversion of freedom, but to be free for the service of others is true freedom in its deep Christian sense, exemplified in the Eucharist.

A chaplain was making his rounds in a military hospital where wounded were being treated. To one soldier he said, "Were you hurt very much, son?" "No, father," the soldier replied. "I thank God, I'm alive. Of course, I'm going home without my right hand, but mother will be glad to have what is left of me." "I'm sure of that," added the chaplain, "and since you have lost your writing hand, shall I write for you and tell her you have lost your hand?" "Father," said the young man quickly, "I did not lose it, I gave it." That soldier was truly a free man, for he freely gave his hand in the service of others. He might have been an ordinary soldier. But history has seen great men who rattled their chains to show that they were free, for they accepted chains on themselves to make others free. True freedom worthy of its name is to be free for others. It means responsibility for others' welfare. Perhaps that is why, most men dread it.

There is a tendency in human nature to be free not for others but for oneself. That is why many are like Adam and Eve, who thought they were free in order to be free from their obligation to obey God's will that had prohibited them to eat from certain fruits in the garden (Gen 3:11). Such people forget that God obliges none to more than he has given us ability to perform. They forget too that if obedience to God becomes at times a torture to us, it also enables us to become "brothers and sisters of Jesus Christ" (Mk 3:35), so that we can even achieve prodigies. Because of the basic human tendency to be free for oneself rather than for others, many choose to blame others for the evils in the world and disown any personal responsibility. Adam blamed Eve for his failure and Eve blamed the serpent. St Paul was blamed of insincerity and selfishness in converting the Corinthians, but he did not lose heart (2 Cor 4:16). The Scribes blamed Jesus saying," he is possessed," because he drove out evil spirits from others (Mk 3:22). Obviously, to choose to think well or ill of others' deeds is one's freedom. But those who are free for themselves normally choose to blame others even for their good deeds. For example, you are rich, and share your riches with the poor, they would say that your charity has strings attached to it. But those who are free for others would choose to believe that you are truly generous and was good intentioned. Yes, I am truly free when I have loved persons and because of my love they become more free and I become less a slave.

Freedom, in the deep Christian sense, is to be free to serve others. It is experienced as duty, as responsibility, as a response to the claims of love and justice. Christian call to freedom is inherently a call to community, a summon out of isolation, an invitation to be with others, an impulse to the service of others. Without such Christian freedom, I am afraid, heavy industry may be perfected in our cities, but not justice and truth in our world. We are free, when we know how to give ourselves to others, without demanding that we possess them in return. We are free when we feel ashamed at the enslavement of our neighbours by the powerful. We are free when we love the welfare of our neighbours more than our own freedom. Therefore married people who regularly exhibit mutual love and dedication are truly free. Peacemakers who seek to overcome malice by genuine concern are truly free. Those who labour for the rights of all, especially the oppressed, are truly free. Those who offer hope to the depraved are truly free. All such people choose to be free for others and are thus free from their own ego.

The Eucharist we are about to celebrate deals with freedom in the best sense, because in the Eucharist we celebrate the giving of Jesus of himself for others. The Eucharist offers Jesus as the model of the truly liberated person. It proclaims that whether or not you are free depends on what you do for others, that true freedom is to share the chains of our brothers and sisters, and that our freedom as the children of God is so great, precisely because we are fast-bound by the perfect law of love. Above all, the Eucharist feeds us with Christ himself. To feed on Christ is not only to know how to free oneself, but to know what to do with one's freedom. When we feed on the corn, the strength of the corn comes into us and becomes our strength. When we feed on Christ, Christ becomes our life. It is he in us that lives our life, that helps the poor, that fights the battles for the oppressed and that wins the crown.

SEEDS OF LIFE

Readings: Ezek 17:22-24; 2 Cor 5:6-10; Mk 4:26-34

Theme: God who sowed the seeds of Christian life in us at baptism, which are growing unnoticed by us in a mysterious way, expects us to sow similar seeds in the hearts of others to make the world a better place to live in.

According to a Chinese proverb, "If you plant for a year, plant grain; if you plant for ten years, plant trees; if you plant for hundred years, plant men". We can also add, "If you plant for Eternity, plant the Word". The Word of God – the Seed of the Christian life – has been implanted at baptism, unknown to the infant, but nonetheless growing within. For the growth of the seed, both God and we have to work together. If God alone, there will be only weeds; if we alone, not even weeds.

On our part we must provide for the seed a fitting soil, and nurture it as it grows, by trying to live our daily Christian life according to the planted Word. Such a life may often be hard and difficult, even demanding great self-sacrifices. But then, God gets the best soldiers out of the highlands of afflictions. Even the bees make the sweetest honey only from the flowers of the thyme – a small and bitter herb. Let us not forget that a price must be paid for extreme specialisation, even in holiness. But the reward will be a plentiful harvest. A woman, for instance, deserves no credit for her beauty at 16, but beauty at 60 is her own soul's doing.

How the Seed of Life implanted in us grows is, of course, a mystery. One may be an expert car mechanic. He knows how to run a car, which keys fit the door and ignition, how to put it in gear and what to do if it stalls, but it is still probably a mystery to him how the car really works. If it is so with a car, is it surprising that how the seed of God's life grows within us is a mystery? But however mysterious, the truth is that it grows. "The seed sprouts and grows without the farmer knowing how it happens" (Mk 4:27). We do not yet fully understand our future destiny, but this we know, that "each one will receive his recompense, good or bad, according to his life in the body" (2 Cor

5:10). "I will plant it on a lofty mountain, it shall put forth branches and bear fruit" (Ezek 17:23). We must therefore believe that the Seed of Life keeps growing in us even though we are unaware of it. At times, one can notice that somebody has grown happier, more fulfilled and more relaxed. This is because the Kingdom of God has grown within him. Likewise we can see another person changed for the better, more self-confident, unselfish and caring for others. This means that the seed is growing.

As God sows seed of new life in us, we Christians are also called to sow seeds of Christian love in the hearts of those whom we meet. Once I was caught in the wrong lane in a traffic jam and I sat and sat and sat and both I and my car began to overheat. Lo, a smiling face in a car in the main stream of traffic nodded unto me and allowed me to get in that lane. That man sowed the seed of compassion in my heart. We can never let ourselves off the hook by saying, "It is not my problem". Neither can we sit back and wait for somebody else to make the world a better place. Each of us can do something loving and loveable for someone else. We should not be discouraged by the apparent lack of result for our efforts because we are sure that the love-seeds we sow will grow in a mysterious way. You don't notice your children actually growing in front of your eyes. You only notice their clothes are no longer big enough for them.

All that God requires of us is that we sow seeds of New Life, namely of faith, of justice, of compassion and love in order to make this world a better place to live. Having done this, we must wait. One cannot force the seed to become a shrub. One can only provide the right conditions for growth. But God in his own time will definitely see to it that selfishness surrenders to sharing, evil gives way to goodness and hate yields to love. If we have patience and hope, eventually the harvest of what we have planted will make its appearance: nations will be reconciled, human rights restored, the vulnerable innocent will be protected, the unwanted cared for and the hungry given food. We may not necessarily see these results in our own lifetime but the next generations will. Hence where will tomorrow's trees come from? From the shoots we plant today. Where will tomorrow's justice and peace get their start? From the seeds we sow today.

12TH SUNDAY OF THE YEAR

STORM

Readings: Job 38:1, 8-11; 2 Cor 5:14-17; Mk 4:35-41

Theme: Whether the storm, which we as individuals or as a Church encounter, be in our personal life or in our Christian missionary work, we can triumph over it if we rely on the supreme power of God over all destructive forces.

A cargo ship carrying slaves from Africa was on its way to America. John Newton was its captain. He never worried whether slave trade was right or wrong. It brought money, that was enough. One night a violent storm blew up at the sea. The waves threw up Newton's ship around like a toy. When everyone on board was filled with panic, Newton did something which he had never done for many years. He prayed. Shouting at the top of his voice, he said: "God! If you will only save us, I promise to be your slave for ever". God heard his prayer, the ship survived and Newton became a priest. He wrote in his later years one of the most moving hymns: "Amazing grace! How sweet the sound that saved a wretch like me". Yes. God who creates all things controls everything. There is no situation that is so chaotic that God cannot subdue and create something surprisingly good out of it. It was when Job realised that God can triumph over all sufferings that he overcame his own suffering (Job 38:11). It is to proclaim God's triumph over all evil including death that St Paul wrote this: "Through Christ's death and resurrection, we are a new creation" (2 Cor 5:17). It is in order to make us realise God's supreme power over all the destructive forces of evil that Jesus stilled the storm (Mk 4:39) in favour of his disciples.

The boat that was caught in the storm with Jesus and disciples in it, is an apt symbol to represent us. Many times storms toss us around like tiny corks on the ocean of life. A storm may arise because of a severe alcohol or drug problem or because of an overwhelming economic or health crisis. A storm may arise because of unexplainable discouragement or despair, or because we feel unappreciated or lonely. At times, the gusting winds of worries about the past and the angry waters of anxieties about the future can scare us out of our wits. At other times, a state of blackness can be frightening, like a thick blanket thrown over you, where suddenly all is dark. At such moments when we feel at the bottom of a slimy pit, Jesus appeals to us to trust in his almighty power to subdue the storm and to rescue us from the domination of darkness. Because Jesus is God made flesh even the tallest waves and the deepest waters together cannot baffle his power.

The boat can also represent the Church, the community of believers. Christ's journey with the disciples in a boat across the sea was a mission to proclaim the gospel of the Kingdom abroad. Their fight with the storm on the sea was symbolic of the struggle that the Church of Christ would face in its mission to overcome suffering, death and evil in the world. But the stilling of the storm by Christ was a guarantee that the Church will always come out successful in its mission, because of the presence of Christ in it. Every follower of Jesus will have many occasions to launch out over troubled waters for some distant shore. If we always wait for perfect conditions, we will accomplish little. A fair-weather Christian will dally, while one with a burning desire to accomplish a mission will risk all in faith. In building God's Kingdom, we must expect storms of ridicule, severe criticism, even violence; yet we go forth. The secret of survival as a church is not a bigger boat but deeper faith.

Whether the storms we encounter be in our lives as individuals or as a Church, we will triumph over them provided we rely on God's power and not on our own. Apparently the eagle is the only bird which renews its strength by renewing its wings. As it gets older, its wings begin to make a noise and its beak grows calluses, which means that it is less able to catch its prey. So it goes to some secure place and plucks out all its feathers and rubs the growth off its beak. New feathers grow. We need to go through a similar process: to shed our feathers of self-reliance, to let go of what we have so far relied on to survive and let God give us his feathers. Let us cry out to God in our stormy moments, but remember that it is so easy to cry out and yet remain in the storm and in so doing still feel engulfed. Therefore, as we cry out, we need to keep our focus fixed not on the storm but on God. Within his encircling power we always stand and on every side we feel his hand. God is never in a hurry but he is always on time. Evil of any kind can do nothing to us without the command of God to whose dominion it is subject.

13TH SUNDAY OF THE YEAR

LIFE FALLING SIDEWAYS?

Readings: Wis 1:13-15, 2:23-24; 2 Cor 8:7, 9, 13-15; Mk 5:21-43

Theme: Imitating God who pursues human beings everywhere to save their imperishable life and following the example of Christ who went about delivering people from all ills, Christians should seek after those who are falling sideways in society.

A man was dangerously hanging on to a tree root over the edge of a cliff: below him rocks, above him a tiger, and a black and white mouse nibbling at the root. The man noticed a strawberry beside him and picked it to eat! This is hunger for life! Life is the one most precious gift we have from God. All that God had created, he saw them good, especially the human life. Yes. Life of every human being has some faults, as all roses have thorns and silver fountains mud. But it is a great life if you don't weaken it. Since God had created human beings in his own image, human life is not perishable, as marble and granite are perishable. "God formed man to be imperishable" (Wis 2:23), and he will see to it that no one loses it on their journey. Hence, where life is bustling God will be there to protect it; where it is withering, he will be there to revive it; where it is falling sideways, he will be there to straighten it. He is thus the God of the tenements and houses of the rich, God of the subways and the nightclub, God of the Cathedral and the streets, God of the sober and the drunk, God of the gambler and of the stripper. He pursues us all everywhere for he is pro-life God.

Illness and death are the worst enemies of human life. Illness is the night-side of life and death is the only disease you don't look forward to being cured of. And yet, God overpowers these two forces of evil in order to save life. That is what Jesus demonstrated during his public ministry. A twelve-year-old daughter of a man named Jairus was critically ill. Her father pleaded with Jesus to come and cure her. When they were on their way, the tragic news came that the little girl was dead. But that would not stop the pro-life Son of God. He still went and raised the dead girl back to life (Mk 5:42). A woman suffering for twelve years from flow of blood came on her own with the crowd, touched the cloak of Jesus in the believe that his power would heal her and it did (Mk 5:29). A woman in Jesus' time did not stand on her own. She was in her father's possession until she was married and then belonged to her husband. To get out in public she needed to have a male by her side and she could make any request only through a male. But Jesus did not mind that she omitted these social taboos of gender restrictions. To him, the releasing of this woman from her bondage of illness was more important than social niceties.

Christ expects his followers too to be pro-life people. The life he wants us to bring to others is not simply 'the life of heaven', some 'pie in the sky', but a life which embraces even our physical, biological and emotional life. Hence St Paul wrote to the Corinthians to give generously in the collections for the needy churches, exhorting them, "Just as you are rich in every respect, also abound in your work of charity" (2 Cor 8:7), because through our collections the Lord can even now heal the sick, feed the hungry and restore people to life. Of course, we need to be pro-life people not only to those with empty stomach and naked body, but also to those with some areas already dead within them. There is something already dead within those who no longer wish to live, those who are so embittered that they no longer look for love in this life, and those who feel so alienated from God and Church that they no longer hope for something from him. It is to these people Jesus says, "I tell you, get up" (Mk 5:41) and it is to these people also whose lives are falling sideways that we need to bring life.

Maybe, we will not have the spectacular power of healing the sick or raising the dead. But all of us are called to do whatever little we can to overcome evil and bring health and love, peace and joy to our fellow human beings. We are in danger of looking too far for opportunities of bringing life to others. In searching for rhododendrons, we may trample down the daisies. For it is the little words you speak, the little thoughts you think, the little things you do or leave undone, that can heal and raise 'the dead' to life. In our time, selfishness and evil look so deeply set to triumph that it will take a miracle to turn things around. However, each of us is called to work our little miracle of love and service. It may benefit only one person, but it will be a sign that Christ, the pro-life God, lives in us who are his followers. May the divine goodness that ever outsoars the narrow loves and charities of earth grant us a loving and generous heart towards all lives that are falling sideways!

14TH SUNDAY OF THE YEAR

"A THORN IN THE FLESH"

Readings: Ezek 2:2-5; 2 Cor 12: 7-10; Mk 6:1-6

Theme: Whatever be the weakness or pain or thorn in our flesh that we have to carry on in our lives, we are convinced that they are powerful symbols of God's dynamic presence amongst us.

The poet William Cowper wrote: "God moves in mysterious ways his wonders to perform". But God's mysterious way seems to be a 'scandalous' or paradoxical way, for he often chooses what is weak, ordinary and painful to make known his presence among men. Ezekiel was a frustrated prophet who in his frustration often scolded and attacked the exiles for their infidelities. But when he received word of the fall of Jerusalem, he offered thc exiles a new message of hope. Because of God's presence in his painful frustration, he rose to the occasion despite his weakness. Jesus was rejected by his own people in his home town (Mk 6:2). And yet Jesus demonstrated God's strength in the very midst of denial and rejection unto Calvary. St Paul was pained when he heard the unjust attacks of his opponents. In addition, he had to carry all his life "a thorn in his flesh" (2 Cor 12:7). But he asserted that "when I am weak, then I am strong" (v.10). All these three great prophets proclaim one simple truth, namely whatever be the weakness or pain or thorn we have to carry in our lives, every thorn is the symbol of the powerful presence of the dynamic presence of God.

'A thorn in the flesh' could be a physical illness. My friend John was a successful executive. But in his early fifties, he was left incapacitated by a stroke. All of a sudden, his speech was slurred and impossible to understand most of the time. He was forced to depend upon others for even the most basic necessities. Frustration and humiliation flashed before his eyes. Used to doing everything for himself, he resented having to depend on others. He did not know why he should suffer this humiliating dependence. But God knew. John, ever since his teens, had been independent, a fighter, a loving husband and a caring father. But he never had any experience of being weak, of being provided for, of being loved. It took a stroke for him to have such an experience. He was a difficult patient, but through it all, his wife, his sons and his daughters stood by him, cared for him and loved him back to life. Health regained was a valued treasure, but a greater treasure was to discover that being loved confers its own dignity. Was not God present in his illness?

'Thorn in the flesh' could take the form of rejection by others. Some are rejected because of colour, race or nationality but when they keep on loving others, they soon see the dynamic presence of God in their rejected condition and win acceptance, love, even admiration. Some are rejected early in life as useless for the future. Bishop Fulton Sheen, the great preacher, was told by his college debate coach, "You are absolutely the worst speaker I ever heard". Ernest Hemingway, the great novelist, was told by his teachers, "Forget about writing; you don't have enough talent for it". Richard Hooker, the author of MASH, had his book rejected by six publishers before it was finally accepted and became a runaway best seller. All such people were not disheartened by rejection, rather they continued to believe in their own worth and persevered in their efforts and God brought out of these rejected individuals the best they could offer to the world. Even our genuine love for others may be rejected, but if we don't give up on love, we will soon possess the supreme happiness of life which is the conviction that we are loved.

'Thorn in the flesh' could mean also the ordinary, routine, humdrum things in life. There is a human temptation in all of us to fail to see God in the ordinary things in life and instead to seek him in the flamboyant, the unusual or exciting phenomenon. Often the longing to touch the presence of God sends us searching for visions and apparitions in faraway or near places, while his guaranteed presence is in the ordinary. Because we instinctively admire strength and expect to find it in our athletes, political leaders and armies, because we live in a society that gives great value to great deeds, weakness is something that we are less able to cope with and our being ordinary and fragile tends to leave us frustrated or depressed. At such moments we must recall that the joy of life depends not so much on what we do, but on what God does through us. And God would never permit any evil, if he could not bring good out of evil. He has in himself all power to protect us, all wisdom to direct us, all mercy to save us and all happiness to crown us.

PREACH

Readings: Am 7:12-15; Eph 1:3-14; Mk 6:7-13

Theme: The mission of the whole Church is to preach the Gospel of Christ, in a credible manner, and with humility, for the same reasons for which Christ sent his disciples to preach in his time.

WHO? It is the mission of the whole Church to preach. When the church begins to preach the Gospel, the devil receives his marching orders, for he can't stand the truth. Some are ordained to preach, others are not, but all the baptised are called to spread the Gospel. God is on the lookout today especially for Christians who will be quiet enough to get a message from him, brave enough to spread it, and honest enough to live it. The beginning and the end of the Christian vocation is this: to know Christ, and in knowing him, to strive to be like him; and in striving to be like him, to love him; and in loving him, to love those who do not know him yet; and in loving those who do not know him, to offer the fruits of his redemption.

WHAT? We are not called upon to invent the message nor decorate the message but to proclaim the Gospel, which is: "It is in Christ and through his blood that we have been redeemed" (Eph 1:7). Preaching which is the richest is the one which is the fullest of the Lord himself. We preach "to bring all things in the heavens and on earth into one under Christ's leadership" (Eph 1:10). Preaching that does not focus on Christ is devoid of divine power and will fall like frost on worshippers. We preach to draw people to Christ through repentance as Jesus himself did. Jesus was not a diplomat but a prophet and his message was not a compromise but an ultimatum: "Unless you repent" were often the first words of his preaching. When his disciples were sent two by two, it was mainly to preach "the need of repentance" (Mk 6:12). Preaching on sin and repentance will offend. If you want to be popular, preach happiness; if you want to be unpopular, preach unhappiness. If you want to be popular, preach resurrection, if you want to be unpopular, preach repentance. But the very fact that repentance is not popular is all the more reason for preaching it. It is not our responsibility to make it acceptable, but it is our duty to make it indispensable.

HOW? Our preaching has to be credible. As they say, a good example is the best sermon. The preacher's life is the people's looking-glass by which they usually dress themselves. On sending his disciples to preach the good news, Jesus "instructed them to take nothing on the journey but a walking stick" (Mk 6:8). By this he did not mean to say to the modern preachers that we should get rid of our cars, empty our freezers, clean out our closets or cut up our credit cards. What he meant was that, if we preach about the coming of God's Kingdom, then our material life has to be simple; if we proclaim the values of the Kingdom such as loving God, depending on him, loving our neighbours and serving them, then we cannot so clutter ourselves with material things that they make us forget our dependence on God or harden our hearts to the poor.

Our preaching has to be humble. One test of a preacher's power is his knowledge that it is not on his own authority he preaches, but on that of Christ (Mk 6:7). It is not to project our own image but the image of God which is his Son Jesus that we preach. That is why a good preacher is heard not seen. A humble preacher will be always conscious of his unworthiness. Amos confessed his unworthiness when he said, "I was only a shepherd; it was the Lord who called me out to go and prophesy" (Am 7:14-15). All of us as preachers are unworthy because all of us are sinners. Only once God chose a completely sinless preacher.

WHY? The reasons for which Jesus sent his disciples to preach remain even today for our preaching. We need to preach in order to discern for the people the meaning of everyday occurrence in the light of God's Kingdom to come; to interpret the signs of the times in the light of the Gospel; to spur people to service in the light of the great commandment to love God and neighbour. Preaching is still the spiritual dynamo of the whole Church programme. When preaching lags, the Church tends to lag. When it mounts up with wings as eagles, the Church and her whole programme begins to move. If it is consistently neglected, it will result in disintegration and the decline of the Church. The power of the pulpit supported by life-witness is still a force and a potential force which must be guarded if the Church is to meet the needs of this time.

16TH SUNDAY OF THE YEAR

BUILDING BRIDGES

Readings: Jer 23:1-6; Eph 2:13-18; Mk 6:30-34

Theme: It is the duty of the followers of Christ, who went round reconciling people with God and each other, to commit themselves, to build bridges between the divided people in the world.

Buddha was once threatened with death by a bandit called Anguliaral. "Then be good enough to fulfil my dying wish", said Buddha. "Cut off the branch of that tree." One flash of the sword, and it was done! "What now?" asked the bandit. "Put it back again", said Buddha. The bandit laughed. "You must be crazy to think that anyone could do that." "On the contrary, it is you who are crazy to think that you are mighty because you can wound and destroy. That is the task of children. The mighty know how to heal and build", was Buddha's reply.

It is the task of children, not of the mighty, to destroy. In the world today, there seems to be a lot of children among grown-ups who go round pulling down bridges that keep people together. They are after dividing people and keeping them apart. They provoke and indulge in conflicts and wars. War not only kills but also scatters. When will our society realise that the real test of power is not capacity to make war, but to make peace? Few people can be happy these days unless they hate some other person. The irrational hostility that some people vent upon one another is nothing but the projection of self-hate, and self-hate is born of empty life. Some store up grievances for so many years that their hearts secretly are repeating those words in *The Merchant of Venice*: "If I can catch him once upon the hip, I will feed fat the ancient grudge I bear him". It is to this world divided by conflicts, wars, hatred and grudge that we Christians are sent to heal and build bridges.

The readings of this Sunday urge us to become bridge-builders between people. One of the tasks which faced the prophets in the aftermath of the fall of Jerusalem was to rebuild a shattered society. So God spoke through Jeremiah: "You have scattered my sheep and driven them away, but I myself will gather them again" (Jer 23:2). St Paul also was concerned with building a new society in which both Jews and Gentiles would find peace as Christ "announced the good news of peace to those who were far off and brought them near" (Eph 2:13). When the heart of Jesus went out to the crowd who were "like sheep without a shepherd" (Mk 6:34) he was bridging the gap of alienation between the poor peasants of Galilee and the religious leaders who never cared for thcm.

More than two thousand years have rolled by, since Christ went round building bridges. But still our society remains divided and hostile. One's inhumanity to another makes countless thousands mourn. Therefore Pope John Paul chose "Build Bridges" as his theme for one of his Masses in the Phillippines. It was a very long Mass. It began an hour late because the Pope's party could not get there by road. They all had to be helicoptered in. The whole Mass lasted three and a half hours. At the end of the Mass, the Pope made this commitment on behalf of everyone present: "We commit ourselves", said he, "to build bridges between all people, between the young and the old, people of different races, different nations, between the rich and the poor, between children and their families, workers and the unemployed and between all religions, churches and nations".

Any multiplication is vexation and division is as bad. Therefore it is the duty of all of us who enjoy the peace of Christ to commit ourselves to build bridges between divided people. It is not an easy task, but not an impossible one provided we keep before our eyes the cross. The cross of Christ will inspire us to look at the disfigured faces, the torn flesh and the contorted limbs of those who are being broken, tortured and killed. Building bridges will not be impossible, if we believe that we are not alone in building. Christ is with us. The Good Friday cross points to the empty cross of Easter Sunday, the cross where the blood has dried, the pain has faded and the broken body has been transformed into a loving stranger, walking in our midst, healing and reconciling. We are called to join him. In the final analysis, humanity has only two ways out – either universal destruction or universal brotherhood.

IS IT NOT A FOLLY?

Readings: 2 Kings 4:42-44; Eph 4:1-6; Jn 6:1-15

Theme: The only adequate response that we can give to God's immeasurable love for us is to build communities of love which offer concrete help and service to those who suffer in human flesh.

A minister who had recently lost his wife took his seven-year-old daughter with him on a foreign trip. They were crossing the ocean on a ship when the captain came to him and asked if he would conduct the Sunday service and speak on the love of God. This was a difficult topic for the minister who was still deep in grief over the loss of his wife. But because he had survived the test of faith, he was able to talk about the immeasurable love of God. After lunch, he and his daughter were standing on deck, leaning on the railing. The little girl said, "Daddy, you said that God loves us, but how much does he love us?" The father looking over the ocean said, "Look in that direction. God's love extends farther than that." Pointing in the opposite direction over endless miles of ocean, he said, "Look the other way. God's love is greater than that". Pointing at the sky he said, "God's love is taller than that", and down at the ocean, "God's love is deeper than that". Biting her lips to hold back the tears, the little girl said, "Daddy, isn't it wonderful that we are standing out here in the midst of it?"

God's love is unfathomed and deathless, untiring, always desiring to stretch forth his hands. No scroll can contain the whole of his love even if it is stretched forth from sky to sky. The bread we read about in two stories in today's liturgy was God's gift to those who sought him through Elijah and Jesus. He catered for their physical needs and did so generously, for when he fed them through Elijah, he said, "They shall eat and there shall be some left over" (2 Kgs 4:44), and when Jesus fed the crowd, he told his disciples, "Gather up the crusts that are left over" (Jn 6:12). This was God's bread for the hungry, but this bread can also be taken metaphorically for God's love which is freely given to those who seek him. God pours out his life-giving love on us according to our need. We experience this love every time we gather around the altar. As we gather we recognise that we are believers but in fact unbelievers, the faithful but in fact unfaithful, brothers and sisters who are often strangers to each other. Yet God in his love forgives us and heals us. When God loves, he always loves and knows that those who deserve least, need it most.

The only adequate response that we, God's children, can make to his immeasurable love is to build our Christian communities in such fashion that they stand as unmistakable signs of God's loving presence among men. We will be able to create such communities if we strive "to live a life worthy of the calling we have received, preserving unity with perfect humility and patience bearing with one another lovingly". (Eph 4:1-2). Peace and union are the most necessary of all things for people who live in common, which requires putting up with one another's defects. There is no one who has his faults and who is not in some way a burden to others. It is easy enough to feel drawn to good and pleasant people but that is only natural love and not charity. A mother does not love her sick, deformed child because he or she is loveable, but because she is his mother. If I take merely a natural attitude towards my neighbour, I can never be charitable in the true Christian sense.

True charity as an adequate response to God's love must take concrete shape in helping and serving God who suffers even today in human flesh. We need not grieve that we live in a time when we can no longer see God in the flesh. He did not in fact take this privilege away from us. As he says: "What ever you have done to the least of my brothers you did it to me". Let us not postpone our loving kindness to others until the evening of our lives or until we can render them in a big way. There was a rich man who complained to his friend thus: "The people do not like me. They say I am stingy and greedy; but I have made my will and have willed my entire property to a charitable institution." The friend replied thus: "A pig came to a cow and complained: 'People speak so well of you. It is true you give milk. But they profit from me much more. They have meat and sausages of different types. Even my feet and hands they eat. Still nobody loves me as they love you. Why?' The cow reflected and said: 'Perhaps it is because of this: I give while I am alive.' Is it not a folly to postpone the good which we can do here and now?"

18TH SUNDAY OF THE YEAR

IS SOMETHING MISSING?

Readings: Ex 16:2-4, 12-15; Eph 4:17, 20-24; Jn 6:24-35

Theme: The basic hunger in the heart of all of us is for God in Christ, who is present in a unique way in the Eucharist, as bread of life, willing to satisfy our deepest hungers, if we follow him.

It happens to us sometimes. We would be hungry for something, but would not know what. We would go to the refrigerator, open the door and look at everything on the shelves, but say, "Not for any of that". We may have everything in life that is important – a family, a job, an income – but still feel something is missing.

We hunger for hundreds of things. First there is a physical hunger which only food can satisfy. You cannot reason out with a hungry belly, for it has no ears. We hunger for feelings of importance, for nobody wants nobody. We hunger for relationships, for without them we are like a lone tree on a hill top at the mercy of every wind that blows. We hunger for faith, for faith is better company than imagination, even for the wife whose husband fails to return on time. We hunger for hope; take away hope from a human heart, and you make the person a beast of prey. We hunger for love, especially in cold climate. Even familiar actions are beautiful through love. But there is one further hunger, a deeper one, that underlies all our other hungers and that is the hunger for the bread of eternal life, which is the hunger for God.

Our hunger for God is actually hunger for Christ, for God is not beyond him but in him. Like man he walked, but like God he talked. His words were oracles, but his deeds were miracles; and so, our hearts yearn for Christ himself. At the age of forty, Tom Phillips was the president of a large company in the State of Massachusetts. He had a Mercedes, a beautiful home, and a lovely family. But Tom was not happy. Rather he was tormented by the moral flabbiness born of the exclusive worship of the bitch-goddess success. Something was missing from his life. But he did not know what it was. Then one night during a business trip to New York, something happened to him. Tom had a religious experience that changed him for ever. Speaking of that experience he said, "I saw what was missing in my life. It was Jesus Christ." Yes. There is deep down a hunger and thirst in all of us that only Jesus can fill. He himself says, "I am the bread of life. He who comes to me will never be hungry; he who believes in me will never thirst" (Jn 6:35).

Jesus the 'Bread of Life' is found in the word of God. Hence the Bible is the greatest traveller in the world; it penetrates every country, civilised and uncivilised. To fill our hungry hearts, we have to enter into the Word of God like a busy bee, which enters a flower here and there, spending some time in each, but emerging from each blossom laden with pollen; it went in empty and came out full. The 'Bread of Life' is of course found in the Eucharist, the Sacrament of sacraments. Scientists tell us that we are what we eat. Incidentally, that is why I stopped eating nuts, which were one of my favourites. If we receive Holy Communion worthily, we not only satisfy our deepmost hungers but also become heart of his heart, and mind of his mind. Jesus can come to us as Bread of Life in so many other ways also. In fact, the very presence of Jesus anywhere and in any manner is food for eternal life.

However, we must not expect this Bread of Life to turn us instantly into deliriously joyful Christians. It is easy for us humans to want 'instant everything'. Supermarkets have shelves full of packages screaming out 'instant coffee', 'Quick Quaker Oats' and 'one minute muffins'. Drive-in restaurants assure us that our orders will be ready in the time it takes to drive from order microphone to the serving window. Banks boast that all our bills for months can be paid in one three minute phone call. Jesus as the Bread of Life is not a similar instant saint-maker. Rather he comes to us constantly inviting us to partake of the experience of true life through effort-filled prayer, the tedious struggle to serve humanity and disciplined commitment to the Gospel values.

19TH SUNDAY OF THE YEAR

AS CHRIST LOVED US

Readings: 1 Kings 19:4-8; Eph 4:30-5:2; Jn 6:41-51

Theme: Those who believe in the real presence of Christ in the Eucharist, will receive his life, which will enable them not only to bear life's trials, such as rejection by others, but also help them to reach out to them in love.

In 1960 a religious persecution broke out in the territory of Sudan in Africa. A Christian black student named Paride Taban fled the danger and went to Uganda. While in Uganda, he studied for the priesthood and was ordained. When things settled down in Sudan, young Fr Taban returned to his homeland. He was assigned to a parish in Palotaka. But his African congregation found it hard to believe that he was really a priest. These people had never had a black priest before. They had always had white priests who gave them clothing and medicine. Fr Taban had nothing to give them for he was poor like them. To make matters worse, Fr Taban had to introduce them to the changes of the Second Vatican Council. These changes bothered the people greatly. They said to one another, "This young black man turns our altar around and celebrates Mass in our own language. He cannot be a priest". Only after a great deal of difficulty did the people of Palotaka finally accept Fr Taban.

Jesus was in a predicament similar to that of Fr Taban. When he said that he was from heaven and gives himself as the Bread of Life, they were scandalised and thought that his outrageous assertions were heretical and blasphemous, totally false and lies. These people had seen him growing as the son of Joseph and Mary and so they believed they knew him and concluded that a man with an ordinary earthly origin and parentage could not have descended from heaven. But their conclusion was based on a superficial knowledge of his life and therefore it closed their minds to truth and their hearts to God. They did not an explanation, rather they preferred to murmur among themselves. Given the incredulity of the people about him, Jesus could have shaken the dust from his feet and walked away. However he was not deterred but chose to stay, to teach them and to offer them his own life.

How often we ourselves have experienced similar rejection based on conjecture! How often we have been the subject of debate and have not been given the opportunity to defend ourselves! How often people have preferred speculation about us than truth and murmured with the crowd! How often our good efforts have met with adversity, bringing our integrity to question, with the result that we have found holding on to our inner convictions with confidence and enthusiasm becoming increasingly difficult! I am sure that all of us have had such afflictions to bear in our lives and have felt them at times so agonising that we wanted to cry to the heavens as Elijah did, "This is enough, O Lord! Take my life" (1 Kings 19:4). But such afflictions greatly lose their sting and the burden becomes easier to bear when we accept the life Jesus offers in the Eucharist. He calls himself "the Bread of Life" (Jn 6: 48). The bread that Jesus offers is not so much a bread that sustains us; rather it is the bread that gives life.

To obtain the life of Jesus from the bread he gives, we must first believe in his word that he himself is in the bread. This is the belief of the Church which she has never changed. Even the threat and revolt of Luther against it did not shake her faith. In the first century, Christians said this, the church of the Middle Ages said this, the pre-Vatican church said this and the post-Vatican Church also says the same. The Church can never explain it how. A little boy asked the electrician: "What exactly is electricity?" The electrician said: "I really do not know, son. But I can make it give you light". Likewise, the Church cannot explain how Jesus is in the Eucharist, but she can make it give us the life of Jesus.

If we believe in the presence of Jesus in the Eucharist, we will receive his life from it and that life will provide us the strength needed to sustain our life's trials. Not only that. With his life, we will also be able to "get rid of all bitterness, all passion and anger, harsh words, slander, and malice of every kind, following the way of life, even as Christ loved us" (Eph 4:31,5:2). Thus, with hearts filled with Christ's own love, we will be daily able to take from our own hearts a few cups of love and one teaspoon of patience, one tablespoon of generosity, one pint of kindness, and one quart of laughter, mix it up, stir it well and then spread it over the span of a lifetime and serve it to others.

THE ASSUMPTION

NOT CHICKENS BUT EAGLES

Readings: Rev 11:19; 12:1-6,10; 1 Cor 15:20-26; Lk 1:39-56

Theme: If we live for the same values which Mary lived for, summed up in her Magnificat, we too, like her, will one day be raised up body and soul to live in heaven with her.

Sin is fatal in all languages, for ever since our first parents Adam and Eve sinned, we are all conceived in our mothers' wombs in sin and are born as the children of darkness. We hate to think that our first parents' sin has got us all into more trouble than science can get us out of. But Mary the Mother of Jesus was an exception. She alone was conceived without sin and was born sinless as the child of light.

In order to have an idea of the shining beauty of Mary's sinless soul, just imagine this. You are sitting on a bench watching the sun go down. As it goes down, it fills the world with golden light. But then it dips lower and lower in the western sky. As the sun retreats, one by one all the colours and all the lights are extinguished and darkness devours all things without a trace. You continue to sit there. Opposite you, there is an open church. It too is plunged into darkness. But then, all of a sudden, a light goes on inside the church. Now against the background of darkness, would not that single light glow with beauty that is simply stunning? Likewise, against the background of humanity steeped in the darkness of sin, Mary's sinless soul shines and it is hard to imagine that anything could be more beautiful!

Mary's freedom from sin ever since her conception required that she be freed also from the ultimate consequence of sin, namely death and decay of her body. It is this freedom that we celebrate on the feast of her assumption. From the theological viewpoint, the feast of the assumption tells us that Mary is in heaven soul and body; that the body of sinless Mary did not decay, but that it went directly from an earthly state to a heavenly one. From a practical viewpoint, the feast of the Assumption reminds us that we too are destined to be in heaven some day, soul and body. Summing up both these viewpoints, the Preface of this feast day Mass says: "The Virgin Mother of God was taken up into heaven to be the beginning and the pattern of the Church in perfection and a sign of hope and comfort for your people on their pilgrim way". Therefore, Mary's glorification is not only a personal privilege but also a reminder that on the last day we too shall rise from the dead and our bodies will be clothed with incorruptibility and immortality. What an encouragement to think that we too are destined for a future glory like that of Mary!

But for that future glory to come true, we need to try to live now, a life soaked in the values which Mary cherished in her life. Her Magnificat sums up her values: "My spirit finds joy in God my Saviour/ He has looked upon her servant in her lowliness/ He has confused the proud and deposed the mighty/ The hungry he has filled and the rich he has sent away empty" (Lk 1:47-48, 52-53). Mary sought her contentment in life solely from God, for she knew that outside God there is nothing but nothing. She was prepared to be a lowly servant of God's will, for she knew that to walk out of God's will is to walk into nowhere. She had nothing to do with pride, for she knew that pride shuts out grace and changes angels into devils. She chose to be poor rather than rich. She embraced both material and spiritual poverty, for she knew that as it is a dry well which makes people know the value of water, so it is only those who see themselves utterly dependent upon God that can fully appreciate the grace of God.

We too are called to live for the same values for which Mary lived, so that we too can share in her heavenly glory. A man found an eagle's egg and placed it under a brooding hen. The eaglet hatched with the chickens and grew to be like them. He clucked and cackled, scratched the earth for worms, flapped his wings and managed to fly a few feet in the air. Years passed. One day, the eagle, now grown old, saw a magnificent bird above him in the sky. It glided in graceful majesty against the powerful wind, with scarcely a movement of its golden wings. Spellbound, the eagle asked, 'Who's that?' 'That is the king of birds, the eagle', said his neighbour; 'he belongs to the sky; we belong to earth – we are chickens.' So the eagle lived and died a chicken for that's what he thought he was. We are not to make the same mistake which the eagle made. We are not born for this earth but for heaven. We are not chickens but eagles!

20TH SUNDAY OF THE YEAR

"AMEN"

Readings: Prov 9:1-6; Eph 5:15-20; Jn 6:51-58

Theme: We graciously affirm that Christ is really present in the Eucharist as the bread of life, calling us to live his life fed by him and to be on earth his visible Body united in love.

A. A. Procter said after a great musical recital: "I do not know what I was playing, or what I was dreaming then; but I struck one chord of music like the sound of a great Amen." Amen is a Hebrew word usually transliterated but sometimes translated. So it is a word found in all languages. Its meaning is: 'So be it!' or 'So it is!' It occurs more in St John's writings than in the writing of any of the other inspired writers. There are four kinds of Amen in St John's writings: the Amen of gracious affirmation; the Amen of grateful adoration; the Amen of glorious annunciation and the Amen of glad anticipation. When we receive the Holy Communion, the priest says, "It is the Body and Blood of Christ" and we respond, 'Amen'; ours is a gracious affirmation. But what do we affirm about the Eucharist when we say Amen?

Our Amen affirms that Jesus Christ is really present in the Eucharist. Of course, Jesus is really present in many ways. For example, he is really present in the community. He is really present in the Scriptures and in all the sacraments. But the phrase 'real presence' normally refers to his presence in the consecrated bread and wine at Mass. The presence of Christ in the Eucharist is unique because in it are contained substantially the body and the blood conjointly with the soul and the divinity of Christ. When the words of Christ, "This is my body; this is my blood" are said over the bread and wine, a supernatural and yet imperceptible conversion takes place, solely by the power of the word of Christ.

Our Amen affirms that Eucharist gives us eternal life. "He who feeds on my flesh and drinks my blood has life eternal", said the Lord (Jn 6:54). Human beings have many basic hungers but the most basic hunger is for food and drink. And Jesus says that our genuine nourishment lies in his flesh and blood; without them, the really 'human person' dies, though he continues to live in the flesh; but with them he lives the life that is really life. Advertisers too make extravagant claims to satisfy our needs for this life such as pleasures of oral gratification, to help us escape from boredom and monotony and to offer security and protection for ourselves and families. Yet, contrary to their claims, what they offer is not the real thing at all, but only an illusion, a substitute. It is only Christ who can show us how really to live and to live abundantly.

Our Amen affirms that when we feed on Christ's life in the Eucharist, we are called to fill our lives with his word and example. In other words, our Amen to the gift of the Eucharist calls us to respond in action and to try to live as Christ lived. This means that we are to "lay aside immaturity and walk in the way of insight" (Prov 9:6). We all know that a mark of maturity is the sense of fellowship with other human beings as we take our place among them; and to walk in the way of insight is to see persons and things through one's heart before the head can see. The gift of the Eucharist calls us to respond also in actions recommended by St Paul. He asks us to "watch over our conduct and not act like fools." (Eph 5:15), and we know only too well that he who provides only for this life but takes no care for eternity may be wise for the moment but a fool for ever.

Our Amen affirms that we who receive the Body of Christ become the Body of Christ and therefore we are called to be truly the members of that Body. Those who have worked long enough in ship-building know that welding is impossible unless the materials to be joined are at white heat temperature. Likewise, unless our love for each other in the Body of Christ is at white heat temperature, we can't forge true union among ourselves as members of the same Body. Yes. In order to be united, we must love one another, to love one another we must know one another, to know one another we must meet one another, especially the poor, at each other's most basic needs, because our love for God can be no greater than our love for the least important person in the Body of Christ.

21ST SUNDAY OF THE YEAR

HOW COMMITTED AM I?

Readings: Jos 24:1-2, 15-18; Eph 5:21-32; Jn 6:60-69

Theme: Our commitment made to God at baptism, which was a commitment made to Christ and to his Church, must be carried out in our life, including marital life.

The number of promises I have made to God ever since I became a Christian are many: some private, others public; some simple, others solemn. What happened to those promises? I must humbly acknowledge that on some of them I have been just standing, on some others sitting. I feel that a few of those promises could have been as well written on wind and on running water. A commitment to God must be at least as binding as those we make at the bank. When Joshua asked all the tribes of Israel, "Decide today whom you will serve", the people in one voice answered, "Far be it from us to forsake the Lord" (Jos 24:15-16). When we were baptised and became God's children, we entered into a covenant with God, and not into an oral contract which is not worth the paper it is written on. If we say we are committed to God as children to a father, how faithful are we in observing at least his Ten Laws, to which the *Catechism of the Chatholic Church* devotes nearly 100 pages, more than one fifth of its length? Sometimes it is sad to think that the law of gravitation seems to be the only law that everybody observes.

Commitment to God our Father naturally calls for a commitment to his son, Jesus Christ. We are not to consider ourselves Christians simply because we think we are. It is our faithfulness to Christ, especially when we are pushed to the wall or when we are ready to quit, that makes our commitment to Christ truly a covenant. The disciples of Jesus were severely challenged when Jesus said, "I am the bread of life". One group finding Jesus' words too hard to take left him and no more walked with him. But the disciples met the challenge successfully and remained faithful to him. When asked, "Would you also like to leave?" St Peter on behalf of all said, "Lord, to whom would we go? You have the words of eternal life" (Jn 6:68). How committed are we to Jesus when his teaching appears to be too idealistic to be practised and too risky to be put into action? At those moments when our faith is challenged, or when some storm threatens to destroy us, we must not fix our attention on the problem but on the person of Jesus Christ. Because he has promised, and that is his commitment to us, that he will not allow us to sink. Do we have faith to believe it, hope to anticipate it, and patience to await it?

The Church is the body of Christ. "He gave Himself up for her", says St Paul, "and cares for her – for we are members of his body" (Eph 5:25,30). Hence if we are committed to Christ, we must be committed to his Church, the people of God. It is in order to renew our commitment to one another and deepen our love for each other in Christ, we gather every week in the church for the Eucharist. Are we faithful to the Sunday Eucharist? Most of God's troubles with labourers in his vineyard seems to be absenteeism. There was a catholic man who would always say to his wife on Sunday morning, "You can go to Mass for both of us". One night he dreamed that he and his wife died and came together to heaven's fate. St Peter asked, "Are you Mr and Mrs Smith?". The couple both nodded their heads. "Well, Mrs Smith can come in for both of you", declared the saint. Church membership is not necessarily an elevator to heaven.

Being committed to the people of God as members of the body of Christ has to find its expression in daily life, particularly in marital life. St Paul urges husbands and wives to model their relationship on that which exists between Christ and his Church. The norm of this relationship is love, faithfulness and mutual respect. Having committed to each other for life, each must "cling" to one another, for "the two are made into one" (Gen 2:24). When the late Mr and Mrs Henry Ford celebrated their golden wedding anniversary, a reporter asked them, "To what do you attribute your 50 years of successful life?" "The formula", said Ford, "is the same formula I have always used in making cars – just stick to one model". Committed couples will not only stick to one another but also forgive each other generously. A happy marriage is the union of two good forgivers. Otherwise, they are in for unhappiness. When I asked a class to explain the meaning of the word "bachelor", one girl wrote, "A very happy man". "Where did you get the idea?" I asked. "My father helped me with my homework", she confessed.

22ND SUNDAY OF THE YEAR

WHAT IS IN OUR HEARTS?

Readings: Deut 4:1-2, 6-8; Jas 1:17-18, 21-22,27; Mk 7:1-8, 14-15, 21-23

Theme: Our observance of the laws of God, which are an expression of God's loving concern and constant presence with us, leads us to love him and our neighbour more and more.

One editor of a small town paper who became irritated with the number of complaints following one of his editorials, decided to run the Ten Commandments in the place of his next editorial. A few days later a letter arrived reading, "Cancel my subscription. You are getting too personal". It is amazing that in every area of life people expect rules and regulations except in religion. And yet God says, "Israel, hear the statutes and decrees I am teaching you to observe, that you may live" (Deut 4:1). God did not give us Ten Suggestions. He gave us Ten Commandments. We can go on breaking them, but we can never get rid of them, for they are written in our consciences. If we disobey them, the disaster will be greater than neglecting the rules of the Highway Code when riding a bicycle. Laws of God are good and necessary, for they are the expressions of God's loving concern and constant presence. However, we are expected to live by the commandments and not die by them. We will die by them if there is no love in our hearts when observing them, for love of God is the root, and love of our neighbour is the fruit.

God's laws are supposed to bring our hearts closer to God and to his people in love. Otherwise, the laws will become only obstacles even to justice and decency in human relationships. Hence, where are our hearts and what is in them? We hope that when looking at us the Lord would not complain, "This people pays me lip service, but their heart is far from me" (Mk 7:6). Christian life is an affair of the heart. Hence we need often to purify our heart and keep it set on love, true love, of course. For, love is the most abused word in our language. It is used to mean anything from self-sacrificing devotion to selfish lust. Therefore in our Christian journey we must go on purifying even our legitimate human loves, such as affection, friendship and eros, until we have learnt to relate all of these to charity, the highest love which is God himself.

As the external observance of God's commandments without charity in our hearts, can become obstacles on our journey towards God, so the performance of religious rituals without charity for its motive, can become an obstruction to holiness. We must not minimise the profound value found in the rituals we perform in Sunday worship. We can even dare say that the truth of religion is in the rituals as the truth of dogma is in poetry. Rituals make religion permeate every action of the day. But in trying to do this we must not allow religion to degenerate into an activity of performance. This is what angered Jesus against the Pharisees. He laughed at them saying, "Empty is the reverence they show me" (Mk 7:7). It is said of a Muslim who pursued an enemy to kill him. In the midst of the chase, the public call to prayer sounded; instantly, the Muslim got off his horse, unrolled his prayer mat, knelt down, and prayed the required prayers as fast as he could. Then he leaped back on his horse and continued his pursuit. It was precisely this kind of legalism that Jesus opposes in us also.

We need to guard against identifying religion with performing external acts. Going to church, saying prayers, reading the Bible and giving to charity do not in themselves guarantee holiness, if we do all these for the wrong motive and in an unloving way. "He means well" is more important than "He does well". What counts is not so much what we do as why we do. If my heart is filled with bitterness and pride, even my best external act will not make me holy before God. Hence we must often examine: Does our observance of laws and performing of rituals spring from loving gratitude to God, bring us to greater intimacy with Jesus, make us love him and our neighbour, help us to practise corporal works of mercy such as, "looking after widows and orphans in their distress", and "keep ourselves unspotted by the world which alone make for pure worship?" (Jas 1:27) Yes. It is our hearts that Jesus is concerned about. Of all rites, the holiest rite is to cleanse one's heart in the company of saints. So long as religion is only outward form and religious rituals are not experienced in our hearts, nothing of any importance has happened. Hence, it would be good if we at times stand before the Lord just with a broken heart how else can he enter into it, anyway?

23RD SUNDAY OF THE YEAR

GOD OF THE OPPRESSED

Readings: Is 35:4-7; Jas 2:1-5; Mk 7:31-37

Theme: God who revealed himself in Jesus as God of the oppressed calls us to be his eyes, hands, legs and tongues so that he could continue to save the oppressed in our midst.

The great Greek Philosopher Cicero said that a tear dries quickly, especially when it is shed for the troubles of others. He was talking about compassion. Compassion is the root of religion as pride is the root of sin. We may dismiss compassion from our heart, but God never will. In fact, the compassion we see in the kind-hearted is God's own compassion. He has given it to us to protect the oppressed for he himself is the God of the oppressed. Addressing his chosen people who were suffering from their exile, he said: "Fear not; your Saviour will come; At his coming, the eyes of the blind will be opened, the ears of the deaf will be cleared and the lame will leap like a stag" (Is 35:4). The Saviour Jesus Christ did come. He showed great concern for all those oppressed by poverty, infirmity, sickness, injustice, discrimination and many other kinds of hardships. Anyone who observed Christ relieving people from their miseries could easily affirm that "God chose who are poor in the eyes of the world" (Jas 2:5). God loves and cares for all of us. But when Jesus made the blind see, the deaf hear, the crippled walk (Mk 7:35), we have a window into the heart of God, a heart that beats faster at the sight of the oppressed.

The cries of the oppressed have not yet ceased even after the coming of the Saviour into our world. Millions are oppressed by injustices of others, the injustices that result from an increase of selfishness and exaggerated nationalism, the injustice that results from a propensity to dominate others beyond the limits of one's legitimate rights and merits, and from a propensity to exploit the whole material progress and the technology of production for the exclusive purpose of dominating others. Many, in most societies, are oppressed by discrimination and discrimination is a way of acting that affects minority people's lives and life chances. People suffer from prejudices of others, and prejudice is having negative attitudes towards particular groups based on false assumptions. Still others suffer from racism and racism is the belief that certain 'races' are superior to others. We sometimes call such sufferers as the 'handicapped' and, in doing so, we indicate how little we expect from them and how little they expect from us.

In the face of such an appalling spectacle of the oppressed, underprivileged and disadvantaged, how can we remain silent and indifferent? If the rejection of others is not my sorrow too, if the anguish of my neighbour in all its forms touches me not, if the lack of hope of my brothers and sisters does not torment me, how can I call myself the child of God who is the Lord of the oppressed? We can't close our eyes in blindness to the hunger of people around to the plight of victims struck by artificial disasters and to the injustices done to immigrants and refugees. We can't turn a deaf ear to the cries of frustration from people victimised because of their colour, to the cries of loneliness from the so called 'untouchables', or to the cries of hurt from people we have injured by our own acts of violence to human rights and dignity. We can't keep our tongue silent when we should speak boldly in defence of the discriminated, of fairness of sharing the goods of the world with the poor.

Therefore our Lord Jesus asks us for a change of heart towards the oppressed. On our own, no real change is possible, but if we allow the Lord to touch us, even hearts of stone will melt into hearts of flesh. By his touch, he can open our eyes, unplug our ears and loosen our tongues. When the Lord touches us, not only we are changed but we in turn are enabled to touch others and lift them from their miseries. Indeed, the Lord of the oppressed asks for our hands so that he might use them to wipe away the tears of the sorrowing; he asks for our mouths to speak out against racial discrimination; he asks for our eyes to see the plight of poverty-stricken people and he asks for our life itself so that he might work through us. And when the Lord works through us, the hatred which divides person from person will end, man's indifference to the plight of the marginalised will end, the greed which urges so many to keep all they have and not share with their neighbour will end; above all, the pride which leads to trust in ourselves and not in God will end.

HOW HARD IT IS!

Readings: Is 50:4-9; Jas 2:14-18; Mk 8:27-35

Theme: Our profession of faith in Christ as the Messiah, leads us to embrace our daily cross as the sure way to life.

Who is Jesus Christ to the world? Well, we can go to a bookstore and peruse the shelves of books marked "Religion"; but be on guard, for some so-called religious books are such that they are not to be tossed aside lightly but be thrown with great force. Or you could for a couple of days see the religious programmes on television, though some television shows are for appearing on, not looking at. You could also on some weekends go to churches where Jesus is the topic of the sermons, but make it a point to listen to a minister who has a sermon to preach and not to one who has to preach a sermon. You will thus come to know more or less what the world thinks of Christ.

Let us be more personal now. Who is Jesus to each of us? We believe that Jesus is to us the "Messiah" (Mk 8:29), the Saviour who is the "Way" to Life. We also know that his Way is "denying oneself", "taking up one's cross", and "losing oneself for his sake" (Mk 8:34-35). How hard a Way it is! I have never seen my congregations sleeping so comfortably as when I preach on this Way. But Jesus like all great leaders had to be honest with his followers.

To know the Way to Life is good but to follow that Way is better. We would be like blind people if we only know and do not follow. Blind people can be taught about colours, that the sky is blue, that the fields are green. But these colours have no meaning for them, for they have never experienced colours by seeing them. Likewise, if we only know the way to life and never follow it, we can't experience the life Jesus promises. It is true also of believing and not practising. So, St James asks, "What good is it to profess faith without practising it?" (Jas 2:14). Yes. Faith without good works has no power to save. If faith is the root of good works, a root that produces nothing is dead. Hence, as a Christian, I prefer to resemble a fruit tree and not a Christmas tree which has only gaudy decorations with no real fruits on it. Jesus himself after showing the way of the cross followed it, fulfilling the prophecy, "I give my back to those who beat me, my cheeks to those who plucked my beard" (Is 50:6).

Life is a tough proposition, for suffering is part of it. The Lord does not ask us to submit ourselves to pains in a fatalistic spirit as though we are doomed to suffer. He is not suggesting that we invite the birds of sorrow who want to fly over our heads to come and build their nests in our hair. We must take all legitimate steps to remove and prevent all unnecessary sufferings. But if, in spite of that, we have still to suffer especially along our journey in faith towards full Christian maturity, we are asked to take them on willingly. To "deny oneself", for example, may be needed to resist temptations, especially in youth. In my own youth I could resist everything except temptation. To "take up one's daily cross", one need not travel very far. Even marital love, at times, could be a cross. How can you go on loving your spouse if his or her love is only a dirty trick played on you to continue the species? Dying is one of the few things as easily done lying down, but "dying to oneself" is very hard, for it means to be sponged out and erased for Christ's sake. However, as the phoenix renews her youth only when she is burnt alive, so a Christian has to come through fire in order not to fade away.

Sorrows for Christ's sake, whatever their source, are a blessing. United with him they become universally redemptive, as his own are. Every pain we welcome destroys something of wickedness. Not that there is any such thing as pure wickedness, for even the most scaring wickedness is only goodness gone wrong. Hence a pain which destroys it is a blessing. Besides, sorrow shatters the illusion of man's self-sufficiency, breaking through the deception that we are in control of our life, and compelling us to look towards God, the source of all comforts. Therefore, "Blessed are those who mourn" is ironically a more necessary message than "Rejoice always in the Lord", for there can be no true rejoicing until we stop running away from mourning.

25TH SUNDAY OF THE YEAR

THE WISDOM FROM ABOVE

Readings: Wis 2:12, 17-20; Jas 3:16-4:3; Mk 9:30-37

Theme: If we are guided by divine wisdom rather than only by human wisdom, we would become more humble, serving one another in love, and thus we would make this world a better place.

Newspapers always excite curiosity, but they often make sad reading, for so much of what they report is about war and violence and many other problems that plague our society. Some of the problems have to be so highlighted that their headlines have to be twice the size of the events. There is the economic problem – since most of the countries are coming up with only a deficit budget, we have to add one more beatitude: Blessed are the young for they shall inherit the national debt. There are political problems, most of which remain unsolved because many of the politicians are ready to do anything to keep their job, even to become a patriot. There are problems in education: some complain that modern universities have become chat-shows but with more people. There is the taunting problem of war and violence: our civilisation is indeed advancing for in every war they kill you in a new way. Modern scientists with their great ability to reason and compute can easily pinpoint most of our problems, but the trouble is that they can't solve many of them.

How can they solve them relying only on human wisdom? Indeed, we need human wisdom. It is wise to act wise unless you are otherwise. But don't we know that human wisdom often degenerates into brute reason which is worse than brute force, and in the process of acquiring it many people make fools of themselves? Besides, human pride and ambition often parade under the guise of human wisdom and, as a result, some foolishly identify even war and violence with courage, though none of us can be sure of our courage until the day of our death. In pride and self-conceit some think they are equal to God. A new patient went to a psychiatrist. The doctor said, "This is your first visit to me. I know absolutely nothing about you. So please tell me about yourself from the beginning". The patient started, "In the beginning I created heaven and earth..." "Stop," said the doctor, "I can guess the rest of your story". Such an inflated self-pride begets envy and jealousy which blind us to our calling to love others and care for them. "Where do the conflicts among you originate? Is it not your inner craving that makes war within your members?" asks St James (4:1). Our silly pride and petty jealousy stirs up hatred which cries out for vengeance even against the innocent, saying, "Let us beset the just one; Let us condemn him to a shameful death" (Wis 2:19-20).

Hence, instead of relying on earthly wisdom, we must look up to the "wisdom that comes from above" (Jas 3:17) which alone can show the way to equality in economics, decency in politics, prosperity in society and peace among all men, not the deep peace of the double bed but the deep, deep peace of the heart. Christ himself spelt out this way when he told his disciples who were arguing among themselves, "Who is the most important?", that "If anyone wishes to rank first, he must remain the last one of all and the servant of all" (Mk 9:35). This means that the way to the peace of Christ is first humility. Humility is not bowing my head so low that I can see nothing but my navel. Rather it is acknowledging one's human limitation and depending upon divine providence. However the person who often looks up to God rarely looks down on any neighbour and hence a humble person will naturally respect and care for fellow human beings. A humble person sees their own brother and sister in the eyes of any man or woman offering loving service to all, especially to the weak and to the poor.

Summing up how the divine wisdom works for peace and joy, Jesus took up a child, as Pope John Paul II often takes a little baby from its mother's arms raising it above the crowd, and said, "Whoever welcomes a child for my sake welcomes me" (Mk 9:37). In saying so, Jesus not only warned us that children are the first victims of war and violence, and not only condemned those who by their acts of fighting and killing teach the young that this is the way to solve problems, but also underlined our need for humble dependence on God as the child depends on its parents, and called us to serve others especially those who are small and weak like little children. Of course such a service will cost dearly. These days, the price of everything is rising, so much that the only way to beat the high cost of living is to stop living. The cost of peace also can be high. Christ's refusal to take up the sword, and his loving service to sinful humanity led him to his passion and death. But then he rose to glory with an explosion of joy and life. Likewise if we dedicate ourselves to loving service, even at a great cost, the risen light and the peace of Christ will fill the earth.

26TH SUNDAY OF THE YEAR

LET THE FLOWER FLOURISH

Readings: Num 11:25-29; Jas 5:1-6; Mk 9:38-43, 45, 47-48

Theme: Since all religions share in divine truth and the works of God in various degrees, we can't condemn anyone outside our own particular faith.

I have often pondered over the fate of Mahatma Gandhi. Where is he now, in heaven, or in hell, or at least in purgatory? He was not a Catholic and Catholics until a few decades ago believed that outside the Catholic Church there is everything except salvation. He was not a Christian: from the day he was refused admission to worship in a Christian church in South Africa, just because he was coloured, he turned his back on Christianity. But even as a Hindu he believed in the unique power of Christ's teachings so much that he said to Winston Churchill that the only way for world peace is that all nations abide by the Beatitudes. He even practised one of the hardest sayings of Christ: "Love your enemies". When Prince Philip was engaged to Princess Elizabeth, Gandhi wanted to give them a wedding present but said to Mountbatten, Viceroy of India, "What can I give, I have nothing?" The Viceroy replied, "You have your spinning wheel, get to work and spin them something". Gandhi made them a tablecloth which Mountbatten sent to Princess Elizabeth with this note: "This you lock up with crown jewels, for it was spun by a man who said, 'The British must depart as friends'". Can this man, just because he did not belong to the visible group of Christ's followers, be separated for ever from God? I hope not.

What drives me to this hope is not my patriotism, though as a true patriot I left my country, I guess for my country's good! My hope is based on the reply Jesus gave to his disciples who complained that some people not belonging to their circle were working miracles. Jesus asked them not to stop the good others were doing, for "anyone who is not against us is with us" (Mk 9:40). What did he mean? He meant that anyone who is attached to God and struggles against the self-centred forces of evil is on the side of Christ, that one does not necessarily have to be part of the visible group following Christ in order to partake of the power of God and that it is wrong to assume that only those who have consciously accepted Christ as personal saviour will be saved and will be able to do the works of God. Thus, Jesus broke through the exclusiveness of all those small groups of believers who think that they have exclusive rights, special access to the full truth.

How often we get so wrapped up in our own organisations or church that it leads to the building of barriers rather than bridges between us and the people of other religions and denominations! Once I was at the General Post Office. I had bought some stamps, went to the high table on the other side of the hall, and was putting the stamps on. Next to me two ladies were talking to each other. I did not want to listen in but I could not help it for they were so loud. I don't know their complete conversation; I only heard one say, "You know, they are Catholics, of course, they think they have the truth, the way and the life, they have no time for us". "Yes", I heard the other answer, "Silly, isn't it?", and after that I heard nothing more. They walked out into the street and I posted my letters. We at times become even jealous of the achievements of other religious groups, like the disciples of Moses did. When they complained out of jealousy that Eldad and Medad who were not of their circle were also prophesying, Moses rebuked them for their envy which at times can be as cruel as grave, asked them to let the flower flourish where it will, and only wished, "Would that the Lord might bestow his spirit on them all" (Num 11:29). Hence, Catholics, Protestants and non-Christians are not against one another but for each other.

In saying this, we are not proposing that we must tolerate everything, for if we do we will teach nothing. Nor are we suggesting that God's grace is distributed denominationally; we still believe that Jesus is the unique reflection of God, the fullness of divine revelation, and the church he founded is the Catholic Church. But at the same time we recognise that all religions share in divine truth and in the works of God. In order to belong to Christ, what really matters is to get rid of anything which leads us away from God and to give "a cup of water to the needy" (Mk 9:41), which is to love God and our neighbour. If we love Christianity more than God and our neighbour, we will soon proceed to love our own sect or church more than Christianity, and then, of course, we will end up as slaves to selfishness by which we will become our own executioners.

27TH SUNDAY OF THE YEAR

TWO IN ONE

Readings: Gen 2:18-24; Heb 2:9-11; Mk 10:2-16

Theme: Totality in love, fidelity to the end, and the use of God-given means, are the conditions for married couples, to find increasing joy in being two in one.

Questioning the children before Confirmation, the Bishop asked one nervous little girl, "What is matrimony?". She answered, "A place where souls suffer for a time for their sins!". "No, no", said the parish priest, "that is purgatory". "Let her alone", said the Bishop, "she might be right, what do you and I know about it?" Yes. What do I, an unmarried, know about marriage?

This much I know: marriage is not an outdated institution for it is a gift from God. Does not the Genesis story portray the first couple being introduced by God in person and joined with his blessing? God knew only too well that, "it is not good for man to be alone" (Gen 2:18). That is why, even celibates like me have a natural tendency to lean towards women, but not far enough to lose my balance. Yet the fact remains that God calls the majority of men and women to become holy and find their fulfilment in marriage through a loving and loyal living together to the end. But it is sad that the rising divorce rate has become a bewildering religious and social problem. We only sympathise with all the divorcees, for marriages though "made in heaven" are lived on earth where, too often, selfishness can overpower love to the extent that marital fidelity indeed becomes difficult.

However, any promise to be true has to fulfil certain conditions as in the case of a seed which is a promise but it has to be first buried in the soil and exposed to rain and wind and sunshine before it sprouts. Likewise, God's promise of fulfilment through marriage has some conditions, namely totality in love and fidelity to the end. As Jesus pointed out: "They are no longer two but one flesh, and therefore let no one separate what God has joined" (Mk 10:8-9). When Jesus said, "two become one" the issue is not how two bodies can occupy one space but rather how married people are destined to live together so closely and give of themselves to each other so entirely that they can be said to form one body. In fact regardless of divorce or death of the spouses they will always be "two in one" in their children. And, of course, such a total giving is to be kept up to the end, because the children need the continued presence of their parents as they grow and the spouses themselves need this continuity to understand one another more and more deeply, to feel secure, to expose one's wounds and to receive healing. In the absence of such a continuity, there will be no reliability of marital love for it will fail to answer when called. Nor will there be predictability of behaviour on which depends one's security and safety.

Hence at a Christian wedding, the couple promise each other, not a Rose Garden but the gift of themselves for ever. Fewer marriages would skid, if more who said, "I do", did. But the Church, while proposing an ideal of marriage, is not unrealistic. It knows that marriage is not like the Hill of Olympus, wholly clear, without clouds. So it is compassionate as well. If the Church's Marriage Tribunal finds that certain marriages were not true marriages, after careful examination, it is prepared to call them null and void. Besides, in order to put the engaged and the married on the way to ideal marriage, it has established pre-marriage agencies from whom to get expert advice from experienced counsellors. It has set up a number of organisations such as The Christian Family Movement, Marriage Encounter, and the Catholic Marriage Advisory Council, which are often instruments of pastoral healing and bring greater vitality into already happy marriages. Indeed all marriages are happy: it is the living together afterwards that causes all the trouble. But of this we are sure: God has made available in Christ the necessary means for Christian couples who are set on the way to successful marriage. Besides the Sacrament of Confirmation which gives strength to live out one's vocation and the Sunday Eucharist which gives further power, Jesus made Matrimony also a Sacrament, of which the couples themselves are ministers, so that not only on the wedding day but each day they can be ministers of God's grace to each other. Without constantly receiving God's grace through sacraments and prayer, Christian marriage is unthinkable. But if God becomes a third party in marriage, it will not be a year of flames and thirty years of ashes. On the contrary, the couple's love for each other, like God its author, will go on and on, intensifying the joy of being two in one.

28TH SUNDAY OF THE YEAR

WHY GO AWAY SAD?

Readings: Wis 7:7-11; Heb 4:12-13; Mk 10:17-27

Theme: Those who have developed a detached Christian attitude towards wealth, will not go away sad, if a part of it or the whole of it has to be sacrificed, for the sake of Christ.

It is always wise to look ahead, but it is wiser to look further than we can see. Further than the material riches which we can see lies Everlasting Life. Though poverty is not necessarily a recipe for contented life, wealth cannot be equated with happiness either. And yet, so many cling to material riches which have a funny way of making the rich greedy and selfish, so much so that such people insist on being happy at all costs, which is one of the surest ways of avoiding being happy. They don't seem to realise that at times the best way not to go mad may be that one does not mind too much when actually going mad. What I mean is that there is an element of hazard involved in nearly everything worthwhile. For example, if I want to explore life on the other side of the road, I have to surrender the security I have on the pavement and brave the risk of getting run over. Hence Jesus tells the rich man in the Gospel (Mk 10:21) that if he wants to become a perfect Christian on the way to eternal life, he must surrender all his riches to the poor. But we feel sorry for this man, because when it had pleased his Father to give him his Kingdom, he wanted only a little piece of toast and went away sad.

After all, in asking "to give away all", Jesus was not condemning material riches in themselves; neither did he call everyone of us to give away everything we have to the poor, nor did he want to make us feel guilty about what we have. He himself had some reasonably well off people among his disciples and he knew well that people have to think of their own needs and of their security. Hence, what Jesus was actually telling us was that because riches give a false sense of security demanding the total loyalty of one's heart, it is dangerous to get attached to them; that the person who has most of the physical needs can become so self-reliant that he forgets eternal life, thus turning abundance itself into a deficiency; and that those who hang on to riches which are more than their need not only forget that they are only stewards of that which is God's, but also allow self-interest to blind them to the needs of others. By implication, Jesus not only warned all those who take advantage of the poor but also condemned the unjust distribution of wealth which is an offence against human brotherhood.

Therefore, the real problem arises not so much from possessing and not possessing material wealth but from one's wrong attitude to wealth. Wealth, as many would think, is not a sign of special favour from God, as a reward for being good; nor is poverty a sign of faithlessness and of God's displeasure. If we have a Christ-like attitude towards wealth, some of us, who knows, may give away everything to the poor in order to follow Christ, as many in the past have done and as some are doing even today; for there is so much material poverty in the world that if all the starving children of the world were lined up one behind the other, starting from your front door, the end of the queue would be twenty-five thousand miles away. With a Christian attitude towards wealth, I am sure, most of us would continue our support of Relief Funds, Mission Work, and Catholic Service Appeal; and many of us, without actually leaving our home and family, would surely keep up our efforts to provide homes for the homeless, employment for the jobless and protection for the defenceless.

Let us face it. The giving up of anything in any form, is going to hurt, as it hurt St Paul when he had to give up his entire past to follow Christ and it hurt him so deeply that he groaned: "God's word is sharper than any two-edged sword" (Heb 4:12). But Jesus, the Wisdom of God, assures us that in return for what we give up, we will be repaid with eternal life and a hundredfold in this life, namely, an inner peace, a deep feeling of fulfilment and an interior joy which seem to escape those who frantically chase after cheap thrills. Hence, if we are really wise, we will "prefer the Wisdom of God to sceptre and throne, for all good things come to us in her company" (Wis 7:8). Why, then, go away sad today, like the man in the gospel, because we won't let go the one thing more the Lord wants from us?

29TH SUNDAY OF THE YEAR

GOD'S MEGAPHONE

Readings: Is 53:10-11; Heb 4:14-16; Mk 10:35-45

Theme: Jesus calls all those who aspire to true greatness to be willing to serve God and neighbour, and even to lay down their lives in service.

The name 'Great Britain' says a lot on greatness. Among other things it points out the basic desire in every person to become great. It is so basic that if one cannot become great, one tries to attach oneself to something that is great. If that too is not possible, some strive at least to look great. Our world too recognises greatness, and so Alfred Gilman and Martin Rodbell, two Americans, were awarded in 1994 the Nobel Prize in medicine. Moved by this universal desire to become great, Ss James and John, in the Gospel, ask the Lord whether they could be a sort of Prime Minister and Chancellor when He became King. Jesus does not blame them for asking this, but points out to them, perhaps to their embarrassment, that true greatness is achieved through service: "Anyone among you who aspires to greatness, must serve the rest" (Mk 10:44). Once again, poor Jesus Christ, the bearer of good news, proclaims bad news to a world where greatness through making a lot of money or by drawing huge crowds at a rock concert seems to be standard. But Jesus means what he says.

Service is not to be understood as meaning only menial jobs, the sort done by domestic servants (in some houses, I know, the servant is treated so badly that when the wife comes in at the front door he goes out at the back). Service is also any noble and unselfish act. It includes one's daily duty taken as God's will for us. We do serve God and human society at large whenever we do our daily task with a sense of dedication and justice, also offering a helping hand to those with whom we live and work. Duty thus performed out of love will never be dull and will give our conscience music at midnight. Yet it is unfortunate that when duty calls, some people are never at home.

Of course duty, however praiseworthy, is not the ideal Christian service. Christ challenges us to go beyond one's duty and serve our fellow human beings without hope of gain or reward, without gratitude or praise. True Christian service is, therefore, that which is done solely out of love without any personal advantage, in order to continue Christ's work of bringing light and hope, help and healing into the lives of others. Such a service will also be unconditional. A rich Hindu gentleman offered Mother Teresa money to build a home for the dying but with a condition that it must be a vegetarian house. But Mother Teresa tries to give every dying person their last wish: it could be something like water from the Ganges, or a cigarette or a chicken leg. In a vegetarian home, she would not be able to give anyone chicken and hence she refused the offer.

It is this kind of service, with no ulterior selfish motive, that must count for a Christian and the service that counts is the service that costs. It means drinking from the cup of suffering Jesus drank, whom God "crushed in infirmity", so that "through his suffering, he may justify many" (Is 53.10). In fact, nothing great was ever done in the world without much enduring. Beethoven was a master composer, yes, but he struggled long hours to get the right note. The only place where greatness comes before suffering is a dictionary. Hence Jesus calls those of us who aspire to higher forms of greatness to be willing to serve others and even to lay down our lives for them.

Indeed, thank goodness, there are thousands of people in our own day, as in the past, who have dedicated themselves to unselfish service after the example of Christ. But these are only like a silver lining across the dark clouds of selfishness or hurtling through the sky. For our world is full of people who hunger not after service but status of prestige, even when they don't deserve it; people who cling to positions of power, as if they are indispensable (yet the graveyards are filled with the so-called indispensables) and people who feel so empty within themselves, because they have lost their way to true greatness that they need some people to lord over or at least an audience to applaud them. It is to arouse this world, which has lost its sense of the other, that Jesus raises God's megaphone of service.

30TH SUNDAY OF THE YEAR

THAT I MAY SEE

Readings: Jer 31:7-9; Heb 5:1-6; Mk 10:46-52

Theme: Christ can open our spiritual eyes, to see our missionary obligation to love others in action, for we were baptised into Christ's love.

If you are truly in love, it will track you down like a cruise missile, making a way out of no way. We see this demonstrated in God's loving care for people all over the world, when he "delivered his people, the remnant of Israel, gathering them from the ends of the earth, with the blind and lame in their midst" (Jer 31:8-9). If you are truly in love, you will be embarrassed if left alone, when the loved one suffers or is in danger. We see this demonstrated in the love of Christ, who "was able to deal patiently with erring sinners, for he himself was beset with weakness" (Heb 5:2), like any one of us. Are we surprised, then, that we who were born of this love of God and were baptised into Christ's love are also given the mission not only to proclaim but to share this love with others? Mission Sunday reminds us that Mission is about loving and sharing.

Love, as you know, is like war, easy to begin but very difficult to stop. That is why Christians, who are fired with a sense of mission to love and care, go even to the extreme of heroic endurance, as it happened in the little African country Rwanda. During the massacre that the militia and rebel forces unleashed against the rival ethnic group, more than 60 priests and missionaries together with many ordinary Christians became willing victims of untold suffering and cruel death, all in the name of love. When mission becomes a consuming passion to love as Christ has loved, some Christians are ready even to scale the skies and fathom the depth of the ocean in order to spread the good news of love, making use of all the available means, including the mighty media like radio and television. Frankly speaking, I am not an avid radio listener, for a radio announcer talks until you have a headache and then tries to sell you something to relieve it. But Radio Veritas is different. It is a Catholic radio station in the Philippines which transmits programmes, ranging from primary health care to religious education, in 16 languages to 21 Asian countries and following a series of its talks on the Catholic Faith, thousands of H'MONG, an aborignal tribe in inaccessible hills of North Vietnam, decided to become Catholics.

One might ask whether every Christian, in order to be a missionary, has to traverse continents in search of famished souls or venture upon the most heroic acts of self-sacrifice? Not necessarily, although in the past a missionary was defined as a person who went to teach cannibals to say grace before they ate him. We can be missionaries being where we are, by means of prayer and by financial aid offered in support of missionary work; by uniting our sufferings and sacrifices with Jesus in the way of the cross; by means of our daily life's duties offered for the success of the missions. It is said of a famous Jesuit, whose sermons converted men by scores, that it was revealed to him that not one of his conversions was owing to his talents and eloquence, but that all were due to an illiterate lay-brother whose only duty was to answer the door bells, which he offered to the success of the sermons. We can turn our families into mission fields through parental care in developing Christian attitudes in the children and in encouraging them, if God calls, to commit themselves completely to the service of Christ and his Gospel.

May we, then, beg the Lord in the words of the blind man Bartimaeus (Mk 10:51) that "we may see" the missionary obligations of our baptism; see where hatred is, in order to sow love; see where injury is, to sow pardon; see where despair is, to sow hope; see where darkness is, to sow light; and see where sadness is, to sow joy. Jesus Christ is God's saving love to be passed on through us; it is not just good advice but the good news, and that this good news is to be opposed is inevitable; to be disbelieved is to be expected; but that it should be hidden under a bushel is intolerable; hence let us pass it on. The Church exists by mission, as fire exists by burning, but mission will not happen unless the Church goes beyond its own life, out into active loving care.

31ST SUNDAY OF THE YEAR

INSEPARABLE TWINS

Readings: Deut 6:2-6; Heb 7:23-28; Mk 12:28-34

Theme: Because loving God and loving our neighbour are inseparable twins, we can't reject God in favour of our neighbour, nor reject our neighbour in favour of God.

They say that goods that are much on show lose their colour; but love is an exception. How often we hear about love in sermons, how deeply radio and television have explored it and how much billboards, stage and screen have exploited it! But still, the subject of love comes up again in today's liturgy. Is it because it will be much appreciated in a cold climate? Not really. Cold or hot, love is for all seasons; love is heaven and heaven is love and naturally no-one is said to have become sick of love. Jesus therefore, repeating the old law, asks us to love God with all our heart, all our soul, all our mind and all our energies (Deut 6:5). If we love God with our whole being, we will worship him even when we work, pray to him whenever we have an opportunity, read his words as well as the newspapers, and listen to his voice just as we listen to radio and television sets. People who love what they are doing with their whole being, for example, master artists, dedicated scientists and outstanding statesmen, love their career with their whole heart, soul and energy. Should we love God less who is the source of all our talents and resources? Yes, love is valuable only when it flows back to its source.

But we cannot love God in a vacuum and so the love command says that we love God by loving others "as ourselves" (Mk 12:31). Otherwise our love will become too spiritual in a 'holy, holy' sense, whereas we ought to be biblically holy which means facing up to the totality of love which includes neighbours. Hence, I often imagine how my love of God would look like, if it had a human form: I believe it will have hands to help others, feet to hasten to the needy, eyes to see the misery of the poor and ears to hear the sighs of the sorrowful. In a London cemetery there were two funerals. The first little coffin was followed by a solitary mourner, evidently a poor mother, for there were no flowers on this coffin. But the other was covered with wreaths and bunches of flowers and followed by several mourners. At the graveside, one of them, evidently the father, took a wreath and a large bunch of lilies from his own child's coffin and laid them upon the other. How beautiful! If loving others after they are dead is so beautiful, how more beautiful it would be if we love them when they are alive!

Therefore loving God and our neighbour are inseparable twins. We cannot reject God in favour of a human being nor can we reject a human being in favour of God. Without love of God, our love of neighbour would become shallow and formalistic; but without love of neighbour, our love of God can become self-centred and individualistic, thus separating religion from life. Hence, however hard it may be, we have to be constantly moving our religion from our throats to our muscles. I used to go to a prison for conducting prayer-discussion among some of the prisoners. One evening a prisoner named Richard was with the group for the first time. It was a windy evening with no heat in the room. An inmate sitting opposite to Richard, having come only in T-shirt and trousers, was shivering. Richard had come with his shoulders wrapped in two blankets. Then, while we were discussing the idea of loving God, Richard suddenly got up, walked to the other inmate and put one of his blankets around him. By that wordless gesture, Richard demonstrated that discussion about the love of God is inseparable from active love for our neighbour.

However, the supreme example of this two-faced love is to be found only in Jesus, for only in him do we see a person, so caught up in the love of God as well as so driven by the love of neighbour that, "He is always able to save those who approach God through him" (Heb 7:25). Inspired by the example of Christ, we are also called to move steadily towards the double command of perfect love which is our final goal. On the gravestones, we often try to express some great values that the dead cherished, such as 'Peace Perfect Peace' or 'Thy Will Be Done' or 'Blessed are the Just'; but what really counts in God's sight is 'How much did they love?' Love though difficult and dangerous, is the one precious value that outlasts all others.

ALL SAINTS

HOLINESS IS LOVE

Readings: Rev 7:2-4, 9-14; 1 Jn 3:1-3; Mt 5:1-12

Theme: We all can become saints each in his or her own way by loving God and our neighbour as Christ has taught us to love.

The Catacombs are a popular tourist site in Rome, for they remind the visitors of thousands of Christians who died as martyrs for the faith during the religious persecution under various Emperors, which lasted on and off for nearly 300 years. The early Christians believed "those who have survived the great period of trial" (Rev 7:14) are saints in heaven, for it was their conviction that if you can't live a saint, you can never die a martyr. But down the centuries, the notion of 'saint' developed to include even those who never die a martyr. Therefore the feast of all saints is a celebration of the memory of all holy men and women canonised and non-canonised, both living and the dead.

Who are saints? They are lovers. They loved God and their neighbour as Christ wanted us to love. They had a heart of fire for God and a heart of flesh for neighbour, because they clearly saw "what love the Father has bestowed on us in letting us be called children of God" (1 Jn 3:1). They were holy because they "showed mercy," because they were "peace makers", and because they "hungered for justice" (Mt 5:1-12), all in love and for love. They were utterly convinced that when love begins to sicken and decay, holiness begins to droop and degenerate.

Saints are the great of this world because they simply loved God than others did, without either the hope of good or fear of pain. Take the example of St Catherine of Siena. When she was offered by our Lord the choice between the crown of roses and the crown of thorns, she chose at once the crown of thorns. She would not have committed the least sin by choosing the roses – our Lord had said that she could take whichever she liked but she knew that the thorns brought her nearer to Christ. She did not say, 'Roses are worldly and so I renounce"; she said 'Roses are lovely, but I would feel silly when my Lord chose thorns'. Saints did not put aside the good things of God's creation because they are seen as evil, but because the absolute goodness of God demanded absolute love from them. They were like little children who put aside a toy when their mother comes in after being away. Their greater love made the love of lesser things fade out.

But the saints were deeply aware that their love for God was not at all love unless it expressed itself in a practical way and so they loved their neighbour as well. They were convinced that as children of God they were born to love others and hence they lived to love and died to love more. Take for example St Peter Claver who worked among the black slaves in South America in the seventeenth century. He wrote: "Yesterday, the feast of the Holy Trinity, a great number of black people who had been seized along the African rivers were put ashore from one large vessel. We hurried out two baskets full of oranges, lemons, sweet biscuits and all sorts of things. Many were sick. A great many were lying on damp earth naked without any covering at all. We took off our clothes, went to a shore, brought from there wood, put it together to make a platform and carried all the sick to it. We knelt beside them and washed their faces and bodies." That was St Peter Claver's love for the slaves.

In our own days, we have seen such a saint in the person of Mother Teresa. When she died, Pope Paul II said: "She has left her mark on the history of our century. She defended life with courage; she served every human being by always promoting dignity and respect; she was a shining example of charity and an unforgettable witness of love that was turned into concrete and unceasing service to the poorest". Mother Teresa had always a smile on her face; her holiness was not dull for her love was full.

We are all called to become saints and we can, because saints like Catherine and Peter Claver and Mother Teresa were ordinary persons like you and me. They achieved holiness not by doing uncommon things but doing common things with uncommon love. We too can in our own way love God and our neighbour and achieve holiness. In the words of the poet John Oxenham: "To everyone there opens a way – a high way and a low way. The high soul takes the high way; the low soul takes the low way. And in between on the misty flats, the rest drift to and fro. But to everyone there opens a way. And everyone decides the way his soul shall go".

32ND SUNDAY OF THE YEAR

SHE GAVE FROM HER HEART

Readings: 1 Kings 17:10-16; Heb 9:24-28; Mk 12:41-44

Theme: Supported by our faith, which is powerful enough to root out the growing disease of the grasping heart, all of us, both rich and the poor, are called to share our possessions with the poorest of the poor.

Money is said to be like muck, not good except it be spread. Hence, a widow in the gospel, who was poor and wise, gave to charity even the two coins which was all she had. Some are against associating money, an unspiritual thing, with worship. Yes, one should look down on money, but never lose sight of it. Even Jesus did not see any conflict between scrutinising the collection in the basket and preaching God's Kingdom and hence drew the attention of his disciples "to observe the poor widow who contributed more than all the others" (Mk 12:43). Besides, we expect religion to speak to people's needs; and who will deny that the materially poor, who have been always with us, are currently in the midst of a population explosion! At least 1.375 billion people in the world live in absolute poverty, lacking the minimum income necessary to obtain the food, clothing and shelter required for mere survival. Therefore, through the example of the poor widow, Jesus is calling us to share our material possessions with those who are oppressed by grinding poverty.

We are called to show them compassion in the name of human solidarity. How often we ourselves experience God's compassion towards us! Whenever we fall from his right hand, we are caught into his left. The compassion we see in the kind-hearted is God's own, given to us to protect the helpless. Without compassion to the suffering humanity, we may believe in human solidarity, but our humanity is in deadly sleep. The widow from Zeraphat was not a Jewess and hence not particularly interested in the prophet Elijah's mission. Yet, she shared with him her pieces of food for a purely humanitarian reason, namely, to help another human being in distress (1 Kings 17:12). Christ's own solidarity with the human race was total, for he identified himself with us in everything but sin, and "was offered up once to take away the sins of many and entered heaven itself to appear before God on our behalf" (Heb 9:28). Therefore, we too are urged in the name of human solidarity to share with the most oppressed in the world, not grudgingly, nor dutifully, but willingly. Grudge givers say, 'I hate to give'; dutiful givers say 'I ought to give'; compassionate givers say, 'I want to give'.

We are called to be generous, when we feel for the poor, in pocket. To be generous one need not be rich. True generosity comes from the heart. Even a pauper, with true spirit of generosity, can give like a prince. The widow of Zeraphat and the poor widow of the gospel belong to this princely class. The gospel is not trying to embarrass the rich into giving more to the church and to charity, but calls all of us, both poor and rich, to be generous to the needy. Unfortunately, in trying to be generous, the poor are handicapped by their own poverty, for the real tragedy of the poor is that they can't afford anything but self-denial; whereas the rich are handicapped by their own riches, for money has a dangerous way of putting scales on people's eyes and freezing their hands, lips and hearts. For the rich, their sense of need progresses in direct proportion to the amount of riches they acquire and as a result they seem to live always in a state of ambitious poverty!

However, our faith is powerful enough to root out the growing disease of the grasping heart. It is so powerful that it can move our hearts to give not only from our luxuries but from our necessities, not only until giving is sufficient but until giving is a sacrifice. Because we believe that when we give to the poor, we give to Christ himself, for he said, "I was hungry you gave me food", we believe that although by giving to the needy we risk becoming ourselves poor, God raises the poor out of the dust, blessing them to be generously open to God and genuinely open to neighbours; and we believe in the promise of Christ that anybody who gives even a glass of water to the needy will be sure of reward in the life to come. May our faith touch our heart and stir within it the fire of love, for some can give without loving but no-one can love without giving.

33RD SUNDAY OF THE YEAR

THE BATTLE CRY

Readings: Dan 12:1-3; Heb 10:11-14,18; Mk 13:24-32

Theme: Christians who deal with their own unjust persecutors with a Christian attitude of love and forgiveness, are better equipped to proclaim and join in the pursuit of justice and peace in the world.

Justice and Peace ring out like a battle cry in the Church and in the world today. Justice is not what the lawyer tells me I may do, but what truth tells me that I ought to do and the truth is that all men are equal, not just in the public baths but in everything that belongs to human dignity. If we begin to ignore human dignity, we will soon ignore human rights and, in fact, we are only too aware of the unjust forces around the world that trample upon the basic human rights of people, some of whom are driven to a state sweltering with the heat of injustice. But justice suffers on a smaller scale too. For most of us being persecuted for justice' sake is not going to mean anything public and dramatic; it is going to mean an endless and boring array of petty harassments of our human right, dignity and freedom within the context of our family, school, place of work and daily human intercourse. How does one react to the injustices in the world and in his own life?

It all depends on the angle from which you look at the source of injustice. Once in the Holy Land, looking at the sky on Christmas Eve, I saw the bottom of the moon hung like a huge orange slice over Bethlehem; but in Newmarket I always see a half moon tipped on its side with its left half missing. So the moon appears different from different angles. Likewise, a nonbeliever may look at his unjust persecutor as his enemy and his first reaction would probably be to take revenge and revenge, I guess, is a kind of wild justice. But Christians look at those from whom they suffer unjustly from a different angle, that of love and forgiveness, because they are aware that they themselves stand before God as forgiven sinners by the cross of Christ, who "offered one sacrifice for sins" and "has taken his seat forever at the right hand of God" (Heb 10:12), placing all those who belong to him in a continual process of sanctification. Hence, the first reaction of a Christian towards injustice must be to forgive without counting the cost.

This does not mean that a Christian is indifferent to the unjust social situations, nor does it mean a panicky withdrawal from oppressive human concerns. But it does mean dealing with injustice from a Christian perspective. Yes, we Christians have the right and duty, not only to proclaim justice but also to join in the pursuit of justice, actively participating in works for justice and peace. We have to begin this work by first being ourselves just towards God. My justice towards God demands that I can only repay God's forgiveness of my sins by forgiving my neighbour's injustice to me. To forgive the injustices of others is not only my justice towards God, but also it is the first step in establishing a just society in the world. For when I forgive my unjust persecutors, I light up a peace around me which will spread to my families, factories and neighbourhood; only such a peace will provide an atmosphere for peaceful coexistence on the basis of human dignity and equality, paving a way for our world to emerge as a global organism, with a common blood steam, a central nervous system, a shared heart and a common destiny.

Our common destiny is that "the Son of Man will come in the clouds to gather together his chosen ones from the ends of the earth" (Mk 13:26-27) and "those who lead the many to justice" through love and forgiveness "shall live for ever and shall shine brightly like the stars for ever" (Dan 12:3). Loving the unjust persecutors is indeed a pain but, if the soul of peace is love, those who seek peace must be willing to take wounds for it as in war. Forgiving the unjust is indeed a cross but only the cross Christ offers to our chaotic world, an opportunity to hew out of the mountain of despair a stone of hope. Without love and forgiveness first offered to the unjust, if we seek justice and peace, we are fighting a battle for battle's sake and such a battle will find little entertainment in heaven.

34TH SUNDAY OF THE YEAR

(CHRIST THE KING) HIS DIVINE MAJESTY

Readings: Dan 7:13-14; Rev 1:5-8; Jn 18:33-37

Theme: His Divine Majesty, Christ the King of peace, justice and truth, has shared his royalty with us, which calls us to join him, in promoting those same Gospel values, however difficult it may be at times.

In modern times kings are almost out, except to describe cigarettes; and royalty is nearly like a chicken whose head has been cut off, it may run about in a lovely way, but in fact it is dead. However, Jesus Christ is still king, every inch king, not just king, but "the ruler of the kings on earth" (Rev 1:5). But his Kingdom is not of this world and that is why we celebrate the feast of our king with no gunshots in the morning, military parade in the afternoon and presentation of arms in the evening. His kingly power is awesome, so awesome that it can put Niagara Falls to shame, but it is a spiritual power. Likewise, his royal authority comes from his being not only a witness to truth, but being the Truth itself. This is why his Kingdom does not seek to increase its wealth but to promote peace, not to expand its border but to establish justice, not to inflate its own image but to lead people to freedom, all in the name of truth. He said this to Pilate (Jn 18:36-37) but, you know, to some people you need never give them hell, instead you just tell them the truth, they think it is hell; so did Pilate.

Christ is not like the old-fashioned kings, some of whom I believe had more titles than subjects. Normally the presence of such a king meant that others were not kings at all; whereas Christ never wanted to keep his kingship all to himself. Instead he shared it with us all. This is what happens at our baptism when the priest, applying holy oil on our head, says, 'I anoint you priest, prophet and king'. Thus Christ "has made us a royal nation" (Rev 1:6) in which each of us is like "the son of man coming on the clouds of heaven, receiving dominion, glory and kingship" (Dan 7:13-14).

Sharing in the kingship of Christ is glorious but precarious, for it is demanding. As Christ bore witness to truth, lived by it and died for it, we too, by virtue of the gift of truth received in our hearts at baptism, are called to speak only the truth, unattended by a bodyguard of lies and of course to spread the truth from pole to pole. Since the truth we have received is not just in our minds but in our hearts, we have not only to speak it but to do it, in justice and love. This means we have to get rid of selfishness and be concerned for the rights and welfare of others, especially of the less fortunate, including the prisoners who languish in solitary confinement facing bare walls day and night. Because the truth of Christ is that each individual, in spite of his/her failures and foibles, is equally and uniquely precious before God and hence can never be discarded. Those who think that truth is only in their minds and not in their hearts will close themselves to their brothers and sisters around. Such persons will consider missing Sunday Mass abominable, but will easily tarry on the way out of the church, expressing no concern for the other members of the same Body of Christ.

But let us admit it; the surest way to be lonesome is always to tell the truth, worse still, to be the truth. Hence Christ stood alone before Pilate, dirty and beaten, but courageous and confident, for he knew full well that truth crushed to earth will rise again. We, too, stamped with the image of our King and trusting in the armour of our royalty, must witness to truth in love. Witnessing may seem difficult when we are struck by serious sickness, impossible when relationships break down, and elusive when we are flattened by despair. But it is at these hard times that our royal status and strength should shine. Besides, Christ the King who is a tower of strength is always with us. Some kings are weak, some are mighty, but Christ our King is Almighty and he is king-sized in his love and mercy. Hence, let us approach his Divine Majesty in all our needs, and ravish our hearts with truth and trust.

YEAR C

1ST SUNDAY OF ADVENT

THE TIME IS NOW

Readings: Jer 33:14-16; 1 Thess 3:12-4:2; Lk 21:25-28, 34-36

Theme: Advent is the time to start living a purposeful life, to watch and pray, to love and share, and to wait on the Lord with hope.

It is fascinating to figure out how the end of the world will come. "The Great Planet Earth", a book by Hal Lindsay, became a best-seller, selling over fifteen million copies, because it contained a set of staggering speculations about the end time. Jesus' own description of the end, with "the roaring of the seas" and "the heaven shaking" (Lk 21:25-26), might indeed be fascinating to some, but frightening to many. However, Jesus spoke about the end of the world, not to scare us, although a good scare is, at times, worth more to us than good advice. Jesus, who always said "Fear not" but "believe" cannot speak of the end time to frighten us. He knew too well that fear imprisons, but faith liberates; fear paralyses but faith empowers and fear sickens but faith heals. Hence Christ's purpose of describing the end, was not to instil fear but to inspire us with the urgency of the gospel message.

The time is NOW, to organise our lives with right priorities. On the night of 1st April 1912, the Titanic hit an iceberg in the North Atlantic and sank. Over 1500 people lost their lives. Suppose I ask, "If you had been on the Titanic when it sank, would you have rearranged the deck chairs?" – surely you would say that it is a ridiculous question; for who in his right mind would ignore wailing sirens on a sinking ship and rearrange its deck chairs? But then, we know that our life on earth is so brief that in the midst of life, we are in death; that our world with all its display of pomp and glory is dissolving. And yet it is possible that some of us are so busy making a living, that we forget the purpose of living, "allowing our spirits to become bloated with indulgence and worldly cares" (Lk 21:34). Is it not like rearranging deck chairs on a sinking ship?

The time is NOW, to "watch and pray" (Lk 21:36), so that prayer opens our eyes to the presence of God, helping us to see everything in proper perspective, and implants in our hearts peace, even in the midst of problems and pains. Prayer is also listening to God's word. How eager we are to listen to the news. Our interest increases depending upon who reads it, for it adds a note of authority. Suppose I turn on TV and see God reading the news! Surely, it would lift me out of my seat. And yet, it is God who speaks every word in the Scriptures. In the days to come, before Christmas, we will feel the powerful presence of God in his Word, provided we believe as Jeremiah did: "See, the days are coming – it is the Lord who speaks – when I am going to fulfil the promise" (Jer 33:14).

The time is NOW, to love and share, in a true Christian way. When God became a human being, he brought all of us into a grand relationship not only with himself but with our fellow men. There are no spinsters and bachelors in the kingdom of God. As Christians we can never walk alone, for we belong. Hence if we want Christ to come into our lives in a living dynamic way, then during Advent our "hearts must overflow with love for one another and for all" (1 Thess 3:12), lifting our spirit of sharing. Sharing does not impoverish us, it only enriches us with a deep sense of satisfaction.

The time is NOW, to wait on the Lord and hope. Have you ever stood on a foreign airport, awaiting the arrival of a plane carrying someone you love; and after what seemed an interminable delay, how thrilled you were to see your loved one emerging, to complete your joy of reunion? Likewise we await during Advent the coming of the Lord into our lives with expectation, until our reunion with him hopefully becomes ecstasy at Christmas. During this waiting period we may experience the end of the world in our personal lives, when for example, a close relative dies or when marriage breaks down or when the job is gone or serious illness strikes; all of which can shake our personal world to its foundation. Even in these moments of desolation and distress, we are called "to stand up straight and raise our hearts" (Lk 21:28), for the Lord is near.

2ND SUNDAY OF ADVENT

THE JOY OF SALVATION

Readings: Bar 5:1-9; Phil 1:4-6, 8-11; Lk 3:1-6

Theme: If we set right in our lives what needs to be set right, the Joy of Salvation will flood our hearts so much that we will be taking it to others.

If there is no joy in being a Christian, probably my Christianity is leaking some where. This joy has its springs deep down inside me, and that spring is Christ. Yes, pleasure is in my power, joy is not. "God, who is leading Israel in joy" does so "by the light of his glory" (Bar 5:9), which is Jesus Christ. Anyone who comes in touch with Christ experiences this joy. Mother Teresa tells us of a young Maltese girl who joined her Order. On the first day she was sent to the Home for the Dying. When she came down, she was radiant. Mother Teresa asked why she was so happy. The girl said, "Mother, I have held Christ in my hands for three hours.

We are waiting during Advent for the coming of this Christ. Of course, Christ cannot come back in the way Mohammed Ali might stage a comeback, for Christ has been never away. He is always with us as he himself said. Hence, what we are waiting for is that Christ may reveal himself and make his presence felt in a new way giving us an intense experience of the joy of salvation.

However, the joy of salvation does not come to us by flashing a magic wand or pressing a Christmas button. Salvation is free, yes, but it is not cheap. We have to work for it, breaking the chains we have bound ourselves with. I don't mean the so called deadly sins, the most expensive ones; but the disposition of our hearts that renders us incapable of even seeing the salvation, leave alone experiencing it. I mean the selfishness that stops us doing a kind act, the resentment that blocks communication, the falsehood that betrays trust, the pride that precludes true regard for others, and the communal prejudice that can destroy a society. So St John the Baptist was right in repeating Isaiah's call "to make ready the way of the Lord and clear him a straight path" (Lk 3:4). The least we could do at Advent is not to put any spiritual obstacle in the way of the Lord's coming. I once asked a born-again

Christian friend how many it took to convert him. “Two”, he replied.” Two, how was that – did not God do it all?” I asked. “The Almighty and myself converted me; I did all I could against it and the Almighty did all he could for it and he won”, he said.

The joy of salvation is not the private property of any Christian; in fact the full value of joy is in dividing it with someone. Besides, it is not right for anyone to consume joy without producing it. Hence we are called ‘to bring this joy to others also, first by promoting justice in the world. It was the dream of God our Father, that with the coming of his son Jesus, his Church, the new Jerusalem, “wrapped in the cloak of justice”, would offer the world “the peace of justice” (Bar 5:2,4); so that “all mankind shall see the salvation of God” (Lk 3:6). Hence it is the sacred duty of every Christian “to promote the gospel” in such a way that the entire world “may be found rich in the harvest of justice which Christ has ripened in us” (Phil 1:11). Are we then doing our part to level-off the sharp peaks of greed and mountain-sized injustice in the world; and to fill in the low, cold areas of depression and despair, that millions suffer in the dark valleys of the gap between the rich and the poor?

Here, I am afraid, you begin to wonder whether Advent is a joyful season or a penitential period! Well, as the French proverb goes, “Great joys weep and great sorrows laugh”, for life itself is made up of marble and mud. It is true that Advent has joyous strains, but it also calls us to struggle in straightening up our lives, using those sources of help that are available. There is help through the sacraments, with an emphasis on reconciliation; there is help through prayer in which we seek sincerely the Lord; and there is help through Jesus’ people around us through whom God speaks. Thus the rough ways, the twisted roads and the steep paths are negotiable for he is coming.

BLESSED IS SHE

Readings: Gen 3:9-15-20; Eph 1:3-6, 11-12; Lk 1:26-38

Theme: Mary was sinless since her conception, but lived a very ordinary human life as we do; as sinless but ordinary, she not only understands our human trials in utter clarity but also serves us as a model we can imitate.

In Michelangelo's masterpiece of sculpture, the Pietá, the woman seems far too young to be the Mother of the dead Son. When someone pointed this out to Michelangelo, he replied, '"You don't know anything. Chaste women retain their fresh looks longer than those who are not chaste. The Madonna was without sin, without even the least unchaste desire, and so she was always young". Today we celebrate the feast of Mary's Immaculate Conception which proclaims that she was preserved from all stain of sin right from her conception.

One of the things Mary said to Bernadette during an apparition was, 'I am the Immaculate Conception'. The 14-year-old girl was not sure of what she heard, but every adult knows what it means. Four years later, on December 8, 1854, Pope Pius IX defined as catholic doctrine the traditional teaching of the Immaculate Conception of Mary. This is in accordance with what God said to the snake: "I will put enmity between you and the woman, and between your offspring and hers" (Gen 3:15). And in today's Gospel, the angel says to Mary, "Peace be with you! The Lord is with you and has greatly blessed you" (Lk 1:28). We are not surprised at this extraordinary favour God did to Mary, preserving her from sin. After all she was meant to be the Mother of God.

Because Mary was preserved from the stain of sin right from her conception, it is wrong for us who are born with sin to think that Mary was not human like all of us. No. Mary lived an ordinary human life like us with all its human joys and sorrows, trials and tribulations, doubts and anxieties. In fact, because of her sinlessness, she became more human than we are. How? We are sinners and what is sin? Sin is blindness, ignorance and the absence of love. Sin separates us from humans, imprisons us in our own cells of selfishness. Most sin, indeed, is loneliness, loneliness from God and loneliness from other human beings, so that the sinner cannot see beyond self. But Mary, because of her sinlessness, could see God and her fellow human beings with utter clarity. She could know by heart the beatings of all human hearts; if we, created in the image of God are human only in as much as we love God and our neighbour, then Mary, who was able to love God and us with her whole heart, because she had been free from sin, was human in its perfect sense.

Thus, in Mary Immaculate, we have a glimpse of what God wishes for all of us. He wants us to love him and our neighbour more and more until we are able to love like Mary. He wants to help us to free ourselves from the loneliness of sin and come into the company of humans and to love them as God loves them. In his book *The World's First Love*, Bishop Fulton Sheen says: "One look at her, and we know that a human who is not good can become better; one prayer to her, and we know that because she is without sin we can become less sinful". Yes. What Mary is by privilege, we are called to become by grace; and what she is by virtue of being the Mother of God, we are called to become like her, aided by the fruits her Son's redemption.

3RD SUNDAY OF ADVENT

CHEER UP

Readings: Zeph 3:14-18; Phil 4:4-7; Lk 3:10-18

Theme: The Lord is coming to cheer us up and to renew us in his love, provided we are prepared, to surrender our lives to him.

It has happened to me at times that when I am in deep desolation, a friend would tell me, "Cheer up, boy!"; but at his word, I would only go into deeper depression; whereas when God tells us, as he does now two weeks before Christmas, "Cheer up, shout for joy, be glad and exult", we actually tend to cheer up, for God's commands, unlike men's, are creative, bringing into effect what they say. Did he not say at the dawn of creation, "Let there be light" and instantly the dark abyss of earth was flooded with light? In fact, God created us, to be people always spilling over with joy, and hence he not only asks us to rejoice but wants himself "to sing joyfully because of us, as one sings at festivals" (Zeph 3:18). Can you imagine anything more crazy than this, that the Lord himself is coming to lead us in our merry dance? So, we'd better all be on the floor to sing and rejoice, especially when we come for the solemn Sunday liturgies during Advent; let us not come with long-faced solemnity, as though we come behind Berlin Walls and Iron Curtains (which in any case have been pulled down).

We must rejoice because "The Lord your God is already in your midst" (Zeph 3:17). When the Lord took human flesh he did not become just one individual; in a sense, he became every individual, dwelling closer to each of us than our thoughts and desires. Yes, as men, we were born broken but our life is mending, for God is acting in us as glue. Besides, the Lord intends to come into our lives more intimately during this Christmas season, in order to "renew us in his love" (Zeph 3.17). Is there any force more healing than that of love? Love always arrives with healing in its wings. It is the arrival of this Lord of love, in ever new ways, that we now anticipate. The delight of children going to see Santa Claus, the buying and wrapping of Christmas gifts, the decorating of Christmas trees, all these Advent activities express this great anticipation of something wonderful to about happen.

The wonderful thing is, of course, about the "Joy in the Lord"; a joy that comes not from any particular position in life but from the disposition of our hearts; a joy of the chainless mind and blameless heart; a joy born of conviction of faith and consciousness of God's love. Because this is a joy in the Lord, this joy is possible even to those who may find the Christmas season itself the most distressing, only because of the demands it makes and the tension it creates. Such a joy is possible even in the most trying of circumstances, and even as we contemplate our present world which was once threatened by a cold war but now by a cold peace. This is why St Paul, although living in prison under the shadow of impending death, could encourage the early Christians, who themselves were under constant threat from political and military powers, saying, "Rejoice in the Lord, I say again rejoice" (Phil 4:4). This means, if my joy is in the Lord, I will smile even when I am chasing my best hat down the street on a windy day. Shall we then beg the Lord that this Christmas may fill us with joy in him?

But whatsoever we beg of God, we must also work for it; our future will be different if we make our present different, but how? "He who has two coats, let him share with him who has none, the man who has food should do the same" (Lk 3:11). What does this mean? We are beautiful people, loveable people, but we are also vulnerable people, especially to selfishness. If in our selfishness we are all the time receiving and not giving, we will be like the Dead Sea which is dead, because it is all the time receiving, never giving anything out and the salt content of the water keeps building up. To make way for the joy in the Lord also calls us to surrender ourselves to God in prayer. "Have no anxiety about anything but if there is anything you need, pray" (Phil 4:6). To those who surrender themselves to him, somehow the good will be the final goal of their ills. Hence let us cheer up and charm it with a smile; one smile in public is worth ten before your mirrors, for it keeps joy in circulation.

4TH SUNDAY OF ADVENT

PEACE ON EARTH

Readings: Mic 5:1-4; Heb 10:5-10; Lk 1:39-45

Theme: Led by the Holy Spirit, if we live a life of loving union with God and neighbour, the peace of Christ will flow like a river into our hearts, turning us into channels of peace for the world.

Ever since Mass began to be said in our churches, we have been singing, "Peace on Earth". It is sad that after two thousand years of mass, we have got as far as poison gas. Even when a peace-treaty is made, it often turns out to be a period of cheating between two periods of fighting. How can there be peace on earth, when there is no peace within individuals? Peace and joy are touches of sweet harmony within a person, harmony between body, mind and heart. When my instincts thunder out of my control, when reason runs wild and the heart desires only what is immoral, illegal and fattening, then I am like an atom, whose electrons have got free of the nucleus. This disunity within a person causes further disunity between one person and another, with the result that one half of the human race is at war with the other half. But all these disunities are symptoms of the most tragic disunity which is the rupture between humanity and God; for God is like the hub of a wheel and when the hub is lost, the spokes of the wheel fall apart. Therefore, peace on earth will become a reality when every human being is reunited with God.

It is in order to reunite all of us with God and set us at peace that Jesus came. At his birth angels sang, "Peace to men of goodwill"; but even before his birth, the prophet foretold that "he shall be Peace" (Mic 5:4). Hence wherever Jesus is, we can expect that sweet peace sits crowned with smiles. The peace that Jesus offers is indeed human peace and that is why his love took on a human form and his peace put on a human dress. Hence, what the nations need most urgently is a peace conference with the Prince of Peace. At such a conference, the world leaders will realise that the peace of God that flows through Christ is far greater than the petty peace they can achieve by themselves. Even we as individuals, when touched by this peace, will easily recognise that Christ's peace is unlike the forced peace that can only be achieved by, say, alcohol; that it is unlike the peace which comes from escaping responsibility through frantic pursuit of pleasures; that it is unlike the superficial joy of prosperity, suggested by slick television commercials. Hence the peace of Christ is very precious, so precious that no money could buy it – even if it could, just imagine what a luxury tax would be upon it!

Therefore let us make space in our hearts for the peace of Christ to flow in. We make space by becoming ever more sensitive to the presence of the Holy Spirit in and around us, like Elizabeth who at the sight of Mary was touched by the Spirit so deeply that she cried out in joy, "Blessed are you among women" (Lk 1:42). We make space by entrusting all our cares to the Lord with a trust like that of Mary who was "blessed for she trusted that the Lord's words to her would be fulfilled" (Lk 1:45). And we make space by erecting within our hearts an interior Castle of Prayer, which the storms of life may beat upon without disturbing the serene quiet within. .

The Prince of Peace is sure to enter into such a space made sacred during Advent. His peace will start coming like the gentle dropping of the morning dew, but soon will flow like a river, inundating our whole self with its blessedness, until we in turn become instruments of peace. Christ's peace is not passive one, such as you can find in the grave. His peace is active, urging us to offer the hand of friendship to all and even pressing us to go into the world, not to buy peace by compromising with evil, but to win peace by resisting evil, especially the evil of injustices, for justice and peace are inseparable. Hence, as long as for millions in the world peace means a piece of bread, true peace will elude us; but once justice is done to all, love which is the soul of peace, will flourish; and the peace of Christ will break out, so that nation can speak peace with nation.

CHRISTMAS DAY

HAIL, CHILD JESUS

Readings: Is 9:1-6; Tit 2:11-14; Lk 2:1-14

Theme: Hail, Child Jesus, God in human flesh, who has made his dwelling among us in order to guide us with his light, to fill us with his peace and to save us for eternal life.

Hail Child Jesus, our Lord and God. You are heir of all things, through whom God created all things, the reflection of the Father's glory. (Heb 1:3). All things bright and beautiful, all things wise and wonderful, you are the God who made them. Might is your power that makes one tiny star to guide the mariner from afar. Marvellous is your wisdom that ripens fruit and golden grain; magnanimous is your heart that sends sunshine and rain, on both the good and the bad. You are unapproachable, yet your height enables you to stoop. Your holiness is undefiled, yet you can handle hearts that droop.

Hail Child Jesus, you are the Saviour of the world. In you "the grace of God has appeared offering salvation to all men" (Tit 2:11). Yes, even to men of today, who have split the atom, conquered space and 'created' new life inside a test tube – you the baby in the manger are the only salvation. It is you who saved us from sin's penalty, its power and its presence. We receive your salvation free, for you have paid. If only the world could believe this! Men go forward in sophistication while falling backward in belief. The God who sent you on earth to bring all men back to himself, must be full of pity as he watches many still searching for a saviour.

Hail, Child Jesus. "The people who walked in darkness have seen in you a great light" (Is 9:1). If we once lose this light, then it is perpetual night. You are funny. Sometimes you put us in the dark to prove that you are light. The restless millions waited for this light, whose dawn made all things new. Even though we know that it is better to be saved by a lighthouse than by a lifeboat, we prefer to remain in the dark and lose our course. How often we have followed false lights and when we have lost sight of them, from our pride we still struck sparks of our own. Lead kindly light, when our light is low, when the blood creeps and the nerves prick. Reach down to our sunless days and help us, that instead of cursing the darkness we may light a candle.

Hail, Child Jesus. "Your name is Prince of Peace" (Is 9:5). Your peace is hard and bitter, for you shed blood to win it. The world too offers peace, but always with a worm inside it; but your peace is pure and bliss. Give us that peace. We know that our bodies will one day be buried in peace; but our problem is our heart, which is restless now. May our world know, that even if it has to go to war for justice' sake, the purpose of all war must be peace; anything short of it is brutality, futility and stupidity. Give us your peace, so that we can break the shell of unforgiveness in our hearts and be reconciled with one another in peace.

Hail, Child Jesus, you are a child of beauty and a joy for ever. At your birth, the angel announced, "tidings of great joy" to be shared by the whole people (Lk 2:10). We see heaven in your manger, in fact something greater than heaven, for heaven itself is your handiwork. You give us the joy of retrospect as we remember all your gifts in the past. You give us the joy of aspect for there is always some aspect of the present that makes us happy. You give us the joy of prospect as we look forward to the future. Your joy is far richer than the wild joys of living. Give us the joy of the peaceful conscience and of the grateful heart; the joy of the teachable mind and of the glowing hope.

Hail, Child Jesus. You are "the Word become flesh and made your dwelling among us" (Jn 1:14). You dwell among us not only in the tabernacles of our temples, but also in the temple of our hearts; not only in the marvellous nature and beauty of people, but also in the poverty of a slum and in the mud of a battlefield. You dwell among us not only in times of success and good fortune, but also when we are sick and handicapped. You dwell among us in order to transform any situation into a place of your glory; thus our kitchens become our cathedrals, factories become temples, our class rooms become our shrines and our hospitals become heaven. We need your continued presence among us, for we live in a world being torn to pieces by the storm of human passions. Be with us therefore to calm our restless thoughts to silence and to conform our spirits to your image.

HOLY FAMILY

THE CENTRE OF FOCUS

Readings: Sir 3:2-6, 12-14; Col 3: 12-21; Lk 2:41-52

Theme: Jesus was born into a human family to stress what a precious gift it is from God and to call the members of all Christian families to play their respective roles in promoting Christian family virtues, especially love that shares joys and sorrows.

Family is the oldest of all societies and the only natural one. God who made the stars and built the world also made man and woman and built the family. The family is the cradle of civil society, for it is within the circle of family life, the destiny of states is formed. It is the family that provides us with a home. Without family, all humanity is homeless. Home is where we live and love together through many changing years; where we share each other's gladness and weep each other's tears. Home is where I can wear what I like and feel like a king by my own fireside, as much as any monarch on his throne. It is in order to make us realise what a precious gift of God is family and to highlight its mission to be the basic unit of the church and society, that Jesus was born into a family and today we celebrate the Feast of the Holy Family.

Our families will serve as the vital cells of the Church and society, if each member in the family plays his or her role as befits each one's status in it. "The Lord sets a father as honour over his children; a mother's authority he confirms over her sons" (Sir 3:2). Parents are entrusted with the responsibility of caring for and training of children. A child is not a vase to be filled but a fire to be lit and the lighter is in the parent's hands. Training has to begin early in life, for, if you want a garden of good fruits, you get the tree young. The best way to train a child is through parental example. The religion of a child depends on what his parents are and not what they say. Children have their duties towards their parents. "he who reveres his father will live a long life; he obeys the Lord who brings comfort to his mother" (Sir 3:3-4). Children must have trust in the guidance of their parents, for a mother's heart is a child's schoolroom and one father is more than a hundred schoolmasters. Children owe gratitude to parents; we never know the love of our parents till we have become parents.

Today we are celebrating the Feast of the Holy Family in which Christ was the centre of focus. Therefore, Christian virtues need to flourish in our families. "Clothe yourselves with heartfelt mercy, with kindness, humility, meekness and patience. Bear with one another and forgive each other" (Col 3:12-13). Parents, be kind to your children: you can soon mend a torn jacket but not so the heart of a child bruised by harsh words. Fathers be gentle: a good father governs his family as he would cook a small fish – very gently. A frustrated young mother heard her children crying and looking over her dirty house, said: "I sometimes wish I'd loved and lost". Mothers be patient with your children; they may tear up a house but they never break it up. "I'm really worried", said one little boy to his friend, "Dad slaves away at his job so I'll never want for anything. Mum spends every day washing and ironing and taking care of me when I am sick. I'm worried". "What about?" asked his friend. "I'm afraid they might try to escape", said he. Children be not selfish.

A family is a Christian family if Christ is at its centre. Where Christ reigns, love abounds. Husband, wife and children form the world's greatest team. Whether this team wins or loses depends largely on the love that binds them. Where love is, joy is shared and sorrow eased. The Holy Family had its sorrows; they had gone to Jerusalem for the feast of the Passover and suddenly the boy Jesus was missing. The parents searched and searched for him in anguish and finally found him in the temple. The astonished mother asked him, "Son, why have you done this to us? You see that your father and I have been searching for you in sorrow" (Lk 2:48). No family is without its own particular stresses and difficulties in the struggle of life. Raising children these days is hard. The one thing that children wear out faster than shoes is parents. A lot of mothers are inclined to believe that it would be much wiser to give themselves vitamins and the kids tranquillisers. To earn enough money to keep up with the cost of living is hard today. It now costs more to amuse a child than once it did to educate its father. A naked terror in many modern families is loneliness. Even before marriage, some leave their parents, with the result that the aged parents are left to spend their time alone, hugging, perhaps, some past memories. However, in the midst of all such family trials, a Christian heart can remain serene, if it loves.

MOTHER OF GOD – JANUARY 1

'I WILL BLESS THEM'

Readings: Num 6:22-27; Gal 4:4-7; Lk 2:16-21

Theme: As we begin a New Year, we thank God for his past gifts, hope for more of his blessings and make good New Year resolutions, confident that the Mother of God will help us on our New Year journey.

New Year is often stock taking time with businessmen, and it is good for us Christians too, to take stock, to look back into the past and to look forward into the future. In fact, January, the first month of the year, gets its name from the Roman God Janus or Januarius, who was represented as having two heads, each having its own pair of eyes. Each face then, would look in the opposite direction to the other. Therefore on this first day of the year, we also trace the good hand and kindness of the Lord that had been guiding us in the past year and thank him for it. And we look for new opportunities and blessings with which God will provide us in the coming year and we hope we will not miss them.

We Christians truly hope that this year will be a bright New Year because we strongly believe that Jesus made flesh is with us and will continue to be with us, saving us and blessing us. When the name 'Jesus' was given to him, it was meant to reveal that Jesus came to save us and bless us. "So shall they invoke my name upon the Israelites, and I will bless them" was God's own promise (Num 6:27). The name of Jesus has power to save us from selfishness, self-pity and self-doubt. It can save us from envy, hostility and animosity. It can deliver us from discouragement, depression and despair. His name can protect us from wasting our resources, when we should be sharing them; from becoming slaves to our appetites, when we should be disciplining them and from worshipping military might, when we should be engaging in a dialogue for peace. The name of Jesus has the power also to bless us with special gifts and graces such as health after long illness, healing after an injury or a job after being unemployed. Calling on his name can bring us blessings such as new strength to go on when we feel like giving up; new experiences of friendship and family, when we feel lonely and left out; new visions and challenges to excite us when we feel listless and stagnant.

As we expect Jesus to continue to save us and bless us in the New Year, he expects us to make some good New Year resolutions. Some of us may not like resolutions because we think we can never keep them. But it does not matter if we fail to keep our resolutions. What is more important is that they be well thought out and that we begin to carry them out resolutely, and carry them out at least once. For example, a nephew resolves to visit his invalid uncle monthly, does it once and discovers how great the experience of selfless loving can be. A mother resolves to be firm with her children without screaming and getting upset, does it once and discovers a new strength within herself. A student resolves to study in absolute disciplined silence for an hour each day, does it once and can hardly believe how much she enjoys it. God does not expect us to keep all our good resolutions without failing. However, he hopes that we will search regularly for new experiences of his presence with us in our determined effort to keep them.

But it was a woman who made it possible for God to be born as man and remain with us as the risen Saviour. "When the appointed time came, God sent his Son, born of a woman" (Gal 4:4). That woman is of course Mary, the Mother of God. Yes. We honour Mary today because it was she who first participated in the dramatic ending of the old and the beginning of the new, when she brought forth Jesus and presented him to the Shepherds (Lk 2:16), Magi and to the whole world. Hence we celebrate the feast of the Mother of God as the crowning of the Christmas Season and we begin the New Year by honouring her. Mary is not only the Mother of God; she has been given to us as our Mother as well, so that we can hold her hand and continue our journey in faith. We need Mary as our Mother to support us on our journey through the New Year. We need her faith when we don't see a way, her hope when we run into a dead end and her love when others desert us. May Mary's memory never leave us, and may her image always inspire us!

THE EPIPHANY CHALLENGE

Readings: Is 60:1-6; Eph 3: 2-3, 5-6; Mt 2:1-12

Theme: The feast of Epiphany, when the light of Christ offered itself to all people, welcomes us who have already seen it to continue to search for its fullness and also challenges us to continue the manifestation of that light to all people.

From the dawn of creation God had been revealing himself by casting aside veil after veil and showing men truth after truth, until one day he unveiled his very face in his Son Jesus Christ. Isaiah foretold (Is 60:1-6) what would happen on that day. "Your light shall come," he said. Yes, it did come and it is still shining. Even on a day of deep and endless sorrows with darkness in its face, a true believer can feel Christ's light shooting through the marrow of his bones. "The riches of the sea shall be emptied out before you" (Is 60:5), he said. Is it not true? Who among us came to Christ and did not experience the riches of God's love, a love that can build a heaven in hell's despair, a love that is unfathomed and deathless, flowing like heaven's life-stream full and sweet? "Your heart shall throb and overflow with joy" (Is 60:5), he said. Yes. That is why, although the casualty list of accidents during Christmas Season may stretch to toilet roll length, we refuse to be gloomy while celebrating the birth of Christ.

Every child brings down something of heaven into the midst of our rough earthiness; but the child Jesus brought down heaven itself and that heaven is for all. That is why the Church of Christ is neither Latin nor Greek but Catholic. "In Christ Jesus the Gentiles are now co-heirs with the Jews, members of the same body and sharers of the promise" (Eph 3:6). We celebrate today the Feast of the Epiphany shortly after Christmas, because at Christmas Christ came into the world and at Epiphany, his coming is announced to all the world. It is in order to convey the image that the Church of Christ is universal, that all nations are at home in her, and that the arms of her crucified Lord are stretched above all races, God drew the Gentile Wise Men from the East to the crib where his Son was born. God excludes none from salvation, if they don't exclude themselves. Christianity is oceanic, you can't contain it in a teacup. Hence, we Christians have a mandate to reach out with Christ's saving mission to all people; missions are a must, not a maybe.

But our mission would not be effective if we ourselves have not really found Christ for ourselves - though we may call ourselves Christians. If we have found him as the Magi did (Mt 2:11), then we would daily offer Christ our gift of 'gold' to his royalty, namely our loyalty and fidelity to him; our gift of 'frankincense' to his divinity, namely our prayer and worship; and our gift of 'myrrh' to his humanity, namely our human sufferings and sorrows. On other hand, if we have not yet found Christ, we should ask: why? Perhaps our faith is not deep enough to keep us searching for Christ in prayer, in the scriptures, in service and in joys and sorrows of this life. How many stories we hear of dogs and cats which have travelled hundreds of miles to return home because of the homeward pull that is present in them! Has our longing for God in Christ lost its pull? Perhaps we are distracted by the myriads of little stars such as money and power, comfort and security, offered by the world as the milky way to happiness. If so, our faith in eternal life with Christ has to be shaken, just as we shake a watch to make it run.

Therefore Epiphany offers us both a welcome and a challenge. It welcomes us to renew our faith and continue our search for fullness of Christ. It also challenges us to continue the manifestation of Christ to the world. It challenges us to share the light of Christ we have received with others who still grope their way from dark behind to dark before, because we believe that in Christ night is day; it challenges us to offer Christ to those who are still searching for meaning in their lives, because we know that the Lord is the joy of every heart and is the answer to its yearnings. It challenges us to become channels of God's grace, because grace that cannot be seen is no grace at all. Should we not accept this Epiphany Challenge? We should because we must be saved together or we will not be saved at all. One wonders what God will say to us if some of us go to him without others.

1ST SUNDAY OF LENT

WE ARE IN LENT

Readings: Deut 26:4-10; Rom 10:8-13; Lk 4:1-13

Theme: Lent is a time of spiritual preparation for Easter, purifying our actions and motives from spiritual obstacles and participating in the Passion and Death of Christ through self-sacrifices, in the belief that with Christ we will rise again.

LENT IS PREPARATION. The loftiest edifices need the deepest foundations. So too the celebration of the most sublime paschal mystery of the death and resurrection of Jesus Christ, needs solemn spiritual preparation. Israel prepared for forty years before entering into the promised land; Jesus prepared for forty days (Lk 4:1-2), to enter into his public ministry, which led him to death on the cross; so too we prepare during Lent in order to enter into the depth of Christ's Passion and then into the fairest garden of the purest Easter joy. We prepare by intensive prayer. To us, prayer ought not to be what dolls are to children, just comforting. We must take prayer seriously, at least during Lent, and find time to be alone with God in solitude for solitude is the audience chamber of God. We prepare through frequent attendance at Mass and the reception of the Sacrament of Reconciliation. Particularly we prepare through daily meditation of God's word. The word of God is not to be adored only as a monument over the graves of Christians. It needs to be engraved in our hearts, while we are still alive.

LENT IS PURIFICATION. If we want to be friends with God, as in all friendships we have to keep it in constant repair. We have to get rid of those spiritual obstacles which hinder us from responding fully to God's love. We must try to remove even our small faults, for men stumble on stones not on mountains. Our actions need purification. In our actions, if we give priority to the physical rather than to the spiritual, we deny, that "man does not live by bread alone" (Lk 4:4). Not only the end of our actions but the means we use to obtain them have to be also good. Jesus refused to cast himself down from the pinnacle of the Temple (Lk 4:12), for that was not God's way to make his mission a success. Life is not a football game, where you may be careful about the goal, but indifferent to the ball. Above all, the motives for our actions need purification. The true motives of our actions are usually concealed like the pipes of an organ.

LENT IS PARTICIPATION. We will fast in Lent. Many of us would deny ourselves some of our cherished pleasures as a penance, for wanting in the past more than our fair share of the good things in life, even though 140,000 children in the world will die of hunger in the next three days. Some of us will give up part of our comforts to the homeless. We will do all these and many other sacrifices not out of duty, for even gold is worthless if given out of duty, but as our loving participation in the Passion and Death of our Lord. Yes, if we are to be remade, reborn and turned around, we need to be first broken to pieces. For a Christian, who does not daily take to himself Christ's death, the crucifix becomes simply a decoration on the wall. After all, suffering does not have the last word. Those who suffer in union with Christ on the cross suffer to end all suffering.

LENT IS PROCLAMATION. In Lent we proclaim that "God who brought our forefathers out of Egypt with a strong hand and outstretched arms" (Deut 26:8) will bring us also to freedom through the cross of his Son, for it was on the cross that freedom's battle against evil, was won. Throughout Lent we profess our faith that "Jesus is the Lord who died and rose from the dead" (Rom 10:9), not only to break our chains here and now but also finally to lead us into the land of the free and the home of the brave. Without this faith, penance will be preposterous. Hence during Lent we have to cling not just to the forms of faith, but to faith itself. Faith is not a feeling but a conviction. At times one wonders whether the best among Christians lack all conviction, while the worst in the world are full of passionate intensity. With an active faith and fire within, Lent can offer us a new beginning and it is never too late to begin. It is better to begin in the evening, than not at all.

THE BEST IS YET TO BE

Readings: Gen 15:5-12, 17-18; Phil 3:17-4:1; Lk 9:28-36

Theme: Those who listen to God's Son Jesus and follow him in suffering and death for the sake of love will be led one day into mankind's glorious destiny.

Our promises made in storms are often forgotten in calms, even if it was a good mouth-filling promise. A doctor said to his patient, "You will pull through, but you are a very sick man". The patient replied, "Please, Doctor, do everything you can for me. If I get well, I will donate thirty thousand pounds to the fund for the new hospital". Several months later, when the patient was completely well, the doctor reminded him: "You said that if you got well, you would donate thirty thousand pounds?" The former patient exclaimed, "If I said that, then I really must have been sick". God's promises are not like ours. He made a promise to Abraham that he would have a great progeny and possess a land of full and plenty" (Gen 15:5,14) and he did fulfil it. Ordinarily the weaker partner in a contract has to accept more obligations than the stronger one. But in the covenant with Abraham, it was God who bore the brunt of obligations, promising, that independent of the faithfulness of the other party he would be faithful.

God is at his best in faithfulness. When we were captives to sin, he sent his Son as he had promised, who made captivity itself captive, so that we can now enjoy freedom; a freedom which has a thousand charms that slaves never know, including the freedom to enter one day into eternal life. Yes, men tore up the roads that led to heaven and Jesus came to make ladders to it. It is into the open face of this heaven that the disciples had a sweet glimpse when Jesus was transfigured on Mount Tabor (Lk 9:29), and that was a sneak preview of our own resurrection to come when "he will change our weak mortal bodies and make them like his own glorious body" (Phil 3:21). But the road we all have to take to our glorious destiny passes over the Bridge of Sighs, as Jesus himself had to pass through passion and death into his glory - a subject of discussion between Moses and Elijah on Mount Tabor (Lk 9:31). The same is true for us. No pain, no palm; no thorns, no throne; no gall, no glory; no cross, no crown.

There is no one in the world, king or pope, without his daily cross. Life is the 'agent' for trials and tribulations which it regularly introduces us to; even when things go well, they are still going poorly, for we are all growing old. All of us must expect some trouble in life. The person whose troubles are all behind him is probably a school bus driver. Every one has a problem; if there is one who has none, you will find him in the cemetery. Just before Jesus went up the Mount, he asked his followers to carry their daily cross and even lose their lives for his sake so that they could save them; and on the Mount God said, "Listen to him" (Lk 9:35). Do we listen? Some people are born deaf, in others hearing is impaired, but there are those whose hearing is nearly perfect but would never listen, with the result "their lives make them enemies of the cross of Christ" (Phil 3:18). But to Christians who listen, the cross would not be a mystery but a revelation; for it discloses how much God loves us, and how much we too should love God by embracing our daily cross.

We say we love God and try to love our neighbour as Christ has loved us. But love is not love until it is vulnerable. Love is essentially sacrificial and that is why the greatest love is a mother's, then comes a dog's, then comes that of a sweetheart. Besides, when we embrace crosses out of love, we are not suffering for nothing. That would be tragic, for the greatest pain is to love in vain. Through our crosses we are destined to a transformation, similar to that of Christ on Mount Tabor. Though our bodies be disfigured now on earth with many defects, they will one day be transfigured. But God's promise is that he will lead us to our dazzling destiny not necessarily through crucifixion on the cross, but through daily sacrifices for love. When some one encourages us, our capacity to achieve our goal expands. Likewise, may this promise of God, uplift our spirits to their fullest potential, for the Best Is Yet To Be.

TURN OR BURN

Readings: Ex 3:1-8, 13-15; 1 Cor 10:1-6, 10-12; Lk 13:1-9

Theme: God whose name is Goodness, also has a limit to his patience and hence waits for us to turn away from sins, lest we are burnt by our own evil.

A lady on a transatlantic flight in a jet became very upset when they hit a strong turbulence. She asked the stewardess, "Are we going to crash?" The stewardess tried to calm her down saying, "Don't be afraid. We are all in the hands of God". The lady exclaimed, "Oh, is it that bad?" to which the stewardess said, "No, it is actually that good". Yes, God is good. He is always good. How many times in the past have we gone to God, for we could go nowhere else and we learnt that the stormy waves of our life had driven us, not upon the rocks, but on to a bed of blessings? As it is in the glimpse of darkened skies that we realise the beauty of the day, so in the daily cares we face, we often come to realise how much God cares. God gave Moses as his name, "I AM WHO AM" (Ex 3:14), which may have other meanings, but surely it also means that God was, is and will be present to us.

It is not surprising then that we who are the recipients of the goodness of God are expected to respond to God's call with a similar goodness of heart. When we were baptised into Christ, as "our ancestors, passing through the seas, were baptised into Moses" (1 Cor 10:2), God called us to put on the mind and heart of Christ. How can our heart be like that of Christ who warned us against too much preoccupation with this world, if its "desires" (1 Cor 10:6) are as greedy as the jaws of hell, with a restless ambition never at an end? How can we reflect the mind of Christ, who came to serve and not to be served, if we sell our souls to self-love, the greatest of flatterers, while our heart for others is as hard-boiled as an Easter egg? How can we say that we drink from the rock of Christ (1 Cor 10:3) who forgave wrongs darker than death, if we store up grudges in the back of our heads as ancient relics? We say that Christ is our way, but when the way becomes bare and rough, we start "grumbling" (1 Cor 10:10), which soon grows to a mighty rumblings.

Therefore we all need to repent and change. What destroys us is not ruthless killing such as the one carried out by Pilate on a number of Gallileans as they prepared for worship; nor some construction accident, such as the one that occurred at the tower of Siloam; but our unwillingness to repent. So Jesus warns "If you do not turn from your sins, you will all die as they did" (Lk 13:3). We do accept that most people do repent of their sins, but frequently by thanking God that they are not so wicked as their neighbours. If only we always compared our wickedness with the goodness of God, all of us would surely repent and our contrition will certainly become like an April violet, filling the rest of the year with buds and blossoms.

God is patient, hoping that we would reform ourselves at least during this Lent, a chance he gives once more. But a doctor who tries a medicine a certain number of times and finds no change abandons the use of the drug. As there is a limit to every effort, so there is limit to God's patient waiting. If we do not produce, at least during Lent, fruits in personal growth, prayer and community service, God may have to "cut down the fig tree to be burnt" (Lk 13:-7). However, reform is not possible all by ourselves. We need grace and we cannot get graces from gadgets but only from God. Hence we need to come to God in prayer during this period of grace. God will hear our prayers, as he heard those of Israel and delivered them (Ex 3:17). If some of our prayers in the past are not answered, probably we put into them too many commercials. But a prayer for conversion will surely be heard. Our faces may be filled with broken commandments and our hearts with sins, as dark as night. Still we must not hesitate to come to God, for God knows how to make use of our sins as manure for the Tree of Life. Hence to the Lord let us turn, lest we burn.

A NEW CREATION – A NEW WORLD

Readings: Jos 5:9, 10-12; 2 Cor 5:17-21; Lk 15:1-3, 11-32

Theme: Since our true happiness lies in belonging to our Father's house and to the human family, we are called to return to God and our fellow human beings, and to be made in Christ new creations for a new world.

A widow who had spent long days and hours in the factory and at home, raising her four children, lay exhausted and emaciated on her death bed. Around her stood the four of them, now grown up men and women. The eldest son, in tears, said to her, "Mother, you have always been so good and kind to us. We want to thank you. We are proud of you". The mother opened her eyes and asked, "Why have you waited so long to tell me that? You never said so before". She turned her head away and died. All of us love children, for they are like olive branches around a table. But some of them can be utterly ungrateful. When the younger son in the parable of the prodigal demanded from his father the portion of his estate (Lk 15:12), his intention was not to insult his father, yet it was like telling him to drop dead. The father, though shattered by this impulsive brashness, still gave him the money. The son left his father's house taking on the world alone, only to come crashing down with a painful bang.

It is a warning to those of us, who have either left or are leaving our Father and his house. Our true happiness lies in belonging to our Father's house. Do we really belong to God our Father? Have we not all been unfaithful to him at some times, making totally inadequate response to his love and "squandering" (Lk 15:13) at least some of our heritage? Do we truly belong to the house of our Father, which is the human society, by our loving care and brotherly concern for each other? Perhaps some of us are like the elder brother of the parable, withdrawn, unapproachable, bitter and afraid to mix with others, finding security in excessive devotion to duty and earning money. To belong to a particular human society may be a bore, but to be out of it is simply a tragedy; for human beings were formed for society and one would not be alone, even in paradise.

Therefore, all of us have gone astray in some sense and need to return to our Father's house. God will surely receive us, for he is not just good but reckless in his goodness. He will be good to us, whether we are like the younger son, a prodigal or like the elder son, a paranoid, when we return to him. When we come to God, let us bring with us that lost part of ourselves which God has been tracking down; once we are reconciled whole and entire with God and neighbour, we will discover that we have returned to a heaven of peace and a new beginning. How our hearts, at times, yearn for that land of new beginnings, where all our mistakes and headaches could be dropped like a shaggy coat at the door, never to be put on again! Indeed, God has provided us with such a land in the heart of his son Jesus. In the past, God "removed from Israel the shame of slavery" (Jos 5:9) and now, through Christ's death on the cross, he has freed us from sin; hence, "if anyone is in Christ, he is a new creation" (2 Cor 5:17).

New creation, indeed, we became at baptism, but as a new broom is said to be good only for three days, so we lose our newness in Christ soon and often by our sins. However, at the sacrament of Reconciliation, our merciful Father again and again welcomes us to reconciliation with himself and with his community, appealing earnestly that we in turn become "ministers of reconciliation" who can "reconcile the world to God" (2 Cor 5:18). This means that we become New Creations, so that we can work for a new world! We are forgiven, so that we cannot only forgive others but even forget their offences; for it is better to forget and smile than to remember and be sad. It is forgiveness that reveals the power of love and it is love that brings about peace. We may call for peace as loudly as we could, but where there is no love, there can be no peace. It is peace not battle that tests the Christian strength, because peace is a daily process, slowly eroding old barriers and quietly building new bridges.

5TH SUNDAY OF LENT

IT'S HAPPENING AGAIN

Readings: Is 43:16-21; Phil 3:8-14; Jn 8:1-11

Theme: The mercy of God is calling us back to drink the waters of life that flow from Christ at the sacrament of reconciliation, as he did to the people of Israel in the past and to the penitent sinners during the life of Christ.

It happened to the people of Israel in the past. Who does not know the appalling miseries and sleepless sufferings they bore? It is true, pleasures too visited them but remember, pain cruelly clung to them. However, every time they fell upon the thorns of life God, the great cloud of mercy, rained compassion to quench the fire that burned their lives. God the mighty liberator parted the waters of the Red Sea for them. The God who worked wonders during their Exodus from Egypt, seven centuries later, worked a new wonder to facilitate their return from Babylonian captivity, saying, "See, I am doing something new. Now it springs forth, do you not perceive it? In the desert I make a way, in the wastelands rivers" (Is 43:19). Who among us can smile in the face of adversity and mean it? So the chosen people cried to God every time calamity hit them, and he came to pluck the burden of sorrow from them.

It happened to penitent sinners during the lifetime of Christ. Christ was the reaching out of God to sinful humanity. That is why, when others wanted to condemn and kill the woman caught in adultery, Jesus forgave her saying, "I do not condemn you" (Jn 8:11). If Jesus overtook even the flying eagle to embrace every sinner, it was because he was the Sacrament of God, the ocean of boundless compassion. The sinners Jesus forgave were only representing the whole of humanity, for all have sinned. When the Pharisees brought the woman accusing her of sin, Jesus said, "Let the man among you who has no sin be the first to cast a stone at her" (Jn 8:7). Jesus looked down to the earth and doodled in it with his fingers, reminding us that all of us are sinners; for dust is the origin and destiny of our bodies. But Jesus does not write our sins on rock to remain for ever, but on dust, to be blown away by the mercy of God, who does not snuff out the smouldering wick or beat the bruised reed.

It is happening again to us here and now, at the sacrament of confession, where the merciful Lord continues to forgive our sins. Many people for various reasons have stopped going to confession. For some, sin is not real; if it is not, why did Jesus say to the woman, "Go, sin no more" (Jn 8:11). Others make excuses for their sins, appealing to sociology or psychology as, for example, when they justify premarital sex as a necessary experience for growth in maturity, although they know that it is better to have a fool to make us merry than an experience to make us sad. Still others find no use in confession, for they have to repeat the same faults again and again. But don't we go to the doctor over and over again for shots or medicine, if we know that we are born with some physical allergies? All of us have some inborn spiritual weaknesses, because of which we fail again and again. Why then should we worry about repeating our faults to the good Lord? After all, repetition is everywhere and nothing is found only once in the world.

Hence, the mercy of God is calling us back to drink the waters of life that flow from Christ. Are we ready to return and open ourselves to God's love? The greatest sin is not adultery but deliberately closing our minds and hearts to God's love and closing in on oneself and away from others in pride and self-sufficiency. In fact we are called to be as enthusiastic in our return to the Lord as St Paul was, who said, "I have accounted all else rubbish, so that Christ can be my wealth" (Phil 3:8). If we do come to the Lord, we will enter into the Palace of Love, where the treasures of the King are kept with all the kisses of love. Kissed by love, we will have truth, which is on the side of the oppressed today. We will have integrity which baffles those full of duplicity; we will have mercy, which blesses him who gives and him who takes; and we will have courage, which narrow souls dare not admire.

CHRIST REIGNS FROM THE CROSS

Readings: Is 50:4-7; Phil 2:6-11; Lk 23:1-49

Theme: Because the cross on which Christ chose to die became a throne from which he would reign over sin and death, we too can win crown and glory through our cross and pain.

Even a cold, untroubled heart of stone will pause to breathe and a noble heart will certainly crack at the sufferings of Christ during his Passion. After being let down by his friends and betrayed by some; after suffering frightening anguish in Gethsemane, after being tried for the offences he did not commit; and after being taunted by blows, spits, lashes of whip and piercing of thorns, he was finally crucified on the cross. On the cross, he was stabbed with nails of black iron, causing gushing wounds, the gaping marks of malice. Clouds of darkness covered his body with blackness. They mutilated his body, the lovely casket of his soul. His death was the most dreadful of all deaths, for he was both Son of God and Son of Man. His sufferings were real, not play-acting, for he was not made of some super-flesh, insensitive to pain, nor of a super-soul which served as anaesthetic. For anyone who doubts that his sufferings were real challenges Christ's honesty.

However, the cross upon which Christ freely chose to die, became a throne from which he would reign. There never was a fairer morning than the golden dawn of Easter Day when he rose; there never was a greater joy than the stunning moment when the angels affirmed that he lives again; there never came a nobler hope that human beings are immortal and human life surges towards infinity, for Christ died and rose for all. Christ reigns from the cross because, after entering into man's sinful state, he twisted sin's own weapon, death, out of its grasp and used it as a means for man's return to God. Christ reigns from the cross because the cross upon which he was the Suffering Servant of the Lord transformed him into the Son of Glory. Christ reigns from the cross because the cross that gathered together all the sorrows in the world into the one Sorrow of Christ in a moment of utter defeat won complete victory over all human sorrows.

Therefore, no tree in all the wood is dearer to us Christians than the tree of the cross; it reminds us that we too can win crown and glory through cross and pain. At times pain pricks us, at other times it hurts us like hell or cracks over our heads like a whip. We find our personal calvaries even in our homes and communities, as the result of violence and harm we do to each other. Some of us place others on the cross, by our hatred and rejection of them. And there are communal calvaries, called social structures, created by the unjust, supported by the violent, exploited by the greedy and abused by the powerful. However, in our suffering, if we jump to the crucified feet of Christ, like a wounded deer that leaps highest, he will console and comfort us and fill our cups to overflowing; for his rivers of might and mercy are all broad. Besides, the same cross which we daily embrace on this earth, will one day bid us to leave this fleeting life, to sit at the banquet of the Lord in heaven.

Until that day of glory, when God will look us over, not for medals but for scars, we will bear our sufferings as Christ did. Christ suffered for love. Our renunciations and sacrifices will be worthless without love, as all the coal and firewood in the world are useless without fire. Christ showed compassion even to his executioners. Likewise, we who cannot do anything with sin can do at least something with suffering, namely, we can take it from others upon ourselves. Christ did not indulge in self-pity during his pains. We may win compassion through self-pity, but the pity of it is, that every horse thinks his own pack heaviest. Above all, Christ suffered with hope that God would raise him. So too, we in our suffering, whether they come singly or in battalions, must hope that they are the means to find our homeward way to our glorious destiny. If we daily put forth such tender leaves of hope we will surely see them one day blossom.

EASTER SUNDAY

HE IS RISING AGAIN

Readings: Acts 10:34, 37-43; Col 3:1-4; Jn 20:1-9

Theme: Jesus is rising again and again in each of us and in the Body of his people; he is rising in the forgiveness we receive from God and offer to others; and he is rising in our daily struggles and trials to be fully human and fully alive.

Christianity is a resurrection religion. It believes that the risen Christ has turned all our sunsets into dawns. Signs of new life can be noticed on Easter Sunday. People come prepared to light a new fire, to sing music, to light candles. New clothes, splashes of colour and maybe a newborn child to be baptised. But let us not misread these signs. These are signs not only that Jesus rose from the dead but also that he is rising again. He is rising in each of us and in the Body of his people, again and again and again. If "being brought back to true life with Christ" (Col 3:1) is to mean anything, it means that the silver thread of resurrection runs through believers of our own time, freeing them to a new relationship with God and to a new bond of love with others, empowering them to realise their own human potential in a new way and sustaining them through struggles and trials, hardships and pains of human life until they triumph. Every time we experience new life in Christ, in that experience Jesus is rising again.

We experience the new life of the risen Jesus when we are forgiven by God of our sins and reconciled with him. "Every one who believes in Jesus has forgiveness of sins through his name" (Acts 10:43). St Peter had such an experience. He denied his Master, but when he was forgiven, the joy of being forgiven surged within himself so much that at the charcoal fire on the beach, he three times asserted his love for the man he had three times denied. We experience the new life of the risen Jesus when we ourselves forgive those who have offended us. The burden of a grudge is a heavy load. As chips on the shoulder burden only the bearer, our grudges limit only our own freedom. But when the grace of Christ's resurrection heals our memories, the load of unforgiveness is lifted and we experience great joy and freedom. Our memories will not be erased, but they will no longer cause us pain. They are rather like the wounds on the risen body of Jesus which were once signs of pain and injustice but have now become signs of triumph.

We experience the new life of the risen Jesus when we are able to pull through our personal calvaries such as severe depression because we trusted in the Lord. You and I know what depression is. It is to feel oneself sinking lower and lower. Yet, even if you reach the lowest depths, if only you place all your trust in Jesus Christ, you will experience an inward peace. Upon the surface a rough tempest may still be raging, but still you will experience a blessed quietness in the deep caverns of your soul. That is the rising of Jesus again. We experience the new life of the risen Jesus when through sheer persistent endeavour we are able to overcome even permanent physical handicaps and live our life to the full. Helen Keller had such an experience. "Be reasonable. There is just no way that a person without sight, hearing or speech could possibly communicate in any meaningful way. We can make you comfortable, but not much more than that", people said to Helen. But she strained and wrestled with every detail of her existence, poured herself into every effort-filled day and there was resurrection.

We experience the new life of the risen Jesus not only as individuals but also as a community. Where there is communal brokenness there is the possibility of communal resurrection. The violence of some of our cities, the inequality of wealth, opportunity and its consequent sense of injustice, the prevailing prejudices, the discrimination against classes and colours are among the many examples of our broken world. But there have been men and women in the world anointed by the Holy Spirit with God's power as Jesus was (Acts 10:38), who have put up peaceful fights to deliver the oppressed people from their communal calvaries leading them to a new life. "There is no way a black person will ever ride in front of the bus in Birmingham. We will keep our customs no matter what anyone else says" warned the establishment. But the Rev Martin Luther King persisted in his movement; 99 percent of black people in Birmingham courageously stood their ground and there was resurrection.

Therefore Jesus is rising again and again. We don't need to wait until we die to share in the power of Christ's resurrection. We can have our personal and communal resurrection here and now.

2ND SUNDAY OF EASTER

"PEACE BE WITH YOU!"

Readings: Acts 5:12-16; Rev 1:9-11, 12-13, 17-19; Jn 20:19-31

Theme: Peace of Christ which is personal before it is social, flows from proper order, giving us wholesome health and freeing us from all fear including the fear of death.

Peace is the first gift of the risen Jesus. "Peace be with you" (Jn 20:19) are the first words he speaks to them. Peace is not 'quiet', the state of nothing going on and not being disturbed by anyone; that is not peace, but vacuum. Peace, as St Augustine would say, is the 'tranquillity that comes from order and order is simply the proper arranging of all the parts'. In other words, peace is the purposeful flow of life. It is a constantly adjusting order of things, such as we see at the crowded intersection in which each motorist and pedestrian gets to where he or she is going without causing any hostile feeling. It can be experienced in a large family with a dozen different tasks to do in the same evening, with each caring about the other and all the tasks eventually falling into place. But for peace to reign in a family or community or in the world, there must be peace first within the individuals. 'Peace demands a mentality and a spirit which, before turning to others, must first permeate him who wishes to bring peace. Peace is first and foremost personal before it is social" said Pope John Paul II. What are some of the signs that a believer enjoys the peace of Christ?

Peace of Christ gives health. It is a healing power. It was with this power that St Peter, after the resurrection of the Lord, healed the sick. "Crowds from the towns around Jerusalem would gather bringing their sick, all of whom were healed" (Acts 5:16). But the health that the peace of Christ effects is more than freedom from physical pain. It is a sense of wellbeing at a profound spiritual and emotional level. Since what happens in a human body is always related to what goes on in other parts of the person, the power of the risen Jesus heals the whole person, by bringing all the parts of the human being, his spirit, emotion and body, into a harmony with each other. The result is that the healed believer finds wholeness of a new kind, an all-embracing condition of wellbeing. The risen Lord effects such a wholesome health primarily by activating within the believer the 'inner doctor', the Holy Spirit, who releases his saving and healing energies. Therefore the advice Carl Gustav Jung (who as we know gave much room to the 'spiritual' dimension in life in his theories) has given to all therapists is quite sound: "The best we can do is to give the inner doctor, who dwells in each patient, a chance to become operative".

Peace of Christ frees us from all fear. There are times when the sea of our life becomes rough, with storms of doubt and tension, of economic and health problems, of loneliness and failure and uncertainty about future, which toss us around like tiny corks on the ocean. However, under the surface of such raging storms, the believer experiences peace when hearing the risen Lord say, "There is nothing to fear. I am the first and the last and the one who lives" (Rev 1:17). Often our fears arise from imaginary worries. There is an old story of an angel who met a man carrying a heavy sack and enquired what was it. 'My worries', said the man. 'Let me see them', asked the angel. When the sack was opened, it was empty. The man was astonished and said he had two great worries. One was of yesterday, which he now saw was past; the other of tomorrow, which had not yet arrived. The angel told him he needed no sack and the man gladly threw it away. Yes. That is what the risen Christ does to our imaginary worries when we open our sack of troubles to him.

Peace of Christ frees us even from fear of death. Not all the preaching since Adam has made death other than death. It is possible to provide security against other ills but as far as death is concerned, we all live in a city without walls. Death is never sweet, not even when it is suffered for the highest ideals. Hence all fear death. Yet we believe that our faith gives us a share in the resurrection of him who says, "Once I was dead but now I live; I hold the keys of death" (Rev 1:18). We believe in eternal life, which is not a pleasing delusion, not an appendage to our Christian faith but it is the Christian faith. We believe that the resurrection of Jesus has touched every phase of human life so thoroughly that our present and future existence is quite secure. After his resurrection, every healing has become a partial resurrection and every change is towards greater life: the child leaving the womb, the adolescent entering the adult life, the adult moving through the middle age crisis and the person leaving this world in death, all move towards fuller life. Thus the risen Lord has freed us from fear of death.

RETURN TO THE CENTRE

Readings: Acts 5:27-32, 40-41; Rv 5:11-14; Jn 21:1-19

Theme: Christ, the centre of our lives, calls us to return to him if we had fallen out of love with him.

Falling in love is charming in life; but there is always some madness in love, and some reason in madness. So, a boy and a girl falling in love married, but after a few years, falling out of love began, because problems arose: bills mounting up, work uncertain, sickness and monotony. He wanted to make love, she didn't. She wanted to go to the theatre, he didn't. He wanted to save money, she wanted to spend it on a holiday. She wanted just to talk, he wanted to watch football. She did not like his family, he didn't like hers. So their love cracked and their life rocked. However, no permanent damage was done, for they realised that they were two separate persons and each cannot be owned or possessed by the other. Hence, they chose to return to love, the centre of their life. Love after reunion was not like their first passion, but it didn't matter. After all, the first passion is only a little foolishness and a lot of curiosity. But after reconciliation their love became truly real.

This is the story of every love. St Peter the Apostle loved Christ. But in the beginning his love was only an emotion, as Grandma feels for a poodle. So St Peter denied Christ three times, but he repented and returned to the centre of his life, Christ, with renewed real love. We too love Christ and love him dearly. If he were to ask each of us, as he asked St Peter (Jn 21:15), "Do you love me?" we would readily reply, "Yes, Lord, I love you; every time I think of you, my heart touches a new high, sighing like furnace". If he would ask a second time, we would respond, "Lord. Yes. My love for you seems to pump me full of vitamins". If he would ask the same question a third time, we would protest saying, "Lord, you know that I love you. My love can conquer all things, including death". Indeed, we do love Christ, but the fabric of our love will begin to unravel when we start our travel along with him. For on our travel we will encounter trials: the presence of trial will tell us how great our love is but its absence will raise the question how long our love will be.

Trial will come when we try to "feed his lambs" (Jn 21:16), not just with the bread of the Eucharist, but with real food and drink. The Eucharist is not just liturgy and ceremony, but loving and sharing, feeding the hungry, sustaining the homeless and mentally sick with acceptance, nourishing our youth by openness, and supporting our aged by high esteem. Trial will come when we are called to join the parish faith-sharing group, Justice and Peace group and similar action groups to build the Kingdom of God. Trial will come when we are urged to smile the risen power of Christ into our secular society, bringing Christian values to play in business, education and families. At times, such trials would hit us like a migraine blotting out reason. At such moments did we bear them in the past as the Apostles did? "They left the Sanhedrin full of joy that they had been ill-treated for Christ" (Acts 5:41). If we could not bear them joyfully, did we accept them at least willingly, at least for the rewards in store for us, the reward of "power and riches, wisdom and strength, honour and glory" (Rev 5:12)? As the evening of well-spent life brings lamps with it, so will our sufferings for the love of Christ.

If our love for Christ has become shaky in the course of our difficult travel with him, he calls us back to him to renew our love. It does not matter even if we have divorced him in our hearts – after all, divorce has become so common today that a wedding is the only prerequisite for a divorce now. Let us only return to him, he will receive us. It is only we who often write off other people; on the strength of one or two unfriendly encounters with them, we rarely give them one more chance. But Jesus is different. As long as there is even the slightest hope of rekindling in us the flame of the smouldering wick, he would not extinguish it. The Christian love story is one of calling, falling and recalling. Christ is recalling us: are we returning to our centre?

SHEPHERDS AND SHEPHERDS

Readings: Acts 13:14, 43-52; Rev 7:9, 14-17; Jn 10:27-30

Theme: Jesus our Good Shepherd invites us to follow him even on rough paths, listening to his voice, spreading his light to others and leading all people into the one fold.

Some handicapped children were asked to make a drawing of their idea of God. One girl drew "an open door" because she always felt locked in; God was an open door to friendship for her. Another painted "a foot" because he could not walk; he thought of God as joy, being able to walk and touch grass with his toes. A third person sketched "a flower" for she believed that God is all beauty. Similarly, Christ gives himself the image of a "SHEPHERD." As our shepherd, he "knows" (Jn 10:27) each of us by name; some of our names may be silly, but they are lovely and he knows them. He gives us "eternal life" (v.28). Some people ask, "Is life worth living?" which is a question for an embryo not for an adult, for life on earth is good though eternal life is best. Christ will "not allow us to perish" (v.28), come what may. People may sometimes give up on us, but never the Lord, for whether we live or whether we die, we belong to him.

Since Christ is our Shepherd, we are his sheep, not dumb animals, but voluntary followers of Christ the leader. Good leaders have become so scarce these days that many people are following themselves. But Christ is a good leader who can change a group from what it is into what it ought to be. To follow Christ means that we "hear his voice" (Jn 10:27) and respond to it. At times he will speak with a voice like the sound of many waters, to proclaim his beatitudes; at other times he will speak in a soft, gentle and slow voice, (an excellent thing in a woman!), in order to comfort us. At still other times, his voice will sound like rolling drums, challenging us to become shepherds like him for others. Above all, to follow Christ means that we bring his "light of salvation" (Acts 13:47) into people whose lives may be as dark as the grave, and we must do this before the jaws of darkness devour them. In following our Shepherd, we may have to face many trials, but one day "our robes washed and made white in the blood of the Lamb, we will be led to springs of life-giving water" (Rev 7:14,17).

Christ the Good Shepherd wished that his followers remain and expand as one united sheepfold, as "he and Father are one" (Jn 10:30). Unity is like fire which can burn down differences. Of what use is it to have many irons in the fire, if the fire is going out? Unity is light; a Church may be like a lighthouse, built of stone so strong that the thunder of the sea cannot move it, but if there is no light at the top, what use is it? We are called not only to remain united by mutual loving and caring, but also to spread this unity throughout the world. Ss Paul and Barnabas did exactly this, when they reached out to the gentiles with the good news (Acts 13:14). If you should ever go to the moon in a space rocket, you would see our world as one lump of earth, water, air clouds floating around in space. Yes, from the moon our world may look as one, but when will it actually become one?

To preserve the unity in the Church and to gather together all people into one fold, Christ needs shepherds like him who can lead his flock. He needs leaders, for he knows that followers will hardly ever go farther than their leader. He needs leaders who are dealers in hope, for his Gospel is the world's only social hope. He needs leaders who are interested in the flock, not in the fleece, and leaders who can hold the helm not only when the sea is calm but also when there is storm in the sea. Vocations Sunday is a day of prayer that such leaders in the faith will never be found wanting among the clergy, the religious and the laity. But shepherding is not a vocation confined only to the leaders in the Church; every Christian is called to be both a follower of Christ and a shepherd for others through love and care. There seems to be three classes of followers of the Good Shepherd: the few who make things happen, the many who watch things happen and the majority who have no notion of what happens in the Church and in the world. To which class do we want to belong?

THE HOUR WILL COME

Readings: Acts 14:21-27; Rev 21:1-5; Jn 13:31-33, 34-35

Theme: Though we pass through some calvaries in our faith journey, the hope of our future glory and the loving support from one another will lead us to final triumph.

We are quickly bored with someone reciting his troubles and we willingly avoid the sight of distress. Perhaps modern living has made us very soft, so soft that when the central heating breaks down or the engine in the car gives trouble, we lament as if it were a major crisis. Yet one has to be realistic. There will be always some distress to plague us in life and, if it is a Christian life, one must be ready to be parched by the heat of trials and drenched by the rain of tribulations. As long as we are not committed Christians, we may feel fine; but once committed to Christ, the troubles will start, as in marriage. They had just become engaged. "I shall love," she cooed, "to share all your troubles." "But darling", he murmured, "I have none". "No", she agreed, "but I mean when we are married". As Christians, we need to remember that the experience of faith, drowned with tears, is the root and anchor of our Christian way of life.

Read the history of the Church. The ink in which many of its pages are written is the blood of the martyrs and every drop of their blood is liquid history. It began with Christ who brought his ministry to a close in scenes of suffering and death. Ss Paul and Barnabas bore witness to Christ in the face of all obstacles and difficulties and even encouraged their disciples to remain steadfast in spite of troubles, for "We must undergo many trials," they said, "if we are to enter into the Kingdom of God" (Acts 14:22). Frequently down the centuries, faith and love provoked persecutions; at other times, they summoned people to heroic sacrifices as in the case of countless saints, who abandoned themselves completely to God in lives of poverty and compassion; at still other times, they aroused great sense of dedication, as in the case of many who emerged from the hell of addiction through faith and dedicated the rest of their lives to thanking God and helping others.

Can we also bear our troubles cheerfully for the sake of faith? We can, if we believe in our future life, and Christianity is the most monumental fraud if there is no future life. On the eve of his death Jesus said, "Now has the Son of Man been glorified and in him God has been glorified" (Jn 13:31). We too will have our hour of glory when we will be great, "enter into new heavens and a new earth", dwell in "New Jerusalem" and when "God shall wipe away every tear from our eyes" (Rev 21:1-4). What a great future awaits us! In this world, some are born great, at least financially, for their parents are very rich; some achieve greatness because of what they accomplish with a lot of effort; and some have greatness thrust upon them because they react heroically and nobly in certain situations. We too, if we react courageously and cheerfully to the crises and challenges of our faith-life, will achieve Christian greatness.

However, we need not suffer alone for faith. As Christians we are friends in Christ and friendship is not a feeling, such as we have when comfortably filled with roast beef; it is loving and sharing. We have a right to expect loving support from one another to sustain our spirits in times of hardships. This is why Jesus asked us "to love each other as he has loved us" (Jn 13:34). It is not one of the teachings of Christ. It is the substance of his teachings. Every teacher and pupil knows that approaching examinations focus the mind and the heart very decisively. One cannot cover every option. The core topics must be highlighted. Jesus, too, just before his death gave his core message and that was on love. Love has the power to bring people back from the brink of death, from hopeless sickness to perfect health and to inspire the people the world over with new hope. "If you Christians," said a Hindu to me, "love the way the Bible says to love, you'd convert India in five years".

6TH SUNDAY OF EASTER

WHO ARE WE?

Readings: Acts 15:1-2, 22-29; Rev 21:10-14, 22-23; Jn 14:23-29

Theme: We are 'Star Gazers' who keep looking up to heaven, 'Caterpillars in Cocoon' who are struggling to grow, 'Relief Ships' who carry the peace of Christ to spread, and 'Path Finders', who keep searching for new ways to build God's Kingdom.

Who are we? We are 'Star Gazers'. We Christians gaze at the stars not to read our day's luck but to see our home beyond them. The film ET is about a terrestrial being from outer space, a friendly being with a glowing heart. In that glow, withered plants start to bloom, aggressive animals become peaceful and a fighting family turns into a nicely caring one. The being cannot communicate in human language, but being very intelligent, it quickly picks up some words. The first word it picks up is 'home' and the first sentence it utters is, "I want to go home"! Millions like me have seen this film, why? Is it because we too don't feel at home here and would like to go to our real home? Jesus too talks about his going home (Jn 14:28). Yes, our home is heaven, "gleaming with the splendour of God" (Rev 21:11). However, God has made his abode in our hearts as well. "If any one loves me and keeps my word, I and my Father will come to dwell in him" (Jn 14.23), says the Lord. Hence we can experience heaven even here on earth.

Who are we? We are 'Caterpillars in Cocoons'. A certain man one day saw the cocoon of a rare caterpillar hanging from a tree twig. He took the cocoon home. A few days later he saw movement inside the cocoon, but the moth did not emerge. He saw the same movement the next day and on the following day, but nothing happened. So he took a knife and slit the cocoon. The moth crawled out but was underdeveloped and soon died. Nature ordains that a caterpillar must struggle to escape its cocoon. It is this struggle that causes it to develop and makes it strong to survive. Something like this happens to us. The indwelling God programmes struggles in our lives, by withdrawing himself sometimes from us to help us grow spiritually. Jesus did this to his disciples when he left them for a while saying, "It is better for you that I go" (Jn 16:7). We can experience at times God's withdrawal in our prayer and in the perceived strength of our faith, with the result they can hardly move a molehill; the same thing occurs at other times in our religious commitments, with the result we derive little joy in any parish ministry. At such moments we have to remember that a caterpillar has to struggle to come out properly developed.

Who are we? We are 'Relief Ships'. We carry with us the peace of the indwelling God wherever we go, to keep the world in one piece. "Peace I leave with you" said Jesus (Jn 14:27). His is not like the peace which the world gives, running wild all over the place. It is a fine inner peace which can hold us secure even when the barque of our soul is buffeted by the severest storms. Jesus gave us his peace to be shared with others. But, before giving it to others, we ourselves must first enjoy this peace. If we are ill at ease in ourselves with no peace of Christ, we will spread only a contagion of conflict around us. "If you are yourself at peace" said Thomas Merton, "then there is at least some peace in the world".

Who are we? We are 'Pathfinders'. The early Church was confronted with a controversy about retaining some Mosaic practices such as circumcision (Acts 15:1-2). But they were willing to be pathfinders, willing to re-evaluate their lives, ready to risk change, daring to make new decisions under the direction of the Holy Spirit. This pattern has been repeated in the Church down through the ages. In our own parish, we may have to settle new questions for its growth. If a parish is going to be relevant in the face of contemporary needs, then we too have to be pathfinders. We may not know exactly what to do, but we must not hesitate to come together to discuss, for the Holy Spirit will enlighten us; we may not know what far-reaching consequences our decisions may have but we should not be fainthearted, for the Spirit dwells in us. Christians who are pathfinders are not content with the routine practice of faith. They search for new forms to express their faith and new ways to apply their Christianity to current issues.

ASCENSION

A RELAY RACE

Readings: Acts 1:1-11; Eph 1:17-23; Lk 24:46-53

Theme: Jesus promised his followers that he would be with them to the end and hence he commissioned them to continue his work on earth courageously, through a witness that has to be personal but which is suited to the needs of every age.

What happened on the day of Ascension was something like what happens in a relay race. In this race, a baton is passed from one runner to another. Likewise, when our Lord ascended into heaven he passed the baton of his work to Ss Peter, James and John. They in turn passed it on to the people who came after them; they in turn passed it on to us and now it is our turn to pass it on to others. "You are my witnesses" (Act 1:8), said Jesus as he ascended. That was said to every follower of his, from the ones who saw his life, death, resurrection and ascension, down to us who have only heard about him, yet have believed. Some Christians think they will sneak comfortably into heaven without bearing witness for Christ. Too many Christians live their Christianity inside their heads; it never gets out through their hands and feet and lips. To witness is to spread the Good News which we can do either by preaching or writing. Even those who feel they can't do either of them, can surely do one thing: they can live Christianity. In fact, witness to Christ in the world for any believer has to begin with oneself.

The secret of success in passing on the Good News in the world lies in our own personal life of witness to Christ's teachings. A great and foolish king complained that the rough ground hurt his feet, so he ordered the whole country to be carpeted with cowhide. The court jester laughed when the king told him of his order, "What an absolutely crazy idea, Your Majesty,'" he cried; "why all the needless expense? Just cut out two small pads to protect your feet!" That is what the king did. And it is rumoured that this is how the idea of shoes was born. This court jester is indirectly telling us believers something about the importance of personal witness. If a believer wants to make the world a joyful place through the Gospel, first it is necessary to live the Gospel one's self; if he or she wants to bring the peace of Christ to the world through righteousness, his or her own soul needs first to be right with God and with neighbour. As the Chinese Proverb goes: "If there is right in the soul, there will be beauty in the person; if there is beauty in the person, there will be harmony in the home; if there is harmony in the home, there will be order in the nation; if there is order in the nation, there will be peace in the world". Yes. A personal witness may produce just a ripple, but that ripple will turn into a tidal wave, and that tidal wave will change the face of the earth in a way we never dreamed possible.

Our Christian witness needs to be personal. Yes. But it has to be also a witness which our contemporary world needs. One of the needs of our times is Christian hope. Of course, everyone hopes in something; if it were not for hopes, the heart would break. However, most people hope in superficialities such as a commercial product or a financial investment. Because of the short span of human life, many hesitate to take on far-reaching hopes. But the Christian hope is far-reaching, for it is an echo of man's end that lies in God. Christian hope is founded upon faith in God, aspiring for the riches of his Kingdom, promised through Christ. So St Paul prays: "May you know the great hope to which God, our Lord Jesus has called you, the wealth of his glorious heritage" (Eph 1:18). Any hope outside this "glorious heritage" is a great falsifier of truth. Because our ultimate hope lies in what is beyond this world, we do not deny the value of what is human; we do not slight what is near because we aim at what is far. But we do resist the temptation to get lost in the enjoyment of what is material and become greedy. People who are greedy have extraordinary capacity for waste, when millions in the world are starving; and because the desires of the greedy are endless, their cares and fears are so too.

Christian witness in our contemporary world is a daunting work; but as it is daunting so it is consoling because the Lord, though absent in the flesh, continues to be with us through the power of the Holy Spirit. In fact, he knew full well that it is only through the power of his Spirit that we can undertake this challenging task with any measure of success. Hence he said, "Remain here in the city until you are clothed with power from on high" (Lk 24:49), and he sent later the Holy Spirit. Yes. The Lord is with us through the abiding presence of the Spirit in the Church. It is not a matter of fact, for we can't see him; but it is a matter of faith, for as believers we can experience his presence. Thus, the ascension is the story not about Jesus being taken away from us, but Jesus being given back to us. The ascension is no time for tears; on this ascension day, we have not come to the church to hold a memorial service for someone who is absent. No. We are here to celebrate. It is a party. It is a feast in honour of the risen and ascended Christ, who is with us now and will be till the end of time, comforting us and guiding us, but also challenging us and strengthening us in our work of bringing the Good News to the world.

7TH SUNDAY OF EASTER

SITTING IN THE SHADE?

Readings: Acts 7:55-60; Rev 22:12-14; 16-17, 20; Jn 17:20-26

Theme: The risen Jesus wished his followers to convince the world of his risen presence by being united in love and by serving others as the messengers of love, in the sure hope of reward that is waiting.

A friend of mine was dying. He spoke intensely about his hopes and dreams for his two children. He was happy about their accomplishments in their studies and jobs. Especially important to him was to teach the kids to care about others and to serve their community. He hoped that they would be able to give something back to the world, to make a difference. As my friend had given a great legacy of serving and caring to his growing children, Jesus too was greatly concerned about the future of those he loved, which he expressed in his prayer to his heavenly Father saying, "that all may be one… that your love for me may live in them" (Jn 17:21,26). Jesus hoped that his followers would make a big impact in the world by their unity and love after he had gone. What Jesus left to them was not just a legacy but an ongoing relationship of unity and a convincing concreteness of love. The words of Jesus' prayer are also words for us. We too are touched by the love the Father had for Jesus and hence we too are sent forth so that through us the world may come to see and to know that love.

The Eucharistic meal we have now is a sacrament which both expresses and increases our love for each other. It is here that we are united with God through Jesus and strengthen our unity among ourselves. It is here that we are filled with indwelling love of Jesus Christ and it is here that we are fed and strengthened to be sent with that love into the world. From here we will go home and have our family meal, which once again must reflect the unity and love among the members of the family. It is love and unity that make a family so precious. The family mirrors God who himself is a family, three in one, whose core is unchanging love which overflows into love for all the human race. If such is the nature of the family, its members need to commit themselves to each other for ever in generosity of love and joy, so that they are enabled to reach out to others beyond the family in concerned service.

Beyond our family lies the whole world which is ready to believe in Jesus if it sees our loving service to all people, especially the least among them. In this, people like Albert Schweitzer are an inspiration to all of us. He, acclaimed the world over as a multiple genius, at the age of 38 became a fully-fledged medical doctor. At the age of 43, he left for Africa where he opened a hospital on the edges of a jungle. He died there in 1965 at the age of 90. What motivated him to turn his back on worldly fame and wealth to work among the poorest of the poor in Africa? he said: "It struck me as incomprehensible that I should be allowed to live such a happy life, while so many people around me were wrestling with suffering". In 1950, he was voted by 17 nations as 'The Man of the Century' and in 1952, he was awarded a Nobel Peace Prize.

But to serve the world, giving witness to the love of God in us, would call for sacrifices on our part, sometimes heroic self-sacrifices. But we are assured of our rewards for what we suffer for others. St John heard a voice saying, "I will soon bring with me the reward that will be given to each man as his conduct deserves" (Rev 22:12). It was the voice of Jesus. At times we have to fight for truth, justice and unity out of love for our fellow human beings. But we are sure to win in the end. Winning is not everything; it is the only thing, for upon it depends our reward. And what would be our reward? Stephen saw it when he was being martyred: "I see an opening in the sky and the Son of Man standing at God's right hand" (Acts 7:56). Yes. Our reward would be a share in Christ's glory at the right hand of his Father. But we can't get this reward for nothing, as you can't make a garden just by singing, "Oh, how beautiful" and sitting in the shade.

PENTECOST

LORD SEND US YOUR SPIRIT!

Readings: Acts 2:1-11; 1 Cor 12: 3-7,12-13; Jn 20: 19-23

Theme: We pray that the Holy Spirit, the Spirit of love, may come on us as gentle breath, if need be even like fire, moving us daily and strongly to live by its guidance but united as one family.

LORD SEND US YOUR SPIRIT. It is not easy for us, Lord, to celebrate the Feast of Pentecost because your Spirit is so elusive like the wind and so invisible like the breath. Pentecost is not only a difficult celebration; it is dangerous too, because once the Spirit enters into a person, he takes complete possession of that person; he demands surrendering of oneself; he urges that person to live according to his inspiration. It is so great a personal responsibility to receive your Spirit, which we fear. It is dangerous also, because whatever the Spirit encounters, he effects something new, and whatever is new often instils fear. But Lord, your Spirit is a Spirit of Love, and love casts out all fear; give us therefore the Spirit of Love.

LORD SEND US YOUR SPIRIT, the source of all gifts. You know, Lord; Pentecost is not just for Pentecostals, any more than baptism is only for the Baptists. Pentecost is for all Christians like us. Send us, Lord, your Pentecostal Spirit. We do not so much ask you that all of us should be blessed with gifts, such as praying in tongues, holding hands in the air, and punctuating with 'Amen' or 'Praise the Lord!'. Lord, give us these gifts as you please. But do give us the Spirit, for it is the Spirit which is the source of all gifts; without it, we can neither be saved nor sanctified. Without it we can neither be true Christians nor can we dare works of evangelisation.

LORD SEND US YOUR SPIRIT, like a gentle breath. As the Spirit descended upon the Apostles, they felt as if you had put a tiger in the church tank. As a result, some like Stephen went to die for you; some like St Paul took a complete turnabout with their lives; some like St Peter did astonishing miracles; some like Philip obtained astonishing conversions; and all of them were no longer afraid to face the world. They were going out and speaking out. Send us your Spirit, if not in the form of a ghost wind, at least in the form of a gentle breath, quietly filling our lungs with supernatural air and our hearts with selfless love.

LORD SEND US YOUR SPIRIT, like fire. Your Spirit descended upon the early Church in tongues of fire. As fire makes clay pots strong, so may your Spirit make us strong in our faith; as fire makes a piece of iron soft, so may your Spirit make our iron will of stubbornness into one of docility and humility; as fire gives light like a candle, so may your Spirit give light to our confused minds and complicated desires; as heat takes away the pain of a sprained muscle or ankle, so may your Spirit take away the pain of our sprained egos and hearts.

LORD SEND US YOUR SPIRIT, that we may live by it. In the ages past, you appeared on Mount Sinai, in storms, smoke and fire and on the day of Pentecost, you similarly came down with great noise, wind and fire. But on Sinai it was to give us your Laws and at Pentecost it was to give us your Spirit. Not that you have abolished all laws, not an iota; but you did want to instil into us a new message at Pentecost, namely that we were born in the Spirit at baptism, must live not so much by the inscription of laws as by the spirit of those laws; that we must seek practical guidance for life, not so much from the laws prescribed in the tablets of stone as from the laws engraved in our hearts. You want us, anointed by your Spirit, to live not from book prescriptions but from our souls turned into a temple of the Holy Spirit.

LORD SEND US YOUR SPIRIT, that we may become one family. As the result of the Spirit coming, the disciples spoke in foreign tongues, yet each nationality present understood them in their own language. What a contrast to the time when people built the Tower of Babel in defiance of God, who punished them by dividing them through confusing speech. Yes, Lord, where your Spirit comes, there is no pride nor arrogance; it comes to restore common understanding and to build a united community. Send us therefore your Spirit so that we may be able to speak the language of love, the only language which can be understood by all, uniting us into one family.

THREE IN ONE

Readings: Prov 8:22-31; Rom 5:1-5; Jn 16:12-15

Theme: Because Trinity is a mystery, it is more beneficial for our personal and community life to ask the question: what is it like to be Triune God, rather than, how is God Triune.

Trinity is not a myth but a mystery. A myth is unreal but conceivable. A mystery is real but incomprehensible. Today is the feast of the Most Holy Trinity, a mystery which has been hidden from ages and from generations but was made manifest by Christ. He spoke of God as his Father saying, "All that the Father has belongs to me" (Jn 16:15); he often called himself "the Son of God"; and he spoke of the third divine person as "the Spirit of truth" (Jn 16:13). Like all mysteries, Trinity is also a mind-boggling puzzle. To some it is an annoying riddle. But we need not be surprised at this, for it is about the all powerful God who made the stars and the planets. It is about a God whose centre is everywhere and whose circumference is nowhere.

It is not only Trinity that is a mystery; in fact, nothing about God can adequately be explained. Even Jesus did not give a direct response, most of the time, to questions relating to God and the supernatural. For example, "What is the Kingdom?" they asked. "A mustard seed," he answered (Mt 13:31). However, in the light of all that Jesus has revealed about God, we are able to have a glimpse into the mystery of the Trinity, and try to explain it in some way, however imperfect that may be. Let us take, for instance, the example of Mr Michael Rogers. At home with his children he is known as daddy and his role is that of a father. At work he is known as Mr Rogers and his role is that of a wage-earner. To his wife he is known as Mike and his role is husband. He is the same man but has three different roles to play. Likewise, God is one but plays three different roles, but in each of these roles he is a different person – while being the same God. God the Father is our Creator; God the Son is our Redeemer; God the Holy Spirit is divine Love within us.

But whatever may be the depth of our understanding of the Trinity, it will still remain a mystery. Hence instead of worrying ourselves about 'how can one God be three persons?' it is better to ask a more useful question, which could be this: "What is it like to be God?" To think of it, it is like asking someone from Tokyo, "What is it like to be a Japanese?" The answer is obvious. You will never know what is it like to be a Japanese, unless you live as they live and learn to see their country from the inside, and see it as they see it. You would have to fall in love with Japan before you could know what it is like to be a Japanese. So it is with God. To know what it is like to be God, we must get closer to God and start living a life of intimacy with him. And to live such a life of intimacy with God is not impossible for Christians, because our God already dwells in every believer. As St Paul says, "the love of God has been poured out in our hearts through the Holy Spirit who has been given to us" (Rom 5:5). God is closer to us than we can imagine. As fish inhabit the sea and birds the air, we live in the atmosphere of the Triune God. Hence, we need not search for him beyond the stars. Would an Arab in the desert, who discovers spring water in his own tent, go elsewhere in search of it?

By living close to the Trinity who dwells within us, we cannot only have some idea about what is it like to be God, but also we will start living like God. This will be so because God as Trinity is like three candles but one light; and anyone who comes near the light cannot but be lit up. If we start living like the Triune God, we will find our life changing for the better. For example, since God as Trinity lives a group life, we too will shed our isolated existence. Since God as Trinity lives a community life, so too will we care for each other and stop saying, "I will attend to myself and God and then mind my own business". In other words, those who are close to the Trinity will start living their lives in the right way. Today so many people claim that they know the way to live, but unfortunately each claim conflicts with the other. For instance, the film and television industries have their gospel; the gambling strips of modern cities have theirs. The print industry and political heavyweights have their own version. In spite of all these confusing messages as to how to live, it is those who live like the Triune God who have learnt the right way.

WHY BODY? WHY BLOOD?

Readings: Gen 14:18-20; 1 Cor 11: 23-26; Lk 9:11-17

Theme: The bread turned into the Body of Christ satisfies all human hungers, while the wine changed into the Blood of Christ cleanses all our sins because it is the outpouring of God's love; and both the Body and the Blood of Christ, are available to us wherever the Mass is said.

Today we celebrate the feast of the Body and Blood of Jesus Christ. The question: "How can Jesus give his body and blood for us to eat and drink?" will remain to the end a matter of faith. It is therefore better to ask, "Why did he give them?". A young man placed a rose on a patch of ground outside the city limits on the third of May every year. If we ask, 'How was he doing it?', the answer would be banal and uninteresting. But if we ask, 'Why did he do it?', we learn that he was placing a rose on the grave of his grandmother whose birthday was May 3, a woman who took him in when his parents deserted him and taught him to be honest and to live without fear. Therefore the 'Why?' question is far more important than the 'How?' question, even with regard to the Eucharist.

Jesus changed bread into his own body for us to eat. Why? I once saw a TV advertisement: "Wonderbread that builds strong bodies twelve ways". Jesus in the Eucharist shared with us "the Wonderbread of the altar" so that we can be fully alive in the Spirit. When we look at this bread of life, Jesus wanted us to know that he is with us to satisfy all our hungers. There is the hunger for ordinary bread: unless this is satisfied, a person will always be in anguish. There is the hunger for meaning: unless this is satisfied a person will always remain dissatisfied and there are many more human hungers. That is why Jesus, in his lifetime, offered to people various kinds of bread to satisfy their different hungers. To the people who followed him in the desert, he offered ordinary bread. To the leper whose body was falling apart, he offered the bread of physical healing. To Mary Magdalene, a public sinner, the bread of forgiveness; to the lonely woman at Jacob's well, the bread of companionship; to Zacchaeus, the bread of conversion; and to the thief on the cross, the bread of reconciliation with God. It is this Jesus whom we see and whose flesh we eat in the Eucharist.

Jesus changed wine into his own blood for us to drink. Why? When we drink this blood, he wanted us to know that our sins are forgiven by his blood. Martin Luther once visited a dying student and asked the young man what he would take to God in whose presence he would shortly appear. The young man replied: "Everything that is good, sir". Luther, surprised, said: "How so, seeing you are but a poor sinner?" The youth replied, "I shall take to God in heaven a penitent and humble heart sprinkled with the blood of Christ". When we drink this blood, Jesus wants us all to remember that the history of humanity has been a long story of wars and sufferings, of bloodshed and injustice; and yet God loved this human being – aggressive, greedy and power-hungry – and often feeding on the blood of fellow human beings, mostly of the innocent, the weak and the silent ones. And yet, God loved this human being so much that he shed the blood of his own Son, so that blood thirsty, violent and unjust people could come to their senses. Hence when we drink this blood, we must remember our Christian obligation to struggle with Christ to remove the violence and the injustice from society by determined action, to heal the hurts in people's hearts by love and acceptance.

All of us know that Jesus instituted the Eucharist at his Last Supper which he had in a large room located in the Mount Zion section of Old Jerusalem, unfurnished now and open sided. Those of you who have been to the Holy Land as pilgrims, may have visited this sacred place also. Most people may never travel to Jerusalem to see where this first Mass was offered but that, of course, is not necessary. The Mass has come to us. In our local parish church we can be present daily at the sacred meal. The essence of the liturgy is not where it happens, but what happens.

WHEN THE SPIRIT COMES

Readings: Is 42:1-4, 6-7; Acts 10:34-38; Lk 3: 15-16, 21-22

Theme: Let us always be in touch with the Holy Spirit, the source of divine power, who came on us at our baptism as he did at Christ's and since then has been coming on all Christians down the centuries.

Mohammed Ali is a great name. He became the 'greatest' heavyweight champion, principally because he had the natural agility and strength that make one a superpower in the ring. Obviously he trained extensively for every fight with vigorous work-outs and diets. However, when he was asked from where did he receive his enormous power, he said that it came from a set of inspirational tapes to which he listened. The tapes were recorded speeches of a black Muslim leader, the honourable Elijah Mohammed. They deal with self-knowledge, freedom and potential. Mohammed Ali would listen to these tapes day in and day out. He claimed that these inspirational messages gave him the power to fight in the ring as well as outside it for his black people.

In today's Gospel we are told about the secret power of Jesus Christ. St Luke tells us about this power. He says that it is the Holy Spirit who came and descended upon Jesus in the form of a dove when he was baptised. "Heaven was opened, and the Holy Spirit came down upon him in bodily form like a dove" (Lk 3:22). The Holy Spirit is the presence of God's power. It is about this power that Genesis speaks when it says, "The Spirit of God hovered over the waters at the beginning of creation" (Gn 1:2). It is to this power Isaiah refers when he says: "Upon my servant, I have put my Spirit; he shall bring forth justice to the nations" (Is 42:1). It is this power of God that came down on Jesus at his Baptism, when "God had anointed him with the Holy Spirit and with power" (Acts 10:38).

Holy Spirit is a power that transforms us interiorly, that stimulates man's thirst for spiritual truth. It is a power of conviction, of cleansing the heart and of strengthening the will. When this power enters into lethargic Christians, they become active and enthusiastic. When this power enters into those who are dead in sin, they become alive. When the Spirit came to Moses, the plagues came upon Egypt; when the Spirit came upon Elijah, fire came down from heaven; when the Spirit came upon Joshua, the whole city of Jerusalem fell into his hands. But when the Spirit came upon Jesus at his Baptism, the Spirit empowered him to heal and to teach, to give up his life on the cross for humanity and finally to rise from the dead.

Ever since our Lord ascended into heaven, the same Holy Spirit has continued to descend upon his faithful followers. If martyrs suffered torture, missionaries worked in foreign lands, married couples persevered in fidelity and monks went into the desert, they were able to do all this in the power of the Spirit. This same Holy Spirit has been guiding the Church in the way of truth and unity; constantly the Spirit renews the Church, to keep the freshness of her youth. It is by the power of the Holy Spirit that soon the priest will change bread and wine into the sacred body and blood of Christ. By baptism we, too, have the Holy Spirit dwelling in us. Whenever we are healed and enlightened, we should realise that this power is operative. Whenever we are enabled to endure difficulties and disappointments, whenever we are strengthened to survive losses and disasters, let us remember that it is by the power of the Holy Spirit. Whenever the Spirit comes into any believer he makes Christ dearer, heaven nearer and the word of God clearer.

Therefore, if a set of tape-recorded inspirational speeches served Mohammed Ali as a secret source of power, to us that source of power is the Holy Spirit. Hence, let us be constantly in touch with the Holy Spirit who will replace the tension within us with a holy relaxation; who will replace the anxiety within us with a quiet conscience; who will replace the bitterness within us with the sweetness of grace; and who will replace the coldness within us with a loving warmth.

2ND SUNDAY OF THE YEAR

NOT ONE, NOT TWO

Readings: Is 62:1-5; 1 Cor 12:4-11; Jn 2:1-12

Theme: If we constantly strive to grow in loving union with God, as a bride does with her husband, we can achieve unity not only within our own Church, but also the visible union of all believers in Christ.

"How does one seek union with God?" asked the disciple. "The harder you seek, the more distance you create between him and you", replied his Master. "So, what does one do about the distance?" queried the disciple. "Understand that it's not there." "Does that mean that God and I are one?" "Not one, not two." "How is that possible?" "The sun and its light, the ocean and the wave, the singer and the song – not one, not two." This is the kind of unity God sought with humankind, a unity which can be compared to the most intimate and ultimate union that exists between a married couple. In fact, that is the comparison God himself used when he called his people Israel his 'Bride' and said, "as the bridegroom rejoices in his bride, so your God rejoices in you" (Is 62:5). Such a union between God and humankind became a reality when God became man in Christ Jesus who, as it were, symbolically confirmed it when he attended the marriage feast at Cana in Galilee. There is something here very important for us to note: if God loves us with such intensity as a new husband loves his bride, so our own loving response to God needs to be like that of a new bride.

It is on the basis of our intense loving union with God in Christ we, the followers of Christ, can build and sustain our own Church unity. As you know, welding is impossible unless the materials to be joined are at white heat temperature. When they are not and if you try to weld them, they only fall apart. Likewise, if our hearts are not aflame with love for God, we will remain scattered, not united, as a Church. Without love for God we cannot love one another, and to gather in a church for worship with no true love for each other is like putting all the ecclesiastical corpses into one graveyard, which will not bring about a resurrection. What would be worse is this: we will start using the gifts God has given us solely for our own selfish purposes and not for the building up of God's people, conveniently forgetting that, "there are different gifts but the same Spirit. To each person the manifestation of the Spirit is given for the common good" (1 Cor 12:4,7). To receive gifts from God and keep them for ourselves is, to say the least, as useless as a football team without the ball, for there will be no common goal achieved. The common goal of God's Church is to witness to his presence in the world through the unity among the disciples.

However, love is exciting but a difficult adventure, so difficult that unaided by grace we cannot transform it from desire to receive, into a desire to give. It is here that we need Christ and he is available to us in the Eucharist. If we approach him for help, he will do something similar to what he did at the wedding at Cana (Jn 2:9). He will take the imperfect water of selfishness in our lives and transform it into the best wine of love for others. To aid our human efforts to build Church unity on the foundation of love, we have another God-given source of help in the person of Mary the Mother of God. Jesus and his disciples were present at the wedding with Mary (Jn 2:1-2) and the community of disciples later awaited Pentecost, united around Mary in prayer. Hence we need to pray through and with Mary for love and unity in the Church. A great treasure in any house is a good mother and Mary does more than what the best of mothers can do in a house.

God wants not just Catholic unity. God's dream is to see the visible unity of all Christian believers. Today there are about 2639 Christian denominations in the world, the result of various disputes between believers. Concern for restoring unity pertains to the whole Church, faithful and clergy alike. Most Catholics may feel that they are able to do little to bring about the visible union of all Christians. But each one by the daily example of a life according to Catholic teaching, especially the teaching on fraternal love, can surely work for the unity Christ willed. Tolstoy tells the story of a man who stopped to give alms to a beggar. To his dismay, he found that he had left his money at home. Stammering his explanation, he said, "I am sorry, brother, but I have nothing". "Never mind, brother", was the beggar's answer, "that too was a gift!" The one word 'brother' meant more to him than money. Yes. True brotherly love to one's neighbour is the greatest force that draws people around Christ, because it is the very love of God poured into our hearts.

A ROSE IN MY HEART

Readings: Neh 8:2-4, 5-6, 8-10; 1 Cor 12:12-30; Lk 1:1-4, 4:14-21

Theme: If we make the laws of God and the laws of the Church our own, the observance of them will not be burdensome but self-fulfilling, for they exist only to enable us to achieve the goals of Christ's mission.

Not all the teeth put into our laws these days are wisdom teeth. Yet we need laws. We can't live without lawyers, certainly we can't die without them. However, a law is not an end in itself but only a means as a valuable support to our human weaknesses. Anyone who goes to law for its own sake holds a wolf by its tail. In particular, the laws of God which Ezra gave to the people of Israel on their return from exile were first thought to be chains, thus caused the Israelites to weep (Neh 8:9). Our God is not a God of law but a God of freedom. His laws are truths which order us to put first things first and forbid us to enthrone baseness upon the altar of our life in order to set us free to love. When the people of God understood this they took the laws of God to their hearts, made them their own and moved from sadness to joy singing, "Your words, Lord, are spirit and life" (Ps 19).

It will be so with us. Until we have freely chosen to make the laws of God as the laws of our being, they will remain as dead weight upon us. As a result, we will either blow up or dry up but never grow up. Whereas, when they become our own, they will awaken in us the freedom to love and mature. Take the law of faith. Our faith is not a wafer-cake but an anchor of strength that is able even to see through death and shines equal to Heaven's glories. We who receive this faith from our parents when baptised as babies are expected to make that faith our own as we grow older. Is there anything more satisfying in life than to see a child confidently walk down the road on his own, after you have shown him the way to go? Hence the law of faith must sooner or later cause a rose to blossom in the depths of our hearts, unlocking the world of riches promised by Christ to his believers.

As believers we belong to the Church, yes, even those who may never have been inside a church. The Church has also its laws for to be the vessel of the Holy Spirit the Church has to be visible, namely, she has to express herself in laws and customs, in 'yes and no' and in 'here and now'. If our heart accepts this with vigorous love, then we can enter through the narrow gate of church law into the vast expanse of the Spirit. The Church is not a tall building with a tower and bells, but the Body of Christ (1 Cor 12:12). Our human body, as long as we carry it around and until we commit it to the deep, lives by certain laws, each part being at the service of the other and all working towards the common good of the body. So, too, in the Body of Christ, each member has a particular role to play, but all are required to join in the common mission of the Church.

The Mission of the Church is the same as the Mission of Jesus. When presidents of the United States are sworn into office, they usually deliver an inaugural address in which, with a dash of vision and sparks of fire, they outline their ideals. Likewise, at the beginning of his public ministry, Jesus made a sort of inaugural speech. It was not tumultuous oratory but it was dramatic and daring, as he spelt out what would be his mission (Lk 4:18-19). He said that he came to seek out the oppressed and outcasts and support their quest for justice; to reach out to the unwanted and unloved and reaffirm their dignity; to listen to the cries of the wounded and the poor and lift them up with compassion. But which president can accomplish his goals without the active support of his citizens? Hence, Jesus needs us, his army of believers, to join his mission. In his inaugural speech, the purpose of his mission came out, and now we must stand up to keep his mission.

4TH SUNDAY OF THE YEAR

HEARING AND SHARING

Readings: Jer 1:4-5,17-19; 1 Cor 12:31-13:13; Lk 4:21-30

Theme: God has dedicated us Christians to receive the Good News and share it with others in brotherly love, unafraid of the opposition it may arouse, since the love of God that has been poured into our hearts is there to sustain in our mission.

How do we hear God's Word? With our ears alone? Our ears may be like a hackney cab with both doors open, but if the word of God is just buzzing in our ears, it is not going to take us across the vale of tears. "Today", said Jesus after speaking in the synagogue, "this scripture passage is fulfilled in your hearing" (Lk 4:21). Do we hear God's Word with our minds alone? Many people have made a tragedy of their lives because they could not make up their minds. Therefore, we are to hear God's Word with our hearts. Only the ear of the heart is like the lover's ear, that will hear even the lowest sound, when God speaks. We have to open our souls to God's words, unless we want to sell our souls and live with a good conscience on the proceeds.

The soul that receives God's Word will experience joy, even though its body may be bound upon a wheel of fire. And it is the responsibility of those who experience the joy of the Good News to share it with their neighbours. To some, Responsibility and Duty are the most unpleasant words that have ever blotted a paper. But God himself lays this responsibility on every Christian at Baptism, saying as he said to Jeremiah, "Before you were born, I dedicated you, and a prophet to the nations I appointed you" (Jer 1:5). Gratitude alone to God, unless our gratitude is just a lovely sense of future favours, should incite us to share the Good News he has given us. And what of the love we profess, a love that is patient and kind, a love that is not self-seeking and never fails?" (1 Cor 13:4-8). Unless our love of neighbour is a gong booming or a cymbal clashing, we will spontaneously come forward to share the Good News, the greatest gift we can offer a person, for it is spirit and life. Those who tend to make excuses, such as I am too young, too busy, too uncertain, too uneducated, should know that several excuses are always less convincing than one. All are required to take part in the building of the Kingdom, for there is work for everyone.

But that work is not going to be easy, for the Good News has a tendency to arouse opposition among the unbelieving and often materialistic neighbours. Give to one in the street a lecture on Christian morality, and to another a pound, and see who will respect you most. At the age of twenty, Jeremiah was called to be a prophet to the nations. Though afraid and hesitant, he did carry out his mission but in the end was exiled to Egypt. Jesus after speaking in the synagogue was expelled from the town by his angry audience. Mother Teresa's name was viciously smeared all over a TV channel. It will happen to us also when we preach, teach and witness to the Good News. But we need not be discouraged. No evil will prevail over us for God has made each of us a "fortified city" (Jer 1:18) and the love he has poured into our hearts "has no limit to its forbearance and its power to endure" (1 Cor 13:7).

Therefore, let us begin our service of the Gospel, and begin where we are, as Jesus began his ministry in his own native land of Galilee. Be not manipulated into thinking that where we are really needed is abroad, or in the board rooms of giant companies, or on the massive campuses of the sprawling universities. Did you hear of the Women's Project of Sr Jennifer of Ruhama , who has been for the last five years going in a white van late at night to the areas of Dublin, well known for prostitutes, in order to help them to regain their self-esteem, and for that she has won this year a People of the Year award? Yes. 'The place where the action is' is the place where there are people to be touched. Who knows? The real need may be where you are standing and the critical place for your service may be where you woke up this morning.

5TH SUNDAY OF THE YEAR

THE MASTERPIECE

Readings: Is 6:1-2, 3-8; 1 Cor 15:1-11; Lk 5:1-11

Theme: We all need to acknowledge our sins and be forgiven by God, so that he can use us, the forgiven sinners, as channels of his love and forgiveness to others.

When St Thomas Aquinas was on his deathbed, his sister asked, "Thomas, what is the main thing to do to get holiness?" And the saint replied, "The main thing is to have a great desire to get it." Indeed, most of us have such a desire, more or less, to become holy and that is why, I suppose, we call so many things 'holy'. We speak, for example, of holy Bible, holy picture, holy rosary, holy water and holy wedlocks though some of them may end in holy deadlocks.

Holiness is Godliness which is the opposite of sinfulness and hence only God can be called 'holy' in the full sense of the word. It is no surprise, then, that the angels in heaven adore God calling him, "Holy, holy, holy is the Lord of hosts" (Is 6:3). But for us human beings to adore God calling him 'holy' appreciating the grandeur of his holiness, we have to be holy ourselves, as one must have musical ears in order to know the value of a symphony. It is not enough to look holy; how holy I look when I am seasick! In the inner depth of our being we need to be holy.

That is our problem, which brings to our situation some sombre sobriety, namely that all of us are sinners, a fact which renders us unworthy to come before God. It may be a gloomy thought but it brings us down to earth. Sin is essentially a departure from God, and all of us are guilty of it. None of us is as spotless as a spring flower. Those who think that they have no fault will not have a friend in the world. See how Isaiah calls himself "a man of unclean lips" (Is 6:5). See how St Paul claims to be "the least of the apostles" (1 Cor 15:9), and see how St Peter protests to Jesus that he "is a sinful man" (Lk 5:8). Hence we too must acknowledge our sins. Not only we have sinned but have stained society with our sins. Sin travels faster than those who ride in chariots. It enters like a needle and spreads like an oak tree. We are therefore called to regret our personal and social sins and to regret deeply is to live afresh. We are not called to remorse, for remorse is impotence and it will sin again. We are called to repentance, for repentance is strong and it can progressively put an end to sin – although of course we will only be finally done with sin in heaven.

Everything can end, for God forgives us. It is unthinkable that the God of mercy will pour water on a drowning mouse. He pardons like a mother who kisses away the repentant tears of her son. All three men, Isaiah, Ss Paul and Peter had fallen but were forgiven and the ineffable joy they experienced when forgiven might well have aroused the envy of the gods! The same forgiving mercy of God, won for us by "the death and resurrection of our Lord Jesus" (1 Cor 15:3-4), today flows for us through the sacrament of reconciliation, once called confession. My younger brother had just made his first confession. When he returned to the pew, he tapped my mother on the shoulder, smiled and said, "I passed". The sacrament of reconciliation is not about passing or failing; it is about falling and rising and getting reconciled with God and our neighbour.

Sins can never be undone, only forgiven. And we are forgiven and reconciled for a purpose. God forgave Isaiah so that he could preach the word of repentance to people (Is 6:8); he forgave St Paul so that he could hand down the sacred traditions to others (1 Cor 15:3); he forgave St Peter so that he could become a "fisherman" (Lk 5:10).

From all these we can see how God is eternally at work, like a windmill, to accomplish the one purpose, which is the salvation of all. As the windmill shifts with every variation of the weather cock, God may vary his purpose to each of us, but the end is the same. He needs all of us to cooperate with his work of salvation, for things don't turn up in this world until somebody turns them up. Hence the Lord needs each of us to work with him. How we work ourselves to death so that we can live! We are called by Christ to join his saving work, for which he forgives and reconciles us so that others too can live. The great and glorious masterpiece of a Christian is to know how to live up to his Christian call.

6TH SUNDAY OF THE YEAR

THE CHOICE IS YOURS

Readings: Jer 17:5-8; 1 Cor 15:12, 16-20; Lk 6:17, 20-26

Theme: Those who, for God's sake, choose poverty rather than riches, dependence rather than independence, detachment rather than attachment, trusting in the support of the Lord, are blessed.

What do you choose, blessings or woes? Whatever we long for is in God, for he is All-Good pulsing power; whatever we want to love is in God, for he is All-Love rushing mercy; whatever we want to know is in God, for he is All-Knowledge flashing wisdom; whatever we want to possess is in God, for he is All-Beauty flowing life.

Therefore, Jesus in his beatitudes (Lk 6:20-26) asserts that those who choose God are blessed and the rest are as good as cursed. The choice is ours, God or something else? To some, the choice of this sort overlooks the complexity of the world we live in where things are not always black or white, but often grey. Yet Jesus insists that we make a choice, for he is not preaching fundamentalism but fundamentals of human flourishing. We are called to make this choice not just at the most critical moments in our life but even as we muddle through daily twists and turns. "Blessed are those whose hope is in the Lord, for they are like a tree growing near a stream" (Jer 17:7-8).

What do you choose, riches or poverty? Jesus blesses the poor and delivers woeful warning to the rich. In doing this, he is not exalting material poverty, which is an evil thing and which all of us must try to eradicate from our midst. But Jesus is warning of the dangers the rich face. The rich tend to be content with their present comfortable existence and, in their self-sufficiency, they tend to forget who their master really is; whereas the poor know that they cannot survive without God. Their material needs speak to them of their greater need for God. The materially rich tend to denigrate their body by pampering it, and in doing so they deny the resurrection of the body (1 Cor 15:15). If Christ's resurrection does not guarantee our own resurrection, our Christianity is empty; if Christians have no resurrection to hope for, then they deserve to be pitied and laughed at. If there is no resurrection, then surely blessed are the rich, more blessed are the full and most blessed are those who laugh now.

What do your choose, dependence or independence? In any civilised society, people depend on one another, for a good crutch is often better than a bad foot. Likewise in the Kingdom of God, it is those who depend on God who are truly "poor" and worthy of the blessings of the beatitudes. Hence, the rich also are blessed, if only they acknowledge their poverty and dependence on God. Are not the rich poor with the poverty of the commonplace, as they daily feel overwhelmed by the sheer drudgery of the routine existence? Are not rich poor from the poverty of their provisional nature, as they are always aware that life is passing and they can't rest in the security of the present? Are not the rich poor from the poverty of their limitation, as every decision they make means that they have to give up other avenues of pursuit? Finally, are not the rich poor from the poverty of death itself? Surely they are.

What do you choose, attachment or detachment? Once, sitting at the dinner table of a friend, I made this comment: "Well, I think that poor people are really the lucky ones". The result was that the ice-cream which was waiting to be served at the end was never brought to the table, and for me ice-cream is the best item in any dinner. Some people don't like the beatitude "Blessed are the poor" (Lk 6:20), because they think that Jesus was referring only to material possessions, when in fact he was mainly talking about the attitude of our heart, whether rich or poor. The religion of Christ is primarily on the inside, for what use is a religion which has all the splendour of ceremonial trappings, but behind them there is only a desert, no trust in the Lord and no love for neighbour? Hence, as Jesus was praising the poor for their trust in God, he was telling the rich not to get attached to their possessions, but to share them generously with the needy. In both cases, it was the matter of the heart, not of the pocket.

7TH SUNDAY OF THE YEAR

THE GOLDEN CHAIN

Readings: 1 Sam 26:2, 7-9, 12-13, 22-23; 1 Cor 15:45-49; Lk 6:27-38

Theme: The sacrifice we make in loving even our enemies, as Jesus, the Son of David from heaven did, will not go in vain.

All our passions and pursuits that stir within our mortal frame are but ministers of love and feed upon its sacred flame. But the kind of love which our world needs today is the sacrificial love which Jesus preached. "Dearest Annabelle", wrote the lovesick swain, "I could swim the mighty ocean for one glance from your lovely eyes; I could walk through a wall of flame for one touch of your little hand; I could leap the widest stream for a word from your warm lips – As always, your own Oscar. P.S. – I'll be over to see you Sunday night, if it doesn't rain". Love is not Christian love until it hurts. Love for our family and friends is good but not enough, for it will be repaid in some way and hence not much sacrifice will be involved. "Even sinners love those who love them" (Lk 6:33). We can't build a better world with a love stripped of self-sacrifice, as we cannot make an omelette without breaking eggs.

It takes sacrificial love to "love our enemies and do good to those who hate us" (Lk 6:27). It happened in New Zealand. A Maori known as 'Warrior Brown' because of her violent temper joined the Salvation Army. While addressing a group of Maoris, she was struck by a potato thrown by one of them. Retrieving it, she returned home, cut it up, planted it and harvested it. On visiting the village again, she sought out the man who had thrown the potato and gave him the potato she had harvested. It takes sacrificial love to "give away even our shirt to one who runs away with our coat" (Lk 6:29). Obviously we are not asked to give away our second family car to some thief who has just made off with the first car; but we are called to love those who hurt us in some way, at least by willing their good and reaching out in forgiveness. "Just as we resemble Adam, the man from the earth", so we are called to "bear the likeness of the man from heaven, Jesus" (1 Cor 15:49), who forgave his enemies from the cross.

This compassionate Christ, whom we have come to know as Son of David, was already prefigured in the person of King David, who penetrated his enemy Saul's camp and had the sleeping king at his mercy, yet showed compassion sparing Saul's life (1 Sam 26:9). The compassion of Christ only reflected the generous compassion of God who is so bountiful in mercy towards us. If God would apply all the rigours of justice that we deserve, none of us would be left standing. We humans may dismiss compassion from our hearts, but God never does. If we are truly children of this God, how can we hand folks over to God's mercy and show none ourselves? Besides, we are asked to pass on to others only the love and kindness which we receive from God. As a lamp has light itself only by diffusing it, so we can remain in God's love only by spreading it around.

But loving the unlovable and pardoning the unpardonable will always be a painful sacrifice and the greatest pain is to love in vain. Will our sacrificial love go in vain? Never. It will come back to us from God, "pouring over into the fold of your garment" (Lk 6:38). An Indian legend tells about a farmer carrying a sack of grain on his shoulders and meeting the good Lord. "Give us some wheat", said the Lord. So the farmer reached into the bag and found one of the tiniest grains he had and gave it to him. God turned the grain of wheat into gold and gave it back to the farmer. Then the farmer was sorry that he had not given the Lord the whole bag. Therefore, if we choose to be not reactive but pro-active people, that is, instead of returning injury to injury, if we generate love where there is hatred and create life where there is void, our Christian love will not only be personally rewarding, but it will also serve as a golden chain that binds together the society we live in.

8TH SUNDAY OF THE YEAR

THE ABUNDANCE OF THE HEART

Readings: Sir 27:4-7; 1 Cor 15:54-58; Lk 6:39-45

Theme: We need constantly to purify our heart, since it is from the abundance of the heart that the mouth speaks, and our mouth can bring forth both good and evil.

When the family returned from Sunday morning service, father criticised the sermon, daughter thought the choir's singing was atrocious, and the mother found fault with the organist's playing. The small boy of the family piped up, "But it was a good show for 50p, don't you think, Dad?" Fault-finding, destructive criticism, rash judgement and gossiping can do enormous harm. Therefore Sirach asks us to guard our tongue and adds, "Speech is a test of a man and reveals the bent of his mind" (Sir 27:5). Some have the habit of talking positively awfully, others awfully positively, particularly when criticising others, "for they see the speck in the eyes of others, while missing the plank in their own" (Lk 6:41). Some people have such a big mouth that they are forced to eat their own words, as a good diet to reduce the size of their mouths. Blessed are they who have animals for their friends, for they never pass criticism. Words are nails for fixing ideas, not for fixing people on a cross by gossiping about them. In most beauty parlours, the gossip alone would curl your hair.

Hence it is true that a lot of mischief that vexes this world arises from words. But it is also true that a lot of good can be done through words. Did you notice how St Paul uses his words in his letter to the Corinthians (1 Cor 15:54-58)? his words are like apples of gold on a plate of silver. He inspires hope when he asks, "Death, where is your victory?" he is grateful when he "thanks God" and he is truthful when he asserts that "the sting of death is sin". Do we encourage people who are downhearted, especially those who carry a thorn in their flesh? Daily we meet people whose hopes, like withered leaves, fall fast. Do our words uplift their spirits? Are we grateful to God and to one another at least through a sincere "Thank you"? St Paul spoke of sin as "the sting of death" although he knew that it would not please many who did not believe in sin. Do we speak out our conviction, or are our words smoother than butter while there is war in our heart, and our words softer than oil but they are drawn swords? (Ps 55:21).

One of the ways by which we can use words for the great benefit of others is in giving advice when asked. Unless one is born a genius like Mozart, all of us seek guidance. But Jesus warns us of blind guides when he asks, "can the blind guide the blind?" (Lk 6:39). Some guides are like the mountain guide I met once who said, "Be careful not to fall here. It is dangerous. But if you do fall, remember to look to the left. You get a wonderful view on that side". Some give you advice without really understanding your situation. "Your methods of cultivation are hopelessly out of date", said the agricultural college graduate to the old farmer. "Why, I'd be astonished if you ever got ten pounds of apples from that tree." "So would I", replied the farmer, "It's a pear tree". The advisory capacity is the only capacity in which some people are willing to serve and we must be wary of such self-righteous advisers, for when such people tell you what they would do if they were in your place, they probably do not know what to do in their own place.

In the use of words, whether in good advice or for any other good purpose, we must always remember that, "out of the abundance of the heart the mouth speaks" (Lk 6:45) and this we learn from trees. Trees are funny creatures for they take their clothes off in winter and put them on in summer, but a thing we can surely learn from them is that as a "good tree produces good fruit so a good heart produces goodness" (Lk 6:43). A kind heart, for example, speaks kind words and one who is humble is of few words who will ask for truth, not flattery. Strong and bitter words reveal pride and a confirmed gossiper is an untrustworthy person for in gossip we reveal confidences. May we then strive to become good persons with a goodness that is real and authentic.

THE TUNNEL-VISION

Readings: 1 Kings 8:41-43; Gal 1:1-2, 6-10; Lk 7:1-10

Theme: Jesus taught us by word and deed to rid ourselves of our habitual ways of viewing other people, with our narrow-minded tunnel-vision, and learn to see them through God's own vision of universal acceptance.

Alexander the Great once came upon Diogenes, the philosopher, looking intently at a heap of human bones. Alexander asked him, "What are you looking for?" Diogenes answered, "Something I cannot find." "And what is that?" asked Alexander. The philosopher replied, "the difference between your father's bones and those of his slaves". Of course there is no difference. We are all equal before God because we are all mortal; but our equality received a great boost when God destined us all to the same immortal life. He offered to all men, be they princes or beggars, Jews or non-Jews, the same salvation in Christ. Centuries before Christ came, King Solomon wished that all people of all nations would one day accept this universal offer from God; so he prayed: "When the foreigner, likewise, who is not of your people Israel, comes and prays to you, listen from your heavenly dwelling". (1 Kgs 8:42-3) When Jesus healed the servant of a Roman centurion (Lk 7:10) who was a gentile, and even praised his faith as surpassing that which he found in Israel, he confirmed God's plan to offer healing and salvation to all people.

God's vision for humankind is not a tunnel-vision but an open one. He treats all human beings as equals in almost all the gifts he gives, especially in the most sublime gift of salvation in Christ. We, his children, are also expected to welcome and accept all people, irrespective of who they are. Jesus himself gave us an outstanding example of how we ought to get away from our narrow-minded tunnel-vision of other people – through God's own vision of universal acceptance. He loved people across every barrier: as a Jew he loved Romans; as a Jew he loved Samaritans; as a teacher of religion he had time for those who had no religion; as the only sinless one, he loved sinners. There was no outsider with Jesus. He gathered together as his disciples those who were not only unlike himself but also unlike each other. Simon the

Zealot had tried to oust the occupation forces; St Matthew was collector of taxes for Rome, the enemy of the Jews; St Peter could blow hot and cold in the same breath; St Thomas had a sceptical approach to things supernatural. These individuals were so different from each other that they had every reason to hate one another; and yet, Jesus took them as a group, established an understanding between them and formed them into his disciples.

To accept and welcome all into our lives does not mean that we pretend that there are no walls between people. But while recognising a wall, we must also find a door. Religion can be a wall. Within Christianity there are many denominational walls. To find an ecumenical door, a Christian has first to agree that laws and customs of a particular denomination do not make its members, as it were, first class Christians. It is not through the law but through faith in the word of Jesus that any one belongs to God. This was the Gospel St Paul preached to the Galatians who very soon forgot what he had preached, which provoked St Paul to cry out: "I am amazed that you are so soon going over to another gospel" (Gal 1:6). Hence, we Catholics need to respect, accept, welcome and collaborate with non-Catholics, because they too believe in Christ. Otherwise we are liable to fall into religious bigotry, a sacred disease, which tries to keep truth safe in its hands with a grip that kills it. As people of universal salvation, we have to show respect for people of non-Christian religions too. Nothing is so fatal to a religion as indifference to other religions. To see a stately Synagogue lifting its walls by the side of an inspiring Cathedral should not make a Christian sad, for there are many mansions in Father's earthly house, as there are in his heavenly one.

Besides religion, there are other walls too, which may make it difficult for us to extend our love and acceptance to all people. One other wall is people's culture. People are culturally different. But cultural walls will crumble, if the people of a particular culture have at least a basic respect for another culture, for the simple reason that in every culture there are wise people who know and there are bold people who perform; that in every culture there is beauty and goodness and hence every culture is halfway to heaven. Still another wall that might pose a challenge when we want to welcome and relate to other people is nationalism. Patriotism is right when it is a lively sense of responsibility to the nation's good; otherwise, it becomes nationalism which is a risk, for it can turn into a silly cock crowing on its own dunghill. There are, of course, still other walls such as colour, race and the rest. But whatever the wall which blocks our loving acceptance of other people, it finally comes down to prejudice born of our ignorance. We hate some persons because we do not know them and we will not know them because we hate them. What a vicious circle! As long as we don't get rid of our prejudices, we won't come out of our tunnel-vision.

10TH SUNDAY OF THE YEAR

PROPHETS OF COMPASSION

Readings: 1 Kings 17:17-24; Gal 1:11-19; Lk 7:11-17

Theme: All the baptised are called to play their prophetic role by speaking on behalf of a compassionate God, through concrete signs of compassion.

A patient from a nearby mental institution recently walked into the local branch of Lloyds Bank, Epsom, and said that he was a prophet and that God had sent him to pick up a million pounds. The unflappable cashier's response was immediate: "I am sorry, sir, God banks with Barclays!". Indeed a prophet is one who is sent by God, but quite a few are false prophets who pretend that they are sent by God.

But Elijah, St Paul and Jesus were true prophets. They were sent by God as his spokesmen to humankind. As God's spokesmen they were not just speaking for God. Their prophetic role went beyond mere spoken words. They used concrete, immediate and meaningful signs in order to make real their message. For example, all three thought that God is compassionate towards humankind and each illustrated it with a concrete compassionate act of their own. Elijah, moved by the distress of the widow caused by the death of her only son, "stretched himself three times on the child and cried out, 'May the soul of this child, I beg, come into him again'" (1 Kings 17:21). St Paul confesses that although he was merciless in persecuting the Church of God, "God called him through his grace and chose to reveal his Son in him" (Gal 1:16). Jesus himself moved with pity for the widow of Nain who had lost her son, "felt sorry for her; 'Do not cry', he said" (Lk 7:13), and brought her dead son back to life.

Not only Elijah, St Paul and Jesus, but we are all prophets, in the strict sense of the term. The whole Church is prophetical and each of its baptised members has a prophetic role to speak on behalf of God. But our prophetic role must not be just passing off the compassion of God through our mouth but passing it on through concrete signs of compassion. Two trucks were standing back to back and a truck driver was struggling to get a huge crate from one truck to the other. A passer-by, seeing his desperate situation, volunteered to help. So the two of them huffed and puffed and struggled for well over half an hour with no result at all. "I am afraid, it is no use", panted the passer-by; "We will never get it off this truck." "Off!", yelled the driver. "Good God, I don't want it off. I want it on!". Yes. We too, the baptised prophets, do not want the compassion of God 'off' our mouth, but we want it 'on' into the experience of people, by ourselves being compassionate in our actions as God is towards humankind.

God is gracious and unconditional in his compassion. In many of his healing actions, Christ first wanted the would-be recipient of the healing to believe. But in the story of the widow of Nain, Jesus did not demand even that faith as a precondition; faith is given as a gift only after the healing. God often comes to help without waiting to be asked. The widow brings out her dead son for burial. Unannounced and uninvited, Jesus restored the young man back to his mother. God also has an option for the poorest of the poor in his compassionate dealings with humankind. In the bible, a widow was a frequent symbol of the poor and the helpless. In the Old Testament especially, women had no job market nor was there any welfare system for them. Hence, when Elijah and Jesus showed compassion to a widow, who had not only lost her husband but also her only son, they indeed cared for the poorest of the poor in their time. If we are prophets with a mission to witness to a God who is so compassionate, our own acts of compassion ought to be like his: unconditional, uninvited and with an option for the very poor in society.

In our world, we will come across many self-proclaimed prophets who will claim to know the future. Do not envy them and do not try to become one like them; after all, if you prophesy wrong, nobody will forget it; and if you prophesy right, I am afraid, hardly anybody will remember it. There are also prophets of doom and gloom, who predict evil consequences and then proceed to do their best in bringing about the verification of their own prophecies. Let us not be enamoured by them either. Instead, as Christians, let us play our role as true prophets who reveal God to humankind as he really is, especially his compassion, not merely through our words but through our own compassionate acts of mercy. The world is dark and human agony is excruciating. Hence a true prophet for our present time is one who acts as an agent of God's own compassion.

11TH SUNDAY OF THE YEAR

THE BIG ERASER

Readings: 2 Sam 12:7-10, 13; Gal 2:16, 19-21; Lk 7:36-50

Theme: God is generous in forgiving all our sins, if we believe in his Son Jesus Christ and repent of our sins.

God is good when he gives, supremely good; even crosses from his hand are blessings in disguise. That is why, in forgiving our sins, he has a big eraser. We cannot sin so as much as God can forgive. We can only sin as a human being, but God can forgive as a God. We sin as a finite creature but the Lord forgives as the infinite Creator. David was the privileged friend of God but grew callous, despising the word of God. His actions, violence and taking of many wives caused subsequent dynastic jealousies. Yet, when he repented, the prophet Nathan comforted him saying, "The Lord, for his part, forgives your sins; you are not to die" (2 Sam 12:13). When Jesus was in Simon's house, a woman known as a sinner, perhaps a prostitute, repented before Jesus by her act of homage. The host believed that Jesus became unclean by allowing a sinner to touch him. But Jesus reminded him that such uncleanness is not important in God's eyes, when a sinner seeks forgiveness. So he said to the woman, "Your sins are forgiven" (Lk 7:48). Perhaps we think such forgiveness is too good to be true. That is because we measure God's corn by our own bushel. Where we would take our brother by the throat, God would forgive him seventy times seven. All God requires from the sinner is faith and repentance. All of us are in need of God's forgiveness. We need only to believe and repent in order to be forgiven.

We believe, of course. But what do we believe in? Some believe in laws and prescriptions and think they will save them. Will they? A doctor had prescribed a sleeping pill for a patient. "Wake up, sir," said the nurse, shaking the sleeping patient. "What's the matter? What's gone wrong?" asked the startled patient. "Nothing. I just forgot to give you your sleeping pill." The nurse remembered only the prescription, not its purpose and so the prescription served only to burden the patient more. The law of God too has a purpose and what is it? Our heart is like a dark cellar, full of lizards, cockroaches and all kinds of reptiles and insects, which in the dark we see not. But the law lifts the shutters and lets in the light and we see the evil. That is the purpose of the law. But the law will not remove the evil; it is the Lord Jesus alone who can do it. The law stirs the mud at the bottom of the pool and proves how foul the waters are. But the law will not cleanse the waters. Only the Lord Jesus can do it. Therefore we must believe not in the law but in Jesus Christ. "We acknowledge that what makes a man righteous is not obedience to the law but faith in Jesus Christ" (Gal 2:16). It is our faith-look at Jesus that breaks our heart, both for sin and from sin, and leads us to repentance.

Repentance like faith is a basic prerequisite for receiving forgiveness from God. Repentance is a part of salvation and when Christ saves us, he saves us by making us repent. God will take nine steps towards us but he will not take the tenth step which is repentance. That is why David had to be reminded of the horror of his sin by a prophet (2 Sam 12:9). A sinner in the Gospel repents openly before Jesus by her act of homage, which becomes the occasion for Jesus to challenges his self-righteous host (Lk 7:45) forcing him to see the mistakes he himself had made as a host. As John Milton said, repentance is the golden key that opens the palace of eternity; but repentance is not hating sin because of the fear of punishment. A person may hate sin just as a murderer hates the gallows but this does not prove repentance. All true repentance arises from seeing Jesus on the cross dying for our sins. Repentance is brokenness of heart which results from seeing sin as an offence against Jesus Christ. In short, repentance is ultimate honesty with one's own sinfulness.

If repentance is ultimate honesty, the first step towards repentance is owning up responsibility for one's own sins. How often people seem to blame everyone and everything else for crimes! A woman complained to a visiting friend that her neighbour was a poor housekeeper. "You should see how dirty her children are and her house. It is almost a disgrace to be living in the same neighbourhood as hers. Take a look at those clothes she has hung out on the line. See the black streaks on the sheets and towels". The friend walked up to the window and said, "I think the clothes are quite clean, my dear. The streaks are on your window". Failures to take responsibility for one's actions seems to have infected all characters in today's readings. David needed to recognise the seriousness of his sin and how damaging his act was both for himself and his nation. The host in the Gospel was more concerned for proper rules to be followed by Christ than for the true and caring hospitality which he should have shown to him. The Galatian community had to be told by St Paul that their mere following of the law would not save them. To repent, therefore, we must first accept responsibility for our evil doing. It is easy to dodge our responsibility, but we can't dodge the consequences of dodging.

12TH SUNDAY OF THE YEAR

THE PIERCING VIRTUE

Readings: Zech 12:10-11; Gal 3:26-29; Lk 9:18-24

Theme: If we keep an eye on the pierced Christ on the cross, we will be able to help others to their human and Christian dignity which we claim for ourselves.

There was once a sweet-maker who made sweets in the shapes of animals and birds of different colours and sizes. When he sold sweets to children, they would begin to quarrel with words such as these: "My rabbit is better than your tiger… My squirrel may be smaller than your elephant, but it is tastier...". And the sweet-maker would laugh at the thought of grown-ups who were no less ignorant than the children, when they thought that one was better than another. The truth is that as human beings, each is equal to the other. Each person has his or her individual worth. None but one's self can be one's own parallel. This is why a human being is more interesting than humanity. God made individuals, not humanity, in his image. In addition to this basic human equality, all believers are equal at still another level. "You are all sons and daughters of God through faith in Christ" (Gal 3:26). Yes, we have our differences: English and Indian, black and white, worker and employer, male and female, because we are not only born equal but we are also born different. However, underneath these legitimate differences, "You are all one in Christ" (Gal 3:28). Therefore, we rejoice in our worth as human beings and in our dignity as sons and daughters of God; but then, we must also treat each other as their human worth and Christian dignity deserve.

Our belief in basic human dignity calls us to respect others in word and deed; without this respect between persons, there is practically nothing left to distinguish men from beasts. If we have some respect for people as they are, we can be more effective in helping them to become better than they are. One way to help others in this respect is to let them enjoy their basic human rights, by dismantling all those barriers we may have erected against others on the basis of colour, race, religion, sex and economic status. Our belief in "all being one in Christ" calls us to interpret others against the background of their being redeemed by Christ for eternal life and to strive to make this oneness real and reasonable, not only in religious terms but also in economic and social terms. If this means sharing with others what we have, we must be ready to share. The truth is, there is no delight in owning anything unshared. Grief can take care of itself, but joy to be joy, needs somebody with whom to share it.

If there is one serious obstacle to our life of witness to the dignity of every human being and to our oneness in Christ, it is selfishness. A great festival was to be held in a village and each villager was asked to contribute by pouring a bottle of wine into a giant barrel. One of the villagers had this thought: "If I pour a bottle of water in that giant barrel, no one will notice the difference." But it did not occur to him that everyone else in the village might have the same thought. When the banquet began, and the barrel was tapped, what came out of it was pure water. The instinct to selfishness is universal and vibrant in all of us. It is this instinct that urges us to put personal happiness as a priority on our life agenda, compelling us to grasp rather than give, to possess rather than share. It is this instinct that destroys justice and equality, the foundations of peace. To prevent this instinct from destroying us, Jesus challenges us to renounce the self: "If anyone wants to be a follower of mine, let him renounce himself" (Lk 9:23). True spiritual renunciation of the self holds us in bounds, not in bonds, for its effect is to reach out to others. We are made for love, justice and peace, and self-renunciation makes room for these virtues to flourish in our lives.

But renunciation is a piercing virtue. We will find it excruciating, even crucifying at times, to deny ourselves in order to treat others as their human and Christian dignity deserve. But we need not be afraid. Jesus renounced his very life so that we might live, and for that he was pierced with a lance. Therefore if we "look upon him whom they have pierced", we will receive the needed strength and support, for "God will pour out his Spirit of kindness and prayer on us" (Zech 12:10) from that pierced side of Christ. Let us keep an eye on the pierced one. He is the Master that we follow. Remember that he is pierced often today in his members: the oppressed, the poverty-stricken, the sick and the neglected. May we look around us at the pierced ones whom we can help to attain the dignity we claim for ourselves.

13TH SUNDAY OF THE YEAR

CHARIOTS OF FIRE

Readings: 1 Kgs 19:16, 19-21; Gal 5:1, 13-18; Lk 9:51-62

Theme: The call of Christ to discipleship is radical. It demands from the follower a total, complete, unconditional and permanent commitment to the Master.

Our Lord made discipleship hard, because he called his disciples to a pilgrimage not to a parade, to a fight not to a frolic. He asks his disciples to put him first, even before the most demanding family ties. When he said to one, "Follow me", the man replied, "Let me first go and bury my father"; but Jesus told him, "Let the dead bury the dead" (Lk 9:60). Because of such demands, Jesus lost many prospective followers. But down the centuries, there have been also inspiring examples of discipleship. Chariots of Fire is a film about Eric Liddell who was Britain's fastest 100-yard runner in 1924 Olympics. Everyone expected him to win the gold medal that year. But then, when the Olympic schedule came out, the 100-yard event was programmed to be run on a Sunday. Because Eric strictly interpreted the keeping of the Lord's Day, he refused to run the race on a Sunday. He put the Lord's Day above an Olympic gold medal and his own world fame.

Our Lord calls his disciples to follow him, accepting all the consequences of this following. He expects his disciple to follow him as Elisha followed Elijah. When Elisha called him, he made a complete break with his former way of life. "He took the pair of oxen and slaughtered them. He then rose and followed Elijah" (1 Kings 19:20). Christ's call is radical, without "ifs" and "buts". Gary, a farmer, is concerned that the insecticides he uses are killing birds and beneficial insects and polluting the air. So far so good. But he does not commit himself totally to safeguard the environment. He says that he would like to switch over to an environmentally safer pest-control system; but he can't, for it is more expensive and would endanger his profit margin and his family's financial security. Gary is an example of a Christian disciple who wants to follow Christ but can't go all the way.

Perseverance in commitment to the Master is to be the hallmark of Christ's disciple. When a man said to Jesus that he would follow him, but first he had to go to his people to say goodbye, Jesus replied: "Once the hand is laid on the plough, no one who looks back is fit for the Kingdom of God" (Lk 9:62). Again we turn to *Chariots of Fire*. Eric Liddell never looked back on his commitment to keep the Lord's Day. He kept only looking forward. He never retraced his steps even in the face of tremendous public pressure. When he had decided not to run the 100-yard race on the Lord's Day, even the Prince of Wales tried to get him to violate his conscience. When Eric absolutely refused, British newspapers called him a traitor to his country. But Eric still refused to go against his commitment.

The Lord asks his disciples to be totally free, in order to be available for the spreading of the Gospel. That is what he said to a prospective follower: "Let the dead bury the dead; your duty is to go and spread the news of the Kingdom of God" (Lk 9:60). And according to St Paul, the best way to spread the Gospel is through works of love. "My brothers," he said, "you were called to liberty, but be careful to serve one another in works of love" (Gal 5:13). Once again we turn to Eric Liddell of *Chariots of Fire* for a model of commitment to works of love. A few years after the Olympics in 1924, Eric surprised the world by going to China as missionary. Later the girl whom he loved joined him. Then came World War II. When Japan entered the War, Eric sent his wife and children to Canada. When Japan invaded China, Eric was arrested and put into a Japanese concentration camp. There he continued his ministry working with the other prisoners. A few years later Eric died a heroic death in the camp.

As disciples of Jesus we are called to share in the cross of Christ, so that we can share also in his rewards. Leave out the cross and you have killed the religion of Jesus. If we want to be free to serve the Master, then we must remember that freedom battle was won on the cross. So "when the time came for Jesus to be taken up to heaven, he resolutely took the road to Jerusalem" (Lk 9:51) to die. Here again we can turn to Eric Liddell. He had his share of crosses but he also had his rewards. After refusing to run his 100-yard race on the Lord's Day, he met with his coaches and suggested that a team-mate run in his place in the 100-yard dash. He would then enter the 400-yard dash, even though he had never run this race in his life. Lo and behold! Not only did Eric win the gold medal in the 400-yard event but his team-mate also won in the 100-yard event. The initial sacrifices Eric had made to respect the Lord's Day brought not one but two gold medals.

The disciples of Jesus are led by the Spirit, because by ourselves we cannot fulfil the demands of Christian discipleship. The freedom we need to follow the Lord all the way is guaranteed by the Holy Spirit. "If you are guided by the Spirit, you will be in no danger of yielding to self-indulgence" (Gal 5:18). Therefore the disciple has to align himself or herself with the Holy Spirit, a choice that has to be renewed daily through prayer. Amazingly, here too, we are supported by the example of Eric Liddell of Chariots of Fire. What was the secret behind Eric's courage never to look back? The secret lies in a remark Eric's widow made in one interview with the Toronto Star. Describing Eric, she said, "he always spent the first – and very early hours – of every day in Bible reading and prayer".

14TH SUNDAY OF THE YEAR

MESSENGERS OF PEACE

Readings: Is 66:10-14; Gal 6:14-18; Lk 10:1-9

Theme: The followers of Christ are called and empowered, not only to personalise the peace of Christ but also to be messengers of peace, in every way possible, especially by working for a just world order.

When Christ came into the world, angels sang about peace; and when he went out of the world, peace was bequeathed. "Whatever house you go into", he instructed his disciples when sending them on missions, "let your first words be, 'Peace be to this house!'" (Lk 10:5). It was the same peace which Isaiah foretold as coming in abundance: "Towards her I send peace flowing like a river" (Is 66:12). What a precious gift of God to humankind is this peace! It is the will of God for us that in the world's most crowded streets, in the din of life, even when the rush and hurry are at their most intense, we should enjoy the peace of Christ in the depth of our heart. With this peace of Christ in my heart, I can look up and I will see no seat of fiery wrath; I can look down, and I will discover no hell; I can look back and I will see all my sins having been blotted out; I can look around and I will rejoice in the knowledge that all things work together for good for those who love God; and if I look even beyond my grave, I will see my glory shining through the veil of the unknown like the sun that shines through a morning mist.

What is this peace of Christ? How do we define it? Peace is a climate in which every person and every group of persons can live the fullness of life that God intended for us when he created us. How does one appropriate to himself or herself this peace? It is by "becoming a new creature" (Gal 6:15), by living the new mode of existence brought about by the cross of Christ, by his death and resurrection. This means that Christian peace comes through union with Christ and by dying to oneself, especially to some of the worst enemies of peace that inhabit and exploit our human nature. These enemies are: avarice, ambition, envy, anger and pride. If these enemies are denied entrance into our lives, we should enjoy the perpetual peace of Christ, because through this denial we will rise with him to live in the power and grace of his risen person. That is peace.

The peace of Christ thus begins in one's heart, but it is meant to flow into the hearts of others, so that the personal peace becomes world peace. Blessed are the peacemakers, they shall never be unemployed, for there is so much need for the peace of Christ in today's world. As Jesus sent out his disciples to pass on this peace to others, he complained that, "the harvest is rich, but the labourers are few, (Lk 10:2), thus indirectly urging all of his would-be followers to become messengers of peace. There are many ways by which we can bring the peace of Christ to others. There is an unusual story of a man who returned to his car which was parked outside a large shopping centre. Lying on the front seat was a note: "Dear Sir or Madam: I fully intended to steal your car until I noticed the 'Peace-Be-To-You' sticker. It made me pause and reflect. I reasoned that if I did steal your car, you certainly would not be at peace and on the other hand, I felt I would not be at peace either, as this was my 'first job'! So, peace be to you and to me. Drive carefully and next time lock your car". The note was signed: "A Would-Be Car Thief".

That is one way of bringing the peace of Christ into our world. But there is another way, perhaps the surest way for enduring peace and that is to work for justice for all; in fact justice is the foundation of peace. We must lay the foundation of justice if we want peace without a worm inside it. Surely the world rests upon three things: upon truth, upon justice and upon peace. All these are really one, for when justice is done truth becomes an actuality and peace a reality. Perhaps we feel that there is not much we can do to solve all the problems of injustice and inequality in the world. However, each of us can at least improve the quality of life for those who are oppressed by injustice. You ask, how? Take for example our belief in human dignity. We can put this belief into practice by treating each other with consideration; by eliminating all sarcasm and prejudice born of racial or colour-consciousness; by affirming others in what they are, rather than in what they have; and by consciously bringing joy and peace through sharing with others what we have and what we are.

Therefore, peace is not made at council tables nor by treaties, but by working for justice in the world. As peace without truth is poison, peace without justice is an illusion. Our efforts to bring peace to others through works of justice may not result immediately in a peaceful world order. But our efforts will be ultimately victorious. The Lord has promised us his power to this end: "I have given you power to tread underfoot serpents and scorpions and the whole strength of the enemy" (Lk 10:19) are his words, that assure the ultimate triumph of the Kingdom.

15TH SUNDAY OF THE YEAR

LOVE: WHOM AND HOW?

Readings: Deut 30:10-14; Col 1:15-20; Lk 10:25:37

Theme: We are called not so much to expensive love but to expansive love that reaches out to all the grief-stricken, with a personal sign that we care.

A seventy-year-old man won in a lottery £65000. He had a bad heart and so the family was afraid that the news might excite him and kill him. Hence they asked the parish priest to convey this news to him tactfully. The priest came and asked the old man: "Friend, suppose you win in lottery a sum of £65000 – what would you do?" The old man said, "I would give you and the church half of it". Hearing that, the parish priest fell over and died. That was a charity shock, too good to be true. We all know the parable of the Good Samaritan as narrated by Jesus (Lk 10:33-37). What the Samaritan did to the man lying half-dead after being attacked by robbers, is too good to be true. In fact, it is only a parable, which means it never really happened. But ever since it was told, it has stirred the hearts of millions inspiring them to love, even love heroically.

Love was the sum and substance of the laws which God had prescribed to his people through Moses who urged them to "obey the voice of the Lord your God, keeping those laws of his" (Dt 30:10). Jesus re-emphasising the Mosaic law of love went further to tell us, through a parable, whom to love and how to love. The lawyer had not asked how one is to be a loving neighbour; he had only asked how one is to recognise the neighbour we are called to love. He asked who, he was told how. We are not provided with a category of persons or a list of individuals whom we must love. It seems, therefore, that Jesus called us to an expansive love, to love without limit – that is, no one is eliminated in advance from our love. But the parable gives us guidelines about those for whom we bear special responsibility to love.

The special people whom we are called to love are the alienated, the marginalised, the oppressed and the disenfranchised. Yes. We are specifically called to care for those who have fallen among 'robbers' who take away people's basic human rights and leave them to live in subhuman conditions. But our 'neighbours' whom we should love are not just these needy strangers but also the needy in our families and parishes. A sad fact is that we sometimes treat the members of our own families who are hurting, worse than we treat needy strangers on the streets. A sadder fact is that we Christians who call ourselves the 'Church' conveniently forget that the "Church is the Body of Christ and he is its head" (Col 1:18). If we could always remember that the members of our parish community all belong to the same Body of Christ, we will constantly look for those among them who are hurting in some way from illness, loneliness, depression, poverty or rejection and reach out to help them.

But how are we to love them? To be a Good Samaritan is a risky business. You do not know where it will end. An act of compassion may lead you into another act of kindness and finally even a caring relationship may blossom. In fact, the power of love demonstrated in the parable lies in the Samaritan's personal involvement in the needy stranger. It is much safer, as you know, to contribute to the collection box or the sponsorship card and leave it at that. But that would be rather a superficial love, not Samaritan-like charity. To call an ambulance or the police to help some needy person, is good; but Christian charity goes beyond that; it gets personally involved in the person cared for.

We shall therefore ask ourselves: are our eyes open to see the pain in other people's eyes? Are our ears open to hear the cry in other people's voices? Are our hearts open to become involved in other people's hurts? Perhaps we often pass by our needy neighbours because of some dislike, mistrust or prejudice; if so, we need to search in our own hearts and see how wounded we are ourselves, how broken we are ourselves, so that we can see in the wounded, in the broken and in the weak our own reflection, and love them. The parable does not command us to go out, risk our lives and become heroes. It invites us to reach out, risk our pride and become compassionate humans. We are called not so much to an expensive love but to an expansive love. Often what the grief-stricken person really needs is not a great expenditure of our energy, of our time or of our money, but at least some small personal sign that we care.

OUR BUSY AGE

Readings: Gen 18:1-10; Col 1:24-28; Lk 10:38-42

Theme: We can't become so confused by the humdrum turmoil of our everyday living that we fail to come to Jesus and listen to his eternal wisdom.

According to a legend, God sent an angel to a holy man with this message: "Ask for a million years of life and they will be given you, or a million million; how long do you wish to live?" "Eighty years", said the saint, without the slightest hesitation. His disciples were dismayed. "But, Master, if you lived for a million years, think how many generations would profit by your wisdom!" The saint replied: "If I lived for a million years, people would be more intent on lengthening their lives than on cultivating their wisdom". Was he not right? Even today, when the average life-span may be seventy or eighty years, people so get involved in living that they forget why they are living; so involved in what they are doing that they forget why they are doing it; so involved in pursuing things which money can buy that they forget about things that money can't buy. If there is one thing money can't buy, it is wisdom and true wisdom comes from the Lord Jesus. Hence Mary sat at the feet of Jesus listening to his eternal wisdom (Lk 10:39), while her sister Martha was preparing the food for him.

Jesus was a guest in the house of Martha and Mary. These sisters, coming from the tradition of Abraham and Sarah who generously welcomed even strangers unaware that they were angels (Gen 18:2-5), were genuine hosts to Jesus. Theirs was not an artificial welcome, for they knew well that when hospitality becomes an art, it loses its very soul. Besides, Jesus was their family friend and their friendship was not like money, easier made than kept. Therefore both went out of their way to extend to him their hospitality but each differently, Martha by preparing food and Mary by listening to his words. However, Jesus chided Martha by saying that she had forgotten something more important and praised Mary for "she had chosen the better part" (Lk 10:42).

Jesus did not condemn Martha for her loving service; how could he? It was he who presented unselfish service as an example of neighbourliness in the parable of the Good Samaritan. Hence Martha was not chided because she served but because she was distracted with all the serving and was "worrying and fretting about many things" (Lk 10:41). In censuring her, Jesus was not promoting prayer against action, nor exalting the contemplative life over and against the active life. What in truth he was reminding Martha and all of us was, that human beings are to live not on bread alone but on the word of God, that Martha was not just busy but too busy to care for anything spiritual, that we should not allow our minds to get so clouded up from turmoils of every day living that we lose sight of our priorities in life and that, when this happens, we must pause at the feet of the Lord and let the murky waters of the mind become clear again.

We are living in a busy age and for most of us our 'business' is important. Two women went on a pilgrimage to Lourdes with the sole purpose of bringing their pains and sufferings to the Lord. But what actually happened? On arrival, the first woman started to see the sights and buy the glittering souvenirs, spending a lot of time and energy. She came to the hotel, put them away carefully and went back again to buy a whole bunch of cards. It took several hours to get them written and posted. After all this was over, she heaved a huge sigh of relief and went to say some prayers; by now she was ready to drop from exhaustion. But her friend, as soon as she arrived, took a little nap, refreshed herself and headed for the shrine. On her way, she saw souvenir shops and cards, but they could wait. At the grotto, she recollected herself, assembled the fragments of her scattered life, laid them before God and returned to the hotel, refreshed in body as well as in spirit. Who was wiser of the two?

17TH SUNDAY OF THE YEAR

ASK, SEEK, KNOCK

Readings: Gen 18:20-32; Col 2:12-14; Lk 11:1-13

Theme: Our persistent prayer to God is to be made in a climate of love and trust, for he is a loving Father who cares for us and will give us the best thing at the right time.

Prayer is the pillow of religion. Only the self-sufficient do not pray, the self-satisfied will not pray, and the self-righteous cannot pray. Otherwise, all of us pray. We pray because we can't help praying. We must pray in adversity as well as in prosperity, for our piety must be like a good well, which must not freeze in winter and must not run dry in summer. A lot of kneeling keeps us in good standing with God; for one thing, you can't stumble if you are on your knees. However, our problem is not prayer but persistent prayer; we easily give up, but Abraham did not. Although the city of Sodom was doomed by God because of its grave sins, Abraham went on pressing God to spare the city, if there were as few as ten just people, to which God agreed (Gen 18:32). In his persistence, Abraham was like the postage stamp sticking to one thing till it gets there. Jesus too teaches a parable about persistence in prayer and then adds, "Ask, Seek, Knock" (Lk 11:9). Hence we must keep on trying with our petitions without getting discouraged. It is only from the valley that the mountain seems high.

However, not all our prayers are answered. An elderly woman who was an enthusiastic gardener declared that she would never believe in the prediction of science that it could one day control the weather. According to her, all that is needed to control the weather is prayer. Then one summer when she was away on a foreign tour, a draught hit the land and wiped out her entire garden. She was so upset when she got back that she changed her religion. God can't grant such prayers which are mere fancies calling him to do our own will rather than his. But you say: 'God does not even answer prayers that are not fancies!' Yes. Many good people ask for cures and don't receive them, seek justice and don't find it or knock for jobs and don't get them. Why? One has to remember that the Lord asked us only to be persistent in prayer believing that God is a loving Father who cares for us; but Jesus did not say that we will get all that we ask and be healed of all our ills, for the simple reason that we are still in human condition and not in heaven.

But let us at the same time make note of this: we will never ask God in vain, because Jesus also said, "It will be given to you ...you will receive ...it will be opened to you" (Lk 11:9). God will always answer our prayer, if not giving exactly what we ask, but surely by giving what we really need and often something of greater worth. For example, we may ask for greater strength to do greater things, but he may give us infirmity, so that we can do better things; we may ask for prosperity, health or success, but he may give us patience, wisdom and peace. Hence ask for things of greater value; ask him to make a sour heart sweet; a foolish heart wise; a timid heart, brave; and a cold heart ardent; you will receive it. Remember, God warms his hands at our heart when we pray. Seek God's will for you more than anything else and he will give the best you could ever imagine. There was an exhausted wood cutter who kept wasting his time and energy chopping wood with a blunt axe, because he did not have the time, he said, to stop and sharpen the blade. Don't be like him. Sharpen your prayer towards God's plan for you and focus your attention on God rather than on actual need, and your prayer will do wonders for you.

In 'Our Father' Jesus taught us also that we must pray in a climate of love and trust, for we are praying to a loving Father who cares for us so much that "he gave you new life in company with Christ" (Col 2:13). Why then, get needlessly anxious about the future while praying? The crosses we make for ourselves by restless anxiety as to the future are not crosses which come from God. God has planned our pathways and is leading us by his hands. He may lead us through fire, but he is only refining the gold; our pathways may be steep and the storm may sweep around us but God can mount the storm and walk upon the wind! Hence, be it trial or test, God knows what is best.

18TH SUNDAY OF THE YEAR

THE JESTER'S WAND

Readings: Eccles 1:2, 2:21-23; Col 3:1-5, 9-11; Lk 12:13-21

Theme: The spiritual goods we acquire by sharing our material goods with the needy are the true riches in the eyes of God and will serve us as provisions for our journey towards God.

It is said that an English nobleman of tremendous wealth gave his jester a wand, saying, "Keep this wand until you find a greater fool than yourself". The jester laughingly accepted the wand and used it on festive occasions. One day, the nobleman lay dying. Calling the jester to his bedside, he said "I am going on a long journey". "Where to?" asked the jester. "I don't know", came the reply. "What provisions have you made for the trip?" the jester asked. The nobleman shrugged his shoulders: "None at all". "Then", said the jester, "take this." And placing the wand in the nobleman's hands, he added, "It belongs to you. You are a greater fool than I". Christian life is a journey, not a home. The end of our journey is not death; death is only a golden key that opens the palace of eternity where God reigns. But have we made provisions that will guarantee our entrance into our eternal home and will sustain us all through the journey, refreshing our spirits when tired and strengthening our hearts so that we may press on to the end?

Indeed, we do make provisions, but they are for the future in this life and therefore they are mostly material provisions. Riches are useful but we need to guard against a greedy accumulation of earthly riches. For one thing, they don't bring happiness in themselves. Many people have found the acquisition of wealth not an end, but only a change of miseries! Secondly, riches are ours only for a time and so the Bible calls them, "vanities" (Eccles 1:2), the original meaning of the word 'vanity' being: 'a gust of wind'. Hence, in the parable of the rich fool, God says to him, "Thou fool, this night thy soul shall be required of thee" (Lk 12:20). We don't condemn riches as evil in themselves, but we can't be blind to the fact that they can be obstacles. Riches by their nature enlarge rather than satisfy appetite; they breed satiety, and satiety, outrage! What is still worse is that they can enslave our spirits so strongly that we are deprived of our freedom to love God and our neighbour. Yes. A great fortune can be a great slavery. One wonders if the rich cannot make themselves freer than those who are not rich, what do they gain by clinging to their wealth?

Therefore we are called not to become greedy and to cling to our riches and other material possessions as if they are an end in themselves, but to use them in such a way that through their use we can acquire spiritual goods as provisions for our spiritual journey towards God. This is what Jesus meant when he warned us "not to store up treasures for ourselves instead of making ourselves rich in the sight of God" (Lk 12:21). And St Paul repeated it: "Let your thoughts be on heavenly things, not on things that are on earth" (Col 3:2). A sure way of acquiring provisions for our journey towards God by means of riches is to love and care for one another and to use our riches to promote justice and peace. The interdenominational Church of the Saviour in Washington D.C. USA, has many wealthy members, many of whom are members of a group called the Ministry of Money. The group meets regularly to see how they should invest their money to promote the welfare of humanity. Recently they decided to invest in companies that research into sicknesses and diseases among poor people; this being an area often neglected by the large pharmaceutical companies because there is no money in it. There is no doubt that this is a commendable way of storing up riches in the sight of God.

Yes; by giving and by giving of ourselves, we make treasures in heaven and become rich in the sight of God. Whatever we give is not lost but is transformed into a treasure of eternity, drawing us forward into the Kingdom. Therefore, if in the past we had been laying up greater importance on material treasures, it is time to change our way. And that is in keeping with what happened at our baptism: "You have stripped off your old behaviour with your old self and you have put on a new self in the image of Christ" (Col 3: 9-10). When we die, we are not going to take with us any of our material wealth. In Kenya, some Africans still follow the practice of removing the clothes from the dead before burying them, in order to dramatise that we leave the world the same way we came into it. Therefore, what counts at death is not the wealth we acquired during life, but the spiritual goods we earned for our long journey towards God.

19TH SUNDAY OF THE YEAR

FAITH ON ALERT

Readings: Wis 18:6-9; Heb 11:1-2,8-19; Lk 12:32-48

Theme: Since we do not know when we will die, it would be wise to be always on the alert, daily living out our faith carrying out the duties God has enjoined upon us, towards his creation and towards one another, with the sure knowledge of the rewards we will receive.

Many in the world build their faith on the holy text of pike and gun. But St Thomas More, speaking to his family in the days before disaster struck the Church in England, urged them to have faith in God: "You have everything in your favour. You are being carried up to heaven by the chins. If you stand fast and firmly stick to God, though you be but half good, God will give credit for the whole," he said.

Faith is "confident assurance concerning what we hope for" (Heb 11:1). The people of Israel who waited on God, "with the sure knowledge of the oaths in which they put their faith" (Wis 18:6), were rewarded with deliverance. By faith, "Abraham became the father of descendants as numerous as the stars," and by the same faith, "Sarah received power to conceive, though she was past the age" (Heb 11:11). Likewise, to each of us Christians, our faith must be the script of joy and our immortal diet. We must always have the staff of faith to walk upon.

Faith is more than believing; it is daily walking with the Lord; it is being "busy" (Lk 12:43), with faith-filled actions. Faith without works is dead and hence the Church must act and not remain cold; a cold church is like cold butter which never spreads very well, nor can it save the world. Speaking recently in Italy, Bishop Simon, the first Hutu Bishop in Burundi warned that Burundi could fall prey to intertribal massacres similar to those that had occurred in Ruwanda. He said that Western powers can be of help, but he also confessed that the Church in Burundi is also responsible for the present situation, because it remained silent so long. "If we in Burundi had taken action 25 or 30 years ago, probably what is happening today might never have come about", he added. What is true of the Church as a whole is also true of us her members. When church services are over, our services must begin. If the Church members rest, the Church rusts.

We are not left in doubt as to the kind of actions our faith has to take on. God has put human beings "in charge of his property" (Lk 12:44), with a duty to care for it, develop it and make use of it for all. Are we failing in this duty? Just consider the ecological devastation resulting from man's greed and selfishness: the World Bank has recently warned that the next global war most likely would be for water, for a billion people in the world today do not have access to clean drinking water; and one of the major trends causing this global water emergency is the increasing level of water pollution. It is obvious that one of the main causes of air and water pollution is senseless wars. At the 50th annual Hiroshima Peace Memorial Ceremony, Tomiichi the Japanese Prime Minister expressed admiration for all citizens of Hiroshima who rebuilt the ruins, "where not one tree or blade of grass remained" after the bombing. Therefore, being in "charge of God's property" means that we take care to safeguard nature's environment; but it especially means that we take care of the poor and the weak in God's world. The Lord even wanted us to be ready to sell what we have for ourselves, in order to help the weaker sections of society: "Sell what you have and give to the poor" he said, and added that "treasures in heaven" (Lk 12:33) will be our rewards.

According to our Lord, there will be reward or punishment for our actions or inaction respectively, when he will come to judge us either at the end of time or at the moment of our death. Hence we would be wise if we always live our faith in action, attuned to our Creator and to his Creation, like a "good and faithful servant whom the master finds wide awake on his return" (Lk 12:37). Living by faith may well be an unending struggle against a mocking faithless world. Even then, we must keep fighting the good fight and run the race with defying faith. If we fall, let us go down fighting as Linford Christie, the Sprinter did. This Olympic champion, in order to retain his world 100-metre title in Gothenburg, ran in the finals but fell prostrate on the track, clutching at the right hamstring which he had strained in the semifinal. "If you have got to go down, it is best to go down fighting" he said, after finishing sixth. This is in a race for an earthly reward. How about in our race for faith-rewards?

ASSUMPTION – AUGUST 15

MISS UNIVERSE

Readings: 1 Chron 15:3-4, 15-16;16:1-2; 1 Cor 15:54-57; Lk 1: 39-56

Theme: The assumption of Mary gives the clearest evidence of fullness of grace in her, brings her spiritual presence closer to us than ever before and serves as a preview of our own transformation after death into a life of glory.

Some are born great, some achieve greatness, of course, some hire public relations officers. But Mary's greatness belonged completely to a different category: greatness was thrust upon her by God. An unmistakable evidence of this was his filling her with his grace which led to her Assumption. The Feast of the Assumption tells us that Mary is in heaven, body and soul. Because she did not sin in her life time, her body like the body of Jesus did not decay. It went directly from the earthly state to the heavenly state. Because of the way Mary bore Christ in her womb and in her heart, she indeed is the "Ark of God" (1 Chron 16:1). Because her "corruptible frame has taken on incorruptibility and her mortal body immortality" (1 Cor 15:54), Mary has defeated death and can now glory in heaven. Because of her faith and love, Mary deserves to be called "Blessed" (Lk 1:42). Yes. Mary is the pride of humanity, the blessed of the ages, the inspiration of the artists, poets and theologians. In our admiring love, we have heaped upon her every praise and honour. But no one has honoured her more than God himself. She is his own virtuous and beautiful Miss Universe.

We cannot fully understand or appreciate the end of a play or film without knowing what went before. We have to know the story that led up to it. If at the end of her earthly life Mary was taken up body and soul into heavenly glory, it was because she was the first and perfect disciple of Jesus Christ in her life. We might argue (or we might not!) that she was not permitted to choose the frame of her destiny, but what she put into it was hers. Hers was a life of faith. Every day, every week, every month, the most widely read journals seem to vie with each other in telling us that the time for religion is past and that faith is an hallucination. But for Mary faith was life and she was made up of faith, which set her free to fly beyond the realm of death. Hers was a life of love which brought with it the normal and more than normal trials and tribulations of human existence. When she first said her 'Yes' to God, she did not guess that Love would prove so hard a Master. Yet, Love is the history of Mary's life, when in the life of many of us love is only an episode.

We know that Mary is our Mother and an extraordinary one, because as mother she is not a person to lean on, but a person who makes leaning unnecessary. In her glorification our Mother has not abandoned us as orphans by leaving us physically. Rather, she is more present to us than ever before in a spiritual manner. Her disappearance from our sight has actually inaugurated a hidden presence that is more powerful than a physical presence and has dramatically extended her influence in our lives. What a source of encouragement to feel Mary's presence by faith when worries and anxieties mount on us. Often life is just a turning around to many of us: one day we are depressed and miserable, another day we are miserable and depressed. What an anchor of strength to know that Mary is by our side at these bleak moments.

Assumption is also the preview of our own future transformation. It is a reminder that on the last day we too shall rise from the dead and our bodies will be clothed with incorruptibility and immortality. Our body! After all, what is it? Just a physical covering, that is all, worth chemically less than fifty pence. Yes. When it is buried it is mortal, but when raised it will be immortal; when buried it is ugly and weak, but when raised it will be beautiful and strong; when buried it is a physical body but when raised it will be a spiritual body (1 Cor 15:53). This is our hope and we do not hope to make some port we know not where or on some impossible shore. Assumption promises us such a life of glory to our body and soul. Compared to this promise, our present life is nothing. I sometimes wish that we discover a computer that can figure out all the things in life that do not add up! The certainty of immortality of our bodies is the rainbow on our tears of grief. Hence let us make the best use of our present life by imitating Mary's life of faith and love, worthy of our glorified destiny. If we do not know what to do with this life, why should we want one which shall last for ever?

20TH SUNDAY OF THE YEAR

COURAGE IN CONFLICT

Readings: Jer 38:4-6, 8-10; Heb 12:1-4; Lk 12:49-53

Theme: When we denounce evil and do good, we are sure to rock the boat, cause division and endanger our own lives; but we are equally sure that God will come to our aid, giving us courage in conflict.

At one point in the conflict in the former Yugoslavia the flood of refugees reached, for the size of the country, staggering proportions. More than 200,000 people fled Croatia and thousands of people fled Krajina in a convoy which stretched for many miles. These were victims of political intrigue and selfish power structures. They flee because they can't speak out; if they do, they will be tortured and put to death. There are countless thousands of others in the world who likewise suffer savage social injustices and they too can't speak out, except cry the cry of despair which could be chilling to anyone who cares to hear. We do hope that our world leaders are genuine as Jeremiah was when they speak for these voiceless people, and are as courageous as Christ was, in their efforts to alleviate their sufferings.

Jeremiah and Jesus lived and died trying to change the course of human history, by denouncing evil and doing good. Jeremiah warned that if people continued in their evil, the nation would fall; but for saying that, he was thrown into a muddy cistern to die (Jer 38:6). Jesus spoke of waging war against evil and of bringing fire of judgement on the wicked; but for speaking like that, he was baptised with death (Lk 12:50). Could we have the same fearlessness and courage to speak and act for what is just, true and good? Why fear when the Lord is near? Fear is the dark room where negatives are developed. We need courage for standing for what is right. Why miss the plum for want of courage to shake the tree? Some ask: Can a single person do anything at all against such an array of world ills? Why not? Each time when a person stands up for an ideal, or strikes out against injustice, tiny ripples of hope are sent forth, and these ripples can build up into a wave that can sweep down the mightiest walls of resistance.

But genuine loyalty to Christ's teachings is sure to rock the boat causing divisions. "I have come for division" (Lk 12:52), said Jesus. For example, if the Church distinguishes between the homosexual tendency and a 'full-blooded acting out' of this tendency (about which she expresses certain reservations), she is accused of inciting homo-hatred of homosexuals; if the Pope objects to contraception, he is ridiculed through a poster which pictures him as a hard-hatted Pope, beseeching people to wear a condom; if you are honest, you will conflict with those who trade in lies and dishonesty; if you try to be just, you will oppose those who exploit the poor and the weak. It happened in Iraq. A general and a colonel, sons-in-law of Saddam, defected with their wives to Jordan in protest against the bloodthirsty president, vowing "to get rid of what is shameful and what caused backwardness in that country". In response, Saddam called them "thieves and traitors". Even Jordan was threatened to face military retaliation for granting refuge to the dissenting group from Iraq. Yes. Gospel values cause divisions.

Yet we Christians know that when we get trapped in the muddy cisterns of threats and oppositions, God will come but to deliver us from them, as he came in the person of a Cushite to rescue Jeremiah from the cistern (Jer 38:10); we believe that our suffering and weeping for justice's sake will endure only for a night, for peace and joy will come in the morning (Ps 30:5). Hence, we fight the good fight with all our might, "keeping our eyes always fixed on the great joy that lies before us" (Heb 12:2). Besides, we are surrounded by "a cloud of witnesses" (Heb 12:1), heroes and heroines of faith to inspire us in our struggle. Therefore, when the world is busy vulgarising such heroes of faith, the Pope goes about canonising them. On 4th June, this year, he beatified Fr Damien, the nineteenth century Belgian missionary to Hawaii, who dedicated his life and died for the lepers, himself becoming a leper, when the rest of the world condemned them as sordid outcasts. Fr Damien was courageous. Courage is the thing; all goes if courage goes.

21ST SUNDAY OF THE YEAR

OPEN BUT NARROW

Readings: Is 66:18-21; Heb 12:5-7, 11-13; Lk 13:22-30

Theme: If we try our best, and try it now, to go through the narrow door of trials as the discipline of God, we are sure to enter our eternal home, prepared by God not for just a chosen few but for all.

God has prepared for us eternal life, where the harsh and long winter of our weariness will end, giving way to the golden summer of delight; where all will be warmth, love and joy. Eternal life is for all, for the Lord says, "I come to gather the nations of every language" (Is 66:18). But who will actually enter? No one can say. "Will there be only few saved?" (Lk 13:23) asked the disciples. Jesus was not prepared to answer. The free human response to the gifts of God also plays a role in our salvation. But one thing is certain: there is no favouritism in the Kingdom of God. When international sports are played, the telescopic lens zooms in on the VIP section. It selects people for reasons of power, prestige, office and privilege, whose prime seats are especially reserved for them, whenever they chose to arrive. There are no such favourites in God's Kingdom. "People will enter from the east and west, from the north and south" (Lk 13:29), from the black and the white, from the rich and the poor.

Though no one is sure who will enter eternal life, Jesus has given us some guides. Of course, he is not like the guide who says, "Well, I don't know for sure, but I have my suspicions". Jesus is definite about his guidance. He says that the "door to eternal life is narrow" (Lk 13:24); hence, one who struggles for it will get into it. This means, those who struggle and suffer for the sake of truth, justice and love will enter into it; those who "endure trials as the discipline of God" (Heb 12:11) who deals with us as sons will enter into it. The word 'discipline' frightens away people these days, though out of the word 'discipline' comes the word 'disciple'. Discipline has the power to transform trials into triumphs, pains into peace, like the modern personal Air Cooler does with the heat. Unlike the conventional fans, which only redistribute warm air, the personal Air Cooler reduces the temperature of the air and gently blows this cooled refreshing air in your direction. So does discipline.

Because the door to eternal life is narrow, some reversals and surprises can be foreseen. "Some who are last will be first and some who are first will be last" (Lk 13:30). The first chosen people may be the last of people. People from four corners of the earth will precede them (v.29). Therefore, those who think that they have privileged entry-permit into the Kingdom because they have some acquaintance with Jesus, because they have shared a meal at the Eucharist, because they have heard some Sunday sermons, because they belong to some Christian establishment or because they are 'insiders', may be disappointed. The poor may step ahead of the rich, the simple surpass the clever and the sinners outshine the pious. That is Christ's warning. Those who heed his warning are safe. Those who do not, may face the kind of fate which Alison Hargreaves faced recently. She was a dedicated and daring British mountaineer; but while making her final assault against the world's most savage mountain, K2, a Pakistani army officer warned her that it would be suicidal to proceed further; but she did not listen. The result was that she died on the mountain; what appeared to be a safe mountain, suddenly turned, as she had been warned, into a raging holocaust of swirling snow and wind.

Therefore, we need to take Christ's warning seriously and "try our best" (v.24) to enter through the narrow door; and we need to start trying now, for "the door will be soon closed" (v.25) to some of us. At times, it takes only a cow to close it! – 300 people died in New Delhi, when a passenger train near Firozabad, northern India, rammed another train that had stopped suddenly after hitting a cow.

We are not alone in struggling to enter through the narrow door. We have countless numbers of Christians to inspire us in this struggle. These men and women have gone before us through the narrow door struggling and suffering, but at the same time living life fully, not pecking away at living. Some years ago at the Commemoration of the 50th anniversary of VJ Day, England remembered and paid tribute to the courage and bravery of such men and women who fought for the Christian values of truth and justice, freedom and peace. As the one thousand children who escorted the Queen up the Mall, candles flickering in the darkness to mark the end of the service, may we light up our lamps of faith and march through the narrow door.

22ND SUNDAY OF THE YEAR

ABLE YET HUMBLE

Readings: Sir 3:17-18, 28-29; Heb 12:18-19, 22-24; Lk 14:1, 7-14

Theme: Genuinely humble people look at the heights and depths of their personalities without becoming proud or discouraged and win favour with God and men.

Do we want to be happy, successful, with a good reputation? Then, we need to "conduct our affairs with humility" (Sir 3:17). The clothing of humility can never go out of style in a Christian world. But the fact is that humility as a virtue has fallen on hard times in our day, while arrogance and aggression, pride and pomp, self-righteousness and self-assertiveness are being paraded as marks of the modern culture, which abhors all simplicity and simplification. Yet humility remains at the root of the Christian life, in which the great Gospel reversals still rank first: to lose one's life is to find it; the last shall be the first; "the humble shall be exalted" (Lk 14:11). However, Sirach and Jesus are teaching us not some kind of pseudo-humility, but genuine humility. Pseudo-humility is pretentious self-effacement and a phoney denial of all our gifts, virtues and talents; and hence it is like a good apple rotten at the heart.

Genuine humility is not something forced from outside. At times, you see some people playing a humble role, because they have to. I am reminded of the man and his wife who went to church one day. Out loud, the man prayed: "Oh, Lord, make me successful and please keep me humble." his wife kneeling beside him, chimed in with a somewhat corrective plea: "Oh, Lord, you make him successful; I will keep him humble." True humility is one's own personal recognition of one's true status before God. As Christians who have personally recognised our true status, we will joyfully accept all our gifts, talents and abilities as coming from God and will use them for our own enrichment and for the glory of God. But at the same time we will not deny his human limitations and weaknesses; we will not rely solely on our own strength, neither will he "seek things beyond his strength" (Sir 3:21); we will candidly admit that we are sinners, but forgiven sinners, while at the same time recognising our continued need for forgiveness. Thus genuine humility is like darkness that reveals the heavenly light, in which humble people look at the heights and the depths of their personalities without becoming proud and discouraged.

It is wise to stay humble, lest we stumble. We need to stay humble also for the rewards it brings. A humble person "wins esteem of his fellow guests" (Lk 14:10); sincere humility attracts but lack of it detracts. Besides, the humble person who often looks up to God rarely looks down on anyone, especially if they were poor, and thus the humble can have more friends. This is why the world considers an able yet humble person as a jewel worth a kingdom. Also humble people "find favour with God" (Sir 3:18), because humility is that low, sweet root from which all heavenly virtues shoot. Pope John XXIII once remarked, "Anybody can be Pope, the proof of this is that I have become Pope." Any great personality like him is humble, for greatness goes with humility. Anyone puffed-up by their "greatness" is like an empty vessel that rattles its small coins noisily. Pride goes before destruction and hence must be kept deflated. A big truck got stuck under a low overhead bridge. Nobody knew what to do, until a small boy suggested that they let the air out of the tyes. This done, the truck, now a couple of inches lower, grazed through. A bit of deflation can help us all at times.

23RD SUNDAY OF THE YEAR

NOT A MATTER OF WHIM

Readings: Wis 9:13-18; Philem 9-10, 12-17; Lk 14:25-33

Theme: To be a serious follower of Christ, which requires the reordering of one's values and relationships, we need the grace of God to aid our human efforts.

A frog found himself trapped on a large lily pad surrounded by hungry crocodiles. His only hope for escape was to hop over the crocodiles to the next lily pad. An owl sitting on a branch overhead said with cool detachment: "Why don't you just take off and fly? Just fly to the next pad". The frog got a running start, flapped his legs as fast as he could, lifted off and came down right in front of the massive jaws of a giant reptile. "Stupid owl!" the frog screamed. "Frogs can't fly". "Please," said the owl disdainfully, "that's an implementation issue. I deal only in concepts." Like this frog, without being forewarned about the implications of executing a plan, a person may begin well but end tragically. Through the stories of the building project and the army strategy (Lk 14:28-32) Jesus drives home the point that becoming a follower of Jesus is not just a matter of whim; it requires careful thought. The follower of Christ must make absolutely clear to himself what level of commitment is required of him.

Following Christ requires reordering of a person's values. For example, a serious disciple must prefer the requirements of the Kingdom to any claim that familial relationships may impose. "If any man comes to me without hating his father, mother, wife, children, brothers, sisters, yes, his own life too, he cannot be my disciple," says Jesus (Lk 14:26). Jesus is not asking his followers actually to hate their parents and relatives. What he is saying is that commitment to the Kingdom must remain absolute so that no human relationships interfere with it. *I Am Third* is the title of the best selling autobiography of Gale Sayers, who ranks among the greatest running backs in the whole history of American football. In his book, Gale says why these three words meant so much to him. They were the motto of his track coach who kept the words on a little sign on his desk. One day Gale asked him what they meant. The coach replied, "The Lord is first, my friends are second, and I am third." From that day on, Gale made those words his own philosophy of life, bought a gold medal, had the words 'I am third' engraved on it and wore it around his neck ever since, like a religious symbol. Yes. To any serious disciple of Christ, the Lord comes first before every other possession, even before his loved ones.

Following Christ requires reordering of a person's human relationships. Onesimus was once a slave to Philemon. St Paul took the slave with him and baptised him. When he sent Onesimus back to Philemon, St Paul wrote to him: "I am sending him back to you for ever not as a slave any more but something better than a slave, a dear brother" (Philem 1:16). Philemon was asked to let the Master/Slave relationship between them cease to exist and be replaced by a kind of relationship that is worthy of brothers in Christ. Thus, the Gospel has power to break such social barriers. Moved by the Gospel "Love one another as I have loved you" a middle-aged woman walked into the slums of a large city in India. She had two dollars in her pocket, no income, and no place to stay. All she had was the conviction that God wanted her to love the poorest of the poor with works of mercy, no matter what their nationality or colour was. That was about 40 years ago. Today, Mother Teresa has 80 schools, 70 leprosy clinics, 30 homes for the dying, 30 homes for abandoned children, 300 mobile dispensaries and 40000 volunteer workers the world over.

Such a following, which requires reordering of one's values and human relationships, cannot be practised if we rely only on our human strength. We need God's wisdom to help us in making and keeping our commitment to the Gospel. We are finite human beings and limited in our strength. In the presence of a guru, a young scientist was boasting of the achievements of modern science. "We can fly just like the birds", he was saying. "We can do what the birds can do!" The guru said, "Except sit on a barbed-wire fence!" Alas! Human as we are, our strengths are limited and we can't do everything even physically; how then spiritually? "It is hard enough for us to work out what is on earth, who then can discover what is in the heavens?" (Wis 9:16). Therefore we need to pray for divine wisdom, so that aided by the grace of God we can succeed in being serious followers of Christ.

24TH SUNDAY OF THE YEAR

WHERE IS HE?

Readings: Ex 32:7-11, 13-14; 1 Tim 1:12-17; Lk 15:1-32

Theme: God is with those who are groping in the dark, sinning against their own fellow human beings, calling them to repent and offering them forgiveness; he is with those who align themselves with the marginalised of society and with those who celebrate their victories over evil.

WHERE IS HE? In the parable of the prodigal son, the father, who represents God, comes out of his house and waits for the return of his wayward son; and after the son rejoins the family, the father once again leaves the house and its party in order to join, this time, his angry elder son and tells him, "All that I have is yours" (Lk 15:31). Yes; Our God is with those who are groping in darkness and fuming with anger; he is not to be found in places of honour but outside, seeking his rebellious sons and daughters telling them, "all that I have is yours".

WHERE IS HE? Saul, a man "filled with arrogance", persecuted Christians; for "he did not know what he was doing in his unbelief" (1 Tim 1:13). But God pursued him, offered him his mercy and turned him into St Paul, who did most to spread the faith in the early Church. Yes; God is still after those who in their ignorance act against Christian faith, persecute others, exploit others, enslave others and kill others; God pursue them, not to punish them but to offer his mercy and forgiveness.

WHERE IS HE? A shepherd in Christ's time was reckoned among the "sinners", because he was suspected of driving his flock onto others' fields and thus increasing his profits. A woman in Christ's time was considered a second-class citizen, the mere property of man. Yet, Jesus chose a shepherd and a woman to play the role of God in his parable of "the lost sheep" and "the lost coin" (Lk 15:4-10). Thus God has revealed his special love for those who are on the fringes of society. God is with people who are dehumanised, counted as digits, and reduced to anonymity, telling them, "You are special, precious and of supreme value to me".

WHERE IS HE? The people of Israel after safely returning to the promised land began worshipping a golden statue of a calf (Ex 32:8) at the foot of the very mountain Sinai where they had made a covenant with God. Hence, in his justice, God announced a crushing punishment; but at the same time, in his mercy, he offered them time to repent and return to him. Yes. God is present even with those who are breaking their exclusive relationship with him, established at their baptism; angry, yes; but still merciful, offering them time to return.

WHERE IS HE? Jesus "ate with tax collectors and sinners" (Lk 15:2), the outcasts of society. He was there because, in the Near East, sharing food together means that the people at table identify with one another and show that they accept each other. So Jesus, by eating with the outcasts, demonstrated the kind of people God is reaching out to through him. Yes. God is at the table of fellowship where people associate themselves with the margins of society.

WHERE IS HE? "There will be more joy in heaven over the return of a repentant sinner" (Lk 15:7). Yes. God is at the party celebrating the return of those who had left his Church; applauding the success of someone in his or her fight against long-standing addiction; commemorating the victory of people over some common evil; praising a courageous community decision, made towards the growth of his Kingdom; lauding the success of a mission well run for the renewal of all. Our God is a God who celebrates, when the wayward are saved, delights when we do the right thing and who finds joy in being generous with his mercy.

25TH SUNDAY OF THE YEAR

"MONEY IS HONEY"

Readings: Amos 8:4-7; 1 Tim 2:1-8; Lk 16:1-13

Theme: Our best Future which is heaven, about which we are to be concerned, does not begin at some distant time after the resurrection of the dead, but it begins now.

Wisdom is a treasure for all time; but the art of being wise is the art of securing the best future and our best future lies in heaven, because we believe that in heaven there will be the presence of all good and the absence of any defect in this good which we call evil. That is why, while common sense suits itself to the ways of the world, wisdom tries to conform to the ways of heaven. Jesus asks his followers to take more interest in their future than the steward of his parable took in his own. The steward in the parable insures his own future by doing favours to others, but this he does by cheating his master. And Jesus commends him, not for his dishonesty but for taking an interest in the future (Lk 16:8). The steward is able to look ahead and see that after he is fired for incompetence, he will have little prospect of getting another job. So before the axe falls, he puts others in his debt so they will be obliged to him when he is unemployed. He foresees his future and provides for it. If our best future lies in heaven, then we must all take active interest in our future .

But, when should our interest in the future begin? After the resurrection of the dead? Certainly not, for that would be a concern for the future at the expense of the present and that we reject. Our future begins now. The future is purchased by the present. In today, already walks tomorrow. The prophet Amos looked at the future of his people and cried out protesting against the values of the present generation. Why? Because he believed that the future is made of the same stuff as the present and he was afraid that his land where greed and dishonesty abounded, where the wealthy exploited the poor and justice was being torn in shreds, was doomed to destruction (Amos 8:7). Hence he argued that unless his people took drastic action against the prevailing false values, there was no future security for them. Yes. Our eternal destiny is a future gift, but it is also a present achievement. It comes one day at a time. We reach it at the rate of sixty minutes an hour. Therefore, we should never forget that the only way we can predict our future is to exercise our power in the present, in order to shape that future. But how?

Jesus makes two clear statements regarding how we should shape our future. One is: "use money, tainted as it is, to win your friends and thus make sure that when it fails you, they will welcome you into the tents of eternity" (Lk 16:9). On the one hand, we are warned against amassing money as if that is the source of eternal bliss. In fact, the opposite is true. Each of us can write a short history of our money in six words: "Here it is. There it goes." On the other hand, Jesus is suggesting that we use money wisely. One way of using money wisely is to give it to the poor. Those who receive it become our friends now and in heaven later.

When we share our money with the poor, we also bridge the appalling gap between the rich and the poor and thus try to create a just society where all people can have "undisturbed and tranquil lives in perfect dignity" (1 Tim 2:2). Helping the poor is justice, not charity, because one person can only accumulate money at another person's expense. Any suggestion that every thing will be put right in the next life, so that people should put up with injustice in this world, is a perversion of Christ's teaching and a refusal to light up tomorrow with today.

Another statement that Jesus makes on how to shape our future is: The man who can be trusted in little things can be trusted in great" (Lk 16:10). Little drops of water, little grains of sand make the mighty ocean. So too, our great doing of little things makes the great life and the responsible use of little things on earth determine our great reward in heaven. Suppose, for example, we don't respect and take care of little things like water, air and soil, and thus cause environmental pollution, how can we expect God to entrust us with great things of the kingdom of heaven? Similarly, when we neglect little deeds of kindness, little words of love or little acts of forgiveness, we are neglecting our duty to shape our future which is a kingdom of love, unity and peace. Yes. The smallest thing by the influence of eternity can be made infinite and eternal. Hence faithfulness in little things is a big thing.

26TH SUNDAY OF THE YEAR

CARING IS NOT SCARING

Readings: Amos 6:1, 4-7; 1 Tim 6:11-16; Lk 16:19-31

Theme: If we always keep the vision of our future glory in focus, it will not be difficult for us to give to the needy now, not just from one's abundance but from one's substance not just bread but any help of which a person stands in need.

When I was a boy, my parish priest used to preach long sermons on hell. If he found that his sermon was not quite hitting any hearts, he would try a little longer, hoping to hit at least some stomachs. Too much stress in the past on the negative aspects of religion, such as hell and damnation, has led many to think of Christianity as a religion of fear and guilt. Teachers of religion would do well to remember that a religion that teaches people to fear the future is likely to teach them to fumble the present. But hell is getting very out of date in today's thinking, though this Sunday's readings remind us of it again. Amos speaks of "exile" into which the rich, who now live in the world of their own, unmindful of the poor, will go first (Amos 6:7). The rich man in our Lord's parable, who did nothing to the beggar Lazarus who sat at his gate, is said to be "tormented in eternal fire" (Lk 16:24). But scriptural scholars think that this fiery language, describing the fate of sinners, could be imaginative and poetic and need not be taken too literally. Therefore, we do not really know what the torments of hell may be, though the possibility of hell is always there, for anyone who chooses to enter.

But for many people in our age, it is not hell fire but God's love and mercy they need to hear. The chief purpose of Amos' warning and of our Lord's parable is to arouse in us a sense of duty to bring God's mercy to others less fortunate than ourselves. Mercy, of course, is not just pity, which at times can be wasted on a poodle, instead of on a child; nor is it a concern to help the needy without any personal involvement. Mercy is a personal concern which demands the giving of one's soul, a giving from one's substance, not just from one's abundance. There is so much poverty in the world. Tonight 1000 million people in the world will go to bed with hungry stomachs. The gap between the rich man and Lazarus is growing into a gigantic abyss in our world. Any religion which does not address itself to the problem of this gap runs the risk of becoming dangerously irrelevant. When you live next to the cemetery, you can hardly weep for any one; similarly, one wonders, whether some have become insensitive to the sufferings of the needy, simply because they have seen so many!

If poverty makes a person subhuman, an excess of wealth can make him inhuman; we Christians are asked not to allow this to happen. John Wesely's rule of life was to save all he could and give all he could. When he was at Oxford, he had an income of £30 a year. He lived on 28 and gave 2 away; when his income increased to £60, £100 and £120, he still lived on £28 and gave the balance away. Some might say: "Jesus' parable of the rich man is not addressed to me, for I am not rich". This is a mistake in interpreting the significance of the parable. This parable is not just about money. Though we may not be materially rich, we all still have something to share with others in need. Therefore, the real question to ask is not "Am I rich?" but "Who is sitting at my 'gate' begging, not necessarily for bread but, may be, for a word of recognition or appreciation, for a bit of companionship or fellowship, a little bit of love or forgiveness?" And the time to give is *now*; one who gives twice gives quickly.

In order to give to the needy quickly and generously, one needs to be driven by a vision. Of course, nearly all have their visions. Some see daggers in their vision and become fatal to society! Some have muddied visions with the result that they see only wretchedness as the end of life; still others have stormy visions and so they fight phantoms and get lost in unprofitable strife. But we Christians have a splendid vision of glory, "the everlasting life to which you were called where the Lord dwells in unapproachable light" (1 Tim 6:16). As long as we live, we can't permit this Christian vision to melt into thin air. To those who daily dip into this glorious vision of eternal destiny, caring is not scaring.

27TH SUNDAY OF THE YEAR

"JUMP SON"

Readings: Hab 1:2-3, 2:2-4; 2 Tim 1:6-8, 13-14; Lk 17:5-10

Theme: Faith is a jump into the arms of God, even when all odds are against us, and if this faith is put into practice and tested in the fire of afflictions, it will steadily turn us into better persons and even give us power to work for a better world.

Faith is more than praying in humble and solemn tone. It is more than trusting when weary and alone. Faith is a jump. A man who loved the Lord was going through deep and discouraging trials and his confidence in the Lord was near to breaking-point. One day he went for a walk in the orchard with his little son. The boy wanted to climb an old apple tree, so the father patiently stood below watching him as he ascended. Many of the limbs were dead and some of them began to break under the youngster's weight. Seeing his son's plight, the man held up his arms and called, "Jump son, I'll catch you". The boy still hung on, then as another branch snapped, he said, "Shall I let go of everything, Daddy?" "Yes", came the reply assuringly. Without any hesitation the boy jumped and was safely caught in his father's arms. This is faith.

Faith is not jumping to a conclusion; it is rather concluding to jump into the arms of God our Father, unconditionally accepting that Jesus is his Son and believing in the words he spoke and in the power he possesses. It is "by this faith a just man lives" (Heb 2:4). It is this faith that can draw poison from every grief, take the sting from every loss and quench the fire of every pain. It is this faith that can be compared, as Jesus does, to a "tiny mustard seed" (Lk 17:6). Because, as the power of a seed does not depend on its size but on the life hidden within itself, so the power of our faith does not depend on its quantity but on its quality. Therefore we would be deluding ourselves if we think that the more prayers we say, the more faith we have, and the more good works we do, the stronger our faith becomes. True faith, in other words, is to the soul what a mainspring is to a watch.

Only with such faith can we trust the past to the mercy of God, the present to his love, and the future to his providence. As a fish that lives among the waves and is not broken or dissolved by them, so with such faith we can live amidst the temptations and tempests of this world and remain uninjured. If we want to grow in such a faith, we need often to use it. I know a rich lady who keeps her priceless collection of jewels in the vault of a large bank; and once a week, the bank secretary, guarded by two plainclothes men, wears those priceless jewels to lunch, in order that this brief but regular contact with the human body may keep the jewels beautiful. So, too, by using our faith regularly, we keep it shining; and the ideal time to use faith is our time of hardships. St Paul tells us: "Bear your share of hardships which the Gospel entails with the strength which comes from God" (2 Tim 1:8). This is because it is in the fire of affliction that our faith is best tested.

Faith not only makes a person undaunted in the face of afflictions in his personal life, but also gives him power to work for a better world. "If you had faith, you would have power to command trees to be uprooted and transplanted into the sea" (Lk 17:6), says the Lord. With faith, we may not be able literally to move trees, but we will have power to overcome obstacles, to do great things for the Lord and the world. How is it that the aeroplane, radio, television and such other modern facilities, which the people of the 17th century thought impossible even to imagine, have become commonplace today? It is because people approached life full of hope, that God is going to be at work in every situation, as they released their faith in him. So, too, if today we work for a better world believing in the power of our faith in God, what appears impossible today will become possible in future, even a world in which there is no more war, no more poverty, no more hatred. Better, then, to be slow of head to understand, than slow of heart to believe.

28TH SUNDAY OF THE YEAR

TRY THANKSGIVING

Readings: 2 Kings 5:14-17; 2 Tim 2:8-13; Lk 17:11-19

Theme: If our gratitude to God for whatever he sends to us is sincere and spontaneous, it will provide us space to recognise his gifts and to appreciate their true values in a deeper sense, as signs of his love for us.

A Christian in great perplexity prayed but found no relief in prayer. Looking up from where he knelt, his eyes alighted on a card with these words: "Try Thanksgiving". He did and the Lord gave him peace and removed his cares. God has two dwellings, one in heaven, another in a grateful heart and hence a grateful heart is always contended. "So much has been given to me", said Hellen Keller, "that I have no time to brood over that which has been denied." God is pleased with gratitude but he gets so little of it. Some can't remember former benefits even when they come to beg for new. God too has a heart which can be hurt by ingratitude and can be provoked to complain: "Were not all made whole? Where are the other nine?" (Lk 17:17). I am afraid that some children of God are like bees who sip honey from flowers and hum their thanks when they leave; but alas! there are others who are like a gaudy butterfly who is sure that flowers owe thanks to him!

Gratitude is a natural virtue; it is the most exquisite form of courtesy. Hence it must be as spontaneous as our heart-beat. You can't extract gratitude as you would extract a tooth. Naaman the military commander of Syria, who was healed of his leprosy by Elisha, the man of God, returned at once with his whole retinue to thank God, declaring, "Now I know that there is no God in all the earth except in Israel. Please accept a gift from your servant" (2 Kings 5:15). Do we thank God enough for all his gifts: the place in which we dwell, the love that unites us, the wealth, the work, the food and the bright skies that make our lives delightful? Is it possible for anyone to count his blessings? When we take time to thank God, it provides us some space not only to recognise the gifts but also to appreciate their values, in a deeper sense, as signs of God's love for us.

We are expected to thank God not only for our happy days but also for the troublesome ones. Because, as even the weariest river somehow finally winds its way safe to sea, so God has a way of weaving glorious destiny even through our troubles. Yes. We are called to thank God even in pains, "in order that we may obtain the salvation to be found in Jesus Christ and with it eternal glory" (2 Tim 2:10). Hence thank him in affliction for afflictions are but shadow of God's wings; thank him in sorrow, for one who suffers, conquers; thank him in tears if need be, for any youth who has not wept is liable to become a savage in later years. Thank him even in death, for death that is born of sin can devour sin. It was after burying numerous victims during those times of war, famine and pestilence that the Minister, Martin Rinkart, composed that great song of praise, "Now Thank We all Our God".

There is a sense in which no gift is ours, till we have thanked the giver, our God. But our thanksgiving has to be sincere; gratitude just out of habit means nothing, less than nothing. "Thanks very much for the beautiful tie," said the child, kissing Grandma dutifully on the cheek. "Oh, that's nothing to thank me for," she murmured. "That's what I thought, but mother said I had to." Our gratitude, to be sincere, cannot be like this, forced or duty-bound. It needs to be heartfelt, like a flower that blossoms from the soil of the heart. A person who is truly grateful to God for everything in life can be said to love God with his whole heart; because such a person will invariably say a whole-hearted yes to life, accepting without reservations all that God had ordained for it. The finest formulation of what it means to love God totally is found in Dag Hammarskjold's words: "For all that has been: Thanks. To all that shall be: Yes."

29TH SUNDAY OF THE YEAR

CAMP AT HIS DOOR

Readings: Ex 17:8-13; 2 Tim 3:14-4:2; Lk 18:18

Theme: To live a fulfilling Christian life, it is necessary to fix a time for prayer in one's daily schedule and to persevere in it, even though God may delay his answers for various good reasons.

We kneel, how weak; we rise, how full of power! Prayer has enormous power. It can influence the outcome of events and it can change the lives of people. On their way to the Promised Land, the people of God were attacked by the Amalekites. So Moses went up the hill and extended his arms in prayer until the victory was won (Ex 17:12-13). Some 500 years ago in London, a number of poor men were praying for liberty to read the Bible. On the spot where the prayer was held stands the building of the Bible Society today. It is not only the materially poor and those who suffer who turn to God in prayer. People from all situations and all walks of life do so. Particularly to good Christians, prayer is the key of the morning and the bolt of the night. As no one can run a Marathon without training, so none can live a proper Christian life without prayer. But to experience the power of prayer we must persevere in praying, camping at his door.

When we persevere at God's door praying, he will come. But our problem is that we live in a society of instant food and instant cures, with the result that we often expect God to take our calls instantly. Too many people pray like little boys who knock at doors, then run away. The judge in the Gospel had probably ignored the plea of the old little widow many times, but she never gave up. She kept making new trips down to the judge's office day and night, till the wicked judge relented (Lk 18:5). If persistence prevails with a judge, who cares only for his own convenience and comforts, how much more will it prevail with a gracious God who loves us his children? Therefore we must not interrupt the course of our prayer on any account; if we do, we would be like a man who allows a bird to escape from his hands – he can hardly catch it again. Prayer is like a journey; to get through even the hardest journey, you need to take only one step at a time but you must keep on stepping.

We need to persevere in prayer, for God can delay his answer. He may delay in order to purify our motives, so that we ask him for what we need, rather than for what we want. He may delay in order to intensify our desire, so that with an intensified desire, we may have the courage to scale the height of excellence, rather than to remain mediocre, after what we had desired has been granted. He may delay in order, "to reprove, correct, train us in holiness, so that fully equipped and competent, for every good work" (2 Tim 3:16) our hearts are prepared to receive his gifts which he chooses to give. It would be a blunder to try to forecast the way God is going to answer our prayer. If God had granted all the silly prayers I have made in life, where would I be now? True prayer is not manipulating God into granting us our requests, but surrendering ourselves to his ways and to experiencing his presence, even without his presents. Hence, we often need to pray for God himself to come and fill our emptiness with his own fullness. In fact, the best prayer is born out of brokeness, for it is a declaration of man's need for God himself.

But whatever we pray for, let us pray with faith. Believe, that God who feeds ravens when they cry will surely answer when his children pray. When faith sets prayer to work, prayer sets God to work. Fix a time for prayer in your daily routine. The demands of modern life are such that unless we schedule a regular time to pray, we probably won't pray at all. Ralph Martin says in his book, *Hungry for God*: "A Real Estate man I know, gets up early in the morning to pray, an aerospace engineer prays and reads Scripture on his lunch-break, a production manager of a computer firm prays after his children are in bed at night". Yes. Prayer is the oil that keeps the lamp of faith burning brightly. I know of no better thermometer to the temperature of faith, than the measure of the intensity of prayer.

"DROP IT"

Readings: Sir 35:12-14, 16-18; 2 Tim 4:6-8, 16-18; Lk 18:9-14

Theme: God is closer to those whose hearts are broken and it is the prayer of the poor in spirit, that pierces the clouds, not that of those who are self-righteous, self-opinionated and conceited.

A man came to Buddha with an offering of flowers in his hands. Buddha looked at him and said, "Drop it!" he could not believe he was being asked to drop the flowers. But then it occurred to him that he was probably being invited to drop the flowers he had in his left hand, since to offer something with one's left hand was considered inauspicious and impolite. So he dropped the flowers that his left hand held. Still Buddha said, "Drop it!" This time he dropped all the flowers and stood empty handed before Buddha, who once again said with a smile, "Drop it!" Perplexed, the man asked, "What is it I am supposed to drop?" "Not the flowers, son, but the one who brought them," was Buddha's reply. Thus, Buddha was calling all devotees to come before God poor in spirit, divorced from oneself, and not to come like the proud Pharisee of the Gospel, who stood before God as an "I" specialist, singing his own praises, off key, of course!

The Pharisee was telling God about the all good things he was doing for him, "praying, fasting, tithing, keeping laws" (Lk 18:12). He was almost demanding God to admire and approve of him. Through this Pharisee, Jesus is warning us against self-righteousness, the devil's masterpiece which has become the family disease of all the children of Adam, clinging to us as skin clings to the body. He is warning us against the self-opinionated attitudes of an egoist, whose self-importance makes his mind shrink while his head swells. He is warning us of conceit, which is not the same as self-confidence, for confidence is keeping your chin up, whereas conceit is sticking your neck out. In short, Jesus is warning us against every form of pride. Oh, how grateful I am to that teacher who gave me her parting advice on my leaving school: "Be not proud of race, face, place or grace!" In fact, pride and grace dwelt never together in one place, for pride dines on vanity and sups on contempt.

The proud place themselves at a distance from others and seen through that distance, others perhaps appear little to them, even contemptible, as the tax-collector appeared to the Pharisee. "O God," he prayed, "I thank you that I am not like the rest of men or even like this tax-collector" (Lk 18:11). How morally contemptuous his words are! Moral contempt is far greater indignity and insult than any kind of crime. We can feel good about our virtues and gifts, but genuine self-esteem is ruined by arrogant self-righteousness that judges others. I once saw a poster of a powerful tawny bearded lion with a caption reading: "It is so difficult to be humble". And yet, it is "the prayer of the humble that pierces the cloud and does not rest till it reaches its goal" (Sir 35:17); because only the humble can fully appreciate the grace of God.

If pride and madness go together, so do humility and sanity. A worried looking fellow walks into the psychiatrist's office, smoking pot and wearing love-beads, bell-bottom trousers frayed at the ends, and shoulder-length hair. The psychiatrist says: "You claim you are not a hippie. Then, how do you explain the clothes, the hair, the pot?" "That's what I'm here to find out, doctor". Sanity is being true to oneself and in our case, it means being humble, praying to God, "O God, be merciful to me, a sinner" (Lk 18:13). Have we not all sinned, as the members of the spoiled race? Sin has made us all mad as well as bad; Yes. Our self is crucified but it is long at dying. We must never forget that God is closest to those whose hearts are broken and he will answer only the prayer of the humble, who alone can declare with St Paul, "The Lord stood by my side and gave me strength" (2 Tim 4:17). So we are offered a choice between being humble and being humbled.

31ST SUNDAY OF THE YEAR

"HURRY DOWN "

Readings: Wis 11:22-12:1; 2 Thess 1:11-2:2; Lk 19:1-10

Theme: Though we are sinners we are still basically good and hence Jesus keeps knocking on the door of our heart, expecting us to open it to him, so that he can reveal the goodness in it and also help it to blossom.

There is a famous painting by Holman Hunt entitled, "The Light of the World." It shows Jesus lamp in hand knocking gently on a door, signifying that he knocks on every human heart. But the door has no handle for, as the artist explained, Christ can only knock; it is for the person inside to let him in; and so the door-handle is on the inside. When Jesus said, "Zacchaeus, hurry down, I must stay at your house today" (Lk 19:5), Jesus was knocking on the door of Zacchaeus' heart and he opened. There are three times Jesus knocks at the door of our hearts in a special way. He knocks, when the Scriptures are read and explained at mass, for he said, "he who listens to you, listens to me"; he knocks in the liturgy of the Eucharist, for he said, "Whoever eats my flesh and drinks my blood, remains in me and I in him"; he knocks whenever we encounter needy people, for he said that whoever helps one of these, helps him. Do we open our hearts when Jesus knocks?

Why does Jesus seek us out, knowing we are sinners? Because each of us is basically still good, good enough to let God come in. When Jesus sought after Zacchaeus, people said, "Does not Jesus know that the food on Zacchaeus table is stolen from our tables? Does not he know that the drinks in his cellar are, so to speak, our sweat and blood? Yes. Jesus knew all that; but he also knew that the goodness God our Creator had placed in Zacchaeus was still there, which no one can take away. "Oh God, you love all that exists; you hate nothing of what you have created, because if you had hated it, you would not have created it" (Wis 11:24). It is this goodness that will last, as long as our human life lasts; it is this goodness that Jesus wants to provoke, call up, and stimulate in us. Even when we feel that we are completely lost, we have to remember that the lost key is still there, but we don't know where; a lost identity-card is still there, but we don't know where; some lost money is still there, but we don't know where. Jesus came to find it for us and to reveal the goodness in us.

Jesus enters into a human heart not only to reveal the goodness in it, but also to help it to blossom so that, "God may make you worthy of his call and fulfil by his power every honest intention and work of faith" (2 Thess 1:11). At times, the touch of Jesus will be so revealing and healing that you can sing only in the words of the poet Emily Dickinson: "We never know how high we are, till we are called to rise; and then, if we are true to plan, our statures touch the sky". Shall we then readily respond to Jesus' knock, when the word of the Lord is broken and read to us; when the body of the Lord is broken and given to us; and when a member of the family of the Lord is broken and comes to us for help?

For Jesus to make any real impact on our life when he enters into our hearts, we have to respond the way Zacchaeus did: we have to face our sinfulness and start changing our ways. How can Jesus justify us, if we won't repent and reform? We have to be willing to let go of certain things to follow the Lord; how can Jesus find a place in our heart, if it is full of love of money, pleasure and power? We have to realise that without Jesus, we could be lost; how can we stand our ground except by the grace of God? We must have faith to see Jesus in our midst; how can we expect to recognise Jesus in the breaking of the Word, the Bread and in the broken heart, unless we have faith? When Jesus called Zacchaeus, "he quickly descended and welcomed him with delight". How eager are we to respond to Jesus, if he wants to stay at our house today?

ALL SAINTS – NOVEMBER 1

ALL ARE CALLED

Readings: Rev 7:2-4, 9-14; 1 Jn 3:1-3; Mt 5:1-12

Theme: The feast of All Saints not only glorifies the canonised saints who were special models of radical discipleship to Christ, but also those countless uncanniness saints who successfully lived a good Christian life on earth, and calls all of us to live by the norms of the beatitudes, though difficult but not impossible, so that we too one day may be saints in heaven.

Devotion to saints is sometimes misunderstood and hence becomes a hindrance rather than help. We should guard against turning the saints into mere objects of cult or using them simply as means of obtaining favours. Of course, the saints can win favours for us but they should first serve as models for us in following Christ. Today we celebrate the feast of All Saints. Saints have played a central role in the growth of the Christian faith. They were people who dared to live the life of a Christian. We honour them today, who in the words of Revelation, "stand before the throne and the Lamb, dressed in long white robes and hold palm branches in their hands" (Rev 7:9). We join Jesus in the

Gospel and call them 'blessed', because in their own way they were poor in spirit, hungered and thirsted for what was right, showed mercy to others and were peace makers.

Strictly speaking today's feast is the feast of the canonised saints. They gave up every material possession and yet they said that they possessed all; they bound themselves by a vow of obedience to God and to his Church and yet they shouted in joy, 'Free at last, Free at last'. They were put under excruciating tortures and yet they sang 'Alleluia'. They were put among the deadliest enemies and yet they hugged them and embraced them. For you and me, cross is to be avoided for it is a punishment, but for them cross is to be embraced for it is a blessing; for you and me, painful experiences teach what one cannot do, but for them, they teach what one can do; for you and me, death is a sunset, but for them death is sun rise; for us the self is first, but for them the self is last; for us, neighbour is the opposite of self, but for them the neighbour is the extension of self; for us God is a giver, but for them God is a lover. Therefore, they were special models of radical discipleship to Jesus Christ.

But there are also countless number of uncanniness saints in heaven. Who are they? They were men and women of flesh and blood like any one of us. They had the same weaknesses and faults and failings as we have and yet they never forgot God and never gave up trying to live a decent Christian life. They went through the turmoils, ups and downs of life as we do, and yet they died in peace with God and went to heaven. Today we venerate them too, as saints of God. This means that many Christians living today a good Christian life will be one day saints in heaven. Why not? Christ did not die just for St Paul, or St Augustine or St Francis. He died also for Mr Murphy and Mr John; he died also for Miss Mary and the little boy Jonathan. Christ died to save all humanity.

All of us could one day be saints in heaven, if only we decide to live by the norms of the Beatitudes that Jesus proclaims in today's Gospel (Mt 5:3-11). Eight beatitudes are eight keys to unlock the treasures of Christian happiness. They are the resume of the Christian character. They are the boundaries within which the Christian life is successfully lived. They are the foundations on which to build our life of faith. They are invitations from God our Father to the destiny of peace and joy.

Therefore, those of us who can now humbly say, 'I need God's help and my community's help', can one day be saints, because Jesus said,

"Blessed are the poor in spirit". Those of us who can say now, 'I am really hurt, but I still love', can one day be saints, because Jesus said, "Blessed are those who mourn". Those of us who can say now, 'I am upset but I am going to remain cool, calm and corrected', can one day be saints, because Jesus said, "Blessed are the meek." If we say now, 'I really want to do the right thing', we can one day be saints, because Jesus said, "Blessed are those who hunger for righteousness". If we can say now, 'I am going to treat others the way I want others to treat me', we can one day be saints, because Jesus said, "Blessed are the merciful". If we can say now, 'I am going to be a bridge-builder for peace', we can one day be saints, because Jesus said, "Blessed are the peace makers".

But let us not forget this: to become saints, though possible for every one, is not going to be easy; to become the citizens of heaven, though it is our right, is an uphill task. The road to heaven is narrow; the journey on this road is tiresome and the Christian life is strewn with crosses. However, this should not discourage us. Hear what St John says: "See what love the Father has given us, that we should be called children of God" (1 Jn 3:1). Yes. The Father has already placed us more than half way on the road to heaven, by making us his adopted children through our rebirth in Jesus Christ.

32ND SUNDAY OF THE YEAR

OVERCOMING DEATH

Readings: 2 Mac 7:1-2, 9-14; 2 Thess 2:16-3:5; Lk 20:27-38

Theme: When we allow ourselves to be loved by God unconditionally as Jesus did, accepting all of its implications, our belief in life after death grows, strong enough to carry us through our mortal life and deep enough to give us the experience of victory over death here and now.

All have a strong appetite for heaven. Every human heart thirsts for eternal life. The very thirst for eternity is an added proof for the existence of eternal life. However the ancients, who also longed to live for ever, were not sure about what happens the day after death. Therefore, they arranged for a life lasting as long as they can be remembered after their death by those left by them, children for example. For the same reason, some built enormous monuments like the pyramids in Egypt to be remembered for ever after. If the ancients did that, some moderns are no better. Have you seen the film *The Day After*, intended primarily to provoke serious discussion about nuclear disarmament? But it went further, raising the ultimate question: what happens to human bodies the day after they are vaporised and atomised by nuclear explosion? The film left the question hanging in the air.

But Christians have strong faith in life after death. In fact, eternal life to a Christian does not begin with death, it begins with this faith. This is why no one ever repents of being a Christian on their deathbed. As one of the strongest Old Testament witnesses to resurrection after death, we hear the sons of a Jewish mother, telling their persecutors, "The King of the world will raise us up to live again for ever" (2 Mac 7:9). We hear St Paul blessing the Thessalonians saying, "May God our Father who in his mercy gave us eternal consolation and hope, console your hearts" (2 Thess 2:16-17). We hear Jesus quoting those very scriptures which the Jewish group which challenged him used as an argument to deny any life after death, to affirm that "the dead do rise to life" (Lk 20:35). Therefore to us believers death is God's delightful way of giving life.

Is our faith in life after death deep enough to sustain us in our sufferings, and strong enough to carry us through our pilgrim life on earth? One wonders whether some of us are like Napoleon who said, "I die before my time; and my body will be given back to earth, to become the food for worms. Such is the fate which soon awaits the great Napoleon". What a contrast are these words to those of Job: "I know that my Redeemer lives and though after my skin worms destroy my body, yet in my flesh I shall see God" (Job 19:25-26). If Job who lived before Christ could say that, we who live after Christ should not only be able just to say it with our lips, but really to mean every word of it and live by it. To a Christian who is rooted in this belief, the best moment of his Christian life would obviously be the last one, because it is the one that is nearest to heaven. Of course, we do not know much about heaven, except that it is for ever, and that nobody there is ever bored, for in heaven God will never hide his face and Satan will never show his.

However, in order to overcome death and enter into eternal life, we must do what Jesus did, not what some heroes of myths did; they seem to have overcome death, by hitting on the mysteries of life, by brewing an eternal-life drug, by eating from the old tree of life, by swallowing a pearl or by taking a miraculous bath. Jesus overcame death not by such means; he overcame death by letting himself be loved by God unconditionally. This is what we too are called to do. We need to allow "the Lord to rule our hearts in the love of God" (2 Thess 3:5), so that daily we live a life of loving and being loved. Such a life calls for accepting our earthly life as a gift to be used every day and making it blessed by living it well; it calls for accepting all the joys and sorrows of life without ever being discouraged; it calls for working daily to build God's Kingdom of justice and peace, demonstrating thereby our appreciation of the temporal order. All this means that as long as we are alive, today is the only day that matters.

33RD SUNDAY OF THE YEAR

THE BIG QUESTION

Readings: Mal 3:19-20; 2 Thess 3:7-12; Lk 21:5-19

Theme: The one big question we Christians need to keep asking ourselves is not when or how the world will end, but how well are we prepared to face the end of our journey.

The newspaper the *Independent* in one of its weekly columns in November 1995, reported that the leaders of million Jehovah's Witnesses had postponed the end of the world until further notice and they had also announced that they would no longer attempt to predict when the end would come, following a series of miscalculations. One of the most important questions that frighten people today is when and how the end will come. With the countdown towards the millennium year 2000, the epidemic of speculation is bound to grow. This interest in knowing about the end of the world is as old as Christianity. When Jesus spoke about the destruction of the Temple, his contemporaries thought that he was referring to the end of the world and so they asked, "When will this happen" (Lk 21:7)? When Jesus spoke of the trials and tribulations prior to the destruction, his listeners thought that at the end of the world the sky would fall, the sun would burst, the moon would disintegrate, plunging the world into a total overhaul. But was this the big question that Jesus was concerned about, as he spoke about the fall of the Temple and which we Christians should be worrying about today? Not really.

Surely, the end of the world will come, but it is yet far, because Jesus warned us, "not to be misled," by those who would say, "the time is near" (Lk 21;8). This means that he was rather urging us to be well prepared for the end, by engaging ourselves in the tasks of the present which are challenging enough to demand our full attention. Surely the Day of Judgement will come; but he said we are "not to be perturbed" (v.9), which means that the Day of judgement should rather serve as a motive to turn back to God and to assess everything that happens to us now in the light of eternity. Surely there would be wars, famines and earthquakes, but they are not to be read as the end of time for, he added, "the end does not follow immediately" (v.9), which means that he was actually asking us to be well prepared for the end by facing courageously our long Christian journey, with all its trials and conflicts, resistance and opposition, sufferings and ordeals, always trusting that the loving God "will not allow even a hair of your head to be harmed" (v.18). Hence the Big Question is how well are we prepared for the end time?

We will be well prepared if we try everyday to live our Christian life well and full; if we do our best to build that part of the Kingdom which God expects from us in the here and now, a Kingdom of peace and justice; if we daily water the seed of love that Jesus has already planted; if we pass on to others the light of faith that he has already lit; if we act as yeast that Jesus has already put in the dough, in order to ferment the world with Gospel values; and if we serve the world as its salt which he called us to be, to preserve the world from every corruption. All this means that we can't sit down doing nothing, just waiting for the end time. It means that we need to keep ourselves always "busy", though not acting as busybodies, "working day and night even to the point of exhaustion" (2 Thess 3:8), in order to hasten the coming of God's Kingdom.

But such an active waiting for the end, calls for patient endurance, because not only problems and pains are part of our everyday life, but we who walk with Christ must also be ready even to lose our life. However, every Christian is convinced that "by patient endurance he will save his life" (Lk 21:19), that by holding on to faith, even when trials arrive blazing like an oven fire, he or she will see "the sun of justice arise for him with its healing rays" (Mal 3:20), that by holding on to hope, though we be crushed by the gigantic forces of evil, we will triumph over them to rise with Christ, and that by holding on to love, at every crisis which we may confront in our life, we will come through our ordeals even stronger in spirit than ever before. This is the Christian programme of preparation to face the end time. Hence the big question is: how well are we prepared to face the end of our journey?

34TH SUNDAY OF THE YEAR – (CHRIST THE KING)

A DIFFERENT KING

Readings: 2 Sam 5:1-3; Col 1:12-20; Lk 23:35-43

Theme: Christ is real King because he is the image of the invisible God, but he is a different King for he died for us on the cross; and so he will be King of our lives, if there is a resemblance in us to what he is and what he did.

Kings and kingships belong to the past, and if they still exist, you can find them in history books. Thank God, we live in democratic times. Why, then, we still keep on celebrating the kingship of Christ? Does it mean that we are longing to get back to monarchy? Not in the least. We call Christ 'King' in a different sense and hence he may not like titles such as 'Jesus Christ Superstar'! This does not mean that Christ is no real King or he is only an ornamental figurehead of the Christian people. If he were not a real King, when he commanded the devils, they would not have obeyed him; when he commanded the dead Lazarus, he would not have come back to life; when he commanded the wind and the sea, they would not have calmed down. Christ is real King but a different one. That is the strangeness of his kingship, which becomes obvious in today's liturgy where, instead of celebrating some glorious enthronement, we read about a man on the cross.

Jesus Christ is real King, first, because of who he is. He is not just "the king of the Jews" (Lk 23:38), but he is the King of Kings, because he has in him all that is best in creation. Gold is called the king of metals, since it is popularly thought to be the most precious of all metals; lion is called the king of the forest, for he is thought to be the noblest of animals. Similarly, Jesus is the King of the human race, since he is the best and noblest human being who ever lived, "the image of the invisible God, the first-born of all creation, in whom everything in heaven and on earth were created through him and for him" (Col 1:15-16). How right Arnold Toynbee was to finish his monumental work on the history of the world with these words: "When we began this work, we found ourselves looking at a great parade of marchers. But as it passed, the marchers all fell, one by one, by the wayside. And now, only one marcher remains, growing larger and larger with each step" And that one marcher is Jesus Christ.

Jesus Christ is a real but a different King, also because of what he did. Some years ago, divers located a 400-year-old sunken ship off the coast of Northern Ireland. Among the treasures they found on the ship was a man's wedding ring, on which was engraved a hand holding a heart with the inscription: "I have nothing more to give you". Of all the treasures found on the sunken ship, none moved the divers more than that ring and its beautiful inscription. The engraving on that ring and its inscription could have been placed on the cross of Christ, for he gave us everything he had when he died on it, by which, "we have redemption and forgiveness of sins" (Col 1:14). Jesus as King is not out to dominate, but to love; not out to rule, but to serve; not out to order, but to seek out the lost ones such as the repentant thief on the cross, assuring him "today you will be with me in paradise" (Lk 23:43). Hence, like the tribes-people who gathered at Hebron of old to acclaim David as their king (2 Sam 5:1-4), so we too can now ask Jesus to be the Lord and King of our lives.

Christ will be King of our lives if he finds in us and in our actions some resemblance to what he is and what he does. Do we love others as he loves us? God has poured his love into us from the cross of Christ, and why should we freeze it? Our heart may be like a cup which can't hold much, but it can overflow a lot. Do we serve others as he serves us? Love rolls up its sleeves to give, for you can't love without giving. Those who are willing to sit at God's table have also to be willing to work in his field. It is unthinkable that the followers of such a King, who was so passionate in the service of others, should spend all their lives in the service of their own passions! Do we forgive others as our King forgives? Forgiveness warms the heart and cools the sting as well. If we are strong in love, we can forgive. Only the weak cannot forgive, because forgiveness is the attribute of the strong.

HOMILIES for FEASTS and SPECIAL OCCASIONS

HOMILIES FOR SPECIAL FEASTS

CHRISTMAS MIDNIGHT

JOY TO THE WORLD

Readings: Is 9:1-6; Tit 2:11-14; Lk 2:1-14

Theme: The joy we experience tonight at the Word made flesh, the light and love of God made visible, is the joy only Christ can give, energising us to care for those who suffer in the world by sharing the light and love of Christ with him.

The most meaningful Christmas sermon ever heard was not preached by any of the early Fathers of the Church such as St John Chrysostom or by Bishop Fulton Sheen, Norman Vincent Peale, Billy Graham, nor by any pope or saint. It was not spoken by any human. It was delivered in song by an anonymous choir of celebrating angels. We find their melodious words in Luke's Gospel: "Glory to God. I come to proclaim Good News to you – tidings of great joy to be shared by the whole people" (Lk 2:10). That message of joy from heaven delivered on the night of Christ's birth is echoed at Christmas celebrations everywhere: the glitter of festive atmosphere and the decorative lights of the Christmas trees, the exchange of gifts as an expression of goodwill and friendship, the greetings that wish other people happiness, the prayers that express longing for peace, the treasured texts that tell of a light that shines for the human race, all help to revitalise the Christmas message of joy.

We rejoice, because on this night, "the Word was made flesh" (Jn 1:14). It is that Word which is a lamp unto our feet and a light unto our path and if we take it out of our homes, the last glimmer of hope is gone. We rejoice because on this night, "the goodness and love of God appeared" (Tit 3: 4) on earth. It is that goodness of God which is equal only to his greatness and it is that love of God which is more delightful to us than all our earthly enjoyments. We rejoice, because on this night, "the light and glory of God" was made visible (Heb 1: 3) on earth in Jesus. It is that light for which restless millions waited, whose dawn made all things new and it is that glory of God which swallows up all the shining achievements of men and women as the brightness of the sun swallows up the light of the moon. We rejoice, because on this night, "the grace of God appeared offering salvation to all" (Tit 2: 11). It is that grace of God without which nothing can be done aright. It is that grace which comes into the soul as the morning sun into the world. It is that grace which cares and stoops and rescues.

The joy we experience tonight is the joy only Christ can give. This is what Isaiah foretold: "You have brought them abundant joy and great rejoicing" (Is 9:3). Without Jesus, it is hard to sing "Joy to the world" even at Christmas, because without Jesus our world is lifeless. The joy which Jesus gives is not the false joy such as we can find in disco clubs or bars, in gambling casinos or rock concerts. It is not the empty joy one may find in X-rated cinemas of self-gratification; It is not the fleeting joy that one can get, when one has a good bank account, a good cook and a good digestion. The joy of Christ is deep, lasting and fulfilling. It is a genuine joy that will sustain us long after our Christmas guests have departed, our Christmas gifts are forgotten and our Christmas cards are burned, because joy in Christ is the joy of salvation. Because it is the joy of salvation, it is an experience of peace and harmony and truth and goodness. It is the kind of experience that we have by a walk in autumn rain, when all of a sudden there is freshness present in the world. Because it is the joy of salvation, there is nothing in affliction which can disturb it. Those who possess this joy, can live in love among those who hate, and live in health among those who are sick.

In the midst of our joyful celebrations, however, we cannot forget either the harshness of the circumstances into which Jesus was born, or the painful and tragic experiences of our own world at this time. What shall we do then? Shall we join the cynics in the world and complain that all our joyful celebration today is mere flight from harsh reality into warm fantasy? No. Rather, we accept the challenge which the birth of our Saviour poses to us, namely, we will resolve to continue his work by making our contribution to the task of healing brokenness, by fostering peace and harmony in human relationships, by offering forgiveness to our offenders, tolerance to our opponents and by bringing a little light and joy into the darkness, confusion and sadness of the world we know.

THE PRESENTATION OF THE LORD

ON WINGS OF PROMISE

Readings: Mal 3:1-4; Heb 2:14-18; Lk 2:22-40

Theme: A Christian who believes in the promises of God will wait patiently and courageously for their fulfilment in God's own good time and live joyfully his daily life on the wings of his promise.

Our life is a long string of expectations. But unfortunately, many of our expectations leave us only disillusioned. Often they are like flowers which fade away leaving no trace; even if few of them yield some fruit, the fruit itself rarely ripens. For example, during the Advent-Christmas season, we were filled with wonderful promises of God about light, hope and peace through Jesus Christ. Yet now in the winter days of January and February, after the Christmas lights and decorations have been taken down and the festal atmosphere has died away, we are tempted to think that the promises of God proclaimed anew at Christmas for a light greater than darkness, for a peace stronger than struggles and for a hope that dispels despair, remain largely unfulfilled in our individual and group lives. Should we then live the rest of our lives as disappointed Christians who have resigned themselves to the ordeal of life? Not really.

God promised at the birth of Christ that men of goodwill shall have peace and that those who live their lives according to his holy will, shall receive salvation in Christ. God will never go back on his promises. His promises are virtually obligations that he imposes on himself. He never made a promise that was too good to be true. For example, God made a promise to Israel that "The Lord you are seeking will suddenly enter his temple and who will be able to resist the day of his coming?" (Mal 3:1) Simeon and Anna waited long years for fulfilment of that promise and their waiting was not in vain. In today's feast of the Presentation we recall how Mary and Joseph came into the temple carrying God in the shape of a helpless child to be "presented in the temple" and how Simeon taking the child in his arms blessed God saying, "Now, Master, you can let your servant go in peace, just as you promised, because my eyes have seen the salvation" (Lk 2:29-30). During those years of waiting, how often Simeon and Anna must have

been tempted to think that things would never change and to despair that God's promises would never come true! But they never yielded to that kind of temptation.

We too like Simeon and Anna wait for the fulfilment of the promises God made at the birth of his Son. He has promised that through Jesus he will free us from sin (Heb 2:15). People hunger for freedom of all sorts such as political and economic freedom. The pity is that with all such freedoms they cannot become even as free as a fish! For true freedom is freedom from sin; for once the freedom from sin has exploded in the soul of every human being who is freed from all miseries including death. God has promised that in Christ we can have salvation (Lk 2:30), a salvation that leads us from living death to deathless life. He has promised his salvation, of course, only to those who take Christ not only as their Saviour but also as Lord of their lives, for salvation is not a cafeteria where you can take whatever you want and leave the rest. Above all God has promised that in Christ we will have 'light' (Lk 2:32). With that light shining in our souls, we need not, like blind men, stumble against one another creating war; with that light, we need not walk in the shadows of fears and uncertainties, for it will be a revealing light that will show things up as disguises and concealments are stripped away, so that we can clearly see what God wants from us.

God will choose his own time to make his promises come true in our lives. We should wait patiently for their fulfilment. Our waiting period may be arduous, even hazardous, as one feels when climbing a mountain. We might feel even crying out like the Psalmist: "Who shall ascend the mountain of the Lord? Who shall stand in his holy place?" (Ps 24:3). And yet, we can't afford to give up our waiting. We do not know why God should make us wait so long for the light of Christ to shine on us. But this much we know: the Almighty does nothing without reason, though our frail human mind cannot explain the reason. God is at work in the world in ways far beyond our power to comprehend. Hence we are not taking any risks when we step out on the promise of God. May the good Lord fill us with deep faith so that we can daily live a joyful Christian life on the wings of his promises.

THE ANNUNCIATION

FULL OF GRACE!

Readings: Is 7:10-14; 8:10 ; Heb 10:4-10; Lk 1:26-38

Theme: God filled his mother, Mary, with his grace because she had emptied herself in order to do whatever he wanted of her, and He will give us a share in the same grace, if we, too, do what she did.

A college student meditated on the Annunciation scene and she wrote about Mary as follows: "Today I saw a water lily growing in a pond. It had the freshest yellow colour I'd ever seen. The lily – a precious treasure was unconcerned about whether anyone noticed its astounding beauty. As I sat there watching it unfold its petals noiselessly, I thought of Mary pregnant with Jesus. She, too, was a precious treasure. She, too, was unconcerned about whether anyone noticed her astounding beauty. But to those who did, she shared a secret. Her beauty came not from herself but from Jesus' life within her, unfolding its petals noiselessly".

It is in order that Mary may conceive his Son that God made her "full of grace" (Lk 1:28). The grace that filled her was that grace, without which men who fall by sin cannot rise up by themselves; it was that grace, which moved St Paul to claim, "I am what I am by the grace of God" (1 Cor 15:10). It was that grace, which finds us beggars but leave us debtors; it was that grace which is a certain beginning of glory in us. And God filled Mary with that grace. The angel does not call her by her proper name 'Miriam', but 'full of grace', thus identifying her with grace itself. In this fullness of grace, she has surpassed all other creatures: because God's giving of himself in some way to all creatures and directly to human beings, reached one of its high points in incarnation. Because of this fullness of grace she gave life as a mother to him from whom she herself received life. The liturgy calls her 'the mother of her creatures'. Dante calls her 'daughter of your Son'.

But Mary had to do certain things in order to be filled with God's grace and become the Mother of his Son. First, Mary had to empty herself completely in order to be filled with grace, and she did. In order to receive the piper's breath and to utter the song that is in his

heart, a reed has to become hollow within. Mary, too, became a reed with a hollow so that through her the eternal love could be piped as a shepherd's song. She became a chalice so that into her the purest water of humanity could be poured, mingled with wine, changed to the crimson blood of love and lifted up in sacrifice. Second, Mary had to make a free choice to obey God's will, that will which wanted her to become the Mother of God, and she did. She had no idea of what kind of haphazard public life her Saviour son would lead; she was asked to make a decision along the line that God proposed which would consume every moment of her life thereafter in ways that she could not imagine. Yet she decided to do God's will saying, "Let it be done to me according to your will". (Lk 1:38), because she always believed that those who take risks in doing God's will will not be disappointed, but will always win favour with God. Her own son Jesus came to this world saying to God his Father, "I have come to do your will" (Heb 10:7) and, like him, she preferred to do only God's will and thus became the first perfect disciple of Christ.

Like Mary our Mother, we too need God's grace to reflect Christ's likeness in us and offer him to the world. We cannot expect God to fill us with his grace as he did to Mary, but we need a share in her grace, for with his grace we are turned into men and women with a strong family likeness to Jesus and without which the human mind itself becomes a nest of wickedness swarming with thoughts of evil. But in order to deserve this grace of God we, like Mary, have to empty ourselves like a reed pipe so that God can live lyrically through us or like hollow in a chalice, so that God can continue Christ's sacrifices through us for the sake of the world. We have to empty ourselves of all the trivialities of this earthly life to fill ourselves with God. If we do not create such a purposeful emptiness within ourselves, we will be driven into the purposeless emptiness of which so many people today complain.

In order to have a share in Mary's grace we, like her, need also to decide to choose God's will at every step we take in our lives. When we take a decision according to God's will, we can't see the future nor the risk involved in taking such a decision. But like Mary we must believe that all will be well for those who do God's will. Speaking by the means of his prophet Isaiah God promised to save his people from physical destruction through a son born to Ahaz and he fulfilled his promise. He promised to save his people from spiritual destruction through a son born through Mary (Is 7:14) and he fulfilled that prom-

ise. So, too, he has promised blessings to all those who do his will. We must trust in his promise and choose to do his holy will and plunge fearlessly like Mary into the implications of that choice.

HOLY THURSDAY

MAN FOR OTHERS

Readings: Ex 12:1-8, 11-14; 1 Cor 11:23-26; Jn 13:1-15

Theme: Jesus who came to deliver us from the slavery of selfishness, not only gave us an example of how to serve others but keeps challenging us to serve, by his continued giving of himself in the Eucharist.

An eighty-five-year-old woman was being interviewed on her birthday. What advice would she have for people of her age, the reporter asked. "Well," said the old dear, "at our age it is very important to keep using all our potential or it dries up. It is important to be with people and, if it is at all possible, to earn one's living through service. That is what keeps us alive and well." "May I ask what exactly you do for a living at your age?" "I look after an old lady in my neighbourhood", was her unexpected reply. What she said echoes what Winston Churchill once said: "We make a living by what we get and we make a life by what we give". The old lady had learnt the greatest of all arts, the art of being a person for others.

Service is the message of Holy Thursday, a message which resounds so strongly in today's liturgy that even those who are normally stone-deaf to the voice of God should be able to hear it. At his Last Supper, Jesus not only served at table but did a dirtier and more unpleasant job: he washed the dust and dirt of the road off the feet of his apostles, a task which, in those days, was done by a slave or a servant to a guest who entered the house. In doing so, he gave a shocking and shining example to his apostles as well as to us all on how to be servant of all. After having given the example, he also commanded us to imitate him saying: "Do you know what I did for you? If I your 'Teacher' and 'Lord' washed your feet, then you must wash each other's feet" (Jn 13:14). And yet, it is sad to see a good many of the followers of Christ, who was passionate in the service of others, spending their lives in the service of their own passions.

Selfishness is a kind of slavery and it is the most common form of slavery. It grows anywhere like a weed in every soil. Selfishness is also the most cruel form of slavery. Selfish persons are incapable of loving others – which is obvious – but the cruelty of it is that they are incapable of loving themselves either. Self-love is the greatest of all flatterers, for it draws a thick veil between us and our faults. Human history itself is the sad result of each one looking out for himself. Jesus was aware of this pernicious slavery and so wanted to deliver us from it into the freedom of loving and serving others. Jesus knew that the service which counts is the service that costs and therefore he instituted the Holy Eucharist in which he provides the spiritual food of his Body and Blood, to sustain those who unselfishly serve their fellow human beings. He also wanted this spiritual food to be available in the Church till the end of time and hence he shared his ministerial priesthood with his apostles telling them, "do this in memory of me" (Lk 22:19). Since that time, the Eucharist remains as the indispensable spiritual food for all those who follow Christ in being men and women for others.

Holy Thursday challenges all of us, high and low, great and small to become persons for others as Jesus was Man for others, ready to serve others even if it is very menial such as the washing of others' feet. We are called to wash not only the feet of those we know or to whom we are related but also the feet of others such as the strangers, orphans, abandoned, homeless, refugees and all those who are struggling to live a decent human life. The Holy Mass in which we participate is not simply a ritual. It represents Jesus giving of himself for others. Therefore we celebrate the Mass properly only if we do so with the same attitude of self-giving in the service of others. If we really believe that we receive Christ in the Eucharist who was man for others, we must ourselves strive to become persons for others.

When Eileen M. Egan, the author of *Such a Vision of the Street: Mother Teresa* visited the Home for the Dying run by her in Calcutta, Mother Teresa said to Eileen, pointing out to the scores of men and women picked up from the streets, "We could not let them die like animals in the streets. We have brought them here so that they could die loved and cared for. Our work calls for us to see Jesus in every one. Jesus has told us that he is the hungry one, the naked one, the thirsty one. He is the one without a home. He is the one who is suffering. They are Jesus. Each one is Jesus in a distressing disguise". If we, too, learn to see Jesus in every fellow human being, especially in anyone who suffers, it will not be that difficult for us to serve them.

GOOD FRIDAY

PASSION

Readings: Is 52:13-53:12; Heb 4:14-16, 5:7-9; Jn 18:1-19:42

Theme: The great message of the passion of Jesus is to live passionately.

Only passions, great passions, can elevate a human soul to great things. The soul of Dr Martin Luther King was such a one. The freedom of the blacks in America became so great a passion with him that he died for their freedom. In the famous sermon he preached before he was assassinated, he declared: "I have been to the Mountain top. I have seen the Promised Land; I am not afraid to die; I am ready to meet my maker". He preached this sermon in the evening and was killed the next day. One would think that he preached this sermon because he had some sort of premonition of his imminent death. But it was not the case. His colleague Andrew Young said later that Dr King preached the same sermon probably a hundred times throughout the country and added, '"the reason that he could preach that sermon so often was that he was always ready to die". He was so convinced of the rightness of what he was doing for the Blacks that he was not afraid to die for the cause. He found something worth dying for. And so he lived passionately and fearlessly.

Yes. Nothing in the world has been accomplished without passion. It was true of our Lord Jesus Christ. He had one passion in his life, he had one cause to live for and that was to save us from our sins and to reconcile us with God. What he lived for was not to save societies or states in general but to save each of one us. It was to save us that he bore our sins on himself. If this is not the Gospel, then we have no Gospel to preach. Because Jesus was fired with this one passion, he lived fearlessly and embraced even death heroically. And what a death he had to endure as a price for his passion! It was death by crucifixion.

Martin Hengel writing in his book *The Crucifixion* says this about the cruelty of the Roman method of execution: "Punished with limbs outstretched, they see the stake as their fate; they are fastened and nailed to it in the bitter torment and evil food for birds of prey and grim pickings for dogs". While suffering his passion and death for his passionate mission, Jesus suffered not only in his body but also in his soul. He suffered in his soul dreadful torments of a person condemned to die. If Christ had not experienced excruciating suffering also in his soul, he would have been the Redeemer only of our body.

Therefore the great message of the passion of Jesus is that we, too, live our lives passionately. Whatever our God-given vocation in life is – whether we are married couples or celibates or parents, whether our life's duty or work is that of a teacher, doctor, nurse, student or social worker, whether our voluntary service for the cause of Christ is working for justice and peace or brotherhood – the passion of Jesus urges us to give ourselves to our present task passionately. Our mind is only our soul's eye, not its source of power. That power lies in our heart, that is, in our passions. When our particular vocation in life becomes a great passion, then it stirs our soul, it becomes at once awe-inspiring and irresistible, drawing us from our firesides, urging us to cast aside comfort and wealth and pursuit of pleasures and enabling us to carry life's daily crosses willingly, empowering us, if need be, even to lay down our precious life for the cause.

A Christian who accepts his God-given vocation in life with passion is truly a dedicated person, who is ready even to lay down his life as Christ did for his vocation. The daily prayer of such a dedicated Christian will not be much different from the prayer of St Ignatius Loyola, who prayed thus: "Lord, take as your right and receive as my gift all my freedom, my memory, my understanding and my will; Whatever I am and whatever I possess, you have given to me; I restore it all to you again, to be at your disposal, according to your will. Give me only a love for you and the gift of your grace; then I am rich enough and I ask for nothing more".

NEW BEGINNING

Readings: Gen 22:1-18; Ex 14:15-15:1; Rom 6:3-11; Mk 16:1-8

Theme: We, who celebrate the new beginning of Jesus raised to life after death and our own new beginning which we had at our baptism, are urged to offer a new beginning to those who are 'least' in society.

In his youth, St Augustine was a profligate. However, through the prayers of his sainted mother, Monica, he was converted and he became one of the great fathers of the Church. One day in his later life, he was walking through a part of town he had frequented in his younger days. A woman recognised him and called out to him: "Augustine! Augustine!" Augustine ignored the call, so the woman cried out again: "Augustine! Augustine! It is I!" But Augustine, turning neither to the right nor the left, kept walking straight ahead saying, "But, it is not I!" Yes, the old 'I' of Augustine had now died to sin. And the "chief character" in his life was now resurrected Christ, "the Christ within" into whose name he had been baptised and was thus given a new beginning in Christ.

The celebration of the death and the resurrection of our Lord Jesus Christ which we have tonight is about 'new beginning' all the way. The night setting of the liturgy, the darkness intimating chaos or death, the light suggesting order and life, all are symbolic of 'new beginning'. The baptism we celebrate in the Easter Vigil is the baptism of new Christians. The Old Testament as well as the New Testament readings suggest or emphasise new beginnings. Genesis tells us the story of the beginning of a new universe; Abraham receives his virtually dead son back to life. The Israelites cross the Red Sea from slavery to a new future. The Lord announces their return for a new beginning in a new Jerusalem. St Paul writing to the Romans describes the power of the Good News to create us anew and to give us a new life, urging us to lead a new moral and spiritual life. Finally, the Gospel presents the Good News of the new beginning of Jesus raised to life after death.

We had our own personal new beginning at our baptism, for at baptism we died with Christ and rose to life in him. At our baptism, we made the promise that we will continue to die and rise in Christ during our life on earth. It is this baptismal promise we renew at this Easter Vigil. This renewal of promise reminds us that at our baptism we were not made Christians once-and-for-all, rather that we made only a beginning to die to our selfishness and rise to live for God and for others. Therefore the process of death to self leading to life for God and others must go on daily in our life. Death to self should not frighten us. For selfishness is the greatest curse of the human race. That is why people in general fall in love with themselves at first sight and it is a passion to which they always remain faithful. And yet, people who are always with themselves become their own tormentors and whenever they look within themselves they are afraid, because selfishness has turned their heart as hard as an Easter egg so that they are no more capable of loving God and others. Hence we resolve to die to self daily, though little by little, and to rise to new life in Christ with renewed love.

We also resolve tonight to carry the Good News that death leads to life, to our brothers and sisters in the world. As the Lord told the first women who met him after his resurrection to 'go and tell' other disciples that he has risen from the dead, he tells us too. Therefore, we are not only recipients and beneficiaries of the Gospel but also the channels by which it is communicated. We tell others not only through words but through actions that they too can have a new beginning in their lives and they too can have deliverance from death. One such action could be to bring all those who are at the bottom of society to the top, that those who are the 'least' in society may become the 'first'. Those who are oppressed, disadvantaged, lowly and those who are last in society because of their colour, race, nationality and ethnic origin could be the people to whom we strive to give an opportunity to rise from their 'death', to rise to the top from the bottom so that they can experience for themselves life coming out of death and have their own new beginning in the risen Lord.

THE SACRED HEART

A GREAT HEART

Readings: Hos 11:1, 3-4, 8-9; 1 Jn 4:7-16; Mt 11:25-30

Theme: Today's celebration of God's love as found in the person of Jesus Christ, urges us to love one another as Christ has loved us.

We often say, "He puts his heart into his work", or '"She is a dear heart", or "I love you with all my heart". In all such usages, the word 'heart' means 'the person'. In particular, 'heart' stands for the 'love' of a person. So it is that people exchange Valentine Cards with 'hearts' on them, to indicate love. Cupid is still pictured as shooting his arrows of love into people's hearts. Heart represents not only the love of a person but also 'emotions' of that person. That is why our hearts beat more rapidly when we meet a long absent friend or a loved one. Thus 'heart' stands for everything we call the 'interior' of a person.

Therefore, our celebration of the feast of the Sacred Heart of Jesus is actually a celebration of God's love as found in the person of Jesus Christ. And we have some idea of God's great love for his people and of the equally great love of Christ for us. There is nothing we Christians could do to make God love us more or love us less, for God's love for us is infinite and unconditional. In the passage, "I taught Ephraim to walk... I fostered them like one who raises an infant to his cheeks" (Hos 11:3-4), Hosea reveals God's love, portraying the relationship between God and Israel as that of father and son. St John, writing about the way God revealed his great love in our midst through Christ, says: "He sent his only Son to the world that we might have life through him" (1 Jn 4:9). We know only too well how Christ won for us by his death on the cross, a death which turned out to be so bloody that when "one of the soldiers thrust a lance into his side, immediately blood and water flowed out" (Jn 19:34). Our Lord Jesus Christ was a great lover. He was the most generous hearted person whoever lived. He never refused a request made by anyone. He went out of his way to cross racial and religious barriers. His heart compassed the whole world in its love.

The great and generous heart of Christ still loves in the same way all humanity and each person in it personally. Even today he calls us saying, "Come to me all you who labour and are overburdened and I will refresh you" (Mt 11:28). One day a mother, a woman of wonderful faith, received an official telegram which told her of the death of her eldest son. It was a terrible shock; she conquered her emotions, ran to the living-room, placed the telegram at the feet of the image of the Sacred Heart and then calmly called her little ones and the servants. She asked that the throne of the Sacred heart be adorned with unusual splendour. She herself helped to beautify the shrine with flowers and candles. Then she asked all to sing with her and she herself led the singing. After the singing they recited the creed and the act of consecration. It was only then, the mother took up the telegram and read it to his children. "Your brother", she said sobbing, "has gone to heaven to the arms of the King. His will be done. Long live his Sacred Heart. May his Kingdom come!" They wept, of course they did, but peacefully and on the heart of Jesus. This was not solely the grief of flesh and blood but a glorious and meritorious one. Our human heart often turns out to be like a ship on a stormy sea driven about by winds blowing from all the corners of heaven. In those moments, if we come to the Sacred Heart, he will give great comfort and strength to suffer the trials of this life lovingly with him.

On this feast day of the Sacred Heart, we express our gratitude to our Lord for the great love that he continues to show in so many ways. But if our gratitude is sincere, we have to promise him that we love one another as he has loved us. "Beloved, let us love one another", urges St John. "The man without love has known nothing of God for God is love" (1 Jn 4:7-8). Besides, if we don't love one another, we deeply sadden the heart of Christ. In order to convey this message, when the Sacred Heart appeared to St Margaret Mary, it was his heart that was crowned with thorns, not his head. Of course, to love is to be vulnerable; to love anything involves risk, for the heart of one who loves may even break. But we have to take this risk for the love of Christ. If we refuse to take this risk and won't give our heart to anyone, then we will have no other alternative except to wrap it carefully with hobbies, pets and little luxuries and lock it safe in the coffin of our selfishness. Hence, let us have a great heart with great love so that with St Augustine we may also be able to say, "To my fellow human beings, a great love; to my friends, a heart of loyalty; to my God, a heart of flame; to myself, a heart of steel".

ST PATRICK

THE BREASTPLATE

Readings: Jer 1:4-9; Acts 13:44-49; Lk 10:1-12

Theme: If we are filled with love for Christ as St Patrick was, we will be consumed as he was with a great missionary zeal to spread the Gospel of Christ in the way in which today's world needs to hear it.

The distinguishing mark of a Christian is his confidence in the love of Christ and the yielding of his total self to Christ in return. We celebrate today the feast of such a person, St Patrick. The famous Breastplate of St Patrick clearly reveals who he was: "Christ shield me this day: Christ with me, Christ before me, Christ behind me, Christ in me, Christ above me, Christ on my right, Christ on my left, Christ when I lie down, Christ when I rise".

St Patrick, the great apostle of Ireland, was the son of a Roman Decurion in Britain. When he was 16, some Irish raiders carried him off into captivity and he spent six years as a slave-shepherd. He escaped and made his way back to Britain and after studies for the priesthood, he returned twenty years later to Ireland in the official capacity of a missionary priest. When he was forty-three, he was consecrated Bishop and started with more vigour and zeal to evangelise his one-time captors. He faced innumerable hardships. A number of times he was thrown into prison with his companions and threatened with death but in the end his success was astounding. When he died at Sabhall in 461, he had established the Church in Ireland on a truly solid foundation.

St Patrick was consumed with holy zeal to spread the Gospel of Christ. His only one preoccupation was to carry the mission which Jesus entrusted to his twelve and the seventy-two, urging them to proclaim the coming of God's Kingdom, but warning them, too, to be ready to face hardships even death in the cause of the Gospel (Lk 10:3). In a sense, St Patrick was like Jeremiah. When Jeremiah was called by God to go on a mission, he at first hesitated because he was a stammerer, protested because he was frightened to face the tragic consequences of undertaking such a mission, though in the end with faith and courage he yielded (Jer 1:4-9). Similarly, St Patrick also knew captivity like Jeremiah and like him he too lacked eloquence and preparation but, full of faith, he persevered through every difficulty in accomplishing the mission God had entrusted to him. In another sense, St Patrick was like St Paul. The vivid experience St Paul had of the risen Christ on the way to Damascus led him to stress in his writings God's initiative in everything and the powerful force of the divine plan (Acts 13:46-49). Like St Paul, St Patrick too saw his mission to the Irish, as part of the universal all-embracing mission of the Church. And, like St Paul, he had to endure his share of opposition for his pioneering work.

The feast of St Patrick urges the whole Church to continue its mission of spreading the Gospel. We all know that this mission is entrusted primarily to the clergy but we often forget that the mission has to be part of the life of the laity, too, in the Church, whatever vocation they may have chosen in their lives. As the Vatican Decree on the apostolate of the Laity states: "The Lord renews his invitation to all the laity to come closer to him every day, recognising that what is his is also their own, to associate themselves with him in his saving mission. Once again, he sends them into every town and place so that they may show that they are co-workers in the various forms and modes of the one apostolate of the Church". Therefore, whoever we are in the Church, we all need to spread the Gospel and its values as Christ taught us.

The Gospel-value that needs to be emphasised at a particular time can change from age to age. There is one Gospel-value that needs special emphasis in our age and which is very dear to the heart of St Patrick. It is the value of the individual worth of every human being, because he or she is the child of God, redeemed by Christ. That is why Jesus prayed even for his persecutors. The boy Patrick, in those trying circumstances as a slave, felt intensely the presence of Christ in him. Thus as a slave he discovered and never forgot that each one, even a slave, is an individual cherished by God. That is why in his famous letter to Coroticus, his persecutor and whose deeds cried out for justice, he offers forgiveness and love because, as he says in that letter, no one is without individual value to Christ. Patrick while spreading the Gospel-value took upon himself the task of creating the awareness that each individual human being is loved by God in a unique way and hence must be respected, loved and treated with human dignity. We, too, as evangelisers of the modern world, where discrimination and dehumanisation of one another abound on the basis of race, colour, nationality and status in life, must work for the promotion of human dignity after the example of St Patrick.

Can we carry on this mission with the same zeal as that of St Patrick? Yes, we can, if our love for Christ is so deep that we are able to say what St Patrick said on his Breastplate: "Christ be beside me, Christ be before me, Christ be behind me, King of my heart. Christ be within me, Christ be below me, Christ be above me, never to part".

ST JOSEPH

"GO TO JOSEPH"

Readings: Gen 41:46-57; Col 3:14-15, 17, 23-24; Mt 1:16, 18-21, 24

Theme: We can go to St Joseph to imbibe his right attitude towards our daily work, to acquire his sense of justice towards God and neighbour, and to share his deep faith.

When hunger came to be felt throughout the land of Egypt and the people cried to Pharaoh for bread, Pharaoh directed all the Egyptians to 'go to Joseph' (Gen 41:55) and asked them to do whatever he told them. When the famine spread throughout the land, Joseph opened all the cities that had grain and rationed it to the Egyptians. This is how Joseph of the Old Testament saved the Egyptians. Today we celebrate the feast of Joseph of the New Testament, the husband of Mary and the foster father of Jesus. Great saints had deep devotion to St Joseph. St Teresa of Avila, among others, assigned special value to his intercession. As his cult grew rapidly, in 1817 Pope Pius IX proclaimed St Joseph the patron of the whole Church. Pope Pius XII often urged the faithful to go to St Joseph for their needs. Indeed, as the Egyptians of ancient times had to go to the Joseph of ancient days, so we too today confidently go to St Joseph of the Holy Family for our various material and spiritual needs.

We can go to St Joseph to imbibe his right attitude and motivation for our daily work. St Joseph was a 'carpenter' (Mk 6:3); He could have been a craftsman or artisan. But it did not matter to him, what work he did, for he believed in what St Paul later said: "whatever your work is, if you put your heart into it as if it were for the Lord" (Col 3:23), it gives glory to God. We learn from him that it is not only prayer that gives glory to God, but work of any kind, hammering on an anvil, preparing a beam, white-washing a wall, driving horses, reaping, scouring, everything gives God glory. St Joseph also teaches us to do our work, whether menial or glamorous, not solely for money but also for love of the society we live in. If you read the book *The Ultimate Seduction* by Charlotte Chandler, you will note two points that stick to your mind when you finish reading it. First, many famous people worked very hard and second, their motivation was not just money but to make the world a better place to live in. God himself did his work of creation out of love for humanity. If we, too, do our work wholeheartedly with a motive of love for God and society, we will find great fulfilment in life as St Joseph found.

We can go to St Joseph to acquire a sense of justice. When the Bible calls St Joseph "the just man" (Mt 1:19) it means more than paying debts. When God justifies us, he so transforms us that we become completely open to all that God wants to do for him. That is why, St Joseph obeyed God in all things. Simply and joyfully he was obedient to God. In marrying Mary, in naming Jesus, in shepherding the precious pair to Egypt, in bringing them to Nazareth, in the undetermined number of years of quiet caring for the family – or; in everything he did as God wanted. When a person is just towards God in this way, he becomes just also towards his neighbours. This we see in St Joseph's treatment of his spouse Mary. When he realised that she was with child, he decided to divorce her, but he planned to do this "quietly." "He being a just man and wanting to spare her publicity, decided to divorce her informally" (Mt 1:19). In our world today, we are only too conscious of the appalling sense of injustice done by one human being to another. The injustice done to an individual is sometimes perceived as a service to the public. There are some, of course, who are just but their love of justice is often no more than the fear of suffering injustice. In such a world, we need the inspiring example of St Joseph who had the constant wish to give God what is his and to every neighbour his or her due.

We can go to St Joseph in order that we may share his deep faith. There is a striking similarity between Abraham, the husband of Sarah, and Joseph, the husband of Mary. Both had their faith tested. To believe that Sarah in her advanced age would bear him a son required a tremendous faith on Abraham's part. To believe Mary had conceived a son by the Holy Spirit required even greater faith from St Joseph. Why does God require from us faith in him, and at times such heroic faith, before he gives us what we need or what he wants to give? This is so in order that we may be convinced beyond all doubt that we are what we are only by the grace of God and that everything we have and may have comes to us as a free gift of God and not as the result of our performance. If we think that we get to heaven by our own work, we are like a man who thinks of climbing to the moon on a rope of sand. In fact even our faith in God is not our achievement but a free gift of God. It is true that God often tests our faith. That is, I suppose, because our limitless faith in God corresponds to his limitless faithfulness towards us. Therefore, we need to raise up our faith lest it lies prostrate, to warm it up lest it is frozen and to rouse it lest it grows torpid. This is also the reason why we need to go to St Joseph.

SS PETER AND PAUL

FAITH AND MISSION

Readings: Acts 3:1-10; Gal 1:11-20; Jn 21:15-19

Theme: The feast of St Peter who represents the faith of the Church and of St Paul who represents the mission of the Church calls us to deepen our faith in Christ and to continue the mission of Christ in the world with renewed vigour.

Peter and Paul are the principal pillars of the Catholic church founded by Christ. St Peter was chosen by Christ to be his first Vicar on earth, endowed with the keys of the Kingdom of Heaven and charged with the role of the Shepherd of Christ's flock. In St Peter and his successors, we can see a visible sign of unity and communion in faith and charity. Divine grace led St Peter to profess Christ's divinity. He suffered martyrdom under Nero in 66 or 67 A.D. He was buried at the hill of the Vatican where recent excavations have revealed what could well be his tomb on the very site of St Peter's Basilica. St Paul was chosen by Christ himself on the road to Damascus to form part of the apostolic college. He was an instrument selected to bring Christ's name to all people, he is the greatest missionary of all time, the advocate of pagans, the Apostle of gentiles. St Paul may well have been beheaded in the Tre Fontane along the Via Ostiense and buried nearby, on the site where the Basilica bearing his name stands. If the church founded by Christ is what it is today, it is so because it has the kind of Faith and Mission that is represented by Ss Peter and Paul.

St Peter represents the Faith of the Church and through St Peter Christ has revealed how essential is faith for the Church to survive and flourish. Jesus was with St Peter for three years. Very early in his public life, he could have made St Peter the head of the Church but he did not. Why? Jesus knew that St Peter was weak, so weak that at one time he was overthrown by the words of a single maidservant. Therefore Jesus waited and waited for the weak man to grow stronger and stronger and for his faith in him to become unassailable. When Jesus asked, "Who do you say that I am?", and when St Peter answered, "You are the Son of the living God" (Mt 16:16), Jesus knew that St Peter's faith had grown rock-like and gave him the keys of the Kingdom. The faith of St Peter grew stronger still when the Holy Spirit came upon the Apostles. His faith in Christ later became a beacon light to all other followers, so much so when a cripple at the Temple gate begged him for some alms, St Peter could say only this: "I have neither silver nor gold, but I will give you what I have: in the name of Jesus, walk" (Acts 3:6).

St Paul represents the Mission of the Church and through him Christ has revealed how important it is for the Church to continue his Mission. What is it that gave St Paul the strength and courage to "pour away his life as a libation" in the service of the Good News? What is it that gave him the zeal and fire "to fight the good fight to the end and to run the race to the finish" (2 Tim 4:6-8)? It was not for any earthly reward nor for any personal profit that he spent every breath of his life; the real reason was his conviction that "the Good News he preached is not a human message but something that he learnt only through a revelation of Jesus Christ". The real reason was his belief that God had created him in his mother's womb was to preach the Gospel: "Then God who had specially chosen me while I was still in my mother's womb, called me through his grace so that I might preach the Good News about his Son Jesus Christ to the pagans" (Gal 1:15-16).

The Gospel that the Church asks her faithful to read on the feast of Ss Peter and Paul is that in which Christ gives to St Peter "the keys of the Kingdom" and the power "to bind and loose on earth" (Mt 16:19).

This passage might be taken as clear evidence to a Catholic believer that Christ gave his authority to St Peter and to his successors. If so, today's feast could be seen as a celebration of the authority of the Pope. But the Church resists this temptation. She rather wants to balance the authority in the Church with her faith and mission. That is why she prefers to celebrate, not just the feast of the authority of St Peter, who also stands for the faith of the Church but, together with him, that of St Paul who stands for the challenge of mission entrusted by Christ to his Church. Thus today's feast is a reminder to all of us that the authority of the Church will be ineffective if there is no faith in her; because only those who believe are obedient and only those who are obedient believe. It also reminds us that faith is not idle; it works while it waits. In fact I can experience my faith only when it is in action: thus the need for all the faithful to be in some way missionaries as well.

THE TRIUMPH OF THE HOLY CROSS

FORGIVING LOVE

Readings: Num 21:4-9; Phil 2:6-11; Jn 3:13-17

Theme: The holy cross of Christ is not only an indictment of the inhuman world that creates innocent victims, but it is also the supreme expression of Christ's forgiving love.

Jesus was as innocent as a child. Yet he died on the cross as the innocent victim of human sinfulness and evil. What is more, he was ultimately crucified because he had taken the side of the innocent victims of his society. Therefore it is wrong to glorify the Cross just because it is a cross, and it is wrong to assume that it is something noble to die an innocent victim. On the contrary, the cross of Christ is an indictment of the inhuman world that we live in, a world that creates victims. The cross of Christ is the scourge of the evil, oppression and abuse of the innocent victims of this world.

However, there is much more to the cross of Christ than just being a scourge of the evils in our world. The cross of Christ also became the supreme expression of Christ's forgiving love. Christ did not die a passive victim of evil. He was active in love till his death. In fact, his whole life from the beginning was an active expression of love for others. That is why, as St Paul says, "Christ, though divine, did not cling to his equality with God but emptied himself to assume the condition of a slave and became as men are" (Phil 2:6-7). It is this love that Christ carried to his cross. Even on his cross his forgiving love was so strong that he forgave even his executioners. It is this love that constitutes the triumph of the holy cross. Its triumph rose to such heights that "those who look upon the Son of Man on the cross" and believe "have eternal life in them" (Jn 3:15). Jesus did not conquer the world with arms. To conquer with arms is to make only a temporary conquest; he conquered it with love and to conquer the world by love is to make a permanent conquest.

In our world today, few people want to suffer passively as victims. There are people such as battered wives, victims of sexual abuse and others who stand up for themselves. This is all to the good. There are also others who want to 'get even' and 'settle the score' by hounding the wrongdoer or abuser and see to it that he pays the full price for his crime. However, we cannot close our eyes to the fact that our world has witnessed down the centuries inspiring examples of forgiving love. The great Indian leader Mohandas Gandhi was killed by a Hindu extremist in 1948. The assassin was standing beside a garden path, his hands folded before him, palms together, in the Hindu gesture of greeting. Between the palms of the assassin's hands was concealed a small, low calibre revolver. As Gandhi passed, the man fired three shots, at very close range, into the leader's body. Gandhi crumpled to the ground instantly, putting his hand to his forehead in the Hindu gesture of forgiveness. More recently, Pope Paul II, during one of his public audiences on a Wednesday in St Peter's open square, was shot by a man. The Pope nearly died but God spared his life. After his recovery, he went to the prison, met his would-be assassin and embraced him in a gesture of forgiveness. Thus the triumph of the cross still goes on today.

Also, the triumph of the cross has less dramatic and more everyday forms. Many who are terminally ill bear their illness with patience and dignity. So many of us extend to others tolerance often against all the odds. Many let go old hurts. Many refuse to play the game of tit-for-tat and settling the scores. For one thing, we don't believe that blood can be washed with blood. Why do we do all these little acts of forgiveness? Because we believe that the cross we bear for the love of others and in following God's will, will finally triumph. Because we believe that there is no situation that is so chaotic that God cannot from that situation create something that is supremely good. Did not God use the bronze serpent, the same serpent whose bite spread plague among the people of Israel, for the cure of that plague (Num 21:8)? Did not the cross of Christ which was an indictment of evil in the world became the source of eternal life to those who look upon Christ on the cross and believe in him? Yes. We know this. The sovereignty of God over evil is so powerful that he can direct any evil to a good and he would never permit an evil if he could not bring good out of evil.

THE FAITHFUL DEPARTED

" FAREWELL, BUT NOT FOR EVER "

Readings: Is 25:6-9; Rom 5:4-11; Lk 7:11-17

Theme: Our prayers for the holy souls who are still being saved in purgatory, assist in their perfect purification before they enter the presence of all-holy God.

In his book *He Leadeth Me* Fr Walter Ciseck tells how Russian peasants remember their beloved departed each year. Families flock to the cemetery as they do for a joyful picnic in the park. "'The graves are cleansed and decorated and then the family sits down to a meal at the graveside. Passers-by are invited to join the meal or to drink a toast." The peasants are utterly convinced that death is not the end of life. Rather it is the doorway to eternal life.

The Russian peasants are right in believing that death is not the end but the beginning of eternal life, that it is the human spirit's glad release, that it is the passing from pain to perfect peace and that it is like the parting of cloud which reveals the sun. But Catholic faith adds something more about the beloved departed. It teaches that there is an in-between state of purification through which the souls of the just pass before finally entering into eternal life. And this in-between state of purification is called Purgatory. There are at least three reasons why we believe in Purgatory.

The first reason is that the vast majority of people who die should not be judged so bad as to deserve hell, nor so good as to deserve heaven. So there must be a kind of middle state where some sort of cleansing takes place. God is holy and his holiness is not just an attribute but it is his very essence. Hence, it stands to reason that souls must be perfectly purified before entering into the presence of such a holy God. The soul in Purgatory may be compared to a freshly cut diamond; it is truly one of God's most beautiful creatures. But it is far from being perfect. Therefore the divine artisan brings it to its full potential by polishing it, that is, purifying it.

The second reason for believing in Purgatory is today's understanding of salvation won for us by Jesus through his death on the cross. Salvation is no longer understood as a single dramatic act of God. It is rather an ongoing process that continues to unfold as one's relationship with God develops. One can't say "I was saved at 2 pm yesterday afternoon". Rather, we affirm that we are being saved as we live the Christian life and as God continues to touch us. This means we are constantly being purified from sin and its effects, becoming more and more holy. Therefore, we can't say that the process of our being saved comes to a stop instantaneously the moment we die. We believe, rather, that death is only one of the processes in our journey into eternal life. If this is so, we also must believe that the saving process also continues in the state called Purgatory.

The third reason for believing in the in-between state of purification called Purgatory is our belief in the 'Communion of Saints'. According to this belief, the person who dies remains in touch with his or her fellow Christians who are still living and remains in a prayerful intercessory role with them. Hence the beloved departed are still active in the whole salvation process. If this is so, we must also believe that they continue to be actively purged and are made more and more Godlike before they finally enter into heaven.

With this understanding of Purgatory as an in-between state of purification, our prayers for the beloved departed make sense. Our prayers assist in their purification to become more like God. Our prayers also remind us that we the living are part of one communion, the Communion of Saints. We are confident that in the all-seeing mind of God, our prayers aid in the perfect purification of the beloved departed. It is in this family, perhaps romantic, sense of continued relationship with the beloved departed, that Cardinal Newman wrote these final lines of *The Dream of Gerontius*: "Farewell but not for ever, brother dear! Be brave and patient on the bed of sorrow/ Swiftly shall pass thy night of trial here/ And I shall come and wake thee on the morrow!”

HOMILIES FOR SPECIAL OCCASIONS

BAPTISM CELEBRATION DURING MASS

A NEW BIRTH

Readings: Acts 16:25-34; Col 2:11-15; Jn 3:1-6

Theme: Since an infant is baptised in the faith of its parents, parents have a duty to help the child to grow in faith so that the child may appropriate all the gifts that are offered in Christ to a child of God.

St Louis of France used to sign his documents not, 'Louis IX, King' but 'Louis of Poissy'. Someone asked him why, and he answered: "Poissy is the place where I was baptised. I think more of the place where I was baptised than of Rheims cathedral where I was crowned. It is a greater thing to be a child of God than to be the ruler of a kingdom: this last I shall lose at death, but the other will be my passport to an everlasting glory". Yes; there is no greater glory than becoming God's child and we all become God's children when we are baptised.

Baptism gives us a new birth, at which we become God's children once we are washed of our sins. Water used at baptism is a sign that our sins are washed away. Baptism cleanses us of original sin with which we are all born and, in the baptism of adults, of every sin committed prior to baptism. As children of God the baptised belong to Christ. The sign of the cross placed on the child's forehead at baptism is the sign showing that the baby belongs to Christ who died on the cross now offering his help and grace to face and overcome the sufferings of life. As children of God, the baptised share in the new life of Christ. The white garment placed on the child is a sign of innocence and the new life of resurrection. As children of God, the baptised receive the light of Christ. The candle used at baptism is the symbol of Christ who is the light of the world. This candle is lit from the paschal candle which stands as a sign of the risen Christ. The baptismal candle reminds us that the light of Christ has entered the child's life; and its flame symbolises the flame of faith which will burn throughout the life of the child. As the children of God, the baptised share in the power of the Spirit of God. The rubbing of the holy oil on the breast of the child at baptism is a sign of sealing the child with the gifts of the Holy Spirit.

Therefore the child to be baptised will receive all these glorious gifts, but on a condition. The condition is that it must have faith, as St Paul reminded the Colossians: "When you were baptised, you were buried with Christ, and in baptism you were also raised with Christ through your faith in the active power of God, who raised him from death" (Col 2:12). What kind of faith should the person to be baptised have? When an adult was asked whether he believed in baptism, he replied, "Sure I believe in it, boss, I've seen it done". That is not the kind of faith we are referring to, but a faith that believes that a person who is baptised receives all the divine gifts we have mentioned above.

Here we have a problem. One might ask: if faith is a basic condition for baptism, how can an infant who has no faith be validly baptised? Yes; but the Church still strongly recommends infant baptism because it believes that baptism is necessary for salvation on the basis of what Christ said: "Unless a man is born through water and the spirit, he cannot enter the kingdom of God" (Jn 3:5). Although the Church finds no clear evidence in the New Testament for infant baptism, it finds some reference to it in the Acts which mentions a new convert who was a jailer at Philippi, and was admitted for baptism together with "his household' (Acts 16:31). This may have included his children, even infants. As for faith needed as a condition for the validity of baptism, the Church believes that infant baptism is still valid because its faith is supplied by the parents and by the church community. This faith, at the beginning given for the child, of course, needs to grow into the full personal commitment of faith through education and formation, above all in the home.

This means that the parents who bring their babies for baptism have a grave duty towards the baptised child. The seed of faith sown and watered in baptism needs their love and care if it is to flourish. The way they live and love, their relationship as a couple, and their beliefs will all contribute to their child's experience of what it means to be a Christian. Here it will be suitable to quote an anonymous author: "A child who lives with criticism learns to condemn, and with hostility, learns to fight. A child who lives with ridicule learns to be shy, and with shame, learns to feel guilty. A child who lives with tolerance learns to be patient, and with encouragement, learns confidence. A child who lives with praise learns to appreciate, and with fairness, learns justice. A child who lives with security learns to have faith, and with approval, learns to like himself or herself. A child who lives with acceptance and friendship learns to find love in the world".

FIRST HOLY COMMUNION

A SPECIAL FRIEND

Readings: Ex 24:3-8; Heb 9:11-15; Mk 14:12-16, 22-26

Theme: First Communion is the first personal meeting with Jesus who is in the Eucharist as our most special friend, to whom we can talk our hearts out and whom we can receive as our spiritual food.

My dear children, you like to go to school. I suppose most of you at some time probably get fed up with school. You don't like all the hard work. Sometimes, you only go to school because your mother makes you go. But even when you get really fed up at school, there is usually one thing that you look forward to – your friends in school. You enjoy going to school to see your friends. Everybody likes to have friends. Of course, there are different kinds of friends. There are friends it is just fun to play with. But there are some friends, may be just one, who are special. With that special friend you like to talk, because you trust him. If you hurt your special friend, you say, 'I am sorry' because you don't want to lose your friend, because saying 'sorry' you become better friends, closer friends.

Now, you should know, children, Jesus is our most special friend, because he is most loveable, he is all love, he is all powerful, and he gives all that we need. Therefore, we must talk often to this special friend and that talking is called prayer. If we hurt him by sin, we must tell him: 'I am sorry' and that is Confession. Every time we hurt him, we must say 'I am sorry.' If we do that, we and Jesus will become better friends.

Do you like parties? Yes, you do. One day, Jesus gave a party to his disciples in Jerusalem two thousand years ago. When the party was underway, Jesus gave some bad news: he said "tomorrow I am going to die". They were shocked, very sad, knowing Jesus will be no more with them. But Jesus consoled them by saying, "Don't be sad. Although I am going to die, I have a way of being with you always". After saying that, he took a loaf of bread, broke it and said, "This is my body, eat". He took a cup of wine and said, "This is my blood, drink". As the Apostles were eating and drinking the Body and the Blood of Jesus, Jesus said, "Do this in memory of me". Now you know how Jesus has managed to remain with us always? It is by means of his Body and Blood which we call the Eucharist or Holy Communion.

In the Eucharist Jesus continues to be our special friend, so we can talk to Jesus in the Eucharist. In the Eucharist, Jesus offers himself to our Heavenly Father for our sins. In the Eucharist, Jesus gives himself to us as our special food. In a few minutes, the priest is going to say the very same words that Jesus said over the bread and wine at that Jerusalem party. He is going to do the very same things that Jesus did on that night two thousand years ago. When the priest has done that, Jesus will be here with us in the appearance of bread and wine, the very same Jesus who died and rose for love of us.

Today you are going to meet Jesus through your First Holy Communion. This is a very important day for you. Today, you become Jesus' special friends; he invites you to his party in the same way as he brought his apostles to that party in Jerusalem. You are going to receive Jesus in the Holy Communion. At his party, you are going to be given the greatest present you will ever receive. You will receive the gift of Jesus himself. So let us thank God for the love of Jesus and let us thank God for this day.

MARRIAGE

FOUNDED ON LOVE

Readings: Gen 2:18-24; 1 Cor 13:1-13; Jn 3:14-17

Theme: The success of a Christian marriage depends on how firmly it is founded on love, how closely that love resembles the love of God, and how steadfastly the partners seek God whose grace is always available in the marriage itself, for it is a sacrament.

There is a great deal that is beautiful in the world. We are deeply moved by the beauty of art and music and enchanted by beautiful nature. However, there is a still greater beauty which is right now in front of us. It is the love of a man and a woman soon to be given in marriage. Love is not only beautiful but joyful because it satisfies a person's irresistible desire to be desired irresistibly, which is best seen in marital love. Love is not only joyful, it is also powerful for it rules without rules and that is why when marital love oils the machinery everything in the household runs smoothly. Why is it that marital love is so beautiful, joyful and powerful? Because it is the reflection of God's own love for us. The springs of love are in God. God's love is unselfish, unconditional and enduring. "God so loved the world that he gave his only Son for us" (Jn 3:16). He loves us not because he needs to receive but because he delights to give; he loves us not because we are loveable but because he is love and he is never wearied by our sins or our indifference towards him.

The success of a Christian marriage depends on how firmly it is founded on love and how closely that love resembles God's own love. St Paul spells out the qualities of such a love (1 Cor 13: 4-8). "Love is never rude", for it respects each one's individuality; when people marry, they don't possess their partner as they possess a fridge or a car; each one must be allowed to keep their identity, like the pillars in a temple where the pillars stand alone but because of that they carry the beautiful ceiling. "Love is not selfish": love seeks to make happy rather than to be happy. Those who enter marriage for purely selfish motives are like the blind leading the blind, both falling into matrimony! Those who marry only with self-centred goals soon find their marriage to be a cage which they were once desperate to get into, but now are equally desperate to get out of. "Love never broods over injuries", for it forgives. A happy marriage is a union of two forgivers. "Love is forbearance", for human love of any sort is often but the encounter of two weaknesses. "Love is trust": nothing makes marriage rust like distrust. "Love never fails": marriage may be inspired by music, soft words and perfume, but its security lies in the couples' determination to be united to the end as "one flesh" (Gen 2:24). Of course, to be one goes beyond sexual union. To be one is not looking into one another's eyes but looking together in the same direction. It is sharing not only of bodies but of mind and soul.

It is obvious to every one that a marriage founded on a love as described by St Paul will not be easy. Questioning the children before Confirmation, the Bishop asked one nervous girl, "What is matrimony?" She answered, "a place where souls suffer for a time on account of their sins". "No, no," said the parish priest, "that is purgatory." "Let her alone", said the Bishop. "She may be right. What do you and I know about it?" Where there is love, there is pain and it is more true of marital love. The course of this love never did run smooth for any couple. We are told that marriages are made in heaven. I suppose that is why there are thunder and lightning in marital life!

But Christian couples need not be afraid. For they have a source of strength to bear their life's trials together. The source is not far away, it is in their marriage itself. Marriage is a sacrament and like any other Sacrament, marriage is not only a sign of Christ's love for the couple but also a means by which he transforms married couple's human love into the love of God himself, so that each partner is able to make Christ present to the other, not only to each other, but also they are able to bring Christ to birth in the Church and in the world. So, trusting in the power of the Sacrament that marriage is, the bride and the bridegroom can begin their life together with confidence.

But it is one thing to trust that the divine power is available in one's own marriage and another thing to make use of it on a daily basis. The way to avail oneself of this divine power is for the couple to strive to live in close union with God in such a way that God is always included into whatever they do and enjoy or suffer. Maybe, they could look at their marriage like a zipper. There are two rows of teeth on a zipper. These teeth fit into one another very neatly. But you need the little zip to draw the teeth together and lock them. Husband and wife need God like a zip, to keep themselves together. This means that they need family religion at home, not as a formality but as a practical everyday response to God. Unless a priority is given to spiritual things, "what God has joined" "man will easily put asunder". It is a pity that because of frenzied concern for success in life, some spouses crowd out God altogether from their lives and because of the quickened speed of travel and pace of life, some spouses find hardly any time not only for being together but also for being together before God. A Christian couple needs to imprint into their hearts and minds at the very start of their marriage the truth that their union with God on a daily basis is a must to nurture their marriage, to sustain their love and to make it grow. Love does not grow on the trees like apples in Eden; it is something you have to make, just like anything else. It is all work on your part, yes, but it is also all grace on God's part.

FUNERAL

"WHERE IS THY STING?"

Readings: Wis 4:7-15; 1 Cor 15:51-58; Jn 11:21-27

Theme: Though death is never sweet, it is only a door to eternal life, for all who believe in Christ will rise again, since Christ rose from the dead.

Whenever a part of life is lost or taken away, it brings grief. What we lose could be a spouse by divorce or a leg by amputation or a car by selling. At any such loss, we experience deprivation and sadness. But a loss of a loved one by death could be devastating, for it lands the bereaved in an irreversible situation that no human being can change. There is always a sadness about departure of the one we love, even if the departure is only for a short time. But the departure at death brings us the greatest sadness because it is the final departure of the one whom we loved and with whom we lived.

We can never make death beautiful by dressing up the corpse in silk or surrounding it with flowers. Not all the preaching since Adam has made death other than death. Nothing throws us off balance like the death of someone very important to us like a father, mother, wife or child. When my father died, I felt as if my whole self had been thrown up into the air and was floating down in little pieces; I never knew how the pieces would come back together. It is possible to provide security against other ills, but as far as death is concerned, we all live in a city without walls. Death is never sweet, not even when it is suffered for the highest ideals.

But the bereaved family and their friends can take some consolation in the thought that you are not alone grieving at the death of someone whom you loved so much. It is as natural to die as to be born. Everything on earth fades fast and death will take us all at last. Death eats up all things both the young lamb and old sheep. You cannot take up a newspaper without finding that death has a corner in it. Death is more universal in that every one dies but not every one lives. None of us knows when we shall die, but all of us know that we must die.

However, these words of comfort are only fragile human words. Words that are more consoling and more enduring come from the Lord Jesus Christ: "I am the resurrection", he says, "If any one believes in me, even though he dies, he will live" (Jn 11:25). Jesus through his death and resurrection has given his followers a share in his resurrection. Belief in the resurrection is not an appendage to the Christian faith; it is the Christian faith. Christianity is the monumental fraud if there be no eternal life. The resurrection of Jesus has created hope for our present and future existence. God is present now in all our material creation, which will one day be completely transformed and brought to its fulfilment. At death what is destroyed is of only passing value and what will be transformed is of surpassing value. This is the result of the resurrection. Every healing is now a partial resurrection and every change is towards greater life; the child leaving the womb, the adolescent entering adult life, the adult moving through the middle age crisis and the person leaving this world in death, all move towards fuller life. This means that our dearly beloved who is dead and who believed in Christ will live for ever.

Our beloved who is dead was a believer. He or she was born and brought up as a Catholic. They nourished their faith through Sacraments. They kept a relationship with God in their own way through prayer. They did whatever they could in the practice of faith. They shared in the sufferings of Christ by means of their own sufferings in life. And finally they have shared in the death of Christ by physically dying. Therefore, they have a share in the risen life of Jesus Christ. Therefore they could challenge death, as all believers challenge: "Death where is thy sting? Death where is thy victory?" (1 Cor 15:55). As you know this is the boldest and bravest challenge that a human being ever rang in the ears of death. Death is here out-faced, called a coward and bidden to do his worst! The human spirit never dies and death can never kill what never dies. If our birth makes us mortal, our death makes us immortal.

(This is the significance of the Mass we are about to celebrate, before we finally bid farewell to the dead. At Mass we recall and represent the death of Jesus Christ which broke the bonds of our own death; and we celebrate his rising victorious from his tomb, thus enabling us to share in his resurrection into eternal life. And so this Jesus our Saviour will once again be present among us.)

We all pray to our heavenly Father for our dead, that our Saviour's death may cleanse them of their sins and give them eternal rest. We shall pray for their bereaved family. Although faith gives the family great consolation and hope in the face of the death of their dear one, it does not remove all the pain of separation all at once. However, faith does enable them to accept the loss of their loved one and continue with their lives, confident that the separation death brings does not last for ever. We pray also for ourselves. We ask that Christ will strengthen our faith in his victory over death so that in our daily struggles and sufferings we may look forward to our own resurrection. For we know if we believe and live in Jesus we too shall never die. We too will share in the new life of resurrection, when we shall all be reunited in the Kingdom of the Father.

WEDDING ANNIVERSARY

THE CIRCLE RING

Readings: Is 63:7-9; Col 3:12-17; Mk 5:18-20

Theme: A wedding anniversary is a time to thank God for keeping the partners united in love, to congratulate them for keeping up the daring promise made to each other, and to encourage them to continue to love one another ever more intensely.

One night before he left, the king was walking in the palace gardens. He stood by the moon-drenched pool, tossing pebbles into the water and watching circles form. How like circles is my love for my queen, he thought. It, too, has no beginning and no ending. The next day, he called in his goldsmith and directed him to make a gold circle to fit the queen's finger. When the king slipped the finished ring on his wife's finger, he told her, "This circle, which has no beginning and no ending, is a pledge of my love for you, which is also eternal." And down through the ages, the giving of a wedding ring has sealed the vows of marriage, and symbolised the purity and endlessness of love in marriage. Dear friends, the wedding rings you both exchanged on your wedding day are still shining on your fingers, on the Anniversary of your marriage, proclaiming the endless love you have for each other.

We thank God for you. His grace has led you all the way to keep you united in love. It is not uncommon these days to see quite a number of marriages fail. Some break because there was no true love between the partners from the beginning; their love was just a shadow of love, inebriation of love, foretaste of love, trickle of love, but never true love. Other marriages break because when the bride swore, shivering and sighing, that she was his and when he vowed that his passion was infinite and undying, one of them was lying. Still other marriages break because, like two children playing by a stream, the couple begin their marriage as lovers, walking in a dream; when the dream is over the marriage is over too.

But you thank God today for he has blessed you with a love that is true and real. Thank him "for all that he has done to you in his mercy and for all the abundance of his acts of faithful love" (Is 63:7). When we drink from the streams, we must remember the spring. You have been drinking all these years from the spring of God's goodness and you are grateful to him. That is why, by the public celebration of the anniversary of your marriage, you are actually telling the family of God which is his Church and to the whole world, "how much the Lord has done for you and how kind he has been to you" (Mk 5:19). Yes. You are right: it is only with a sense of gratitude to God that your life is going to become richer in every sense.

While we thank God for his gracious assistance to you in finding true happiness in your marriage, we also congratulate both of you. You chose the right partner according to God's plan. We congratulate you not so much for choosing each other as for allowing to be chosen by one another. Because there is a world of difference between choosing and being chosen. A married person who believes he or she has chosen the partner is like a Christian who thinks he or she has chosen

God. Any such love is liable to evaporate into choosiness and selfishness. Whereas couples who allow to be chosen are like Christians who realise they have been chosen by God and this is why your marital life has been full of joy, thanksgiving and praise. We congratulate you also for the most daring promise you made to each other on the wedding day and for keeping that promise thus far. They were daring because, when you committed yourself for future life together, you did so without knowing how much of riches and how much of poverty, how much of health and how much of sickness, how much of victory and how much of failures, how much of happiness and how much of sadness would be in that future.

However, on this anniversary day, do not dwell too much on the past, neither on its joys or sorrows. Do not keep asking, 'What have we done?' but ask also, 'What are we going to do?' Because the past is no more yours. What is yours now is the future. If you want, think of your past as a bucket of ashes and determine to use the ashes as manure for a greater future. And your future will be greater and brighter if you resolve today to continue to love each other more intensely than ever. Marriage is not a finished affair. No matter to what agc you livc, love must be continuously consolidated. Do not think you have exhausted your love. The one thing we can never get enough of is love and the one thing we can never give enough of is love. Keep showing your love to each other in the ways St Paul recommends (Col 3:12-13) "Be kind": Yes. It destroys one's nerve to be kind every day to the same human being; but, as sun makes ice melt, so kindness causes mistrust to evaporate. "Be patient" when pains visit you. Sometimes a tragic event holds a marriage together; but often, it is the threads, hundreds of tiny threads of pain which sew people together through the years and that is what makes a marriage last. Continue to 'forgive' each other's frailties, irrespective of how hurtful they might be. To love and to be hurt often and to love again: this is the brave and happy marital life.

ORDINATION JUBILEE

THE OTHER CHRIST

Readings: Is 61:1-3; 2 Cor 5:14-20; Jn 21:15-19

Theme: Our Jubilarian has strived so far to live up to his priestly calling which is to be on earth an 'other Christ' and hence we thank God for all that he has done to him and pray for more grace to be showered on him in the years to come.

St Francis of Assisi resisted all suggestions that he should be ordained a priest, and in this way he taught all his followers how lofty and holy a dignity the priesthood is. Only with reluctance did he allow himself to be ordained Deacon. One day he said to the friars: "If I met an angel and a priest walking together, I would salute the priest first and then the angel. This puzzled some of the friars, no doubt because they knew priests who were evidently not so holy as angels. So St Francis explained: "I would salute the priest first because the angel, although so great, is only God's servant, but the priest actually represents Jesus Christ."

Because a priest represents Christ on earth, if the end of a human being is the glory of God and the end of a Christian is the greater glory of God, the end of a priest is the greatest glory of God. It is true that all Christians are 'other Christs'. But the priest's ordination consecrates him in a special way to be the representative of Christ in the Christian community, through living a Christ-like life, preaching the Gospel, dispensing the sacraments, shepherding the faithful to form a community of love, sharing and witnessing and offering his whole life as Christ did as a sacrifice for God and his people. In particular, it is in the Mass that a priest's role as the 'other Christ' is most fully expressed, for it is at mass that he represents Christ's offering of the perfect worship to the Father.

To represent Christ on earth and dedicate one's life, like him, to serving God and his people cannot be easier because priesthood is a life-mission without intermission and a priest is expected to employ all his passions in the service of others and not spend his life in the service of his own passions. A priest's work is varied, demanding, lonely and often hard. The priest's life, like all professions, is often humdrum and concerned with mundane affairs like raising money for the upkeep of the church. He is something of a GP, expected to be a counsellor, friend, small business manager, spiritual director, preacher, parish politician, school governor, school teacher, youth club leader, registrar, employment referee. No task, however secular or unusual, which builds up Christian community, is foreign to the priestly ministry and hence, some days of a priest's life could be full of tensions. In fact, many priests at one stage or other during their ministry will be tempted to give up.

But most do not give up. What keeps them going, and still more, happy and fulfilled in their vocation? Basically, it is love for Christ and for his people. A priest who loves Christ is in an unassailable position. True love, as we know, is always costly. But a priest who loves Christ much shall trust him much and hence be able to suffer much. Little privations are easily endured when the heart of a priest is better treated with love than his body with more luxury. St John Vianney used to say, "it is always springtime in the heart that loves God". That is why, Jesus, before appointing St Peter as the chief shepherd of his Church, made sure that he loved him very much by asking him the same question three times; "Do you love me?" (Jn 21:17) The love of a priest for Christ naturally flows into his love for his Church, as it was with Christ, and of this love St Paul wrote: "Christ loved the Church and sacrificed himself for her" (Eph 5:25). Just as Christ's love led him to die on the cross, so the priest is prepared to give his very life for the love of the Church.

We thank God today for our Jubilarian. We thank God for calling him to be his priest and in doing so he has made him his messenger, a wind and that this gentle - at times strong - wind is still blowing. We thank God for making him his minister, a flame of fire and that this fire of love is still burning brightly. Many are stubborn in pursuit of the path they themselves have chosen, but few in pursuit of that which God calls them to follow, unaware that if we are not in the place where God has called us to be, we are like a dislocated bone: we suffer and we cause suffering. We thank God for his consistent aid given all these years to our priest to walk perseveringly on the path of vocation which God chose to give him. A constant danger with some modern priests is that they become so immersed in the work of the Lord that they neglect the Lord of the work. We thank the Lord for helping our priest to secure, in the midst of his daily priestly concerns, a sustained prayer life which is the heart of a priestly vocation.

Let us pray, too, for our Jubilarian. May God continue to help him to grow more and more passionate in his commitment to love, more fiery-eyed in the vision of God's Kingdom with an insatiable thirst to serve. We pray that God may ever deepen the sense of mission in him, for the sense of mission sustains a man's soul as food sustains his body, that he may steward his priestly powers in ways that do not bind others but which free them to take their place in the Kingdom. May God stir up and strengthen the gifts of his grace in him and make him always open to that grace, in which alone lies his hope and joy.

RELIGIOUS PROFESSION

THE CONSECRATED

Readings: Song 8:6-7; Rom 12:1-13; Mk 10:17-27

Theme: Those who consecrate themselves to live by the evangelical values taught by Christ, counter the evil caused by the opposite worldly values and, in return, receive the blessings of the Kingdom.

One of the commonly-quoted biblical sayings is, "Sufficient unto the day is the evil thereof" (Mt 6:34), because there is so much evil in the world. The evil of this age is getting worse all the time. It is much like our atmosphere which is becoming more and more polluted with gases and exhaust fumes. The fear of one evil often only leads you towards a greater evil. The belief in a supernatural source of evil is not necessary; men alone are quite capable of every evil. Just to mention a few: the evil of egotism is one. Most of the troubles in the world is caused by people wanting to be important. Egotism is an odd disease: it makes everybody sick save the one who has it. A Christian psychiatrist told me that egotism is the anaesthetic that dulls the pain of stupidity. Sexual permissiveness is another evil. Many want to satisfy their sexual instinct without love and call themselves civilised. Lust for material possessions is yet another evil. Possessions pamper many minds, but few things eat into the soul of one so devastatingly as the love of money. Wealth may be gold, but it is a chain of gold, stronger than any chain of iron.

Therefore our world needs some men and women to stand up against such evils, not just to condemn them orally, but to counter their effects by consecrating themselves to evangelical values of poverty, chastity and obedience, the direct opposites of those worldly values which are the sources of many evils in the world. This was the need that Jesus had in mind when he asked the rich man in the Gospel (Mk 10:21) to give up everything he had, renounce all those values which this world cherishes to its own execution and follow him, so that he could become perfect and enter into the Kingdom of God. But we feel sorry for this man because when it had pleased Christ to give him the Kingdom, he wanted only a little piece of toast and went away sad.

But down the centuries, there have been countless Christians who have consecrated themselves, through vows, to the evangelical values proposed by Christ. These men and women are called the religious. Through the vow of poverty, a religious surrenders all his possessions and promises to live completely dependent on God's providence. By this vow he becomes like Christ, poor. Through this vow, he shares the life of the poor, proclaiming thereby to the world that it is better to be a child of God in poverty than to be a child of evil in riches. Through the vow of chastity, he "offers his living body as a sacrifice, truly pleasing to God" (Rom 12:1). By this vow, he gives God an undivided heart, becomes free to give himself completely in unselfish service of others and repudiates at the same time all those pledges of love which are easily made at weddings but soon turned into perjuries of love blown null and void by sexual permissiveness across the land and farthest seas. Through the vow of obedience, the religious imitates Christ obedient unto death and becomes a fit instrument of Christ in his Church. Through this vow, he proclaims to the world that it is not what we do that matters, but what God chooses to do through us, and as God uses broken things such as broken soil and broken cloud to produce rain, so he can achieve great things for his Kingdom through our broken ego.

What do men and women gain by following Christ as religious? Joy, peace, fulfilment and the Kingdom. Poverty may be inconvenient but it is no disgrace, for the "poor inherit the Kingdom of God" (Mt 5:3). To the poor in spirit, God provides for every need, and providence always orders that condition which is best for our eternal good. In the heart of one who obeys God in everything, there is always peace, for the heart is right when it wills what God wills. The obedient are truly free; obedience is not servile or blind, but requires on the contrary the greatest freedom of the spirit. There is joy in being chaste. Chastity enables a person to love God with one's whole heart. If it is true that we are shaped and fashioned by what we love, then by loving God we become godlike and when one loves God with his whole heart, his heart is turned into a paradise on earth for God dwells in that heart. By sacrificing marriage a religious may loose family happiness, but in return he or she receives a community of religious brothers and sisters, all united in Christ for the same purpose. Where there is such a communion, there is something more than human; there is surely something divine.

We thank God for giving our brother (sister) such a blessed vocation. We pray for him. We pray that he may love God with "a love that no flood can quench and no torrents can drown" (Song 8:7). We pray that, as the dry earth yearns in thirst for the raindrops and as the honeybee yearns for the scent of the flowers, so God may become the object of the yearning of his religious soul. We pray that he may daily strive "not to model himself on the behaviour of the world, but let his behaviour change, modelled by a new mind" (Rom 12:2) to live a new life in Christ. May the Lord Jesus Christ draw all the fragments of his life into the bright mosaic of his purpose and daily water him with plenteous streams from the riches of his grace.

THE FOUNDING OF A PARISH

MY PARISH IS MY FAMILY

Readings: Acts 4:32-35; Eph 2:19-22; Jn 17:20-21

Theme: In an ideal parish, its members not only receive rebirth to become children of God and all the spiritual nourishment needed for their faith journey, but also they work together to make their parish a community of love, a communion of hearts and the centre for a community apostolate.

As the Chinese proverb says, '"A journey of a thousand miles must begin with a single step". Yes, everything must have a beginning and everything has its seed. Today we celebrate the beginning of our parish family. Philosophers and politicians have agreed that the bonding together in family groups is both instinctive and necessary to human welfare and therefore essential to the health of a society. This is true of natural families as well as of spiritual families. Our parish is our spiritual family.

It is in this spiritual family we had our second birth at our baptism, were raised to the dignity of children adopted by God becoming members of God's own family with the result that we are now privileged to call God 'Father'. In this way, our parish has become our spiritual mother and no Christian can have God for father, without the parish for mother. A parish is not only a mother but a father too. As a father in a natural family provides for the needs of his family, so the parish provides for us the spiritual nourishments through different Sacraments which are channels of the life-giving grace of Christ. Our parish is our family where we meet also our brothers and sisters in Christ. When we become God's children at our baptism, a special bond is formed not only between us and Christ as our elder Brother, but with one another as children of God. Thus we "are no longer strangers and aliens. No, you are fellow citizens of the saints and members of the household of God" (Eph 2:19).

What a privilege it is for us to belong to such a family of God which is our parish! But do we really belong to our parish? To belong to a parish is not to hang onto the parish by the membrane of an old childhood memory; I do not belong to my parish just because I pull off my hat every time I pass by my parish church. There are some who know which is their parish but usually go to attend services in another parish and thus remain anonymous to their own pastor and to their own parishioners. Can we have our family roots in one parish and family relationships in another? True belonging calls for developing close and if possible intimate faith-relationship with fellow parishioners. We cannot form such a relationship by the occasional showing of one's face at Sunday services. The Diocese has specified territories to each parish, to help the parishioners really to belong to at least one Catholic community, small enough to form intimate fellowship and thus to derive all the joys of belonging to God's family.

Parish fellowship, in order to stand the test of time, needs to be founded on love in Christ. Where does the natural family start? It starts with a young man falling in love with a girl – no superior alternative has yet been found. So too our spiritual family must start with our falling in spiritual love for one another. With that love, it will not be that difficult for the members to strive to develop their parish into what God wants it to be, that is, a community and a communion. As a community the members will readily come forward to share their talents, time, energies, even of their possessions, to care for one another's needs, and to join in common prayer and worship, which were the characteristic marks of the first Christian communities (Acts 4:32-35). As a communion, they will seek greater and greater parish unity, thus fulfilling the desire of Jesus that "they may be one as we are one" (Jn 17:21). Already being united with Christ, they will seek also union of heart and mind with their fellow parishoners, like the lines that lead to the centre of a circle uniting there and not like the parallel lines which never join.

But we strive to make our parish a community of love and a communion of hearts not solely for our own benefit, but for the good of the world as well, "that the world may believe" in Jesus as one sent by God to save this world (Jn 17:21). This means that a member of this parish cannot remain merely as a piece of church furniture. All its members have an apostolate to do, the apostolate of witnessing to the presence of Christ in our midst, not only by proclaiming his Good News from this parish, but also by continuing Christ's mission of mercy and charity, such as feeding the hungry, healing the sick, reconciling the brokenhearted, uplifting the downtrodden and ministering to the most needy in our society. The Church of Christ is basically a missionary church and so must be the local church which is the parish. As the Second Vatican Council says in its document on the Laity, "The parish offers an outstanding example of community apostolate, for it gathers into unity all the human diversities that are found there and inserts them into the universality of the Church". Therefore, according to each one's ability, the members of this parish ought to be fired with an apostolic zeal to cooperate in all the missionary enterprises of this parish family. In fact, when this parish was born, no one ever thought that it was vase to be filled, but a fire to be lit.